Praise for 'My Nile Odyssey'

"The memoir is a vivid cameo of a rarely seen Sudan, of a loving family hit by numerous tragedies, of eccentric characters, old souks, camel markets and of a fabulous historical heritage that is only just being unearthed. I found it a richly rewarding, memorable read and would unhesitatingly recommend it."

H.E. Ambassador (Dr) Alfredo Maiolesi, Secretary General of the World Organisation of States, International Parliament for Safety and Peace (Italy)

"Kamil`s love of his home country shines through, yet he does not shy away from describing the horrors of the civil war and conflict in Darfur. His commitment to human rights and lasting peace in Sudan are an inspiration."

Dr Miranda Brown, international advocate and human rights defender (UK/Australia)

"This memoir is a must read for those who believe and those who doubt that North, South, East or West, the world is one."

H.E. Ambassador Dr Martin Ihoeghian Uhomoibhi, Joint Special Representative/ Joint Chief Mediator of the United Nations – Secretary General and African Union Chairperson, African Union – United Nations Hybrid Operation in Darfur, Sudan (Nigeria)

MY NILE ODYSSEY

Kamil Idris

First published in Great Britain as a hardback original in 2017

Copyright © Kamil Idris

www.profkamilidris.co.uk

The moral right of this author has been asserted.

Design, typesetting and editing by UK Book Publishing

ISBN: 978-1-910223-96-3

www.ukbookpublishing.com

MY NILE ODYSSEY

The life and death story of a child labourer's
rise to international leadership

Kamil Idris

A Memoir

Dedication

I wish to send with this memoir a message of hope to all
those in the wider world, whatever their system of belief
or religion, who believe in the community of nations,
the sanctity of life and the brotherhood of mankind.

I would also like to dedicate this book to my wife Azza, my
children Mohamed, Dinas, Dalia, Dahd, Mumin and Munib.

And also to my larger family and the extensive network of my
close relatives and friends.

Acknowledgments

I wish to pay tribute to my late father Eltayeb Idris and
late mother Amouna Haj Hussein, and to my sister
Samira, brothers Farid, Siddig and the late Izzeldeen for
their tremendous encouragement. Also to my late sister
Awatif, late brother El-sir and my brother Abdeen.

The help and support of Hugh Dias was immense.

I am also thankful to UK Book Publishing,
in particular, Jay, Ruth, Dan and Judith
for their advice and professionalism.

My apologies in advance for any ommisions or
mistakes in the compilation of the memoir.

Contents

Foreword

I take great pleasure in writing an introduction to this important 'memoir' because of the role it could play in the ongoing cultural enlightenment of Sudan and also of the wider world.

The story is a testimony to the achievement of the human spirit in overcoming adversity and a testament to the importance of self discipline, the hunger for knowledge and the universal values of brotherhood that transcend nationality and religion.

The family cameos, the human context, reveal a Sudan perhaps rarely seen by the outside world. The instinctive kindness, dignity, courtesy and welcome to the stranger are a powerful antidote to the headlines of civil war and violence. Here are families and communities, Bedouins, traders and simple fishermen full of charm and character, bound together in celebration and mourning, still in touch with their rooted traditions and proud of their ancestry.

The memoir is also a treasure chest of fascinating diversions into history and philosophy. For example, DNA proof of the common origin of human beings; the rich and still to be fully uncovered archaeology of Sudan and its one time greatness as the centre of an ancient civilisation.

In one of these diversions Kamil argues that there are aspects of life that atheism finds difficulty in addressing.

While modern secular thought tends to deny any role for metaphysics, studying it as parapsychology, religion allows for the acceptance of spiritual energy. In the memoir the telepathic calls of his grandmother Zainab, the extraordinary apparition of the dates' giver and the contact with dead souls are pointers to a dimension of life that defies rational explanation. Religious faith simply acknowledges this and through revelation provides guidance to humanity. It is true that religious faith has been abused and intolerance and sectarianism have been a source of conflict and despotism, but this does not detract from the fact that it has also been, in its truest form, the founder of civilisations, the building block of morality and the cement of society.

I salute the note of optimism for the revival and future progress of Sudan in the memoir and would fully endorse Kamil's message by emphasizing the following points:

We need: An ideological synthesis between religion and secularism; a cultural accommodation of diversity; a government based upon participation, accountability, transparency and the law; an economic system which realizes development and abides by social and regional justice; a balancing of the relationships between Arab, Islamic, and African regions and International relations based on peace and justice.

I also salute the memoir's optimism for the future of Africa with the qualification that no amount of Marshall Aid will make a difference with despotic and corrupt regimes while they are still able to deny human rights and abuse their nations' wealth.

In addition, international terrorism has metamorphosed into reactionary criminal brutality with multiple tentacles, namely: so called states, *lmarat*, a network of activists, and destructive lone wolves. There are multiple causes for this and bombs alone will not be the only answer. What is needed are ideological convictions that champion the values of humanity, respect for the sanctity of life and dialogue.

I commend this memoir for its courage in facing these unpalatable issues and for its vision of a future based on brotherhood, acceptance and a rejection of violence.

This profound message is not wishful thinking. Kamil's portrait of a kindly, gentle, accepting community, and his practical menu for change, is evidence that a tolerant and open society is achievable and that global healing can become a reality.

Imam El-Sadiq El-Mahdi
Former Prime Minister of Sudan
1966-1967; 1986-1989

Prologue

Some months before his death in 2013 I had a conversation with Nelson Mandela. I think he knew that he was dying and wanted to share with me his vision for the future, not only for Africa but also for the entire world. His hopes were not based on airy idealism but on a fusion of his own heroic example and realistic economic and political strategies. He called me "a true son of Africa" and urged me to write this autobiography. I was flattered by his request, even though I felt my memoir could never match up to the scale of his own magnificent achievement in uniting his own country and inspiring millions across the globe.

However, he reminded me that my experiences with leading world statesmen and women, and my profound optimistic faith in human nature, were precisely the same as his and that I should echo his beliefs by telling my own story. We were both aware of the dire problems that were afflicting the world but he thought that a positive, uplifting message of brotherhood, reconciliation and compassion could be a powerful antidote to intolerance, racism and bloodshed. To be honest I thought this would be an impossible task but I was humbled by his confidence in me and promised that I would honour his wishes.

Essentially the book is a cameo of an affectionate and loving family seen through the eyes of a growing child; a snapshot of a rarely seen and unexpectedly gentler Sudan; and also historic, ancient Nubia. However, it is also a confession of hope for a brighter future for my nation and hopefully, an echo of the great Mandela's dying wishes.

In the beginning was the family. My childhood was enriched by loving and caring parents, older brothers and a sister, and a colourful parade of relatives and eccentric friends who visited and stayed with us as often as they wanted, forming an 'extended' family. I learned to swim but was nearly drowned when trying to cross the River Nile. The premature deaths of my father, half-sister, aunts and close friends were devastating blows to my happiness and I sought solace and distraction in hard work, self discipline and child labouring in a bottling factory, among others.

As a young teenager I journeyed to Cairo on the top of a train to find more work and was stranded on the shores of Lake Nasser where I was threatened by a gang of fishermen who thought I was a djinn or ghost. As a student I flirted with communism but rejected it in favour of my deep and forgiving religious faith. I studied ferociously hard at universities, dabbled in journalism, and eventually rose high in the United Nations as a Director General of WIPO and UPOV, became a leader at the United Nations Law Commission and, with all humility, a trusted, respected academic and global diplomat.

In Sudan I tried to champion free speech and human rights, and after standing as a Presidential Candidate in the 2010 elections faced inevitable clashes with the security services.

I escaped from virtual house arrest in a frantic dash to freedom with my family and eventually was able to return as an accepted moderating and unifying figure.

My life story then is the backbone of the book, but there are many relevant digressions concerning people and events which captured my imagination and that have been seminal in forming my character.

In fact it was shortly before the completion of this memoir that I lost one such persona and a huge gap opened up in my life. My beloved elder brother Izzeldeen passed away. I was at his bedside during his final days and marvelled at the number of people who came to the house to offer their support and sympathy. He knew he was dying and his calmness and bearing were extraordinary.

What followed was even more remarkable. For more than 15 days after the funeral the family had to erect huge tents as thousands of mourners came to pay their respects. The only way we could cope was to accept the help of the charitable young people in the neighbourhood who volunteered to help with the service, the arranging of all the chairs and tables and the continual cleaning and sweeping of the courtyard. I knew my brother was a highly respected man but these unprecedented numbers amazed all the immediate family. The sincerity and goodwill shown were of immense help in coping with the sadness of his passing and I will cherish the memory of those final days. It was a confirmation to me of the deep spiritual roots of the wonderful people of Sudan.

نادي الشاطئ الرياضي الثقافي الاجتماعي
تأسس عام 1930م

نعي أليم

قال تعالى: (وَبَشِّرِ الصَّابِرِينَ . الَّذِينَ إِذَا أَصَابَتْهُم مُصِيبَةٌ قَالُوا إِنَّا لِلّهِ وَإِنَّا إِلَيْهِ رَاجِعونَ . أُولَئِكَ عَلَيْهِمْ صَلَوَاتٌ مِّن رَّبِّهِمْ وَرَحْمَةٌ وَأُولَئِكَ هُمُ الْمُهْتَدُونَ). صدق الله العظيم

بمزيد من الحزن الآسى ينعى مجلس إدارة
نادي الشاطئ الرياضي الثقافي الاجتماعي المغفور له بإذن الله :

عز الدين الطيب إدريس

رئيس النادي الأسبق الذي حدثت وفاته أمس الثلاثاء، وكان الفقيد من الإداريين المؤسسين للنادي، وكانت له اسهامات طيبة، وبفقده فقد النادي ركنا من أركانه الهامة.
اتصف الفقيد الراحل بطيب المعشر ودماثة الخلق وعفة اللسان وصدق الإخاء ونقاء السريرة والتفاني والإخلاص في العمل وكان محبا للجميع.
ونحن إذ ننعيه نسأل الله العلي القدير أن يتغمده بواسع رحمته وأن يسكنه فسيح جناته مع النبيين والصديقين والشهداء وحسن أولئك رفيقا وأن يلهم أهله وذويه وأصدقاءه ورفاقه الصبر وحسن العزاء..

إنا لله وإنا إليه راجعون

My late brother Izzeldeen Eltayeb Idris, a great loss.
He was as genuine and pure as the river Nile

My country stands at the crossroads of Africa, a link between Europe to the north and the great heart of the continent to the south. Through it runs the green ribbon of the Nile, the life force of the country and a direct link with antiquity, its rhythm and presence unchanged since the days of the Pharaohs. It has been a constant source of wonder and inspiration in my life. Even from an early age I have been drawn to the mystery and splendour of its waters and whenever the dark angels of worry and doubt were circling I would wander to a quiet stretch of its banks to find calm and solace. To me it is almost an intimation of immortality, a living metaphor, another character in the story, whispering its timeless secrets and informing the present with the grace and strength of old times.

However, in recent years the historic and ancient Sudan has been trapped in poverty and ravaged by a vicious civil war, enduring horrific episodes with commonplace suffering and ethnic intolerance. As a balance to all this brutality I have tried to include tales of happier days when for centuries peoples of different faiths – Muslims, Jews, Christians and others – lived in mutual respect and harmony.

So it is a tale of a huge country with immense natural resources and potential, proud of its diversity, culture and its unmatchable heritage when the Nubian kingdom of Kush, our ancestors in Sudan, once ruled as Pharaohs of Egypt and beyond.

The memoir is an attempt to shine a bright candle in a dark world. It is to explain, confess, forgive, inspire and act as a summons to action. It would be easy for cynics to dismiss these thoughts as futile, as political wallpaper, but here is TE Lawrence, author of Seven Pillars of Wisdom:

> "All men dream but not equally. Those who dream by night in the dusty recesses of their minds may wake up in the day to find it was vanity, but the dreamers of the day are dangerous men, for they may act their dreams with open eyes to make it possible."

I think in that sense Mandela was an exceptional man because he really believed, like Gandhi, that open violence was a cul de sac, a one way street to nowhere. Change and progress could come about only through mutual respect, dialogue, tolerance and understanding and not through beheadings, executions and an intolerance of different faiths.

I shared his core beliefs and hope that my own story can light another candle to stand beside his own bright flame in lighting the way to the sunlit uplands of the future.

And why 'My Nile Odyssey' as a title? I don't think this will take too much detective work. Look out for strong currents, crocodiles, pirates, train roofs and the mighty Sahara desert for the answer.

Sudan before 2011

The vast territories of Sudan and the Republic of South Sudan which gained its independence in 2011

Chapter 1

Shades of Darkness and The Good Samaritan

And say… my Lord; have mercy upon them that brought me up when I was small.
(Quaran.17.24)

My vision for education: to nourish a child's sense of mystery and wonder.
(Kamil Idris)

It was the best of times and the finest of days, but balancing on the top of a train in 50°C can kill you. You can slide off as it hits bends. Low hanging wires can slice your head off. You keep to the middle and are constantly looking ahead for bridges. Sometimes you spread yourself flat on your stomach and drift away into an uneasy doze but if you fall off, the train won't stop. It won't know you're gone. If it's high summer the lethal, Sudan 50°C midday sun can bake you alive and at night the temperature in the winter desert can drop to near freezing point. To ward off the ferocious sun you keep pouring water from a pitcher over your head and you face the front so the slipstream wind from the train offers some relief from the oven-like heat. You begin to lose concentration. You cling on for dear life.

I was thirteen and travelling back from a 48-hour trip north to Cairo, where I had been working in a small printing factory during the school holidays. The pay had been miserable,

1

I was hungry and tired but soon I would be back home in Omdurman. I couldn't wait to see my mother and brothers and sister again and enjoy some home cooking and a bed. There had been no windows in the factory and the other twelve boys and I had had to work a 14-hour day in the airless, stifling heat. My job had been to assemble school text books and at times I had nearly fainted when the noon sun hit the roof of the building and turned it into an oven. After only a day or two a couple of the young boys had left but I decided I would try to tough it out and stayed, as I was also fascinated by Egypt and wanted more time to explore it.

I had entered the country, like most newcomers, insecure, nervous and brimming with youthful innocence, but the helpful advice I received at the station from strangers had reassured me that Egypt was a friendly and welcoming place. What I hadn't expected was the harshness of the working conditions. I had been a child labourer in Omdurman but had always had the haven of home at the end of the day. Working in that particular factory in Cairo had been a brutal wake up call.

We slept on old mattresses on the factory floor, our diet had been mainly stale bread and dates, and there were no toilet or washing facilities. I had had enough and it was now time for home. The evening before I left I asked Atif, a street hawker friend who sold cheap jewellery, sweets and dried fruit, to come with me to buy a ticket at Cairo station.

"You don't need one."

"What do you mean?" I asked.

"You don't need one. There's a better way."

"What way?"

"Don't worry. Just do what I used to do," he said.

"Bring peanuts and some water."

"Why peanuts?"

"Because they're cheap and they fill you up."

That night I hardly slept. I knew what he and some others were planning and I was sick with worry. They were going to jump on the train at the last second and sit on the roof for the entire journey without a ticket. The last time I had made the journey from Khartoum to Cairo on top of the train three young boys had fallen off. I heard later that one of them had survived but the other two had died of thirst in the desert.

We would be travelling from Cairo to Aswan, taking a ferry to Halfa and then a train again to Khartoum. It was going to be a long and tiring journey and we would have to work on the ferry to pay our way. Even this could be as dangerous as the train. It would be crowded and the only places where we could sleep would be on the side edges of the boat. If we rolled over in our sleep we could easily drown. We could survive the journey, but only if we were careful and kept our wits about us. Now we were sitting on the roof of the train and rattling south. In Cairo station we had positioned ourselves at the back of the train and waited for it to inch forward before leaping up the steps of the last carriage and clinging to the roof. It was important to stay right in the middle and keep flat for as long as possible. The porters had spotted us and shouted when the train chugged off, but they were halfhearted and in the end just shrugged their shoulders. If we wanted to die, fair enough. It was not their business. I did manage to get some fitful sleep and kept my balance by lying flat and spreading out my arms and legs.

Eventually we arrived at Aswan, then took the ferry to Halfa where we had to walk a few kilometres in the boiling midday heat to pick up the connecting train south. Once again we had to manoeuvre and negotiate our way onto the roof of the train. The best way was to open our arms to the inspectors and depend on their indifference.

We were now on a much older train and the rocking to-and-fro of the carriages meant we were in constant danger of being shaken off. In addition the inspectors had warned us that in some sections of the route there were low hanging wires which could slice our heads off! We were travelling through the night for some of the journey and to help us concentrate and keep awake we had filled our pockets with small tomatoes and some salt. We were able to 'refuel' at the ancient town of Shendi where

3

some kind people gave us some dry bread and water and one or two boiled eggs.

Somehow we survived and in the early morning sunlight the train rattled slowly into Khartoum station. I waved to my mother and scampered down from the roof, but as she hugged me she began to cry. I thought she was just worried about how I had been risking my life but it was because she couldn't believe what had happened to her youngest son. I hadn't realised I had lost so much weight and from then on she began to cook vast meals for me. I was delighted to be home and was treated like a returning prince. It was so reassuring to be back in the bosom of my family, although my sense of independence had taken root. I had had a taste of the glamour of travel, of lands beyond the Sudan and in the coming weeks and months I became restless. I was Icarus. If I could survive on the roof of a train I could go anywhere. I wanted to zoom across the Mediterranean to see Europe; then the Atlantic to see America. The world was waiting to be discovered.

I was born on 26th August 1954 in Omdurman, an ancient trading and fishing village on the west bank of the confluence of the White and Blue Nile rivers, and now the once historic capital of the country. The name my parents gave me, 'Kamil', means 'complete' in Arabic, an impossible label to live up to, as I know only too well that I am as fallible as the next man, and 'Idris' was an early prophet mentioned in the Holy Qur'an. It means 'patient' or 'capable of high office'.

In the wider world that year there was relative calm after the horrors of the Second World War, but the tensions between the democracies of the West and communism continued to rumble. The USA was testing atomic bombs on Bikini Island in the Pacific and had launched its first nuclear submarine. John Foster Dulles, the US Secretary of State, warned of "massive retaliation" in the event of a nuclear strike from the Soviets. It also outlawed its own communist party. The unpredictable Nikita Khrushchev had become Premier and had ordered the building of what Winston Churchill called, "an iron curtain", stretching from the

Arctic Circle to the Adriatic, virtually imprisoning hundreds of millions. The Soviets had also tested their first hydrogen bomb, much more powerful than the atomic bombs at Hiroshima and Nagasaki.

In Africa there were stirrings of revolt and demands for change. Abdul Nasser gained power in Egypt, survived an assassination attempt, and disbanded The Muslim Brotherhood and communists, branding them "corrupting forces". He issued a dramatic challenge to Britain and the colonial powers by closing the Suez Canal, threatening their vital flow of oil. France sent 20,000 troops to quell a nationalist uprising in Algeria and it also started to withdraw its forces from Vietnam, while the US increased its numbers of military advisers to the South. In South Africa President HH Verwoerd stated in a speech that humanity needed to be racially defined and organised under "the supremacy of the white race". At the same time Nelson Mandela was devising plans for the ANC's underground operations.

Talks on the unification of Germany stalled when the four powers couldn't agree on a formula. Morocco and Tunisia were moving towards independence. Fidel Castro, Che Guevara and 28 Cuban revolutionaries were arrested in Mexico City and in two years' time The Sudan, after gaining independence, would be plunged into a vicious civil war.

Such was the world I was born into. I was fortunate to be surrounded by a loving family but from early childhood I began to be plagued by nightmares and dark premonitions about the future. The boundaries and defences against these fears were my affectionate, extended relatives – a riot of uncles, aunts, cousins and grandparents – and of course my early days of schooling.

The other defining boundary was the mighty River Nile. It flows for 6,650 km from its sources to the delta in the Mediterranean and is the longest river in the world.

As soon as I reached boyhood it bewitched my imagination and in a way it still does. Seen from space it looks like a huge lotus flower. Alternatively it can be seen as a striking cobra with its head spitting poison into the sea. It is the heart and nerve

centre of Sudan and Egypt, the backbone of Africa and an
unparalleled theatre of human diversity. It's impossible to classify
because it ignores human borders and means so many different
things to different people. For Egypt and Sudan in particular it
has been a ribbon of life, flowing through a desolate wasteland of
rock and sand, and it continues to defy understanding because
of its dramatic geographic differences. In bygone ages it was
considered a God, much as the Hindus consider the Ganges
today, and it was so long that no single tribe or culture knew its
full scope. In the 1960s its mountain gorges in the south were
still being mapped and its source is a question mark even now. It
dominated and coloured my childhood and has been a spiritual
companion throughout my life. It still casts its spell today.

I loved growing up in Omdurman. It stands opposite its
bigger brother Khartoum at the confluence of the White and
Blue Niles, possibly one of the most dramatic interchanges in
the world. If I looked south I could visualise the land of the
fabled Prester John, founder of an ancient Christian empire
in Ethiopia and the great green heart of the continent. If I
looked north I was in the land of the Pharaohs, pyramids, and
Cleopatra. If there is a demographic contrast in Africa it is here.

Southern Sudan's green, fertile plains, swamps and
mountains are inhabited by diverse ethnic tribes speaking a
multitude of languages and dialects. The north is hot, dry and
partly scorching desert, populated again by a variety of tribes
and cultures. Before the division of the country into North and
South Sudan in 2011 they formed three quarters of the total
population and they gave the country its name, 'Sudan', which
some people think is an ancient Arabic word meaning 'the land
of the black peoples'.

Omdurman was at the junction of these two fabulous
worlds. When I was a boy it was smaller and more intimate, and
wandering through its old streets and districts, even now, is like
journeying into the past.

Rickshaws and donkey carts still jostle for space. Muslims,
Christians, Jews and others rub shoulders with eyes, not on each

other, but on exotic wares from all over the world.

My eyes were mesmerised by all the silver and gold jewellery, pots and pans scattered in great heaps, piles of multi-coloured carpets and mounds of exotic fruits. In the olden days of the souk there would be lion and leopard skins, ostrich feathers, gold from Ethiopia, spices, ebony, ivory, herbs, drifting clouds of wood smoke and incense.

It was an enchanting, intoxicating brew. This was my world, my family, my home and the Nile.

My father, Eltayeb Idris, had been born in the north of Sudan in 1915 in the Al-Zawrat area. He was from a tribe called the Danagla Khazrag and could trace his ancestry back 1,400 years, when part of the Khazrag tribe had migrated from the Arabian peninsula during the times of the Prophet (PBUH). He had been born into difficult times though. His father, Alsheikh Idris Abdel Hafeez, had moved from Dongola to Omdurman in the early years of the twentieth century and had settled in an area favoured by the disciples of the Mahdi revolution, and the house that he built there is still standing today.

My paternal grandmother was Haja Al-Nima Al-Sayed. When she was a small child in the 1890s the British and then later the British Egyptian Condominium were both occupying and administering Sudan. Their conduct towards the ordinary citizens was, on occasions, brutal and the insensitive behaviour of the Egyptian tax collectors became an insult to the Sudanese. This gave rise to a growing sense of injustice which in turn led to a major uprising, spearheaded by The Mahdi, whose Dervish army overran General Gordon's defences at Khartoum. Before he died my grandfather, who had been sympathetic to the movement during the uprisings, moved his family from Dongola to Omdurman and settled in an area close to the Mahdi's tomb. Later, he had just enough money to have a house built nearby which my father inherited.

My mother Amouna was a tall, slim woman with a pale complexion, a classically aquiline nose and dancing brown eyes. She was proud of her long black hair and once told me that when she had been a young girl she could comb it down until it completely covered her back. Like my father she too could trace her family back through the generations, and she had strong Turkish and Egyptian origins. She was a confident, honest and creative woman with an unconditional love of all her children. She was strict with us though and one disapproving glance was enough to stop us in our tracks from whatever boundaries we had crossed. Her voice was firm and gentle and I never once heard her shouting at us. Physically she was a demonstrative and affectionate mother, instinctively hugging us when we left or returned from journeys.

Whenever we were about to leave she would even make a footprint from sand as a lucky memento, a good omen for the safe return of her children.

She was a skilful cook too and in the kitchen there were always huge pots of soup and meat stews on the go. The pots used to bubble, gurgle and simmer for hours on the top of our wood burning stove and she would hover over them with a massive brown spoon, frowning or smiling as she sipped for taste. Fresh vegetables were her passion and each morning she would trip down to the markets by the Nile, returning with full baskets of cucumber, pepper, peas, potatoes, carrots and onions. She also loved corn and okra (a vegetable called 'lady's fingers' in the west) when they were in season, and on special occasions she would bake her own bread and delicious biscuits, the gorgeous smells perfuming the whole house.

In the corner of the kitchen was a 'sahara', an antique wooden storage box where she kept pieces of fresh and any left over bread wrapped in old newspapers. I never knew whether she kept it for us or the chickens and goats outside.

It didn't matter to me. I would take a piece of hardened bread, dip it in the maturing soup and relish the flavours.

Her favourite time of day was sunset when she would open our doors for visitors and dispense hot food and tea to whoever dropped in. We had a sort of 'open house', not just for relatives, but also for friends. This was the generous side of her nature, and it would reach a peak in the winter when people were needy or sick in the cold and occasionally rainy days. Then she would visit them, cheering them up with armfuls of food and sunny smiles. She had little money but whatever she had she would give freely, whether it was to the local woodcutter, the woman who helped her wash and iron the clothes, or the occasional tramp who knocked politely at the door. She had a special place in all our hearts but none of us knew of the tragedy that would soon devastate us, my mother in particular.

My father was a tall, broad-shouldered man with large brown eyes and black hair tinged with grey. He had 'presence', a special combination of dignity and calm, especially when he wore his reading glasses. Traditionally minded and patient, he was very much in charge of the family, chain smoking packets of *Rothmans* and *Benson and Hedges* cigarettes and exercising his authority like an indulgent teacher trying to control a classroom of unruly children. It is strange now to think that I can remember details like that after all these years. To a child the golden packets of *Benson and Hedges* were attractive, expensive imports from mysterious cold lands to the north and I can still recall the moment when we boys were able to read on the side, "Especially manufactured for Sudan"!

We loved him – subtle and humorous, he was always generous and impeccably dressed in the railway uniform of a dark blue suit and highly polished black shoes.

Although well read, he was a quiet person of few words, speaking only when needed, and though he kept a distance between himself and his children, we were aware that his love for us was as unconditional as our mother's. He was very much a man of his time, leaving the cooking and housework to my mother because his work took up long hours of the day. He wasn't gregarious or sporty and he relaxed from his job by reading newspapers and classical literature which he kept in a pile by his chair. My mother sensed he was very tired when he came home from work and that he needed quiet moments to change his clothes and pray. Afterwards, when he had settled down, he would help us with our school work, outlining the complexities of mathematics and explaining how to pronounce foreign words in English.

He took his religion very seriously and was a man of deep and sincere faith but I never heard him preaching or insisting that we should do this or that. It sounds like a cliché but he lived by example and the only piece of advice he gave us directly was that if a problem arose in life we had to face it head on and not run away from it. This was the time when we had been moving house.

My father was a Senior Director of the then prestigious and efficient railway corporation of Sudan, built by and inherited from the British in the 1890s, and he was taking up the position of General Manager of the Northern section in Karima, 400 km north of Omdurman. The whole family – my father, mother and three elder brothers Farid, Siddig, Izzeldeen and sister Samira and I – were to start up a new life. Looking back, I'm not sure if they were happy at being uprooted from their home but at least we were all together.

It was a long journey, especially for a five-year-old. I remember staring from the train window at vast mounds of shimmering yellow and caramel coloured sand and rocky outcrops that stretched for 3,000 miles until they reached the Atlantic coast. This was the pitiless furnace of the Sahara, the Alatmour desert, where temperatures could be above 50°C and below freezing in winter, a place criss-crossed by nomads, camel trains and legendary tribes such as the black robed Bedouin and Taureg. My father had already triggered my sense of wonder, telling me in his deep rich voice of ancient trade routes, oases and 'haboobs', huge sand storms that rolled out of the empty vastness, choking the land for days on end and, somewhere in the gigantic wastes, the size of the entire United States of America, was the fabled city of Timbuktu. On the other side of the carriage, to the east, I could just make out the beginnings of greenery and palm trees, edging the banks and waters of the legendary Nile – the river had already had a special magic for me and would become an intricate part of my boyhood life.

The wheezy old train and the heat was rocking me to sleep. As I was holding my sister's hand my head sank into my mother's shoulder and my eyes began to close. For some strange reason I can remember to this day the mysterious dream I had on that train. I dreamt of my boyhood play by the banks of the Nile where I had learned to catch fish, build great sand castles and where I had nearly drowned when being taught to swim. I had heard tales of gigantic crocodiles that patrolled the river banks, pulling animals and even humans into deep flowing pools; of travelling to far away places and the names of exotic cities and countries, of struggles and challenges in my life. I dreamt of human beings who looked like angels and long sea and air journeys.

But demons were also circling and gathering like vultures. Nightmares had already invaded my childhood heaven and dark angels drifted in and out of my subconscious.

Another dream I had was again on the train when we were returning to Omdurman.

I had a premonition of my father's death, of being lost and alone on the banks of the Nile and of a cruel illness that would attack my mother. When I awoke I was confused and panic stricken. Maybe it was a childhood fear of the unknown and the unsettling emotions of having moved house, but I felt that the world was a threatening and menacing place. An inner voice, a rescuing angel, some childhood instinct, flooded in and I pretended all was well. I drifted off to sleep again.

This time I dreamt I was walking barefoot in the desert with an old man who seemed to be lit up and glowing. I saw three sets of footprints in the sand. I asked him who the third set belonged to but he ushered me to be quiet.

After a long, tiring walk we arrived at a huge expanse of water. The old man hadn't said anything but then he spoke. "The first footprints were mine, the second were yours and the third belonged to the waters you see now. This is the River Nile. It is the river of life." This was all very strange to me.

I never mentioned these recurring dreams to anyone but ever since I have wondered where they came from. I had other, brighter dreams too, and the daylight visions of my family and the solidity of my father's presence were reassuring. Even as a small child I was already thinking of my future life. Where would I live? Would I marry? What would I do to earn a living? I knew I wanted to travel and see more of this strange and captivating landscape that I had been catapulted into and I sensed that whatever the journey I did make, it would be a world away from that of my family and ancestors.

At last the train chuffed into Karima. The journey was over; the train shuddered to a sudden halt and we were taken to our new home. This was a large, strange, oldlooking place, built in the 1890s by the British to house the chief of their new railway. Painted grey on the outside with a massive entrance hall, it had a large sprawling garden at the front and a fruit orchard at the back with guava, orange, lemon, mango and palm trees. It was looked after by an old, dignified man called Ami El-Feel who greeted us with gentle courtesy. It was an impressive looking building but from the start I sensed something spooky about it. Perhaps I was developing into an over sensitive child, but my worries were soon confirmed.

Some weeks later there was some cautious gossip from our new neighbours who whispered that it was haunted by spirits and a 'Djinn', and my mother and grandmother who later came and stayed with us experienced some scary times in the house. We also had a domestic helper, a young man called Rabih. He wanted to tell us stories about how haunted the place was, but Ami El-Feel would glare at him, put his fingers to his lips in warning and shuffle him away.

One dark and windy night in Karima, the palm trees were whistling and whooshing outside in the garden and I nestled up to my mother on the sofa. My father was away on railway business and we were alone together. My brothers and sister had mooched off to a different room and I felt deliciously comfortable having her undivided attention all to myself as she told me stories that I still remember to this day. The first one was about our previous home in Omdurman. Apparently a crowd of children, including one or two of our cousins, had been shrieking wildly outside of the house because they had seen my grandfather chasing something. When my grandmother went out to check what was going on my aunt was yelling that the old lady by the window had suddenly left. Neither my mother or grandmother believed in djinns (ghosts) but they both swore that they had seen this old lady turn into glittering fragments of light and just melt into the river. Maybe this is just a story and a reflection of overworked imaginations, but it stayed with me and added to my growing realisation that there are more things in heaven and earth than we think, and that there are unseen powers beyond our comprehension.

Another weird incident happened in Omdurman when I was still only four and was sleeping in the same room as my mother. I was desperate for sleep but fought to stay awake to listen to her stories about the desert nomads, the ancient trade routes and the terrible accounts of vanished camel trains and sand-whipped relics of antique kingdoms. I decided that I was going to get up and ask my mother to stop because I was now really asleep, when I was suddenly hurled into the air by my mattress. It lifted me straight up and then plonked me back down on my bed. I was terrified and screamed out. My mother rushed over to calm me down, insisting that I had been dreaming, but she couldn't explain why my mattress was now in a completely different place and position. It sounds silly now but it hadn't been a dream and both my mother and I stayed awake for the rest of the night, wide-eyed with terror, until my father returned home in the early hours of the morning.

When we were in Karima my father would take the family on trips into the desert on the Friday weekends. I never quite knew where we were going, but as he talked an astonishing vision of early Africa began to unfold.

After a stifling hot car journey we arrived at the Pyramids of Meroe, a few kilometres south of Karima. There had been no metalled or tarmacked roads, just bumpy tracks which sometimes vanished in mounds of windblown sands, and I was terrified that we would end up driving into the desert and die of thirst. There are approximately 200 pyramids scattered on the west bank of the Nile, which are burial chambers and monuments of kings and queens, and had been built during the second and third centuries BCE. We were in the centre of the Nubian kingdom of Kush which rose to prominence in approximately 1000 BCE following the collapse of the 24th Pharaonic Egyptian dynasty to the north. Here was the heartland of the kingdom which came to be known in classical literature as 'The Island of Meroe'. Because of the remoteness, the pyramids are well off the international tourist routes, but the few visitors that do make the trip often leave spellbound. I was probably too immature to appreciate all this fabulous history, but something must have lodged in my mind and when I was older I began to ransack university libraries to find out more.

I soon adapted to my new life in Karima. I was not ready for a main school so I went to a small informal religious one where I remember we all had to sit on the sandy floor and look up at an ancient cracked board. Here we learned how to write our first words in Arabic and recite some verses from the Holy Qur'an. It was not a good introduction to education… there were no windows, and the only light sources were the door and a tiny window in the roof, so it was dark and oppressively hot.

The discipline was non existent. Pupils and parents would wander in and out of the classroom at will. I didn't stay there very long and my real schooling began back in Omdurman when I was six years old.

After a year away we moved back to Omdurman and I was happy to be once more in my real home where I was soon to start school. One chilly evening in December, my father took me on a trip to a nearby shop to get some bread, cooking oil and soap. The shop was owned and run by Taifoor, an abrupt, short man with a small scar on his right cheek. He peered at the world through a pair of ancient black glasses making his eyes look like outsize grapes. I had already encountered Taifoor on a previous visit and was wary of his appearance.

I was completely bored by the walk but thought it a good opportunity to get my father to open up a bit and tell some stories on the way. However, he just walked quietly on and eventually we reached the shop. This was no more than a converted garage made of mud bricks on the side of a small one-storey house. There was no proper door and my father had to stoop to enter the dark interior.

Out of the gloom stepped Taifoor, eyeing us bleakly and saying nothing. He was dressed like a Dickensian villain, with a long, khaki shirt and short black trousers covered in spots of oil and food stains. The 'shop' was unbelievable. Cigarettes, matches, out-of-date food, toys, pencils, charcoal, ink-stained exercise books, hammers, nails, old newspapers, screws, bicycle pumps, bottles of paraffin and assorted other junk were in haphazard piles that reached the ceiling. We could only see some of all this because the counter was almost head height and formed a sort of barrier between Taifoor and his customers.

My father, not in the least unnerved by his appearance, politely asked for the fresh bread, oil and soap. There was a pause and Taifoor, with a low grunt, shimmered back into the darkness on what I thought would be a hopeless quest. To my amazement he appeared with each item in a small cardboard box. He then took out his account book.

"Do you want to pay now or later?" he asked. I think this was his attempt at appearing efficient, although it wasn't working. Loose dirty papers were falling out of the book and Taifoor was scribbling frantically into what was left of it with a stubby pencil.

"I'll pay you now, Taifoor." My father thanked him, wished him goodbye with elaborate courtesy and we began the walk home. I was amazed at his approach and asked him why he had been so polite in the face of what I thought had been rudeness. He gave me a short reply, which I think summed up his innate understanding and sympathy for people. He told me he found a quotation in a biography which had struck him quite forcibly, which stated that, "Most men live lives of quiet desperation." I was baffled by this at the time, but when he added that Taifoor was not a wealthy man and was just trying to make a living, I began to understand what he meant, and that despite his manner he was a kindly and generous man.

Then an astonishing thing happened on the way back.

I saw a semi-naked man crouching on the pavement. Rain water was dripping from his shoulders and he was shivering violently from the cold. His only piece of clothing was a grey blanket wrapped round his waist. It was clear from the thinness of his ribs that he was starving. My father followed my gaze and immediately he took some of the bread we had just bought, wrapped it in a small cloth and offered it to the man. I will never forget the expression of gratitude in the man's eyes as his bony arms stretched out for the gift. Then, to my horror, my father began to take off his turban and a shawl and started to dress him. At first the man shrank back in embarrassment, but after a while he relaxed, bowed his head and allowed himself to be helped. We were near a bus station and as all this was going on small crowds, including some staring schoolboys, had gathered to watch.

They were arguing and shouting, not at my father, but amongst themselves, and they were clearly confused by what they were seeing. Suddenly they went quiet as an old man held up both his arms to speak. I think he must have been a religious teacher of some sort because he was able to command immediate silence. I couldn't hear all of what he was saying but I found out later that he had called my father's behaviour "blessed conduct", and that if only we could all behave in such a manner the world would be a kinder and better place. I saw that my father was listening intently to what was being said and as we walked home I gripped his hand tightly. I was so proud of him.

Typically, my father said nothing about the incident on our way home. He didn't need to. What he had done made a huge impact on my young mind. I never forgot his example and my respect for him soared from that moment. I think in holy writings there is the story of the Good Samaritan, the man who finds a stranger who is not of his faith or tribe who has been robbed and is bleeding and unconscious by the side of the road. Instead of leaving him to die he tends to his wounds and gives him refuge. Such was my father.

Chapter 2

Tales of the First Children of the Earth

Wisdom is the perfume of the wise.
(Kamil Idris)

What shall we tell you? Tales, marvellous tales, of ships and stars and islands where good men rest...

(James Elroy Flecker. English poet. 1884-1915)

T he Nile defined and coloured my childhood. I think the ancient Greeks would have called me a 'nympholet', someone whose imagination is dominated by running water. I have never tired of watching or even thinking about it and I feel there is something miraculous in its ever changing moods, at times gentle and benign, at others furious, tempestuous and wild. In my mind it is a symbol of permanence, even of eternity, its very air charged with echoes of the past. I could sit on its banks for hours just absorbed by the neverending flow, lost in wonder at the way each tiny droplet was on its own journey to the sea far away to the Mediterranean in the north. If I looked up I could see egrets, kingfishers, swallows, green bee eaters, pelicans and red beaked flamingos swooping and diving in their endless quest for food. Higher up huge flocks of white storks would be migrating, using the river as a navigation highway on their great trek to breed in Europe.

Perhaps it was then that I made an unconscious promise to myself that one day I would follow their route myself to explore unknown lands.

The river was also an avenue into the past. I was old enough to know that when the first ancestors of Africa arrived awestruck on its banks, it had already been flowing, down the long distances of history for hundreds of thousands of years. I thought this was wonderful. I think most people have precious memories of times when life is lived in complete harmony, perhaps when they were young and there was never a crack in the heart, and I find it soothing and reassuring to relive those golden moments when I was a small child fishing from its banks. When I was older it became a habit to find quiet stretches of the river, well away from the frantic bustle of the city, where I could sit still and just be calmed by the waters. The chaos of many worries would slip away and for a few moments the peace of the centuries would hush my soul and I sensed a great silence that whispered of the dawn of mankind. The scene I would be looking at was prehistoric, as unaltered as the stars overhead in its elemental simplicity. I would also discover that the ancient Greeks had had another wonderful word, 'temenos', for what I was seeking. To them this described a sacred place, a sanctuary with its own healing graces, and I treasured this sense of spiritual connection with them.

I still had my strange nightmares but the river seemed to usher them away as it just kept on rolling calmly along.

An English poet called these moments 'relics of joy'; visions of the past recollected in tranquillity, providing ballast in the rough storms of existence. The Nile had cast its allure over me. Its scale and unmatchable history stirred my blood. It was 'old man river' and as a young boy it was my whole world. I was also fascinated by the way the White and Blue rivers coalesced and flowed smoothly on, the white creamy waters of the former eventually joining with the brown alluvial silt of the other. In my later teenage fancies I imagined that their intermingling might be a sort of metaphor for all the problems of mankind.

The destiny, the journey, the endless tensions of race and religion might be harmonised, even though there would be strong currents, floods and dangerous cataracts on the way. Was the great peaceful delta thousands of kilometres to the north another metaphor for heaven and were the sources symbols of all our births? Whimsical thinking, but I stored it away in my young mind.

This was a time just before I started school and I spent many happy days with other boys fishing on its banks and swimming to Tutti Island. This was about 8km² of fruit orchards and vegetable farms overflowing with fresh produce and inhabited for centuries by the Mahas tribe and others – traditionally farmers and fishermen. I loved it. On good days, with earthworms as our main bait, we were able to haul out dozens of oval-shaped fish called bulti and sharp finned perch. They weren't giant size but we were proud of our skills and would carry them home in baskets for the evening family meals. My mother would whoop with delight when I tipped the fish on to the kitchen table. After I had gutted them she would grill them on an open fire in the outside yard and my elder brothers would slap me on the back calling me a 'true fisherman' as they wolfed them down with fresh bread and salads.

This was heady praise from them as they could also tease me about being the youngest and weakest member of the family. There was nothing malicious in this, it was just their way of reminding me who was whom in the pecking order – who was boss. I remember those days so clearly now and whenever I smell wood smoke, herbs and cooked meat in the evening dusk, the years are whisked away and I am a small child again in the bosom of my family.

I had made many friends with other boys on the river banks but the one I remember most was El-hadi Adam.

He was also called 'Wad Nas Elbahar', meaning 'Son of the Nile people'. He was about eight years old, tall, smiling and well built with hands and nails permanently covered in mud. He was an intelligent pupil at school but had had to leave early to help his parents. I think his confidence came from the fact that he knew that his future would be the same as his father and grandfather, and he was quite happy about it. His family were poor, managing to scratch a living right next to the river, but they were kindly and had the manners of aristocrats. Outside their small hut they grew seeds and seasonal vegetables, along with another six or seven families close by. Their whole lives were dominated by the river. They cleaned themselves in it, washed their clothes in it and caught as many fish as they could, eating what they needed and selling the rest.

It was a fragile existence though, as high rainfall up river would send raging floods turning their huts into floating boats and washing their tools away in the currents. I was amazed by the way they accepted this as part of the trials of life. They never seemed to be afraid as the river levels rose and rose.

It struck me then, even as a small child, that life was a struggle and very precarious. I was amazed at their calm fatalism. They seemed to know that they were in the hands of Allah and that all manner of things would eventually be well – a simple philosophy which I found very reassuring. I was learning many lessons on this river bank and was amazed at the resilience of these poor people and the simplicity of their lives. To them the floods could be destructive, but they were also life-saving, because when the waters settled, the soil was oozing with nutrients and minerals. When the time was right they would once more plant their seeds in its restored richness, as their ancestors had done for hundreds of years before them.

Their humility and faith in Allah was matched by their kindness. They were a generous and welcoming family and often invited me to share meals of delicious lentils, fish, home-cooked bread and mint tea with them, prepared on an open fire outside their hut.

I remember that one morning while we were sipping tea, El-hadi Adam had been watching me carefully with a strange look on his face. His gaze had wandered to the river. He suddenly jumped to his feet. "Come on," he shouted, "you're going to learn to swim!" I was terrified.

We were fishing a few hundred yards past the confluence and the river, though shallow on the edges, was also about eight metres deep in midstream, and there were strong currents. That wasn't my only fear – although I had never seen one, I had heard horrific stories about the man-eating crocodiles that patrolled the river shallows. They would swim underwater and hang motionless like dead logs, waiting for a passing meal. You couldn't see them until they exploded onto the bank and dragged you under. I had also heard the story of an explorer who had found a young boy crying beside a dead crocodile which had eaten his grandmother. The boy had sold it for a small sum with her body still inside it! The crocodiles had slitty yellow eyes and rows of sharp white teeth like piano keys, and their sense of smell was so powerful they knew immediately when you had stepped into the water. I was terrified but El-hadi Adam swam about without a care in the world and started laughing when I mentioned them. He was now in the water shouting at me to come in.

"What about the crocodiles?"

"To hell with the crocodiles!" he yelled.

"But they'll eat us. Anyway I'll drown!" I protested.

"You won't drown and if they come for us we'll hit them on the nose and eat them!" he replied.

I wasn't convinced. I waded cautiously into the river, half expecting to get my legs bitten off, but nothing happened. The water was warm – there was only a tiny current and El-hadi Adam came swimming towards me.

He stood up and said I had to put my head under the water in what he called a pre drowning exercise. I was reluctant but he gently forced me to sit down and pushed my head under. I spluttered and coughed but found I wasn't dead and the crocodiles hadn't appeared. My fears began to vanish and somehow, two days later, I was swimming alongside him, and although not nearly as strongly, at least I could stay afloat and move. Other young boys began to join us. I remember some of their names to this day and often wonder what became of them. They were Ismat Abbas, Ahmed Hamid, Osama Dar-Sileih, Kardash, Salah Abbas and his cousin Mahmoud.

We were now a sort of gang with El-hadi Adam as the self-appointed leader and of course, being young and silly, we were looking for challenges. One day he announced that we were going to swim across to Tutti Island and visit the farmers there. I thought he was joking, but he wasn't, and the gang began to walk towards the river. I held back and was terrified. I was the smallest and youngest and I knew I would have to swim for at least an hour as the river was full at the time, and more than 1.5km wide. I also knew there was a strong current about half way across… but I couldn't lose face in front of the others, so I trudged along at the back. I was ready to run away, but I took a deep breath and plunged in. It was fine at first as I could paddle a long way out and I swam only when the water was deep enough. However, when about half-way across, I began to be swept downstream by the current, swallowing water and choking. I tried as hard as I could to fight my way back but my arms and legs were getting heavier and heavier and I was drifting downstream. The whole group realised what was happening and turned in panic towards me. Two of them splashed their way back and started pushing me forward. I tried to hold my head high out of the water and after a while I was able to continue on my own. As we reached the island they began shouting and cheering me on. This really encouraged me and somehow I made it to the shore.

I crawled up the bank on all fours, spitting out water and feeling so proud of myself. What we hadn't realised was that all the way across we had had an audience of farmers on the island watching us. These old men were very poor. Their only clothes were long, white shirts and the short, tattered trousers they were standing in, but they gave us a royal welcome and invited us to share their midday meal. The food was delicious. Freshly caught fish, cooked tomatoes, carrots and cucumber were cooked on an open fire, followed by water melon and mint tea. In return we offered to help them with their work on their farms but they smiled and refused. We were their guests they said and wouldn't dream of accepting the offer. We stayed and chatted with them for about three hours and they told us stories about their fishing experiences.

They explained that there were in fact crocodiles, but most of them were well upstream and they were man-eaters. Then there was this terrible place called 'The Sud', a vast, insect-ridden, primeval swamp where the Nile hardly moved and the only sounds were the splashing of the hippopotamuses and crocodiles, and where explorers disappeared and were never seen again. There were stories that the natives decorated their spear shafts with the testicles of unwelcome intruders, and there was a king who was so proud of his huge fat wives that he would make guests measure them with a special tape. There were massive perch, bigger than grown men, aggressive predators and highly prized by sports anglers, and terrible snakes that could swallow pigs. Then there were catfish, great slimy creatures that lived on the bottom of the river and were horrible to eat because they lived on dead and dying fish and any rubbish that would sink to the river bed. They also could grow to a huge size and drag little boys under the water, drowning and then eating them...

We listened wide-eyed in wonder, but it was now getting towards late afternoon and time for home.

Enchanted by the welcome and the food, I had forgotten about the return trip, but I was now far more relaxed and was able to cross the river without any major crisis, though the older boys did keep a watchful eye on my progress. I was waiting all the time for a crocodile or catfish to grab me by the ankles and eat me alive, but nothing happened. When I got to the far bank I was so tired I could hardly drag myself out of the water.

However, in a way this was a very important moment in my life. I had accepted a challenge and had been able to keep up with my elder peers without showing too much fear, and this gave me enormous confidence. We arrived on the far bank and by the time I marched proudly back to my home all my clothes were dry. I didn't tell anyone about where we had been because I would probably have been grounded, but I did boast about it the next day to my best friend at school, Omar Khatir. I think he was shocked and maybe a bit envious. He gave me dire warnings about how the river could suddenly flood and that I had to be careful. Ironically he was drowned himself a few years later near the place I had been telling him about, even though he was a strong swimmer.

Later, in 1974, I read something in a local paper that made ice run through my veins – I had to stand still for a moment. In the very waters where I had been swimming a grown man had been dragged from the river bank and eaten by a huge crocodile. I hadn't known that they could run at 40 kph and twice that speed when erupting from the water!

My only other memory of fishing in the Nile was the day when a friend called Mahgoub swallowed a perch bone and it stuck in his throat. He was slowly choking and couldn't spit it out. We were panicking. A man driving a Coca-Cola wagon saw what was happening, lifted him into his cabin and rushed him to the hospital. Mahgoub survived and the man drove us back to the fishing bank, sharing his sandwiches on the way. The kindness of strangers…

It wasn't just the Nile that had beguiled my childhood and opened up the world for me – I had also been mesmerised by the fabled souks or markets. Situated at the confluence of the White and Blue Nile rivers, they were hundreds of years old. There were rambling, chaotic labyrinths of street sellers, traders, and merchants; of small wagons called 'carros' driven by monkeys; of Muslims, Christians, and Jews, all busy selling their wares and forgetting their religious or tribal differences.

Whenever I was there my senses danced with delight. I smelled ginger, cinnamon, frankincense, tamarind, coffee and even myrrh. I remember seeing silks and ceramics from India, glass and precious stones from China, whale bone, textiles and bright metals from Northern Europe.

My parents would explain everything to me as we picked our

way through this wonderland. Some goods were displayed on blankets and others on wooden stalls.

I have carried this mental picture all my life of my childhood days when Khartoum, with its markets, souks and shops, was a dynamic, bustling mass of traders, customers and merchants all happily engaging with each other in a sort of gigantic festival of bargaining, lively haggling and goodwill. This was the universal brotherhood of commerce where religious differences were put to one side in the interests of mutual benefit and tolerance.

There were Muslims, Christians, Jews, the "Alshawam" from Syria and Lebanon, Armenians and Greeks, competing with one another to see who could open their shop first. In the suburbs of the city gypsies lived in neighbourly co-existence with Copts and Muslims and I can still hear the ringing of church bells in Almasalma in Omdurman and Alamlak in the north summoning them to church on Sunday mornings.

The early nights in the markets were especially active and older readers will remember dazzlingly lit shops such as Kont Muklis, Vanian Sons, Abdalla Al-azrag, and Surkisian selling high quality jewellery, silver, gold and precious stones.

There was also Jumhuria Street and Al-suk-al-afrangi where clothes, furniture and household goods tempted the passers-by. The Arab market featured huge mounds of fruit, spices, coffee, vegetables and perfumes and after shopping there were the delights of the Gordon Music Hall, or family entertainment at cinemas such as "The Blue Nile". A casino, also called "The Blue Nile", on a beach near the river was especially popular as a place where families and friends could relax over soft drinks such as ginger and double cola to exchange the news of the day. Here the rich city people also gathered, such as Osman Salih, Abdelmoniem Mohamed Abu-Elila, Mamoun Elbireir, Elsir Abbas, Garu Vanian, Elsheikh Mustafa, Kont Muklis, Saad Abu-Elila, Elshingiti and Taha Elroobi who all represented the generous values of society.

The big mosques in Khartoum, Omdurman and the Idrisi mosque in Almorada were always busy. I can still hear the heavenly singing voice of Hassan Attiya and then Sheikh Siddig Ahmed Hamdoun's beautiful recital of Quaranic verses, listened to on the radio by millions in cities and villages all over Sudan. The one that struck a deep chord within me was, and still is, from Quaran-Alkafirun, verse 109:6 "Lakum deenekum waliya deen." (You are allowed your religion and I am allowed mine.) Underlining this essential message of tolerance were the other key themes: Quaran-Aal-i-imraan (The family of Imraan) Allah! There is no God but he – the living, the Self-Subsisting, Eternal. It is He who sent down to thee (step by step), in truth, The Book, confirming what went before it; and he sent down the law (of Moses) and the gospel (of Jesus), as a guide to mankind and He sent down the criterion of judgement between right and wrong.

This is the picture I treasure because it is one of hope for the future. I know we cannot arrest time and turn back the clock but in a troubled and constantly changing world we should always have a vision before us of sunlit uplands where harmony, tolerance and kindliness are the supreme virtues and it is my rock solid conviction, as I mention again and again in the memoir, that that precious goal is achievable.

There were special markets too. I remember in particular Gold Street, Spice Street, Clothes Street and Silver Street.

I was told that the best silver was sold by the Rashaida, an eastern tribe specialising in precious rings, amulets, bracelets and pendants. Mingling with all the delicious smells of wood smoke, incense and spices were excited voices disputing the prices. I knew very few of the dialects and accents but could recognise the traditional pantomime of haggling.

"How much?"

"Ridiculous!"

"Give me your lowest price!"

Typically a crowd would form around a potential sale and the buyer and seller would drop into actor mode, well aware of the importance of providing a mini-theatre for the onlookers and desperate not to be seen as losers.

Bluffing, counter-bluffing and outraged walking away were all part of the fun. Eventually a compromise would be reached after much drama, and applause would even break out when the deal was finalised with slapped handshakes.

I also noticed that trust and honesty were essential. I loved the story of a jeweller who had noticed a young girl eyeing a silver bracelet. She was obviously not sure whether she should buy it, so he allowed her to take it home without payment, trusting that she would return the next day with her decision. This she did. She bought the bracelet.

Back home in the evenings my father would gather his children around and he would tell wonderful tales. In those days we had no television, but we did have an antique brown *Grundig* radio and would listen to the local stations and then twiddle with the dials until he found the BBC World Service. My father would usually choose what programmes we tuned in to, and as he was interested in the news and current affairs my awareness of politics and social issues began to develop.

At other times in the evenings he would switch the radio off and we would settle round him, knowing exactly what was coming next, but longing to hear it again. He would relate the ancient stories of Africa, as old as time itself. They were folk memories that had been passed on from generation to generation, an oral tradition that my father was perhaps unwittingly continuing himself. He would go back to the very beginning, to the very earliest days of the human race which had begun, according to legend, in the rift valley to the south (in present day Kenya). He told us about the Bushmen, thought to be the descendants of the oldest tribe in the continent, the nursery of mankind, and possibly the first inhabitants of the world. They were the original nomads of antiquity and at one time their territory had stretched from Kenya to the Cape of Good Hope. They, or their ancestors, had crossed into Arabia and the Levant and over thousands of years had moved further north into Asia and Europe. These were the people who eventually reached Australia, and even America, by crossing the

Bering Strait.

The stories set my mind reeling. Were they the descendants of Adam and Eve? Was that just a story? Was there a direct genetic link between the present day Bushmen and their descendants? The story also challenged the contemporary view that it was the Europeans that had 'discovered' Africa. If the anthropologists were correct, it was the other way round – it was the indigenous Africans who had discovered the world. They were the great grandparents of humanity. I didn't know the answers to all these questions but I listened open-mouthed. At the time many of my friends would make jokes about these stories, calling them old wives' tales. However, modern day research, based on DNA samples, has confirmed that the whole human race was once one tribe and that Africa was the mother and father of humanity.

There were more stories about other war-like tribes, probably descendants of the original ones who attacked the Bushmen. The Bushmen were pushed south, fighting all the way until they settled in the only places that they felt safe – mainly in the Namibian desert. My father told us that they were still there and that their myths and legends were helping to sustain them as they faced the inevitable collisions with the modern world. They lived a primitive but enduring life – expert hunters and gatherers, nurturing the wisdom and knowledge of their ancestors, whose creation stories had uncanny links with the deepest thinkers and poets in the rest of the world. According to their beliefs the supreme god Kang created the world, but death and destruction entered when mankind became presumptuous and arrogant. They believe that he lives in the sky and that his invisible spirit resides in all living things. One particular Bushman story my father told me stuck in my mind: Kang's wife gave birth to an eland, a beautiful antelope, but it was mistakenly killed by two of his sons. Kang demanded that the animal's blood be boiled and the remaining fatty issue was scattered over the landscape, in turn becoming other antelope and animals for his people to hunt, kill and eat.

Their explanation for existence and all the mysteries of life was contained in the phrase, 'There is a dream dreaming us' – an outlook I was later to discover in The Tempest by Shakespeare, in the enigmatic lines from Prospero, the philosopher king, at the end of the play when he declares, "We are such stuff as dreams are made on, and out little life is rounded with a sleep."

On other nights my father would astonish us with his knowledge of the history of African tribes. Their names were as numerous as the stars, but the ones that I remember were the Ashanti, the Berbers, the Taureg and Dogons of the Sahara, the Pygmies in the dense equatorial forests, the great warlike Zulu kings and the lion hunting Masai. In Sudan there were the Nubians, the Beja, the Fur, the Nuba, the Baggara, the Dinka, the Nuer, the Shilluk, the Danagla, the Shaigia, the Ja'aleen and many others, each tribe with its own language, traditions and fierce sense of independence.

His voice seemed to change slightly when he told us about the Nubians and I sensed they held a special place in his heart. He told us that it had been the Nubians who had founded the fabulous Kingdom of Kush and the pyramids of Meroe were echoes of the grandeur of their civilisation.

To me this was an exciting revelation. We had visited the pyramids before when we were in Karima, but I had been too young to appreciate them. Now I began to realise that the Egyptians weren't the only ones that had built vast shrines and temples to their dead. In Meroe over 40 pyramids, all made of reddish brown volcanic stone, glow magnificently in the evening light. Some have their tops blown off, the work of Guiseppe Ferlini, an Italian who blasted off the core of one of them in 1834 and discovered some treasure. He then wrongly assumed that the others had hidden gems and dynamited their tops off as well, an act of vandalism that would probably have earned him a prison sentence today. It is hard to imagine now but the civilisation lasted for a thousand years, finally fading away in about 400 CE. Nobody really seems to know why the culture declined, but at one time Meroe was the centre of a world-wide trade and a place of mighty industry. It controlled the entire Nile valley and from its foundries and mines sent iron and gold to India and China and other parts of the world.

Nearby was Gebel Al Barkal, a sandstone mountain which the Egyptians believed was the birthplace of Amun, their mythical god of creation. Rising at the southern edge of their empire, they thought this mountain was where the Nile began (and therefore all of creation), and in 1500 BCE they built a temple to Amun. It wasn't really a mountain, but at 98 m high it soared dramatically above the flat desert, was a landmark for traders on the great routes to the Mediterranean and Arabia, and was a pointer to the safest crossing of the Nile. The Kushites developed into a formidable military power and invaded Egypt in 747 BCE, founding the 25th Pharaonic dynasty. They had absorbed the Egyptian culture and, as well as expanding the temple, built pyramids in Meroe as tombs for their dead kings. The engineering was sensational in that they aligned the tops of the pyramids to a pinnacle on Gebel Al Barkal that in turn lined up with the rising of the sun on the exact day when the Nile floods began to recede.

One of the kings, Taharka, built a huge golden inscription, a message to both the gods and mortals, the pinnacle of which reflected the sun's rays and shone out for miles into the surrounding desert. The colours have faded over the years, but if you look closely, you can still see the original words high up on the pinnacle. I found this mesmerising and marvelled at the craftsmanship involved. It required almost superhuman intelligence and planning to create these magnificent monuments and throughout my life I have been lost in wonder and praise for their creators.

They and the Nile have pride of place in my imagination, and I sincerely hope that others will come to Sudan to gaze on these fabulous relics of civilisation and their splendour as I have done since childhood.

It wasn't just the stories that were part of the magic.

One day my father took me to the camel market on the

outskirts of Omdurman and I felt as though I had lifted a veil into the past and was centuries back in time. The market was a sprawling confusion of farmers and traders in dusty blue and white robes, with women at tea and coffee stands. Hundreds of camels stood around in tethered groups with ropes around their ankles and legs to stop them running away. They had sneering, arrogant expressions and great velvety mouths which they would suddenly bare, spewing forth a mass of disgusting yellow teeth and stinking breath. These were the 'ships of the desert', able to endure the fiercest heat and sandstorms with long dark eyelashes that helped to keep out the flies and sand. They could also be very bad tempered and I was careful not to go too near them. In times gone by traders from the north would have brought balsam oil, European made paper, textiles, scents and spices, dyes and small amounts of military supplies in exchange for the camels.

Just like in the souks, the selling and bargaining was furious and dramatic, as sand dusted nomads matched wits with the merchants.

These were the men who would buy the beasts en masse and drive them north to Egypt on the fabled 'Darb al Arba'In', the forty days road. This was a 700 year old trade route that connected the market with Asyoot, just over the Egyptian border – a round trip of about three months.

The whole safety of the drive depended on hitting the two oases en route at Selima and Kharga. If they missed or were hit by a three or four day sandstorm, they would be in deep trouble. I learned that camels can go up to 30 days without water but a human will last only a matter of days.

These men had the look of genuine experts – tough, lean, their eyes forever on a distant horizon. Proud and independent in their bearing, they were the true masters of the desert and they gave me the impression that borders, politics and the sick hurry of modern life were irrelevant to their lives.

Stirred by my father's stories, I wanted to know more.

I sensed that in some places I was standing on ghostly

ground. The monumental past was all around me. Its neglected stones and statues were permanent, insistent invitations, and all I had to do was take a trip back to absorb their splendour. For me the past has never been a foreign country and I felt the presence of vanished generations all around. We cannot recreate the past but its presence, if the imagination is allowed to wander, is tantalisingly within reach. I thought it was a tremendous thing that the Nile was the river where early man had once stood and gazed, saw that the land was good and built his first campfires. I was overwhelmed by these feelings of close communion with the dead, but to get closer I had to be patient and listen. I had to ask old people for their memories, and find out for myself.

I found it extraordinary that Khartoum was the place where a Roman expeditionary force had been sent by the Emperor Nero in 61 CE. They had reached Meroe and then given an escort up the White Nile, but the swamps and insects of the Sudd had defeated them and they turned for home. I was fishing on the very ground where British gunboats had pounded the vast hordes of the Mahdi, when thousands of men had been massacred by a terrible thing called the Maxim Gun. This had been the appalling Battle of Omdurman in 1898 when my grandparents had been children. It all had started when the Egyptians and British had ruled Sudan as a protectorate during the late nineteenth century. In 1883 the region erupted in rebellion when a charismatic, inspirational Muslim leader called Muhammed Ahmad identified himself as the 'Mahdi', a descendant of the Prophet who would redeem and purify the Islamic world.

The son of a boat-builder, he was convinced that he had a divine mission to rid Sudan of the colonial powers. His most loyal followers were from the Baggara tribe from the region of Kordofan, west of the Nile. With some captured rifles and cannons they defeated an Egyptian force of eight thousand at Shaykan, the capital of Kordofan, and now with an army of 30,000 followers, marched towards Omdurman.

The city was defended by General Gordon, a tough British

officer who refused to surrender. When the city was overrun he was killed and the British Parliament sent troops to quell the uprising and avenge Gordon's death.

Among the troops was a young subaltern called Winston Churchill. He was also acting as a newspaper reporter and later wrote a detailed account of the battle. The battlefield was at Kerreri, only 11 km north of Omdurman, and Churchill took part in one of the last cavalry charges in British military history.

The army, made up of 26,000 British and Egyptian troops, and commanded by Major General Kitchener, had 20 Maxim Guns and was supported by ten gunboats. The Maxim Guns were terrible weapons, each capable of firing 600 bullets a minute, and Kitchener planted them in the front line of battle. He arranged his men in a semi-circle on the west bank of the Nile with the gun boats at anchor just behind them. Three miles away across an empty dusty plain were 60,000 of the Mahdi's army, mainly Ansar or 'servants of Allah'. Their leader was the Khalifa Abdullahi, the successor of the Mahdi. The Ansar had been told by the Mahdi before he died that his special blessing or 'baraka' would turn the enemy's guns to water and they would be victorious in any battle. They made a colourful and terrifying sight, their front line stretching nearly five miles across the desert plain. Most of the warriors were in white tunics with black patches sewn on the front and back and each contingent had its own highly coloured flags of red, green and blue. There were other white flags embroidered with quotations from the Holy Qur'an.

Churchill, watching on his horse from a nearby ridge, described the scene:

> They looked like dark blurs and streaks, relieved and diversified with an odd looking shimmer of light from the spear points. A tremendous roar came up in waves of intense sound, like the tumult of the rising wind and sea before a storm.

The battle began but before the Ansar got within sword and spear range they were mown down like grass.

According to one eyewitness:

> They could never get near and refused to hold back. It was not a battle but a mass execution.

The bodies were not in heaps, bodies hardly ever are, but they were spread evenly over acres and acres. Some lay composed with their slippers placed under their heads for a last pillow, some knelt, cut short in a last prayer.

They suffered the most terrible injuries with arms and legs scattered at random and men staggering around with their bowels hanging down and faces cut to rags. In a little over five hours it was all over. As many as 11,000 of the Mahdi's army were dead and approximately 16,000 wounded. The Anglo-Egyptian losses were only 500 dead and wounded. A British officer recalled one of the final, climactic moments of the battle when the courage and bravery of the Mahdi's army was almost beyond description:

> One of the finest things I've ever seen. They hadn't a chance… but not one man faltered, each rode to his death without flinching.

He was describing the doomed charge of 200 Baggara horsemen who galloped towards the Maxim Guns, knowing full well that the day was lost. The bullets hit them like hail and not a single one survived. Another officer was deeply moved by their gallantry. "You never saw anything so stirring and so recklessly brave…"

Churchill was astounded by the enemy's courage and refusal to turn back, but was moved to tears at the callousness of the aftermath when the wounded were left to die where they lay. He wrote to his mother:

> Our victory was disgraced by the inhuman slaughter of the wounded and Lord Kitchener was responsible for this.

Later Kitchener entered Khartoum in triumph and had many of the Khalifa's leaders and followers killed. As a final insult he had the Mahdi's bones dug up and thrown into the Nile. Churchill had had great respect for the Mahdi, calling him "heroic" and a great charismatic leader, and this treatment of his dead body appalled him. Later in his life he would urge his victorious troops always to show magnanimity and compassion for a defeated enemy – perhaps the battle of Omdurman was influential in forming these views.

I treasured these memories of my father and his wonderful tales of Africa and battles long ago. I say 'treasured' because he passed away shortly afterwards. It was 1960 and he had been in the special wing of the then British Hospital in Khartoum, suffering from the effects of high blood pressure. We were visiting him at exactly 1.45 pm. It is strange how I remember the time so exactly, even though I was very young. Perhaps in moments of crisis the mind is sharpened and the senses go on high alert. I don't know. My father had stood up from his chair, and had walked me to the window of the room. He pointed out a small supermarket in the street below and said that, if he could save enough money, he would buy it for me when I was older. Then he handed a small picture of himself to me, urged me to work hard at school and to live a good and honest life. I was a bit puzzled by all of this but forgot about it as it was time for lunch and we all had to leave. He had by now apparently fully recovered from his illness and was due to be discharged from the hospital the next day. He waved us goodbye and settled down in his chair for an afternoon nap.

A couple of hours later we were just finishing lunch at home when we heard hysterical shouting. It came from the house of our uncle next door and we stood up in shock as a second cousin, Abdeen Ali, vaulted over the tall wall separating the house and began yelling and shouting in our hallway. The hospital had phoned him with terrible news. He covered his face in his hands and wailed. I couldn't make out the words at first, but my mother and sister started screaming and crying. Abdeen Ali was telling us that my father was dead.

Within minutes what seemed like hundreds of relatives and friends were pouring into the house. We were frozen in shock, holding hands and unable to believe what was happening. My vivid memory of that moment is of my small self poised motionless, staring up into a mass of weeping faces. My feet felt locked to the floor, perfectly still. I was like a feather in the still centre of a whirlwind.

Only I wasn't a feather – I was a devastated young son whose whole universe had just been shattered. People say that children are very resilient in the face of tragedy, but my father's death rocked me to my core, and even though my mother was still there I felt lost and abandoned. A week later an old man who somehow hadn't heard the news asked me where my father was and I cried for nearly a full day.

Apart from my immediate family it was the local children who tried to comfort me. Some of them were from poor families wearing old worn-out clothes and going barefoot, but they would smile and pat me on the back, urging me to join in with their games. I would climb trees and go on fishing expeditions with them, and as the days and weeks passed I tuned back into life. I think this was also the time that I began to understand how much my mother was grieving and I made a decision that somehow I would help and support her as much as I could.

This was a very depressing period for all the family because we had loved and depended on my father for everything. He had handled all the financial and legal concerns, and no one had a clue where all the required papers were. According to tradition it would be his closest brother who would handle the will and the inevitable claims on the property, and so my Uncle Gurashi became the executor and official caretaker. As a family we were in a very precarious situation, because the only obvious source of security was the house we were living in, but even that was under threat.

There were legitimate family claims on the house that had to be sorted out, and as the weeks passed we would hear a court messenger knocking on the front door with papers for my mother to sign. She was understandably still in a highly nervous and emotional state and didn't want to appear in person in court. We were in a confusing situation, but we had someone in the family who was a force to be reckoned with. Enter my aunt Hayat, my mother's closest sister, a tall, kindly, imposing, fighting matriarch to her fingertips. She stormed into our lives with tremendous energy and defiance as if on a divine mission, and she quite simply rescued us from our depression and sense of hopelessness. I was too young to understand the complexities, but she pored over the paperwork, scribbling furiously in the margins and guiding us through the maze of legal jargon. She argued. She challenged. She remonstrated. She was a gift from heaven, transforming our lives and restoring our confidence. I have never forgotten her in my prayers.

One of the other ways we got round the crisis was by selling off some small assets. However, we didn't want to attract too much attention from our neighbours while doing this and we had to be discreet. My mother had a small amount of inherited gold secreted away in an ancient eighteenth century safe. The other members of the family knew little about this because she had hidden it in a crack behind one of the walls in her bedroom.

Unbeknown to us, she had been leaving the house secretly and selling it to a gold merchant in the old souk in Omdurman. The gold was now all gone, but beside the safe was an old-fashioned sewing machine which she thought might fetch some money. This had been a wedding gift from her mother and it had sentimental value, but she realised that we needed the cash it might bring. She couldn't hide from us the fact that she was selling it, and when she returned from the market she complained that she had sold it for less than its real value.

Next was the turn of the old safe. Before it went we took out the items that still remained in it – some texts from the Holy Qur'an, and our birth certificates. These were put safely in a large cupboard drawer but have since been lost! The safe was so heavy it took six men to carry it out of the house, and by this time the neighbours were crowding round outside wondering what on earth was going on. With much heaving and shoving the safe was loaded onto a wooden cart and a donkey led it away to the market.

These were very hard times, but my mother, strengthened by the presence and determination of her sisters Hayat, Huda, Fahima and her aunt Zainab, began to recover her strength. We had one spare room in the house and she decided that she would rent it out to help make ends meet. Being close to the Nile it was in a desirable spot and might attract the attention of young couples.

Another relative who made a great impression on me was Zainab, my mother's aunt. Sometimes we called her 'Haboba' or 'grandmother', and she was quite happy answering to both names. She was a tall, heavy-set woman with a fleshy face, strong, sparkling brown eyes and another confident, uncompromising matriarch. She was of Turkish origin and it was clear to me that she had once been a very handsome woman. Now retired from teaching art, crafts and sewing, she relished her role as a senior member of the family. For some reason, maybe undiagnosed asthma, she was always a heavy and noisy breather, and she would arrive puffing and wheezing in our house, laden with all sorts of food and presents from a shopping trip. She would stride down to the river bank markets to buy from the local farmers, but the journey was really something of a trial for her.

I loved her twice weekly visits. Gasping for breath, she would plonk her 'guffa', a home-made basket, on the kitchen table, and I would stand on tip-toe to see what delights she had brought. There were hand-made sweets, peanut butter, spices, coffee, vegetables and fresh milk, and sometimes traditional games involving coloured cards and counters. She would then start chattering and gossiping away, mainly to her nieces and granddaughters, and begin to prepare a great meal for all the family, clattering the pans into submission and issuing orders like a sergeant major. Naturally she was the chief cook and she would insist that everyone should eat together. Her speciality was mulah asida, a local speciality of crushed meat, marinated in herbs, spices and a small amount of milk. It was sensational.

When she laughed her whole body would shake and wobble, and as she boiled and stirred she would offer the wisdom of age to nobody in particular. The phrases were proverbs as old as Moses, distilled by her own experience of life. "Oh my God life is very short!" "Oh, laughter is the best medicine!" "Oh if we do not find what we like, we should like what we find!"

She was a one-woman hurricane in our lives, and we loved her very much. I was fascinated by her and would ask tentative questions about her roots, her history, her pupils and her own education, but she would give me sideways looks, answer in vague generalisations (sometimes very sarcastically), and totter away. I thought there might be some tragedy in her life that she was hiding and maybe the extrovert side of her character was her means of defence. I never found out.

My aunt Fahima was another widow who came to live with us from early days. She had Turkish, Egyptian and Moroccan blood in her veins, and to me she was very beautiful, but her jet-black hair and deep brown eyes couldn't hide the deep sadness of her expression when she thought no one was looking. Her husband had died after only two years of marriage and they had had no children. I remember she always dressed in white traditional clothes and she had a gentle and very dignified manner, with a soft musky voice. When the really black moods descended she would become quiet, retire to her bed and stare at the wall for hours, sometimes for days.

We tried not to disturb her and were as understanding and affectionate as possible. She repaid our concern by taking a genuine interest in our progress, especially at school. I think she began a slow process of redirecting her life and channelling all her motherly instincts into the well-being of her little nieces and nephews.

For some reason, maybe because I was the 'baby' of the family, she seemed to take a special interest in me.

When I was in bed she would come into my room and talk or read me stories, and she would never leave until she was sure I had gone to sleep. Like Zainab, she became a totemic figure in our lives. She seemed to be able to sense when I was worried about exams at school and she would stop whatever she was doing and sit quietly next to me.

One day she said she had a surprise gift for me. Once again we were in the middle of the Mawlid period honouring the Prophet Mohammed (PBUH). She wanted me to go with her to the huge celebration site in Khalifa square, where she would buy something special. I was one happy boy at this invitation, as my childish wish was to have a sugared green and pink toy horse to bring home and show my friends. I would then spend a wonderful hour sucking it to pieces. I was also delirious at the thought of being part of the festivities that would take place the next day. In addition to the religious observances, this was a time of street processions, coloured lights, acrobats, magicians, performing monkeys, drumming, flutes, whirling dervishes, dancing and high spirits, where the dust literally rose in the air as the celebrations continued far into the night.

Somehow Fahima had found out that my one ambition in life was to have this sugar horse and she had been saving up her precious coins to buy one for me. I knew she had very little money, even though she pretended to be well off, but I put this to the back of my mind, and that night I was so excited I couldn't sleep. The next morning we walked hand-in-hand to the celebrations. The distant noise of the drumming, the whoops of the crowd, the smell of incense and the cloud of greyish brown dust ahead of us launched my senses into overdrive. When we were walking Fahima didn't say much and had to hold my hand firmly as I pulled her along. I couldn't wait! Fahima too was on a mission, and she began to inspect all the different shops and wooden stalls with an eagle-eye, finally stopping at one with a vast array of coloured dolls and sugared-knights on horseback. She seemed to be negotiating a price with the stall holder, a round-faced, sweaty man wearing a vivid green sash over his jalabiya, but I couldn't hear what she was saying. I watched the man closely. He seemed very self-important, even arrogant, and it was obvious he didn't have much time for her. Once or twice she would back away and take money from the small leather wallet in her left hand, counting it carefully. The look on her face was now tragic. Her head drooped, her eyes began to water and suddenly we were marching away from the stall on our way back home. She wouldn't look at or speak to me, but I didn't need any explanation – the price for the sugar horse had been too high and she had totally miscalculated. I couldn't help but watch the other children waving their multi-coloured sweets and toys in the air, yelling, whooping and dancing along to the music of the whirling dervishes at the centre of the fair. Even though I was the only one without a toy I was desperate to join them in the fun, but when I asked Fahima to stop she gripped my hand hard and marched away on the long walk home. I could see she was crying but she pretended that the dust from the road had irritated her eyes.

When we arrived home my mother was shocked but she read what had happened in an instant. She saw my downcast expression and that was enough. Fahima walked quickly to a bedroom without saying anything. She was still weeping and lay on her bed with her face to the wall.

I was devastated, but also felt desperately sorry for her, because the humiliation had been total and she knew she had let me down badly. I wanted to hug her and tell her everything was fine, but she stayed in her room for two days refusing to eat or drink. Eventually she reappeared and we all pretended that nothing had happened.

However, not long afterwards, Fahima's grief returned.

She stayed in that room for hours, then days, and no amount of encouragement and sympathy would bring her out.

We just couldn't raise her spirits, and finally she died.

I remember her as a very dignified lady, and I think perhaps the double blow of her young husband's death and the embarrassment of losing face in the marketplace were just too much for her to bear. Perhaps some people do die of a broken heart.

It was one of my first lessons in realising that adults were vulnerable and sensitive, and it also taught me that the good things in life are sometimes too far out of reach.

Chapter 3

Hard Times as a Child Labourer and the Strange Genius of Abdulahi

All happy families are alike. Each unhappy family is unhappy in its own way.
(Leo Tolstoy. 1828-1900)

One tree collapses and the whole village worries, while the forest grows silently by itself.
(Kamil Idris)

The sudden unexpected deaths in the family were blasts from hell and cast a black cloud over the whole family. I was confused and devastated and could see that my mother was close to despair. She was now a widow with a young family to feed, and I was too young to help with the upkeep.

I was now nearly six years old and it was time for school, the same one my older brothers had been to. I had picked up very little in the dark, scruffy one in Karima, where we had had to sit on the sandy floor. All I had learned there was a smattering of Arabic, enough for me to write my name and some basic sentences. For some reason my elder brother Farid had taught me three random words in English: 'bicycle', 'cupboard' and 'elephant'. He had an unusual way of teaching me to spell 'cupboard' correctly, making me pronounce the silent 'p' sound by holding a piece of paper to my mouth so that he could hear it properly. This was my first introduction to the English language and I was so proud of being able to write in two different alphabets at the age of five.

I had also learned the names of most of the countries of the world and their capital cities. I had been taught them by an extraordinary man called Abdulahi Al Aweer.

His nickname was 'Abdulahi the Naïve', though some people also called him 'Abdulahi the idiot'. He had no fixed home and was quite happy to wander round the town spending his time in other people's houses, where he would be fed and looked after, and he wasn't in the least upset about his nickname. He was a tall, thin, greyhaired man with the cleanest clothes I have ever seen. He had spare ones in different houses and he would wash them in the Nile, borrowing people's irons to make mathematically straight creases in his shirts and trousers.

It was impossible to tell his age. He could have been anywhere from 35 to 65. He seemed to eat nothing at all and would sleep wherever he could, usually on a mattress outside someone's house. I'm sure a modern psychologist would have a technical term to describe his condition, but our common-sense view was that he had just lost his wits.

Nobody knew where he came from, but it was rumoured that he had arrived one day after travelling many miles from the north and that he came from a wealthy landowning family, the owners of thousands of palm trees.

People accepted him because he was gentle and harmless, and maybe the strangeness of his behaviour made them feel normal. His own internal landscape must have been a peaceful place as his calm eyes looked out placidly on the world and he had a smile for everyone.

He loved coming to our house for two reasons. Firstly, because my mother fed him, and secondly because he adored listening to the BBC news in English and Arabic on our radio. This really intrigued me because it suggested that he wasn't quite as stupid as people thought. Somehow he had picked up a knowledge of English and was able to understand everything that what was being said. He regarded the radio as a sacred object and before listening to the news he would carefully wipe the table it was placed on and polish the dials with a clean handkerchief. He would then sit with his right ear next to it and close his eyes. I can see him now twiddling a dial to get the clearest signal from the BBC. I was dazzled by the names of all those cities that we could reach, even though they were in foreign languages: 'Bordeaux', 'Munich', 'Helsinki', 'Athens', 'Rome', 'London'. Intoxicated by the romance of their names, I wanted to become a migrating bird and fly up the Nile and cross the Mediterranean to visit them.

Meanwhile Abdulahi had found London. His concentration was intense and he would shake his head from side-to-side whenever something terribly tragic like an air crash or earthquake was announced on the news.

Over time he had become a living, mobile English dictionary and on occasions my mother would try to catch him out by asking what 'difficult' words meant. "Abdulahi, the man on the radio said something was 'sacrosanct'.

What does that mean?"

"It means it is holy or sacred," he would answer, "and shouldn't be insulted."

One of his party tricks was to recite a list of the countries of the world and their capital cities. For some reason he adopted me as a 'pupil' and would insist on my learning them as well. As soon as the news was finished he would grin across at me and bark out the names of five or six countries, and I would have to answer with their capitals.

"Soviet Union?"

"Moscow."

"Spain?"

"Madrid."

"Morocco?"

"Rabat."

"Chile?"

"Santiago."

"Egypt?"

"Cairo."

By this stage my mother was helpless with laughter and I could see that for a while she had forgotten her grief.

I also remember that Abdulahi had some sort of special understanding with Taifoor the shopkeeper.

Taifoor had a small, ancient radio which he kept hidden in a box behind his counter, and Abdulahi would sneak behind it and tune in whenever he could. While he was doing this he would help himself to the piles of nuts and fruit that were within arms' reach. Taifoor would discover him but instead of losing his temper he would sit beside him and they would discuss all the world's affairs together as if they were the wisest statesmen in the universe. Once one of my brothers overheard them discussing a Churchill broadcast together, but when they realised they had been seen they stopped immediately.

We were fascinated by Abdulahi and made up all sorts of fantasies about his early life and background. I imagined that he might have once been a university professor or teacher and had received a tragic blow to his head. Whatever the reason for his condition, I had a real soft spot for him, as his lessons in English vocabulary were to provide a dramatic bonus when I started to go to elementary school.

This was not long after my father's passing and I was very reluctant to leave the sanctuary of home. The dark cloud still hung over all the family and I had become nervous and withdrawn. I think my brothers and sister noticed this and thought that a change of scenery would help to distract my mind. I had a half-sister called Awatif who gently suggested to my mother one day that as I was only five, I could wait another year before going to school.

Awatif was a tall, beautiful young woman who already had three sons of her own. She lived about 10 km from us and she was a great support to my mother who, like myself, was still in shock. I trusted her completely, as I had often seen my father talking to her as if she had been an adult, probably asking for her advice. I waited for a decision, hoping against hope that I could have one more year at home with my mother. Unfortunately it was my brothers who made the final move.

On the first day of what should have been school I was lying snugly in bed, looking forward to another blissful day at home, when all three marched into the room. They lifted me up bodily, ducked away from my kicking legs, ignored my screams, dressed me, and carried me all the way to the elementary school – about half a kilometre up the road. My mother was following behind, head bowed, obviously overawed by this display of masculine decisiveness. By this stage I had calmed down but my brothers were not going to let me run back to my mother.

They gripped me by my arms while we waited for the headmaster to appear. I think my mother was embarrassed and upset, not just by my behaviour, but also because all the other children had arrived with their fathers and were waiting quietly.

The school building was a ramshackle ruin. It was just a square block with few windows, open gaps in the walls for doors, and an old wooden gate. I think the headmaster was ashamed of it as when he appeared he looked tired and dishevelled. He was called Mr Gaili and he was one of the first completely bald men I had ever seen. He was very tall, had a huge black moustache, and wore a pair of dark brown trousers attached to some loose-fitting braces. I could see that everyone was not too sure about leaving their children in the place. We were shown to our classroom and the other parents waited behind for a while. However, my mother and brothers slipped silently away, my mother whispering that I would have to find my own way home at the end of the day. She gave me a parting hug and whispered in my ear that I should always be confident and that she loved me so much. Then I was alone.

I was now in a state of acute anxiety but it was going to get worse… The door of the classroom was hanging off from its hinges and we had to wait while a senior pupil bashed it around before we could go in. The room was gloomy, dusty, covered in cobwebs and most of the chairs and tables were balancing on three legs; some had fallen over completely and were lying on the floor like upturned turtles. There were spiders everywhere. Although it was still early in the day, the room was stiflingly hot and the roof seemed to be made of some sort of glowing zinc.

My eyes began to adjust to the murk and I spotted four small shutterless windows allowing some light to fall on the floor. This was just a covering of bricks and some sand, and at the front was a stained and dusty blackboard.

The floor and desks were covered with broken sticks of white chalk.

All the newcomers gathered together in a silent huddle, like nervous sheep waiting for the knife. Nobody moved.

The only sound came from a creaky fan whirring monotonously from the ceiling. Nothing was happening, so I stared up at it. It was making all sorts of threatening noises and I was convinced it was going to fall down and decapitate one of the children.

Then a tall, bearded, grey-haired man marched into the room. He glared down at us from a red, sweaty face and barked, "Good morning, everyone. I am your teacher Sheikh Siddig. Sit down on a chair, and if you can't find one, sit on the floor!" There was a rush to grab a chair. I managed to find one quickly and sat down. This was not a man to play around with. One or two of the other boys were now crying and I stared rigidly ahead at the giant in front of me. As he looked over our heads, a boy whispered to me. "What's your name?" I was terrified of replying and stared straight ahead.

"I'm called Osman. We can go home. We can run away…"

I wanted him to shut up. What if the teacher heard him?

"Are you coming with me? We can go home."

I didn't want to get into trouble on my first day and was about to whisper back when Sheikh Siddig boomed out a question. "Now, does anyone here know how to write his name?"

No answer.

"I repeat. Does anyone here know how to write his name?"
No answer. Total silence.

When he asked for a third time he started laughing
sarcastically. "Well, we'll have to start from the beginning then."
Taking a deep breath, I raised my right arm and he fixed me
with a laser stare. "What is your name?" he asked.

"Kamil."

"Kamil what?"

"Kamil El Tayeb Idris."

"Can you write your name?"

"Yes, Sir."

"Where is your house?"

"I live by the river Nile."

"Do you know El-hadi Adam?"

All the other boys began to stare at me and I panicked.

Who was he talking about? In my confusion I had forgotten
about my friend who had taken me fishing and taught me how
to swim to Tutti Island.

"Yes, I know him," I replied. "I see him from time to time."

Sheikh Siddig's eyes narrowed and I bowed my head.

"He was in this class. He was very clever but he had to leave
to make his living, poor boy." The conversation continued. He
asked me about my family and told me he had known my father
well. He ignored the others and I felt my face colouring with
embarrassment, though I did begin to bask in my new role as
class communicator. I was asked to come to the front of the class
and write my full name on the blackboard. I picked up a stub of
broken chalk from the floor and copied it out in Arabic. When
I had finished Sheikh Siddig told the class to give me a round of
applause.

"Do you know anything else?"

"Yes. I know the capitals of some countries and can write
three words in English."

"Amazing! Tell me some names and write the three words on
the board!"

I said in English, "Khartoum, capital of Sudan. Washington,

capital of The United States of America. London, capital of the United Kingdom," and "Cairo, capital of Egypt." Underneath I wrote 'bicycle', 'cupboard' and 'elephant'. More applause. Sheikh Siddig didn't know it, but that was all I was capable of… I had reached my limit.

"Very good. Well done, Kamil. Is there anything else you want to add?" This was an unexpected blow. I couldn't write anything else, and my mind was as blank as the rest of the board. What could I do? All I wanted was to return to the safety of my seat. Where was my mother? Yet I was caught. I paused and remembered something I had heard one of my relatives say at home. I lowered my arm, stepped away from the blackboard and handed the chalk to Sheikh Siddig. "Yes. The Nile is the capital city of my heart."

There was an intake of breath from the other children.

Sheikh Siddig smiled down at me and the bell rang. All of this had happened so quickly that I was in a state of numbed shock. I had no idea where the inspiration for that remark had come from, but from then on I knew I could react instinctively in a crisis – that I could summon my wits in front of that terrifying thing, an expectant audience.

We were allowed out for a break and all of the children crowded round, slapping me on the back and laughing.

Without realising it, or even wanting it, I had become a spokesman and someone with instant status in the class.

It was very bewildering. All I had done was simply repeat and write a few words on the board, but my performance in front of the teacher had delighted them. My euphoria didn't last too long because while we were on our break we had been told to eat our breakfast. Where was my breakfast? I didn't have any… why had my mother not realised? However, I was not alone this time – only a few of the children had been given anything to eat and they had already disappeared to the corners of the small playground, shielding their food from view. Thankfully two of the older ones took pity on us and spread some egg sandwiches on the floor to be shared out. I might have been the quickest to get a seat, but I was slow on the uptake, and by the time I got to the front they were all gone.

The bell rang again and we were back in the classroom.

I wondered what was coming next but Sheikh Siddig announced that, as this was the first day, we would soon be allowed to go home. I was disappointed because I thought there might have been more opportunities to show off, but all the other children started cheering. "But before you all go, I want to take a list of your names."

It was when we got to the third name that there was a knock on the door. To my intense surprise it was El-hadi Adam. I hadn't seen him for a long time and as he stood framed in the doorway he seemed taller, but also somehow quieter and sadder looking. "Excuse me, Sheikh Siddig. I have come to take someone home."

"You are very welcome, El-hadi Adam. Of course you can take someone home. We are leaving early anyway. Who is it?"

El-hadi Adam's lower lip began to quiver and he looked directly at the row where I was sitting. He began to cry and the class fell silent. Then he lifted his gaze to the back of the class and asked, "Is Kamil here?"

What was he doing? He knew I was there; he had just looked straight at me!

"Of course he's here. He's sitting right in front of you!" Sheikh Siddig was becoming impatient. Tears were streaming down El-hadi Adam's face.

"I'm so sorry. Kamil's sister Awatif was having a baby and she has died."

I was in a dream, a screaming fog. I found myself walking to my house with El-hadi Adam. He was silent and looking straight ahead. We didn't know what to say to each other, but we were both crying openly and people stopped and stared at us as we passed by. We heard the wailing and weeping before we got to the house, as it was already full of friends and relatives. Everyone was appalled and stunned by the news. They couldn't believe that such a beautiful young woman had been taken away. My mother, Aunt Fahima and sister Samira spotted me and started hugging me, but I broke off and disappeared into the crowd.

Then I saw something which broke me to my core.

Sheikh Siddig had arrived with the whole of my new class and was standing with them outside the house. Many of the young children were crying. I knew they couldn't do anything to bring Awatif back, but the fact that they were offering sympathy and their own kind of help was so comforting. This was yet another nightmare in my short life and for days I was unable to believe what had happened. All I wanted was to stay at home and it took me a long while before I was able to return to school.

These were tough times for me, but somewhere I found the resilience to carry on. I don't know where it comes from, but it seems that there is a life force in all of us that pushes us on, a divinity that helps to shape our lives, especially when we are very young. This was yet another blow to my childhood happiness, but I realised that I had to go back to the classroom and accept what had happened. I also knew that concentrating on the lessons helped me to take my mind off the tragedy.

Eventually I found that the subjects became absorbing in themselves. My mind at that age must have been like blotting paper, because I found it easy to remember facts and whatever was taught in class seemed to stick in my mind straight away. While other children had to revise at home for tests, I could quickly summon up the answers. I began to love school, especially maths, science and history.

We were taught in Arabic and had some lessons in English. There was also football, volleyball, basketball, and at the weekend fishing and swimming.

I loved school from the beginning. The teachers were kind and helpful and I relished the challenges of learning poetry, prayers and facts off by heart. Every day was a new adventure – solving mathematics problems, remembering dates and discovering strange and fabulous things about the countries of the world and the rich heritage of Sudan. I don't know where my delight and curiosity came from – maybe deep down I knew I had somehow to help my widowed mother, as well as cramming my mind with wonders. Whatever the reasons, I had grasped from an early age that if I worked hard I would be rewarded and she would be proud of me.

Learning was a joy and the hours spent reading and studying were intoxicating. Even though I was still very young, I devised a daily routine and vowed to stick to it.

It wasn't hard to keep it up as I made sure that there were enjoyable breaks with plenty of time for family fun and swimming and fishing with friends on the banks of the Nile.

A daily schedule is outlined below, and I can honestly say that devising it was one of the most rewarding things I have ever done. It gave me a framework and sense of purpose and as I grew older I adapted it to secondary school and then university with some modifications.

Working hard during term time and playing and planning hard in the holidays kept me refreshed, mentally agile and eager for more knowledge.

A Typical Day At Junior School

5.30 a.m.   I wake myself, wash, dress and say my morning prayers.

6.00 a.m.   I listen to the news on the local radio station. All the family are now awake and my mother prepares some bread and milk and hot tea.

6.15 a.m.   I go to my tiny room where it is quiet and I rehearse the different periods that we will be having at school that day. I make sure that all the homework has been completed and if there is a test I check that I know all the necessary facts. The tests could be on Holy Qur'anic verses, history, poetry or mathematics. Each period at school will be 45 minutes long and there are normally five to six of them.

7.15 a.m.   I start the ten minute walk to school and on the way mentally check again that I know everything.

7.25 a.m.	I arrive at school and greet my friends. We chat and joke for a few minutes.
7.30 a.m.	The bell rings for assembly in the courtyard. The headmaster emerges and checks that we have the right clothes, shoes and bags.
7.45 a.m.	First three lessons.
10.00 a.m.	Breakfast. The sandwiches are either brought in old newspapers from home, bought from the school shop or there is 'sharing'. This was a wonderful early lesson in generosity and teamwork. Anybody 'without' is always offered something from someone else and will always make sure that the favour is repaid later.
10.45 a.m.	More lessons.
2.00 p.m.	End of school. Walk home and mentally revise the day.
2.15 p.m.	Cold shower, especially in the hot summer months. Change of clothes.
2.30 p.m.	Chat with my mother, Aunt Fahima and sister Samira. They are always interested in what has happened at school and if I was making good progress. All of them are full of praise if there are any positive comments from the teachers and they really help to boost my self confidence.
3.00 p.m.	Family lunch. This is the highlight of the day. All the family sit at a large low-lying round table and we normally enjoy basic simple food. If we have unexpected guests or visitors my mother and Aunt Fahima like to be generous and if they have enough time will prepare more lavish meals of meatballs, salads, okra and plates of freshly cooked bread and rice, with small dishes of lemon, pepper and salt nearby. They love doing this and will insist that the guests join us, grabbing their arms and almost forcing them to take a seat. When the main course is finished on these special occasions there will

sometimes be bowls of mango and melon followed by hot tea in small incense scented cups. I can look back on these times with tremendous nostalgia. I sip the tea and absorb the familiar stories, the jokes, the nicknames, the singing of traditional songs, the group prayers, the kindly teasing and all the precious intimacies that bind a family and community together.

4.00 p.m.   Back to my small quiet room to complete any homework. I always make sure that there are no distractions like radios or magazines and try to concentrate hard. Later on in my junior school I begin to write a diary and have kept writing additions to it to this day.

6.00 p.m.   I take a break and gather round the radio with the rest of the family to listen to the BBC World Service There is a communal hush as the chimes of Big Ben in London strike six times. They are solid and powerful and the old Grundig radio shakes slightly at their deep tones. Then the announcer begins. "Huna London." ("This is London.") This the most serious moment of the day for Abdulahi and as the headlines and news come through he reacts as if he is the Prime Minister of the universe, pursing his lips and shaking his head at the bad news or nodding wisely and smiling if it is good.

6.15 p.m.   Outside to meet friends. Visit others' houses. Generally relax.

8.00 p.m.   Back to my room for more study and reading my favourite books. I remember two in particular: I loved the story of Animal Farm, even though I didn't appreciate its political slant until I was older, and I have to admit that I read Treasure Island with a beating heart. Pirates, daggers and a character called 'Blind Pew' haunted my childhood, and for a while I preferred to sleep with the light on.

9.45 p.m.   Chat with my mother, brothers and sister and so to bed. I always kept a small transistor radio under my pillow and if I twiddled the dials carefully I could pick up Radio Luxembourg, Radio Monte Carlo and the BBC World Service, and I would sometimes forget to switch it off. My sleep is sound but I can remember times when there would be a loud knock on the door of the house, either late at night or in the early morning. This was never a welcome sound as the knocking was made with a stone on our steel door and would usually be news of a death or serious illness in the family. Another noise I remember is the clip-clopping of horses' hooves as the Alsawari (the police) patrolled the streets at night keeping us all safe from harm.

Sometimes I would wake just before dawn and gaze up at the fading night sky with the stars still just twinkling.

I thought of all the generations of travellers, nomads and fishermen who had navigated by the unchanging position of the north star and of the vast areas above my head that had no end – a mystery that my human mind couldn't comprehend. Then I would hear my mother bustling about in the kitchen preparing our breakfast. Another day had begun.

I know that some people reading this will think it unusual that a young boy could be as self-disciplined as this, but I should explain that the family traumas and sadnesses had concentrated my mind to such an extent that I found the ordering and structure of the day quietly reassuring. Also, not everyday was precisely the same – there were random variations and I never lost my natural appetite for play and adventure.

After a few months my friend Osman, who had wanted me to run away with him on the first day of school, sidled up to me one morning break. "You want to escape?"

"Not again! I don't want to escape – I'm very happy.
Are you crazy?"

"No. I'm not crazy!" He hung his head and turned away.
"My mother and father," he started to say.

"What?" I asked.

He was embarrassed and didn't want to continue, but he explained that the family was very poor and that he was going to leave school to work in a factory to help support them. His story made me think – I wasn't going to leave school now that I was enjoying it so much, but I knew that money was also short in our family, and since my father's death my mother was struggling to support us. With the death of my father all his wealth (excluding his house)

'mysteriously' disappeared. It was not possible at the time for an enquiry to be held. My mind was racing.

"Where is this factory?" I asked Osman.

"It's an hour's walk," he replied, "about 6 km."

The next day Osman and I walked to the factory after school. He was hoping to work full-time and I was going to ask to be part-time, in the afternoons and evenings after school. We were still small children, barely seven years old, and I didn't feel our chances of getting work were very good.

The factory was a dismal, depressing-looking place made of mud brick with outside walls topped by broken glass to stop thieves. It reeked of oil and chemicals and there was a large, rusty iron gate guarded by three bored looking men. We took a deep breath and walked past them. They looked us up and down but said nothing. They knew why we were here.

The manager, an imposing, fleshy man with a boxer's broken nose, inspected us, sniffed a bit, turned his back and announced, as if he was doing us a massive favour, that we could start at once. Osman would have to work an eleven-hour day and I could arrive from school at 3.00 p.m. until the evening. Osman's pay was less than ten dollars a month – I would be getting less. It wasn't much, but at least it would be of help to my mother.

Our job was to squeeze sesame seeds into a piping machine that poured out a small stream of oil. Then we had to bottle the oil and stack it in large wooden crates. There was no ventilation or toilets in the factory, and the other 15 or so workers were old and tired and simply ignored us. The work was repetitive and very boring, but I kept thinking about the wage at the end of the month and how my mother would be pleased.

I also had thought of a plan to earn some pocket money from my elder brothers. They were very clothes conscious and loved to have mathematically straight creases in their trousers and shirts, just like Abdulahi. I told them that I would take over the ironing from our mother and they could pay me for each item done. They thought this was very funny as I had no experience at all, but they handed their garments over. We had a massive old iron that was heated from inside with hot coals. To keep the coals glowing you had to blow on them every now and then. Once it got so hot that I burned a hole in one of the black trouser legs when trying to get a crease straight. My brother was furious!

"Look what you've done! I can't go out in those," he screamed. "You've ruined them!"

My mother consoled me. "Don't worry. I have faith in you. Remember you were born with early signs of teeth and you walked well before your brothers did." I was a bit mystified by this, but I think she was trying to tell me that I wasn't as stupid as my brother thought. Then I had an idea. I went back to my brother.

"I have an idea," I said.

"What?" he asked.

"I've got a black biro here."

"So what? Are you going to write me a letter of apology?" enquired my brother.

"No," I explained. "If you scribble your skin with the biro where the hole is no one will notice it."

He stared at me for a few seconds as if I really was crazy, then he smiled. "Well done, Kamil. Good thinking."

On some nights at the factory I stayed until very late, well after all the others had gone home, and only one of the guards was left. It was quite scary by myself but I stuck it out and would walk home alone in the dark. I had told my mother all about this and she allowed me to stay out late. However, one night I got the fright of my life. I was about 20 minutes from home when two stray dogs started following me. They were thin, hungry-looking and growling softly in their throats. I started to walk faster but they started to trot. I was really scared and began to run. Now they started barking and I could see their white teeth shining in the gloom. I sprinted down a side street, a short cut I knew, jumped over a garden wall and ran for the safety of home. I could hear the dogs behind me, but they had given up. After that I always took a different route home.

It was a miserable life working in a factory like that, but I was proud of the fact that I could please my mother. I would hand over all my wages to her at the end of every month and she gave me a small allowance back. Soon I had enough to buy myself a treat. I had always wanted a smart pair of shoes, and once I had saved enough I went down to the souk and haggled for a black pair. I was so proud when I walked back home in them. I had earned them myself through persistence and hard work. Now and then I would stop and sweep the dust off them – just like my father used to do.

The workload at the factory became too much for Osman and he left, but I decided to continue for as long as I could. By this time my mother was worried about my schoolwork, but I was able to keep up and pass all the tests. I discovered that I could get up early in the morning to study. I kept a small notebook in my pocket and I would read or memorise things from it under the light of an electricity pillar on my way home or going to school. I could even snatch stolen moments to study in the factory when the boss wasn't looking. My teachers, unaware of the pressures I was under, were very happy with me, and I was able to reach the top positions in my class – something my mother was so proud of.

It wasn't until later in life that it dawned on me that millions of children have their childhood stolen from them. I was fortunate in that I had the choice of whether to work or not, but in some countries little ones are forced into labour. The stress, fatigue and deprivation of freedom and play are appalling and they are at the constant mercy of cruel bosses who sometimes will not even pay them.

Throughout the 1960s I was a child labourer, working in oil, paper, chemical and toothpaste factories. The conditions were dreadful, as there was no sick pay. We worked long hours and there were no safety requirements.

I was under continual stress, worrying that if I made a mistake I had no comeback and would lose my job.

Perhaps it was these early experiences of mine which attracted me to the Marxist philosophy. I probably saw it in its simplest terms, but its championing of the working class made a good impression on me. It wasn't until I was a few years older that I rejected it, because its in-built contradictions and dismissal of the spiritual aspects of life made little sense to me.

The years in elementary school passed very quickly.

Although I was living a sort of double life as a pupil and a child labourer, I still had the energy to join in with the rough and tumble of the playground and classroom. I made friends that I still think of today, even though we would have childish squabbles and fights. Mostly we were kind and generous with each other, sharing confidences and worries, and I will never forget the way some of the children continued to cut up their sandwiches at break time to share with the ones who had nothing – another lesson in simple charity. This concept of sharing extended beyond food to notes and thoughts, and to clothing and other essentials in life. It highlighted for me the importance of partnership, shared responsibility and communication which I have tried to carry with me throughout my life.

One or two of my friends even showed signs of early business skills. Muawia Jabir would collect money from us to buy falafal, salad and bread at discounted prices. At break-time we would sit in a circle to share it out as Muawia would sit next to (or even hide) the choicest pieces for himself.

It was at this time that one of my best friends, Omar Khatir, was drowned in the Nile. It was a Friday morning, a school holiday, and he asked me to come swimming with him. However, I was too busy at the factory. He went with two of his friends but got trapped in a small whirlpool and three days later his body was found 2 km downstream.

This was another terrible shock and to deal with it I once again immersed myself in schoolwork. It was a distraction of sorts and at this stage I would like to pay tribute to the men who taught me all those years ago.

Some are now dead, but I have vivid memories of them.

Dr Muaz Elsaraj was a great man who spent his entire life teaching a range of subjects but principally English. His top priority was the success of his pupils, and he worked incredibly hard to improve the school system. He was a genuine pioneer in education, eventually starting his own private university where his firm paternal approach to teaching was a winning formula. Ustaz Elgadi was an excellent headmaster and gifted mathematics teacher.

Mature, wise and thoughtful, he was a complete gentleman and greatly respected by the children. Ustaz Omer Haj Eltom and Abdelgahani Adam were devoted and distinguished English teachers. They had their different methods and personalities and complemented each other brilliantly. Ustaz Atta was our Arabic teacher and passed on his love of poetry and proverbs with his enthusiastic and encouraging approach. Ustaz Awad had a modern, dynamic approach and was able to teach many subjects across the curriculum, and Ustaz Kamal Muzamil was a hard-working and highly dedicated science teacher. Last but not least I remember Ustaz Abdel Wahab Elsharami, a giant in teaching and affectionately remembered.

There were golden days, cherished well into adulthood.

Some of the best times were in the winters or the rare days

when it would rain. We would play, frolic and shriek in it for sheer joy, competing with each other to see who could cover himself in the most mud. Then I would sprint home and enjoy a quick cold shower, my mother clucking furiously at me for dirtying my clothes and carrying the mud into the house.

Afterwards she would make huge cups of dark tea, dipping in old dry bread and my elder brother Izzeldeen and I would sit on either side of her silent and content, basking in her affection while we drank. It is a strange thing but I have kept a mental picture of the scene all my life and in moments of dark times it is a wonderful solace.

I was now old enough to recognise that my extended family was much bigger than I had thought, and new characters started to appear on the stage. There were aunties and uncles from everywhere. There was my mother's older sister Huda, tall, energetic and warm hearted. She lived nearby in her own house and was a constant visitor. Her husband had died before the independence of the country and they had had no children. She loved it when her little nephews and nieces visited her. We always looked forward to seeing her because she had a huge fridge stacked with different kinds of cheese, yoghurt and chilled water. Her younger sister Suad was very like my mother in her quiet dignity and even temper. She would never let us leave her house before she had stuffed us with her home made cakes and sweets.

Sometimes Suad, my mother, Huda, Fahima and Aunt Hyat would gather together writing and reciting poetry, laughing and telling stories. These women were like angels from heaven in my life. The aunts were bolts from the blue, unexpected, affectionate and fiercely protective of us all. I think they even competed with each other to be the most generous. If we were given one bar of chocolate by Huda, Suad would have to give us two – discreetly.

Then there were the uncles, my mother's brothers.

They were just as loyal and devoted but in a more masculine way than my aunts. My mother's brother Abbas was the senior male of the family and a senior administrator in the Post Office.

He was a serious man, aware of his status, but gentle and considerate. In the evenings he liked to place his chair in front of the house and, coffee or tea in hand, watch the world go by with his friends. Mohamed was a senior civil servant, another man of immense kindness and charity, and a writer of poetry in his spare time. His pockets were always jingling with coins and whenever he came around he would give generously. Then there was Abdu, a foreign affairs officer, perhaps one of the most decent men I have ever known.

He was very sentimental, even melancholy, and if anyone was ill he would visit every day until they recovered. Amir was a laughing, crinkly-eyed uncle who worked as a hospital administrator and was loved by all. There is not enough room to mention everyone, but this was my beloved family. I treasure their memory and the quotation from Tolstoy at the beginning of the chapter captures the essence of the happiness I felt in their presence.

Meanwhile, back at school my teachers still did not know that I was a child labourer, and I was proud of the fact that I was helping my mother without losing ground.

In fact, I was forging ahead, and I knew my teachers were always encouraging me on. However, all good things have to come to an end, and soon it was time for us all to begin secondary school. I had adored the elementary one and couldn't believe that the new one would be as good, but I was ready for new challenges.

I was now nearly 13 years old, having completed four years in junior (elementary) school and another four years in intermediate school. It was the summer holidays and I was itching to travel. I hadn't told my mother, but I was planning a working trip to Cairo, over 1,600 km to the north.

Chapter 4

Crocodiles, Pirates and Djinns

Your thoughts define your character.
(Kamil Idris)

How but in custom and ceremony are innocence and beauty born?
(WB Yeats. Irish poet. 1865-1939)

There is in every man, deep down in his nature, something simple and primeval, a memory of an earlier and fresher life. Hence hunting and fishing, travelling and sailing on the sea are things of an enduring interest to mankind.

(John Buchan, An extract from "Musa Picatrix")

School was over for the summer. I had just turned 13 and with my mother's reluctant blessings I set off for the long journey north to Egypt. If I found work there I knew I could survive and save some money, as long hours as a child labourer had inured me to tiredness and boredom. I had no job to go to, but an older friend had told me that the best thing to do was ask around when I got to Cairo Railway Station. He said I would be perfectly safe and to just keep on trying. I trusted him, but the long journey could take two days by train and involved an almost 24-hour lake crossing on a rickety old steamer.

The trains were always packed with people and their mountains of luggage, and some brave young men would chance their luck by riding on the roofs of the carriages.

There were no safety checks and the train inspectors turned a blind and sympathetic eye to these risk-takers. If they fell off, the train would just carry on, leaving them facing death in the desert. I had to promise my mother that I would buy a ticket and never join these roof riders, but money was short and I planned to pay some of my way by helping the crew on the ferry with all the loading and unloading, and maybe making tea for them. I put all my trust in providence and a great word I had learned from my grandmother Zainab – 'resilience'. I think when you are very young and take risks there is some unseen power that watches over you like a guardian angel. It certainly looked after me. I just felt I could make it and stand on my own two feet.

I took with me on the train a small bag with some boiled eggs, dry bread, dates and a bottle of tap water, and I sat opposite a middle-aged woman with kindly, laughing eyes and an honest face. She sort of adopted me as a surrogate son and insisted on sharing her own food with me and other young boys. Eventually I got to know her well. She told me her name was Haja Al-Sura, and I think she was a widow as she was travelling alone and obviously wanted to talk with someone. I think she was also a bit deaf because she kept calling me 'Kamal' instead of 'Kamil'. I liked her very much and I think the feeling was mutual, because when she left the train at Al-Zidab station she told the inspector that I was her son and that he had to look after me for the rest of the journey! Before she stepped down from the train she opened her zuwada (her travelling food bag) and pressed some tomatoes, dates, and a flask of tea into my hands. She said that she had enjoyed meeting me, that I should always remember the importance of education and good manners, and that we would meet again – if not on earth, then in paradise. She made a great impression on me and deepened my trust in the warmth and generosity of ordinary people.

I wouldn't have said that she was poor, but she wasn't well off either. I have never forgotten her kindness and am absolutely convinced that she is now in heaven, hopefully sharing her food with the angels.

After this journey I travelled every summer and with experience I became a trader to pay for the trips. By now fully streetwise, I would buy small quantities of Persol sunglasses, Nacett razor blades, and nuts from the souks in Omdurman, selling them in Egypt in exchange for cotton bed sheets which I could then trade back home.

On the ferry I continued to bargain for a free passage by helping the crew with luggage loading and preparing mint tea for them. Eventually, on some of the return trips, I had enough money saved to travel fourth class inside the train. This was just sitting on a hard wooden bench, but at least I was away from the scorching heat of the roof and I no longer had to worry about overhead wires decapitating me, or falling off and dying of thirst in the desert. I was still convinced that providence was on my side, although there were occasions during these journeys when I was nearly killed.

I can remember to this day the terrifying time when I left the ferry to go for a stroll onshore. About half-way across the lake the boat made a random halt at a small landing station. Nobody knew why we had stopped, but when I asked how long we would be tied up a crew member said, "At least two hours… maybe the whole night." It was unbelievably noisy and crowded on the ferry, with people packed tightly against each other and all sorts of goods, fridges, chairs, motorbikes and cartons of food all piled on top of one another. I needed some space and distance from it all and decided to wander ashore.

It was early afternoon and the air was still ferociously hot. Although there was little to see except some sparse vegetation, a few palm trees and two old roofless ruins, it was a relief to get away from the noisy ferry. I had to be careful – the fishermen of

Tutti Island had told me stories of the snakes and scorpions that loved to live near water, and of course the crocodiles. I think I was most afraid of the snakes. Apparently there are about 39 different species in Sudan and ten of them are killers. There is the demon night adder, the black mamba (that can slide across the ground as fast as a human), and the hooded cobra that spits poison into your eyes. The one I was most terrified of was the black mamba, because it was the only one that would follow and attack you for no reason – it could even climb trees! The others would only get aggressive if they thought they were being threatened.

I found a clear space under a palm tree and sat down.

I looked up. Was that a black mamba eyeing me from the upper branches? If I kicked that rock at my feet would a scorpion bite my ankle? Was I sitting too near a mother crocodile's nest? I kicked the stone but there was nothing there, and as far as I could see there were no snakes above me. Anyway, I knew they came out mainly at night and I would be gone before it got dark. I relaxed. A cooling breeze wafted over my face and I closed my eyes. Just 100m away the mighty Nile drifted away on its leisurely journey to Cairo in the north. I was on a boyhood adventure and all was well with the world… and what a world it was. The dazzling azure sky above me, the soft susurration of the wind and the vast waters of the river soothed my mind. I breathed in the clear desert air and, still with eyes closed, raised my head to the sun and fell into a deep quiet sleep.

I was at one with my beloved Nile and a great calm gentled my soul.

For a while I was in a sort of trance – almost as if I had left my body. I was above the earth, looking down on a pristine panorama, a Garden of Eden of sweet sounds and exquisite delight. I think there must be times in everyone's life when there are experiences such as these, tranquil moments when a veil is lifted and nature seems to say, "Look – this is a snapshot of paradise." There seemed to be a tape in my head which I could rewind to childhood days. In my dream I was once again a small boy sitting in the school without walls and in the evening listening to my father's wonderful tales of the first dawn of Africa, being rocked gently to sleep by the ancient train on the way to Karima. I have already mentioned that fears and nightmares had plagued my childhood, but the Nile was my fighting brother, my ally in life who spoke of a more lasting and eternal world. It held the magic of all the ages and as long as I could store it in my imagination it would accompany and strengthen me through the darkest of days.

I can't remember how long this daydream lasted but eventually the vision faded and it was time to return to the ferry. It was now late in the afternoon and the fierce heat of midday had gone. I stood up, stretched my arms and legs, brushed the dust off my trousers and strolled back to the banks of the lake. For about a minute I thought I was still dreaming. This had to be a dream… This was a nightmare and I would suddenly snap awake. The ferry was gone! Which world was I in? Was this reality? Yet it was a few hundred metres away, and this was actually happening. I was not asleep.

I shouted and screamed for it to come back, but of course it was useless. Even though it was hopeless I kept looking at it until it disappeared. I willed it to turn around and rescue me. I shouted and shouted, but all I could hear was a small echo of my own voice. The wake of the boat had churned the water up and the tiny waves rippled back towards me. "It's too late," they seemed to say. "It's too late and you are abandoned and alone." I thought that maybe someone would notice that I was gone. However, that was no good either – there were too many people on board for just one boy to be seen as missing. I couldn't believe this was happening and slumped to the ground, my heart thumping in shock and disbelief.

I tried to keep calm. There was no point in crying or feeling sorry for myself. I had to think. I balanced up my possibilities of survival and rescue. I wouldn't die of thirst – the lake water was there, but what about the crocodiles?

I couldn't see any, although I knew that they were there.

Apparently there were thousands of them in the Nile and they had been known to snatch people from the banks when people went down to drink or clean their clothes.

On shore they could be just as dangerous. If I went anywhere near a nest the mother would rip me to shreds.

The chances of the return ferry in a week's time stopping at this middle-of-nowhere jetty were absolutely nil. I could die of heat-stroke or starvation. The two roofless old ruins were falling to pieces and would provide little protection from the midday sun. Anyway, there were probably snakes or scorpions lurking in the dusty corners and brickwork. There were no roads and no signs of human life.

I began to pray. I prayed that God would somehow come to the rescue of a poor little boy, lost and alone in the wilderness. I thought of my mother and brothers and sister sleeping peacefully back home. In my confusion I had a sudden vision of shadowy images of the old palm trees outside our house in Omdurman, of Abdulahi, El hadi Adam, of the gateway to my school and all my classmates. They all seemed to be standing together as if gathering round my dead body.

Then I saw the rock – a huge structure to my left, a few hundred metres away dropping right into the water.

It sounds incredible now, but I am convinced I heard the voice of Zainab warning me to be careful and watchful.

"You are close to death but be brave," she said. "There are dangers here – wild animals and even djinns – go to the rock! Go to the rock!" Maybe I would be safe there. It was still just light enough to be seen and I ran towards it.

I tripped and cut my knee, but it wasn't a large wound and in my panic I didn't feel any pain. Nevertheless, small drops of blood were being left on the ground and I hoped that hyenas or wolves wouldn't smell them and begin to track me. As I got nearer to it, the rock seemed to loom up in the dusk like a small mountain. If I could get near the top I would be safe from crocodiles.

I had to be ultra cautious, as in places the rock dropped

steeply into the lake. I needed to find a way up that wasn't too sheer. The wind had died down by now and the surface of the water was as flat as a plate. Then I saw the ripples. About 30m out, they were moving slowly towards me, and now and again air bubbles were plopping next to them. They say that crocodiles are sensitive to vibrations in the ground and perhaps my running had alerted one of them. I edged further up the rock. Surely a crocodile wouldn't follow me up the slope? Looking down I was just able to make out a dark shape in the water. The crocodile was massive, lying as still as a dead log of wood, aiming its nose straight up at me. I knew it had over 60 dangerous teeth, that there were thousands of them in the lake and that they could weigh as much as a small car. Anchoring its tail it could rear three metres out of the water and grab me. I climbed further and looked down. The beast had sunk away but I knew it was still lurking under the surface.

I found a level piece of ground about halfway up, had a quick look for crevices or cracks which might be hiding deadly creatures, and sat down. My knee was bleeding, but the cut wasn't too deep, and there was so much adrenalin pounding through my body that I still couldn't feel any pain. So far there were no signs of hyenas. I had read somewhere that breathing slowly helps to calm the nerves and clear the mind. I really needed to do this, because I had just remembered that I had left my bag of worldly possessions on the ferry and I would probably never see it again. My passport, a small amount of money, a change of clothes and some bread and fruit were all gone! I buried my face in my hands and started to pray once more.

I have never prayed so hard in my life. If Allah were to listen to me, I would have to stay concentrated so that any prayers would be heard and I would be helped. However, strange sounds at the sides of the rock interrupted them.

From a small jungle of bushes and trees I heard weird chattering and shrieks as the night animals and birds began to wake up and prowl around. I knew that the owls, rats and foxes were harmless, but I wasn't sure about either the wolves or the packs of jackals that had been known to attack vulnerable humans. And as for the snakes…! I drew my knees up to my chest and glanced around for a stick. I needed some form of protection, however primitive, but there was nothing at hand. It was also getting very cold. Maybe I could build a fire – it would keep the wild animals away and keep me warm, but I had no matches or tools.

I lay down on the rock. It was still just warm from the sun and I wrapped my arms together and tried to sleep. I was so tired and I must have nodded off for a few seconds. Zainab was once more with me. "Stay on the rock," she instructed me, "stay on the rock!" Then a bright light dissolved her – was that the morning sun already?

My eyes stung as a beam of light scanned my face. Behind the beam was a dark shape and from the shape came a voice.

"It's a djinn! Allahu Akbar!"

"It can't be a djinn. It's too small."

"It's a djinn. A real one. Be careful!"

This was no dream. I was wide awake and could just make out four figures in the moonlight. One of them was shining a torch all over my body.

"This is a djinn! What are you doing here?" called one of the figures. "This is our rock. You are a djinn."

"No I'm not a djinn," I replied. "I'm lost. I was on the ferry."

"You are a djinn. Which ferry?" they asked. "There is no ferry! The ferry has never stopped here!"

"I was on the ferry and it left me," I protested.

The figures continued to interrogate me. "No. You have no things. You are lying. Where are your things? You are a djinn! Why have you come here?"

A deep voice came from the back. "Djinns can go anywhere. Don't you know that?" Four men were now talking amongst themselves. I thought the safest thing to do was to stay quiet and not move. The only way I could think of surviving was to play for time. I knew a few things about djinns from my father's stories and some books at home. Djinns were ghosts – they could appear in any shape or form, and they could cause trouble. Some people called them evil spirits and there were hundreds of stories about them, stories that went back thousands of years.

These were four superstitious fishermen, and if they thought that I was a real djinn, they might attack me. It was still dark but I could just make them out. They wore old, shabby clothing, they also had knives and axes glinting in their belts, and with what seemed like metres of cloth wound round their heads. Their beards and tanned faces reminded me of pictures of pirates I had seen in books at home. Perhaps they were smugglers or even djinns themselves. To my terrified young mind all these were possibilities. The one with the torch seemed to be the leader, the other, standing well back from me, looked like the most dangerous and violent. If anyone was going to knife me it was him. In my mind I called the first one 'Torch' and the other one 'Bluebeard'. To survive I would have to convince Torch I was a human.

Bluebeard moved nearer. "It's small," he said. "It's the son of a djinn." He drew out a large curved knife from his belt.

"Wait a bit," Torch intervened. "If it's a djinn it could tell us about the treasure. Tell us about the treasure."

"What treasure?" I asked. I hadn't a clue what Torch was talking about.

"The treasure. Djinns know where the treasure is," he said to me.

"I'm not a djinn!" I protested. "I don't know anything about treasure."

"Yes you do. You know about the two boats that were wrecked here. They got some treasure ashore and buried it somewhere. Where is it?"

"I'm telling you I don't know!"

All four of them were now standing over me, Bluebeard's knife dangling in his hand. What they didn't know, was that I was hatching a plan in my mind, but I needed to buy time.

"All right I will tell you. But first you must all sit down and please put the knife away." I don't know where the words came from. I was barely 13 and was telling four angry grown men what to do. They stared at me for a while and then Torch sat down. This was a signal for the others to relax, although Bluebeard kept standing, glaring at me over Torch's shoulder with his knife half-hidden up his sleeve.

I gambled that I knew more about djinns than they did.

"Before we talk about the treasure," I explained, "I need to ask you some questions. If I was a djinn were you going to kill me?"

They stared at the ground for a while then Torch looked up. "Maybe. You could be an evil Djinn."

"Yes, but I could be a good one. You know that some djinns are friendly to humans. Do you know what happens to humans who kill a good djinn?" I asked the group.

No answer. They didn't know that I was making most of this up." They come to their houses at night and steal their children. They put them to sleep and drink their blood. Or they will poison their water. Anyway, you never looked at my arms or hands."

"Why would we look at your arms or hands?" one of them asked.

"Because when djinns are in danger the tattoos on their arms move up and down and their hands turn blue."

There was a collective gasp at this revelation.

Torch leaned over and grabbed my arm, declaring to the others, "He has no tattoos."

"No. Because I am not a djinn."

Bluebeard spoke up. "I think you are a clever djinn. We know djinns can change shape and tell lies like you are doing, and I know how to kill you. I have a silver knife and all I need to do is dip it in lamb's blood and you will die."

"Where is your lamb?" I countered. "Anyway, if you did that I might have djinn friends that would avenge me.

I know a special one who can take humans, make them small and put them in a bottle. If you killed me other djinns would find you and you would take a long time to die."

Torch was deep in thought. "Do you want some water?" he asked. "You must be very thirsty." I wasn't sure what he was up to, but after running so hard I was very thirsty indeed. He handed me what looked like a brown bag. It was a cow's bladder full of water. It tasted a bit slimy but I was so parched after all the activity and I drank my full.

"Let me see your feet," he then snapped.

"What?"

"Let me see your feet!"

"Why?" I asked.

He grabbed my right foot and ran his hand along the sole and then spoke to the others. "He doesn't seem to be a djinn. His toes and heel are not upside down. Anyway, djinns don't drink water."

I couldn't believe I was listening to this. They actually thought that a real djinn never drank water like humans and had toes and heels in the wrong places! "I keep telling you I'm not a djinn," I explained. "I am a human. But I can tell you about the treasure."

"Where is it?" they asked.

"You will find the treasure twice," I teased.

"What do you mean?"

I was now just about convinced they were not going to kill me and told them that if they let me live and helped me, they would find a special type of treasure in their souls. Their acts of kindness would be seen by God and their chances of paradise in the next life increased. I was just a poor lost boy – not a djinn – and helping me on my way would be an act of great charity. This would be a special, spiritual kind of treasure. Djinns would also notice this and perhaps in the future, when a good one appeared on the rock, it would help them find the other treasure.

They were quiet for a moment then Torch stood up and led them away. They didn't go far and Bluebeard was still glaring at me. I couldn't follow their rough dialect but I sensed that Torch was persuading them that I might not be a djinn.

"Okay. We think you might be a human, but we are not

sure. We will help you, but you will have to stay with us for two days before we move on. Don't wander away tonight or the hyenas or wolves will get you. Now we are going to eat and then we sleep." In no time at all they had a small fire going and cooked some fish. I didn't know what type it was, but it was from the Nile and tasted delicious. That night I lay slightly away from the men, but the rock was too hard for me to be able to sleep much. I noticed that they took it in turn to look after the fire and keep a watch – there was always one wide-awake. When Bluebeard's turn came he kept staring at me. I prayed that he wouldn't come over and slit my throat. I shivered, kept one eye open and pretended to be asleep.

The next day was spent chopping firewood and watching them fish. They clearly knew all about the crocodiles and when casting their lines stood well back from the water. They also had nets which they threw in a wide semi circle, watching the floating corks on the surface for any sudden movement from below. That evening after we had eaten I asked Torch about the ruined huts. He was quiet for a moment and then said, "Don't ask about them. We don't want questions about them. By the way, tomorrow morning we are going to look for the treasure. You will have to give us a sign."

"But I'm not a djinn," I reminded him.

"No, but you might be half a djinn. We think you have some power." This was worrying. If I didn't give them some sort of help they might kill me. As long as they thought I could help them find the treasure I would stay alive.

That night I lay on some old rags that Torch had given me, but the rock was still too hard and I slept for only a few minutes at a time. When I was awake I tried to think of plans to escape but gave up. My situation was hopeless. I also thought about the old ruined huts. Why had Torch been so anxious not to talk about them? Maybe they thought there were djinns there. It was more likely that there was some sort of smuggling going on. I had heard rumours on the ferry that some fishermen were trading stolen gold and antiques and selling it to dealers in the north.

During the long night I thought of something that might lure the men away from the rock and leave me alone for a while. I told Torch that I had had a vision or dream.

It was a strange one and didn't mean that I was a djinn, but I had dreamt that the treasure was near a large, almost triangular, rock standing apart from some other small ones. It was fairly easy to see because of its unusual rusty colour. I wasn't sure whether it was upstream to the north or downstream to the south, but it was on this side of the lake, within a kilometre of where we were camping. He became very excited and called the others over, making me repeat what I had told him. Of course once again I was making this up, but at least it gave me more time to think of a rescue plan.

They couldn't wait to start looking and soon they had disappeared downstream to look for the rust-coloured rock. They split up and I could hear them shouting instructions to each other. I was alone at last – but what was I to do? Torch had given me strict instructions to stay on the rock and keep the small fire going. I wasn't to move until they returned. Ignoring these warnings, I wandered down to the shoreline, praying once more for God to help me. I was staring gloomily at the water when a movement to my left caught my eye.

It was a small boat and I could just make out three men in it. I waved frantically and to my relief they waved back, rowing towards me. I prayed that they would hurry, because Torch and the others could be returning emptyhanded at any moment and would realise they had been tricked. The men glided their boat to the shoreline and helped me on board. There were three of them and they fired questions at me. I explained that I was on my way to Egypt, that I had been left behind by the ferry, and that I had lost all my money and clothes. For a moment it looked like they thought I was a djinn too, but they seemed more worldly wise than Torch and company. There was doubt in their eyes but I managed to convince them that my story was true. When they heard about Torch and the others they exchanged knowing looks and rowed quickly away from the rock. Maybe they knew they were smugglers. Soon we were out of sight and round a bend in the lake.

The leader was a shrewd, dark-faced, kindly looking man in his seventies. "I am Amin," he explained, "and these are my two sons, Jabir and Samir. You can come with us and we will put you in a safe place where you can maybe reach another ferry. You look tired. You can sleep there."

He pointed to the forward part of the boat where there were some blankets and a small platform. For the next few hours I slept like a baby, and in my dream I once more heard Zainab's voice. "Stay in the boat, stay in the boat!"

When I woke and continued my story, they couldn't believe that I had been all-alone and had survived two nights amongst the snakes and wild animals. Later on I realised that Amin and his sons were probably the descendants of the Nubians, certainly superstitious, but also intensely proud of the reputation their tribe had of showing tolerance and generosity to neighbours and travellers. There had been centuries of intermarriage since the earliest days, but the two sons, who showed immense respect for their father, had curly black hair and shared with their father the large almond-shaped eyes and fleshy lips that spoke of their ancestry.

They were hospitable and sympathetic, insisting that I shared their fried fish and bread, although before long I could see that their minds were also on the lost treasure.

They repeated the same story as Torch – that long ago the boats had buried the treasure somewhere along these banks. How they could link this with my being with them was a mystery. Maybe they secretly thought I was a good djinn who had become lost! Nevertheless they weren't threatening, and when I told them about the spiritual treasure their eyes lit up in wonder. I could tell that this meant a great deal to them, even though I knew they would go looking for the actual treasure near the triangular red rock when Torch and his friends had left. I spent almost two days with them as they sailed across the lake to the next port of call near Aswan. They took turns when navigating and at night one was always awake while the other two slept, all expertly aware of the shifting winds and sudden currents. During the day we spent much of the time throwing fishing nets out, making sweet tea and talking.

When the shadows lengthened we moored close to the shore and the two sons busied themselves in lighting the small fire in the boat while their father began to prepare the evening meal. Amin sliced up some tomatoes and onions, added some salt, divided up the bread, fried some freshly caught fish and we finished with some guava and water melon. I don't know whether it was the clear air or the combination of my hunger and the freshness of the food but the taste was unforgettable. There was no sound except the water lightly slapping on the side of the boat, the droning of insects and the distant barking of a dog.

Amin placed some aromatic incense on the dying fire as his sons stretched out on their blankets. The rich smell mingled and wafted with the wood smoke and all was quiet with the world. It was time for the old tales to begin.

Many years later I realised that the evenings I spent with these simple fishermen were among the most wonderful in my life. No words can ever do justice to the extravagant beauty of the Nile's sunsets. I have travelled in many lands and noted their wonders but the ancient, heart-breaking majesty of the river stands above them all. The merciless midday sun had waned and there was only the slightest whisper of wind. All along the banks the animals had begun to stir and waken from their afternoon torpor while the herons, white egrets and cormorants patrolled and scanned the waters, hunting for their evening meal – wild geese swirled in great squabbling flocks, seeking safe ground to roost for the night, and darting swallows quartered the air like aerial ballerinas. The setting sun, acting as if it were a divine artist, cast its magic on the waters. Miraculous colours – purples, golds, reds, crimsons, greens and blues shimmered on the glass-like surface – shades and subtle tints that seemed hardly of this world. The shifting shades gradually gave way to a pearly grey, then a darkish indigo and the first shy stars began to blink and twinkle. Finally came the clean, luminous moon, the inspiration for a thousand myths and tales. It was like a friendly visitor, casting a silver-grey glow on the darkened waters and adding a touch of wonder to the overwhelming stillness and quiet.

I saw that the fishermen were just as enchanted as I was by this fabulous pageant, although they must have witnessed it thousands of times before. They closed their eyes, not asleep, but lost in their own private thoughts like me. Their reaction surprised me, and I began to feel a bit guilty at having inwardly ridiculed their childish superstitions. These illiterate, simple men had not had much education, but they had an innate gentleness and a reverence for the mysteries and wonders of life that demanded my respect. Later in life when I was about my business and pursuing my ambitions, I kept in mind their practical wisdom and dignified stoical courage in the face of extreme poverty and their daily struggle for survival.

Then the stories began. Amin had a deep velvety voice, embrowned by years of smoking, and there was a lilt and natural rhythm in his telling of the old tales. It was clear that the sons knew them by heart but, like children, they were willing to hear them again.

It was enchanting. Biblical narratives, legends, folk tales and myths coalesced in a non-stop journey through history.

I was told of beautiful female djinns with magical voices that lured men into whirlpools and dangerous rapids. The fabulous temples of Solomon had been built by djinns and when they were destroyed by the invading Persians, the holy priests took the gold and silver from the storerooms and threw it in the river. On some nights when the moon was full, a golden boat was seen and blue fish swam all around it. Many people had tried to reach the boat, but it would disappear in a puff of smoke. There were other stories of kidnapped brides, sacrificial virgins and great kings and queens more powerful than the Egyptians. Amin told us of the crocodile god Sobek, a great protector of fishermen, and of the buried treasure which all men who live by the Nile still look for. They believe that strange, vertical-eyed creatures, half human, half fish, rise to the surface to look for brides to marry, and when a baby is born the parents and relatives throw handfuls of milk pudding into the Nile to thank the local gods.

There were other stories about the building of the great dam in the 1960s. This had been a gigantic project to harness the Nile, making it the third largest man-made lake in the world. President Nasser had given the building contract to the Soviets after he had quarrelled with the Americans. Due to the rising waters, thousands of Sudanese people from low-lying towns and villages had had to be relocated. Many were reluctant to move from their homes and some had decided to stay and risk the floods.

Thousands of animals, trees, and townships disappeared under the waters. In some places the only traces of their towns and villages were the tops of minarets peeping through the surface of the vast lake. Amin's voice trembled when he said that there were even many people who had refused to move and had been drowned by the rising floods, though this was never made public at the time. The fishermen were worried that over time all the mud flowing with the river could silt up the whole lake – what would become of them then, as all the fish would die? This project inflicted huge damage on the cultural heritage of Sudan, to say nothing of the effects on individual people in the area.

His sons were now asleep, probably dreaming of virgins and beautiful female djinns, but he was still very much awake. I pointed up to a very shiny star. "Which one is that?" I asked.

"That one? That is Sirius," he replied, "the brightest star of them all. It is very sacred."

"Why is it sacred?"

"Because it can disappear and when it returns we know that The Nile will flood. It has special powers. Did you know that there is a belief that when the goddess Isis cries for her dead husband Osiris, her tears water the river and it overflows? We know about Isis, but we also believe in Hapi, the Lord of the river, and Anuket. She is very special, like Sirius," he explained.

"Why is she special?" I replied.

"Because she is the daughter of the sun god Ra, and she holds the whole of the Nile in her arms. She is the first lady of heaven and makes the land and river fertile for all of us. Can you see that grey path above your head?

Some people call that the 'milky-way', whilst others believe that it is made up of dead souls drifting toward paradise."

"Do you believe all this?" I asked the man.

"Why not?" he said. "Do you know that some men are atheists?"

"Yes," I answered.

"But sometimes they are not atheists at night, are they?" he added. "In the dark they become frightened. Look up at those stars. Where do they end?"

"I don't know."

"They don't end. There is nothing beyond them. They go on forever. Isn't that a great mystery?"

I lay back and looked up at the stars. They were indeed a great mystery. I cannot forget those nights amongst the humble fishermen. I think it was a combination of their kindliness and Amin's wonderful stories that helped to form my early conviction that, despite the bad dreams and demons, and the outrageous cruelties of some deluded men, the universe is a benevolent and friendly place and there is a divine order that guides and watches over our world. A divinity shapes our lives, and in my mind I was beginning to form a belief that these encounters with the majesty of the natural world were hints of a further, hidden, absolute truth. The memory of the generosity and hospitality of these simple fishermen and their intimate connection with the splendour of those nights continued to nourish my faith in human nature and its creator.

I cherished the time I was with them and when they left me on the shore they pointed the way to Aswan, gave me a cheerful wave and wished that Allah would be with me. I wanted to give them something for saving my life, but I had nothing. I had only three small items in my pockets. I was embarrassed to hand them over, but it was the least I could do. I bowed to them and solemnly held out in my hands a box of seven or eight matches that Torch had left me, a piece of 'muswak' or wood for cleaning my teeth, and a small slab of soap I had kept in my pocket. They were also embarrassed but accepted them with the profound dignity of the poor, conscious that in my own poverty-stricken state these were precious gifts. I never forgot their kindness. If I could I would have given them some money, but I think their honour would have been offended.

I now had about a 16km walk to Aswan in the midday sun. I had lost touch with the ferry, and of course I would never see all my clothes and goods again, but at least I was alive and I knew that I could find water in the gula pots outside people's houses. This was yet another timeless tradition of the generosity of the local people to the stranger, especially the weary traveller. I had to stop many times because of the heat, but as I neared Aswan people came out of their houses, curious about this young, dustcovered boy in their midst. When I told them my story they pressed bread and oranges into my hands, shaking their heads in disbelief.

Eventually I reached Aswan and, realising that the ferry had long since gone, I asked for directions to the railway station. I thought in my innocence that if I could tell someone my story they might help me along on my way. I saw a large brown door with 'Inspector's Office' written in bold red script on it. I knocked gently. No answer. I knocked louder and this time the door was opened by a huge, redfaced man wearing a black suit and white shirt, just like my father's. A cigarette was dangling from his mouth and he smiled when he looked down at me. Then, remembering his dignity, he frowned at being interrupted from his work by a mere child. The smile vanished – I had forgotten how dirty and tired I must have looked. "Yes. What do you want?" he asked. I told him about the ferry and losing all my belongings. He wasn't impressed. "I'm sorry but there's nothing we can do," he said, "perhaps if you go to the police they might help you." He was about to slam the door in my face when I asked, "Did you know my father?"

"What?"

"Did you know my father?" I repeated.

"Why would I have known your father?" he asked.

"Because he was a Director of the Sudanese Railway System," I explained. "He's dead now."

The man looked at me suspiciously. He took a deep whiff of his cigarette, puffed the smoke out over my head and stared at me with narrowed eyes. "What was his name?"

"Eltayeb Idris," I answered. I could see that he was still unconvinced.

"What sort of cigarettes did he smoke?" he enquired.

"Benson and Hedges. In golden packs of twenty."

"And what is your mother called?"

"Amouna," I replied.

He turned away and walked towards his desk. He took a long look at me then opened a drawer and brought out a small, creased black and white photograph of a group of men. As he handed it to me he said, "If you are who you say you are, you will know the name of the man in the middle of the back row."

"Yes. I know him. This is Ami El-Feel. He helped us with the garden in Karima."

"Well, well, well." The smile returned. "So you really are Eltayeb's son. I think I can see a likeness. I knew him very well. When I visited him in his house he told me all about the djinns! He was a good man – God bless his soul." The man went quiet for a while and his eyes began to moisten. I thought he was about to cry but he cleared his throat and in a gentle voice bent down with his face close to mine and asked me, "And what is your name?"

"Kamil," I answered.

He paused and looked me over once again, as if in doubt about what to do next. "Come in, Kamil. We will see what we can do."

I was told to sit in a corner of his office while he spent over an hour phoning and waiting for replies. One of the calls must have been to his wife because I heard him say that they might be having a small visitor for the night. The other men working there grinned at me, obviously amused by my filthy clothes and cheek in knocking on this important man's door. I was given some sweet tea and a biscuit and eventually the Chief Inspector put down the phone and beckoned me over to his desk. "We are in a very fortunate position, Kamil. Your bag, with your passport and money, is waiting for you in Cairo station. Some honest person has handed it in." I couldn't believe it! I felt like leaping on the spot for joy. "There's something else. As a mark of respect to your father you are allowed to travel free for the rest of the journey."

"I don't know how to thank you," I said, and taking a huge risk I continued, "but if you don't mind, I have one request."

"Yes?"

"You know there are some poor boys who have no ticket and have to travel on the top of the train. If there are any on the way to Cairo, would you allow me to take two or three of them down and sit with me inside?"

"I think so. I'll order the inspector to make some room. Just this once though! By the way, if you have any problems, here is my telephone number."

I was back on track. I wanted to give the man a huge hug. This would have been the natural reaction of a young boy, but my recent terrors with the smugglers had rocketed me into adulthood. Holding my back as straight as I could, I shook hands with him like a young man would. He was true to his word. On the journey north I was able to bring down twin brothers called Hassan and Hussein from the roof, and they sat goggle-eyed in amazement with me all the way to Cairo. Later we worked together in a printing factory as child labourers, but that is another story…

This is the vest of my childhood. I took it with me when I was on top of the train stranded in the desert – it witnessed some of the dramas by the Nile

Top from right: Farid, my mother Amouna, Siddig; sitting: Kamil, Samira and Izzeldeen in 1962 in Sudan

My mother Amouna Haj Hussein, a great mother without whom I wouldn't have survived; an example of sacrifice, patience and commitment

My beloved father El-tayeb Idris wearing his official uniform as a Director of the National Railway Corporation

My wonderful aunties

My aunt Fahima Haj Hussein

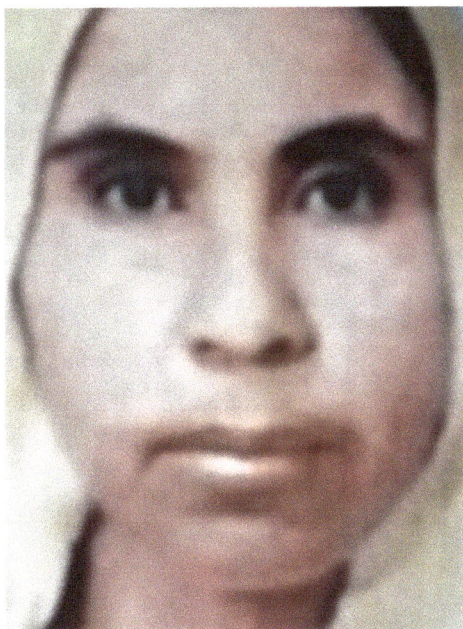

My aunt Hayat Haj Hussein

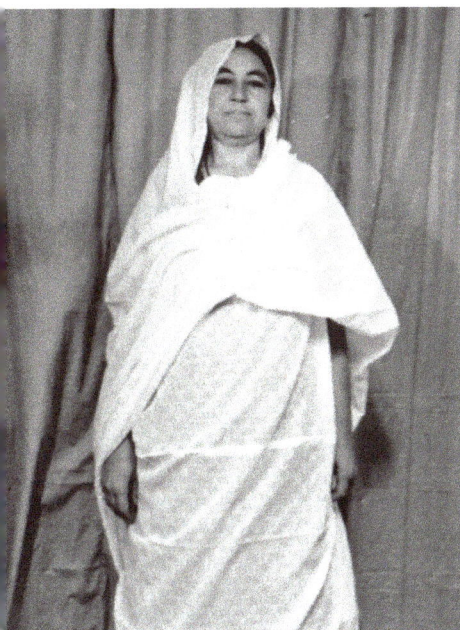

My aunt Huda Haj Hussein

My aunt Suad Haj Hussein

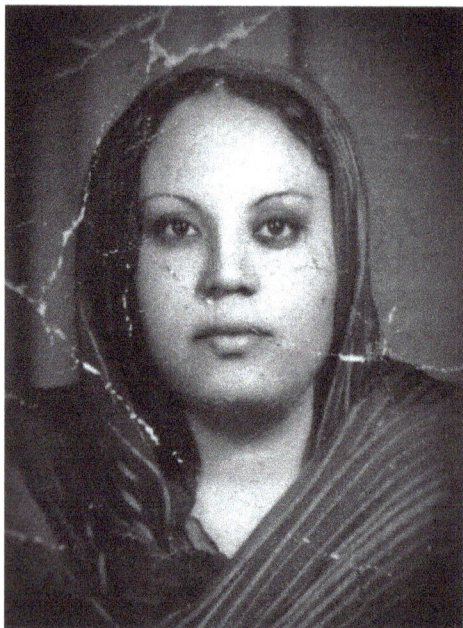

My late mother-in-law Fathia Mohamed Mabrouk who died young; an Angel from heaven

My late cousin Abdelhalim Mohamed Mabrouk who also died young; most kind and most helpful

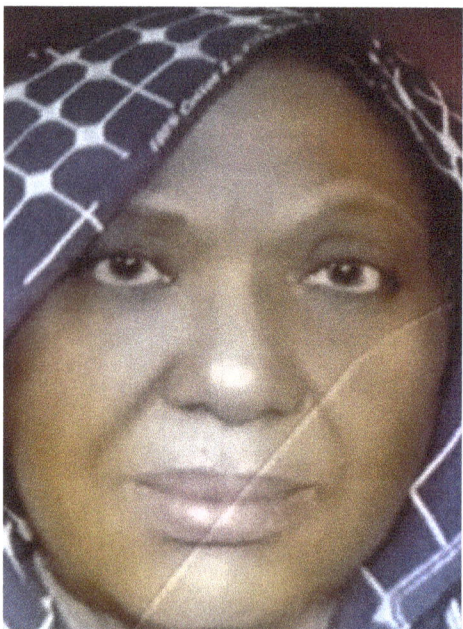

My niece Insaf Mohamed Haj Hussein

My mother Amouna again

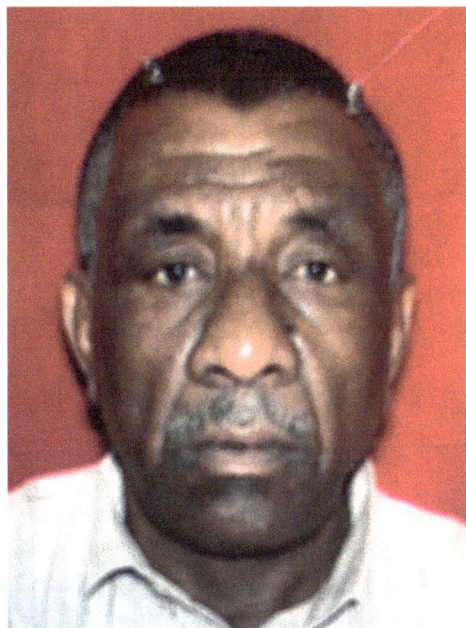

My late brother Izzeldeen Eltayeb Idris.

My father-in law Major General Mohi-Eldeen Ahmed Mabrouk, a great example of leadership, perseverance and dedication

My uncle Abdu Haj Hussein

My uncle Abbas Haj Hussein

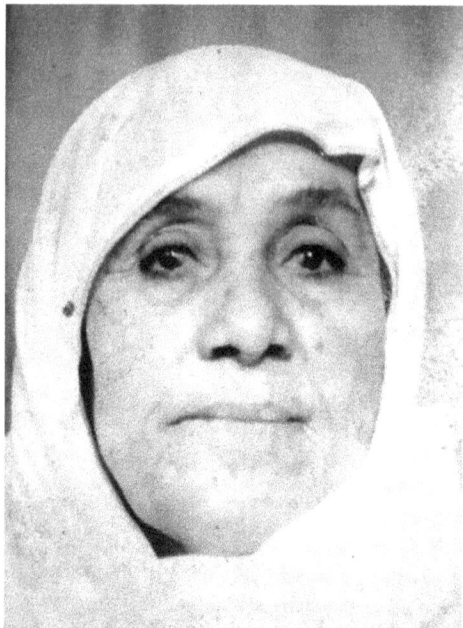

My late grandmother Zainab, my mentor and teacher ("stay on the rock, stay on the rock!")

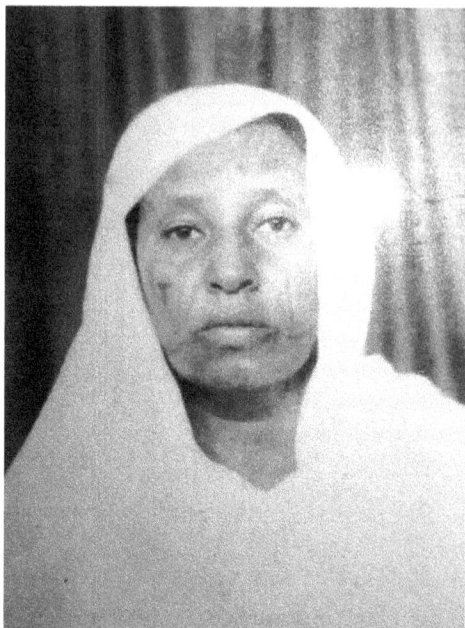

Bint Khairy, wife of my uncle Qurashi Idris

My uncle Qurashi Idris

My cousin Mohamed Qurashi Idris

My cousin Ala-Eldeen Qurashi Idris

My cousin Abbas Qurashi Idris

My uncle Amir Haj Hussein

My uncle Mohamed Haj Hussein

Salah Gurashi Idris, first class administrator and leader. His passion was in supporting and helping people

Mohamed Ahmed Elmadih, father-in-law of my brother Farid. Not only a faithful and generous neighbour, but also an example of integrity, dignity and respect

Ambassador Abdel-Hadi El-Siddig, a bosom friend and a polymath extraordinaire

With my beloved wife Azza in 2016, at an adventure animal park in County Durham in the UK

Our wedding – the happiest day of my life with my precious new bride, Azza. She was never awake after me and never slept before me and has been a constant and loving companion throughout my life

My family standing outside my home in the UK. Standing: my daughters Dr Dinas Idris and Dr Dalia Idris, my wife Dr Azza Idris, my daughter Dr Dahd Idris and myself, Professor Kamil Idris. Kneeling: my three sons: Mumin Idris, Munib Idris and Dr Mohamed Idris

Dear Mum & Dad,

It takes two special people
to make one wonderful marriage,

May every wonderful memory
and dream come true
fill your heart with happiness
to last a lifetime,

Thank you for always being there,
for everything that you do,
for the love you give,
The care you show & for being
such a wonderful mum & Dad.

Happy 30th Anniversary,

With lots of love,

Dinas
Nazin & Ziad

Dahel &
Dalia

Munib

Duaa &
Mohamed

Munib

WISHING *you both* LOVE
AND LOTS OF HAPPINESS TODAY.

HAVE A *beautiful*
30th ANNIVERSARY
of
your Marriage

30th anniversary of our marriage

Chapter 5

Lost in the Desert, Bedouins, and the Depth of Despair

Life consists of two days; one for you and one against you. So when it's for you don't be proud or reckless and when it's against you be patient, for both days are really the same.

(Imam Ali. 4th Imam, Cousin of Mohammed (PBUH))

There will be bumps on the road, but the strong march on.

(Kamil Idris)

My last childhood job was in a book-binding operation in a small factory in Cairo. Work was now occupying a primary place in my life and I had got used to the harsh conditions and long hours. I always tried to give 100% to whatever I was doing, not finishing until the work was complete, and taking a pride in the task – even if it was mundane and boring. However, it was then that Zainab played a major role in shaping my life. I had always been very close to her and talked to her often when she came to visit. When I had returned from Cairo I told her about the book-binding and photocopying. She was immediately inquisitive, then suspicious, and finally she investigated. She found out that the whole operation (unknown to me) was not entirely straightforward and that it might be producing questionable products. She insisted that I should be wary of working at the factory again. I followed her advice and kept away. I thought this was another important lesson and the seeds of an idea began to grow. I began to understand that the workings of the mind are precious assets which must be protected and must be given proper respect.

One day Zainab arrived at our house earlier than usual, her basket spilling over with the usual treats. She was in a serious, excited mood and asked us to all sit down on the 'angareb', a large traditionally made wooden bed. She then began to lecture us in true teacher style and it was clear that there would be no interruptions. She began by reminding us that in our culture it was expected that men and boys should share meals together, enjoying themselves playing and chatting. Apart from schooling, girls were to stay at home, almost in custody, supported by their fathers and brothers until they left to become married. Zainab took a deep breath and told us that this was unhealthy and unnatural. She asked if that from this moment on we would support her in a community action to liberate women from this form of life. She wrote long letters to the local authorities, gave talks to social clubs and even joined in discussions on the local radio. One of the messages she insisted on highlighting was that all the great religions of the world allowed women basic rights, dignity, freedom and full participation in society, and that we should do the same.

I didn't know it but at the time this was a very progressive view in an essentially traditional and conservative community. In retrospect she could have been taking quite a risk in airing her views so openly. I admired her for this early introduction to feminism and also for the fact that she had tried to put her opinions into practice.

It was now obvious that she had thought carefully about the timing of her visit and her pleas for action. She straightened her back, cleared her throat and went into no-nonsense teacher mode once again. She reminded us that it was Mawlid, the birthday of the Prophet Mohammed (PBUH), and lectured us on his message of peace, forgiveness, tolerance and love for all humankind. We would enjoy a day of singing, eating and dancing, but first we should say some holy prayers. Afterwards she told us the miraculous story of Amna bint Wahb, the mother of Mohammed (PBUH), who became pregnant on the first night of the Arabic month of Rajab. The birds would greet her with their music and when she went to drink from a well the water would rise up to the top in honour of the Prophet (PBUH). There were other wonderful stories which I had heard before at school, but Zainab's retelling of them was special. She had the great teacher's gift of adding drama and conviction to what she was saying. She emphasised that this was a day which would help to unite all humankind, regardless of religious beliefs, differences or tribal roots.

I watched closely as she took from her basket some vivid green clothes that she had inherited from her father.

She explained that this was the colour of the angels and of our heavenly inheritance. I found all of this mysterious, although also comforting and inspiring. What she was telling us was that we should respect and show tolerance to all religions despite their differences, and that every single human being was a creation of God.

Zainab had now finished and the family was thoughtful as we absorbed this powerful message. We all sat silently for a few minutes as she closed her eyes and bowed her head. Then it was time for the festivities to begin and she marched towards the kitchen. During dinner that evening she ate practically nothing and was certainly not her talkative self. She sat quietly in a corner of the front room and watched and listened as we sang our songs and played our games. Later, as we were getting ready for bed, she invited the children to sleep in her room and we moved some mattresses onto the floor and settled down for the night. I was worried that her heavy breathing would keep me awake but I was the first to drift off to sleep. I was really looking forward to the next morning as she had told us that there would be more games and stories and I was so excited.

I was the first to wake up, even though it was not quite light. I looked across to her bed and saw that her lower legs were hanging down. I went across to see if she was all right. She looked to be sleeping and had the traces of a smile on her face, but when I touched her arm it was ice cold. Zainab was dead. This was yet another blow to my childhood heaven – to lose my father, Awatif and Zainab in such a short time was a devastating shock, and I ran crying into the arms of my mother.

Then came another sledgehammer blow. My mother was diagnosed with a vicious illness and told she had only two weeks to live. It seemed as if there was a malicious devil forcing me to stare into hell. I started to ask myself deep questions about life. Why would a beautiful, gentle creature like my mother have to suffer so much pain and die before her time? Had we as a family been especially selected for terrible treatment? What had we done to deserve all these deaths? We prayed and prayed, and my aunts and uncles gathered in support. The response my mother made to her condition was inspiring – she faced the future with great courage, and in fact she managed to beat off the illness. How I don't know, but I think willpower and determination must have played a part in her recovery. Amazingly she lived for almost 50 more years, but she was under a permanent shadow as the illness could have reappeared at any time. As she once told us, "Death keeps no calendar…"

As a defence, I once more threw myself into school work and as many activities as I could. Here I must mention a special man who had an influence on my developing social awareness. He was called Abdel-Khalig Mahgoub, and he was the then Secretary General of the Communist party of Sudan, one of the strongest political forces in Africa at the time. He lived a couple of kilometres from us and invited me to his house for discussions about politics and the relevance of Marx and Engels. I was under no pressure to join the party and I had only a basic idea of what the philosophy entailed, but I kept an open mind and was intrigued by the answers it posed to the problem of poverty. What I did respect was the man's intelligence and integrity.

I think it was a youthful flirtation which didn't really lead anywhere. In fact in later life I became increasingly aware of its limitations and contradictions as a political philosophy.

In retrospect I do not think this was all that unusual, as in the wider world millions of young people like myself were involved in similar discussions, questioning their own democratic, capitalist systems. This was the time of the Vietnam War, of student riots in Europe and America, the Cultural Revolution in China, and rebellion against authority in general. There was street fighting in Paris, London, Chicago and Washington, and Soviet tanks smashed into Prague to smother a popular uprising. In the United States the murders of John and Robert Kennedy and Martin Luther King, followed by the assassination of Prime Minister Verwoerd in South Africa, shattered the status quo and seemed for many to signal the start of the apocalypse – the end of the world.

While these cataclysmic events were happening, I still attended the mosque with my brothers and continued to pray for my mother, but I was also grappling intellectually with a ferment of new ideas. I saw no conflict between my religion and what I sensed was the idealism of communism, but its contradictions and rejection of the spiritual dimension eventually persuaded me otherwise. A regrettable footnote to my involvement was that Abdel-Khalig Mahgoub was executed on the orders of President Nimeiri following the 1971 attempted coup d'état – a demonstration that freedom of expression carried significant dangers.

I didn't allow this intellectual struggle to affect my studies, even though I continued with factory work. By now I had experience of textile manufacturing, papermaking, paint and oil production, and ready-made clothing in the outer industrial areas of Omdurman. I also had begun experience of teaching English in Cairo. On the ferry journey back after my first visit, I had met an older Egyptian man who heard me using some basic words in English. There weren't many words, but he didn't know that, and he said if I was coming back to Cairo the following summer he would find me a job teaching English in a summer school. Of course I jumped at this chance and determined that the first words my students would learn would be 'bicycle', 'cupboard' and 'elephant'.

I would also teach them the names of the capital cities of the world.

I was now in my mid to late teens and thought of myself as an experienced traveller, but on one of the annual train journeys to Cairo I got the shock of my life.

The memory of being left behind by the ferry was a recurring nightmare and I was determined that nothing like it should ever happen again. But it did…

In 2015 a sleek air-conditioned train can make the 1,000 km journey from Khartoum to the Egyptian border at Wadi Halfa in about twelve hours. In the 1960s it took 36. I spent many of these hours balanced precariously on a carriage roof of the old steam train as it rattled and rocked its way across the desert. The line had been built by the British in 1896 to allow General Kitchener's army to move south from Cairo to Khartoum to secure the country. It was an extraordinary feat of engineering because at one point it connected a vast and unexplored region of the Nubian Desert which was thought impossible to cross. Only the Bedouin would venture into it, and they usually avoided it in the summer months when temperatures could reach above 50 degrees C. This was the area where the Nile made a huge loop southwards.

From space it looks like a gigantic question mark – cutting the loop involved a 350 km trek from Abu Hamed to Wadi Halfa across a featureless wasteland of flat plains, acacia scrub and volcanic rock. It has a reputation as one of the most inhospitable and deadly places on earth and was known as the 'death passage'. With luck camel trains could cross it in eight days but everything depended on finding the few wells that broke the journey. If they missed them…! Experts and locals thought Kitchener was crazy to even think about building a railway across it, but he assembled 3,000 labourers and dozens of engineers and set to work. In blistering summer heat 3 km of track were laid per day and the line was completed in just over a year.

I was now in the very middle of the place when the train I was on made an unexpected stop. I was used to this. For reasons known only to its drivers, the train would suddenly halt in the middle of nowhere, usually for about ten minutes to a quarter-of-an-hour, while some sort of repairs or adjustments were made to the engine. Feeling the need to stretch my legs, I clambered down from the roof and walked towards the end carriage where I thought I might stock up my water supply from a fellow traveller.

I had had to clamber down a bank to reach it and was just climbing back up again when the train made a sudden screeching grunt and lurched off without me. I scrabbled away, slipped in the sand and fell down the bank. Within seconds it was travelling too fast for me to catch up. My companions on the roof yelled at me to run as fast as I could but it was no use. Snorting clouds of black smoke, it chugged away into the distance.

Once again I was alone and terrified in the desert. It was the silence that began to unnerve me. For a moment I imagined I was dreaming and this was another of my nightmares. But no, it was really happening. I slumped to the ground and wailed at my fate. Surely this couldn't have happened again? I tried to keep calm and weighed up my chances of survival. It was now around ten o'clock in the morning and the temperature was already rising into the 40s. There were a few rocks around that would provide me with some shelter from the midday sun and I did have a wide-brimmed hat over my head. However, there wouldn't be another train for at least a week, by which time I could be a skeleton in the sand. There was a belief that humans could last three days without water and three weeks without food, but in this heat I could be dead within 24 hours.

I had my rucksack with some money and passport, and just enough water and food for a day or so, but I had no chance of walking to Abu Hamed or Wadi Halfa – they were just too far away. My only hope was to stick to the railway line and chance my arm that the train had made another stop somewhere. It was the only thing I could think of doing and I shouldered my bag and trudged off following the tracks. After an hour or so I was becoming delirious from the overhead sun. I could see nothing but a shimmering ocean of golden sand and black rocks. I headed for a scrubby acacia tree and found a tiny spot of shade where I drifted off, half asleep, half praying for God to help me.

I dreamt of an old man with long hair and long beard. He was spraying small grains of flour in the middle of the desert. The wind was blowing them in all directions. He asked me to recollect them. I said it was impossible, they were gone away. He said they did exist and determination would bring them back. I stood and started running left and right following the wind and collecting the air.

After a while piles of grain were in front of the old man. He said, "You see I told you nothing is impossible."

When I awoke it was beginning to get dark. I knew that this was the time when the wild animals stirred themselves, getting ready for the evening hunt – jackals, hyenas and even wolves were known to roam the area in hungry packs.

The heat was now bearable and once more I heard my grandmother Zainab's voice: "Keep walking. Keep walking by the tracks." I set off walking parallel to the railway line, looking out for a stick to protect myself in case of attack. There wasn't much wood around, but I did pick up an old piece of metal. It would have to do. I had now been alone for eight hours and had only a small bottle of water and some bread and cucumber left. Then I saw a small red light glowing, maybe half-a-kilometre away on my left. As I came closer I realised it was a camp fire and in the gloom I could just make out the shadows of two or three square-shaped tents. I had stumbled upon a Bedouin camp!

Five or six men in long white robes rose to meet me. I stopped walking. There was an awkward silence as they stared

closely at this dusty apparition from the darkening desert.
Eventually one of them uttered the wonderful words, "Ahlan wa
sahlan," meaning, "You are welcome."

This was the traditional greeting to the stranger who would
then be treated as an honoured guest. I had heard tales of the
legendary hospitality of these nomads and I mentally blessed
them and said a prayer of thanks to Allah. A woman appeared in
traditional veiled clothing. She avoided eye contact and handed
me a bowl of water and some warm camel's milk. I was then
invited to join the men's circle round the fire. Their manners
were impeccable. Not a word or question was spoken as I sat
down and was offered some of their bread and vegetable meal.

When I was finished the leader, a lean, white-bearded,
powerful looking man in his 70s began to find out who I was.
He introduced himself as Sheik Tahir and the others as his sons
and brothers-in-law. Where had I come from?

What had happened? My answers brought gasps and groans
from the others. When I had finished, Sheikh Tahir remained
thoughtful as the others waited for him to reply.

"This is not uncommon," he said. "We have heard of it
happening before but you are beloved by God because this is
not our usual camp. We were moving across the railway line but
some wild animals blocked our traditional route. You are a very
fortunate young man to have met us." I bowed my head and told
him how sincerely thankful I was. He just smiled and told me
I was now another brother in the family and that I could travel
north with them for a few days until the next train station was
reached.

The night then continued with some stories around the
campfire. If I listened carefully I could understand most of the
dialect. Their language was rich, poetic and from an older world,
and the tales were similar to the ones I had listened to with the
fishermen. Each one seemed to have a 'message' or moral. The
poor would always win in the end, confounding the rich; true
love would triumph; djinns, gods and goddesses flitted in and
out of human lives; animals had magical powers; and honesty,

generosity, trust in Allah and hospitality were the supreme
virtues.

I slept well that night on homemade carpets in a tent
separate from the women, and in the morning I was allowed
to work with two young nephews as they tended their twelve
camels. I learned a lot from them. I think they delighted in
showing off their knowledge to a city dweller and grinned when
I backed away from one of the grumpier animals. There were
only two female camels, kept for their milk and breeding, and
the boys made the males do all the carrying work. Occasionally
they would feed them nutrient-rich sorghum grass and massage
their necks to help them digest it. If they wanted them to kneel
they would make weird gurgling noises and the camels would
collapse like folding tents onto the ground hissing, bubbling out
froth and gurgling themselves in protest.

They told me that the best ones were young males between
four and seven years old, and that they had to shackle some of
them by the ankles at night in case they ran away. When they
became too old for work they gave them a quick death as they
faced them in the direction of Mecca and slit their throats.

We travelled in the very early mornings after our prayers and
rested during the roasting midday hours.

There was more travel in the late afternoons, and I began
to look forward to the times after we had eaten when the
stories and discussions started around the fireside. I was
astonished at the breadth of topics that would be covered in
these conversations. Though barely literate, these were highly
intelligent people with an abundance of intellectual curiosity.
They had a reverence for and acceptance of the great miracles
of life. Islam provided them with answers, but they continued
to speculate about the infinities of space, the distances between
planets and the daily mysteries of birth and death. Later,
as a student and eventually a professor, I delved deep into
philosophy, and I am confident in saying that these people
would have been perfectly at ease in the discussions. An added
dimension to these evenings was the glowing fire and the huge

canopy of stars above us. There were no city lights to dull the glow and gazing upwards at the vast blackness, studded with countless millions of stars, was something that is seared in my memory.

After six days we had reached the next stop on the railway line and as the engine wheezed to a stop the whole family, including the women, gathered round to say goodbye. Sheikh Tahir beckoned to the inspector and asked him if he would treat me as a guest on the train and if I could be allowed to sit inside. Such was his natural authority that the inspector immediately agreed. Then two women came forward and pressed some fresh bread and milk in an aluminium container into my hands. Finally Sheikh Tahir presented me with a special gift – a leather shoulder bag which I still treasure today. I was overwhelmed by the kindness of these people, one or two of whom were now in tears.

Like the lake fishermen, these simple people had a profound influence on my life. Academic education is a fine thing but the values I learned from them – gracious manners, kindness, respect for their elders, generosity and hospitality to the wandering stranger, infused my very being. They had no books, but they had saved my life and had reinforced my trust in the essential goodness of human nature.

* * *

After Cairo it was back to school where I was making genuine friends and gaining more self-confidence as I joined in all sorts of activities.

Sport, particularly basketball, ping-pong and football, were all outlets. I was a reasonable footballer and played up front for the school team on a few occasions, but much of my free time was taken up with my responsibilities as President of the Student Union. We were left wing at the time, part of what was called The Democratic Front. We felt – and my experiences of appalling working conditions had convinced me of this – that even though the communist party manipulated the movement, we were championing the rights of the poor and the struggling.

Somehow I even found time to do some acting as well, joining a professional group called Apadamac which performed plays and gave recitals in and around the area.

I was still only 16 and very much the junior of the group, but for a while I enjoyed a gypsy-like existence as we travelled from town to town in a ramshackle old van.

The director of the drama group was Mahjoub Abbas Sid-Ahmed, a brilliant, cultured scholar and deep thinker who held open house at his bachelor home in Khartoum north. Although still at school, I was invited into his circle of intellectual friends and was able to join in the evening discussions. I remember him as a smiling, witty man who would often collapse with laughter when the talk became over serious. He was a genuine, cultured polymath, interested in everything under the sun, especially literature, politics and drama. He once directed me as the central figure in a play called 'The Blacks' – this was not quite what it sounds, and its central theme was freedom of expression and human rights. In a way, belonging to the circle was like being at a mini-university with the bonus that there were no exams to be taken at the end of the year! Mahjoub later married Suad Adam, a highly respected English teacher, and her brother Mustafa became part of the group. Others that are treasured in my memory are Jaffar Abbas, Mahjoub's older brother and another deep thinker, and the late El Khatim Adlan, a philosopher, intellectual and a mover-and-shaker in the political world. There was also Gadoora, a gentle, self contained, perceptive man, adored by all, who listened quietly and offered profound insights into whatever was being discussed.

I look back on my schooldays with tremendous nostalgia and have no regrets, no chips on the shoulder, no burning resentments that many people seem to carry with them through life. I still had my dark moods or "black dogs" as I heard Abdulahi Al Awir once call them when he was quoting Winston Churchill. Somehow, through hard work and keeping busy,

I managed to keep them at bay and the brave presence of my mother helped me to keep my worries in perspective.

Abdulahi continued to intrigue me. He was a walking dictionary in himself, though he never paraded his knowledge, and we regularly listened to the BBC World Service together. The large dial on the *Grundig* radio was very much part of the fun because it spun across a panorama of all the other major radio stations in the world and Abdulahi would delight in tuning in to random foreign stations to see if he could pick up any additions to his vocabulary. He rarely did and usually settled back with the BBC World Service and it was in one of their broadcasts that I listened to the story of Churchill.

Abdulahi had a special reverence for him. "A great man. He saved the world from evil…"

I once mentioned to him that I was talking to communist leaders. He lifted his head, thought about saying something, but remained quiet.

The silence was non committal but I sensed he disapproved.

One day El-Hadi Adam told me a strange story about him. He had been walking by the Nile when he noticed a man sitting on a rock about 150 metres from the bank. The river was quite shallow and he was so intrigued he paddled out to talk to him to see if he was all right. The man had his back to him but as he got closer he realised it was Abdulahi. He was reading some notes aloud to himself.

When El-hadi Adam asked if he was all right Abdulahi turned round in shock, stuffed his notes into his pocket and blurted out, "I've forgotten all my French and Spanish…"

Then he added, "I was only joking, only joking…"

He was such a mystery to us. It only deepened one day at school when the history teacher, Mr Siddig, announced that that morning we were to receive a distinguished visitor. Instead of our usual forty five minute lesson we were going to have a lecture about the history of Sudan.

He disappeared and to my astonishment walked back into the classroom with Abdulahi Al Awir. He was dressed in an immaculate white jalabiya, a turban and shawl. His tiger skin shoes were locally made and expensive and his entire bearing was composed and dignified. All the students were now respectfully standing and after Mr Siddig introduced him as a distinguished historian Abdulahi took the floor.

I knew he had recognised me but he looked over my head and pretended he hadn't. He had the voice, delivery and presence of a genuine scholar and experienced lecturer and he talked to us without notes about a key period in the history of Sudan called "The Funj". He mentioned a famous book written by a man called Al-Fagih Muhammed al-Nur Dayfallah. He insisted that if we were to really understand our country's history it was essential to read the book. It was an extraordinary collection of two hundred and eighty stories, including births, miracles and life stories of holy men and Sufi saints. Initially they had been part of an oral tradition but now they were available in written form.

There was silence when he had finished and he folded his hands and looked down at his feet.

"Are there any questions?"

Nobody put a hand up so I raised my arm. Again Abdulahi pretended he didn't know me.

"Yes?"

To test him I asked him a question in English. "Are all these stories true?"

Without hesitation he answered in the same language.

"Every single one."

Before he left the school he did an extraordinary thing.

He said if any of the students wanted further information, or wanted to consult him he had a telephone number. He then gave out our own home number, 53791, which, of course, some of my friends recognised. Then he walked out with Mr Siddig. The class was silent.

When I told my family that afternoon about all of this they were stunned. He was due that evening to hear the 6.00 p.m. news and he was now late for his ritualistic polishing of the table and radio. We were anxious to question him and find out about his mysterious past but he didn't appear. We waited and waited and the next day went to search for him. A neighbour who had just come back from the souk told us some terrible news. Abdulahi, the scholar, the wisest and gentlest of men, the wandering philosopher king, had been killed instantly the previous evening in a road accident. What was worse, he had no relatives to claim him and his body was to be used as a cadaver in the University medical school.

We missed him so much. He was an enigmatic, beguiling man, not quite of this world but a giant from another one. I never found out what that world was and I never discovered where he came from, but I sensed it was a wonderful one.

He wasn't the only character to visit our house.

Others I remember were Salah Karar, a tall, thin man who had his own small barber's. When he wasn't shaving people's chins or cutting their hair he would close his shop and walk around the district talking to as many people as possible. He had educated himself beyond school and had an intelligent, enquiring mind. He was always asking people for their opinions on all sorts of matters, politics, dreams, history, the welfare of their families and so on. He continued in this manner even after he became totally blind in later life. Then there was Walid who was completely deaf and dumb. He was from a good family and like Salah Karar he had a lively curiosity about life following all the local and international news with great interest. He communicated by using his own invented signals and drawings. Other characters were Elgid Qurashi, a Sufi of genuine integrity and lovable absent mindedness. He once arrived at a function during Ramadan with a large case of ice for the evening drinks and left it outside the building in the hot sun where it melted. It was as if he lived in another richer world of the spirit and the real world was a source of difficulty for him. He was always smiling and, like my grandmother Zainab, told wonderful Sufi stories. There were hundreds of them but one stuck in my mind. Here it is:

"A poor man in rags went to the palace where there was a great banquet. The King said he should be admitted out of courtesy but no one wanted to sit next to him and he was placed at the lowest end of the table by himself.

He left the banquet and borrowed some fine clothes and jewels from a wealthy friend and returned a few hours later. This time he was greeted with great respect and ceremony and shown to the head of the table to sit with the honoured guests.

"This food is so delicious I must rub some on my clothes," he said, and each time he took a mouthful he smeared some of it on his sleeves and front. A nobleman sitting next to him was astonished.

"Sir, why are you rubbing food on your beautiful clothes?"

"Oh," he answered with a smile. "It was these clothes that brought me food in the first place and they have to be fed first."

There were many other characters in addition to the ones above: There was the fish merchant Ahmed who sold all his wares from the back of a donkey; Yahia the milkman and his clanking aluminium cans. He delivered daily, kept all the accounts in his head and settled the bills at the end of each month, never making a mistake. There was Abdulla the bread man, weighed down on his wobbly old bicycle with loaves of every description and the mighty Abu-Al-Roos, a volunteer gravedigger with the build of an Olympic weightlifter, who suddenly dropped dead in his late thirties for no apparent reason. All these individuals are gone now which I think is a shame. They were more than mere tradesmen as they knew everyone and would stop to chat and pass the time of day while making their rounds, bringing colour and eccentricity to the neighbourhood.

At this point in my memoir I want to pay tribute to our closest neighbours in Omdurman. The native Americans have a saying that it takes a whole village to bring up a child and I know exactly what they mean. Our house was surrounded by friends who mirrored that 'village' and who became like an extended family. Doors were always open and if a stranger or visitor arrived in one house, food and drink from neighbours would appear as if by magic. In times of hardship things were shared with no embarrassment and no questions asked. A death was met with mutual sadness and support and the whole "village" would rejoice at a marriage or the birth of a new child. It was a wonderful thing to have absolute trust in so many people and I like to think that I was able to take that trust into my adult life, using it as a springboard in my dealings with the outer world.

I treasure the memory of these people who lived so close to our house and I would like to name as many as possible: There was Qurashi, a kindly man, a senior civil servant, devout, precise and fair in all his dealings; Abbas, my friendly uncle and a senior civil servant in the Post Office who loved to sit outside his house in the evenings to watch the world go past. He kept spare chairs, a transistor radio and a flask of coffee or tea for any passers-by who wanted to stay for a chat. Then there was Omer, a devout and holy man who had queues of people outside his doors gratefully accepting his charity; Al-Madih was another fine, charitable giver, devoted to his family and a man of complete integrity. He worked in the oil industry and his wife and children had the rarest of smiles.

There was Mohamed Osman, a business man whose children became talented artists and teachers and Guma, another civil servant. These two men were both as welcoming and generous in their dealings as the others.

Then there was Hassoun, an Imam and a profoundly learned and respected man who would offer discreet and wise advice on religious matters. He and his family were famous for helping anyone in need.

Finally the ones who lived next door to us were the brothers Ahmed Dar-Sileih, another senior civil servant, and Addalla Dar-Sileih a senior military officer, and the finest neighbours you could possibly have. Words fail me when I try to describe their generosity. Sadly Ahmed died about the same time as my father and the families became united in their grief, even tearing down the wall between the two houses to symbolise their closeness. Their children became like extra brothers and sisters to us and the two mothers supported each other as if they were twins. The wonderful Abdulahi Al Awir was welcome in all of the houses, sometimes arriving unannounced, sometimes sleeping on a mattress in an outside courtyard; always courteous, beautifully mannered and composed. We all loved him.

The memory of these people also brings to mind my teachers. Much of their hard work went unseen by the parents but the pupils knew and were quick to appreciate their commitment and dedication, particularly when they would take many hours out after school to help anyone who asked. I had learned from them, and of course from my family, my neighbours and even the memorable eccentrics, that a reaching out, a search for the new, the unknown, for truth and authenticity and a strong work ethic are unbeatable combinations for success and happiness. They became anchors of goodness in my life, exemplars of kindness and charity that I was able to store in my memory and try to live up to. They were a perfect complement to that other eternal friend of mine, the Nile.

May Allah bless them all.

Chapter 6

North to the Cold Islands, Victoria Station and James and Elena

A shared commitment to the ideal of disinterested scholarship, devoted to the development and transmission of a civilisation, pursued in a community free from ideological intimidation.

(Roger Kimball, an American art critic and social commentator's definition of a University)

When men speak badly of you wrap yourself in your own virtue and integrity.

(Kamil Idris)

"You're not going!" My mother was horrified when I told her I was planning a trip to Europe during the two month school holiday. She was sitting in her favourite chair in the kitchen and she paused to look me up and down. "You're too young," she said. "You can go to Cairo but not to Europe. It's too far. Anyway, it's too expensive. You'll get lost as well."

"I won't get lost," I replied. "I have a map and I know the way."

I had known this would be her reaction so I had planned everything down to the last detail. "Look. I have saved money from working in Cairo. My good friend Saleem wants to come with me. He has a brother in England, a doctor in a place called Manchester, and his wife is a nurse. They will look after us. We can fly to Beirut and then hitch-hike or get trains to the UK. It will be easy."

"It won't be easy. Do you know how far it is from the Lebanon to the UK? You'll both get kidnapped or murdered. You're too young. You're not going. The plane might crash. Where is Manchester?"

I could see I was getting nowhere. Just then my elder brother Farid wandered into the kitchen. He had been listening to the conversation and was smiling to himself. I knew my mother regarded him as the man of the house after the death of my father and that she would listen to what he had to say. "He'll be fine," he said.

"He won't be fine," said my mother, "he's still only 14."

"He's nearly 15 and he's old enough to take care of himself. He's been to Cairo, hasn't he?" I could have hugged Farid. My mother was wavering.

"Let him go. There are two of them and if they stick together nothing will happen. Besides, it's time he grew up. Your baby son is a young man now." My mother slumped deep into her chair. I could see that Farid's words had hit her hard. Here was her youngest child straining to leave the family nest. Deep down I knew she wanted to protect her last baby and prolong her own role as the protective, loving mother, but she was facing the inevitable – her offspring's instinctive urge to meet the outside world and spread his wings.

I seem to remember that she was near to tears. She looked across to Farid and then at me. She sniffed, swallowed hard, placed her hands in her lap and stared at them closely as if they were providing her with an answer.

"I will let you go, but only under two conditions." She breathed deeply, trying to control her quavering voice.

"The first is that you will write to me every week telling me where you are. The second is that you never ever go anywhere or do anything on your own. You stay with Saleem all the time."

Farid wandered languidly out of the kitchen leaving my mother and me alone. Her watery eyes were blazing with love and I went across to embrace her. "Please be careful.

You are my last child and I don't want anything to happen to you. You *will* write to me!"

"I promise," I replied. "There's only one thing.

"What?" she asked.

"I don't have quite enough money for the flight."

"What?"

"There's nearly enough. I just need a little more."

I thought she was going to change her mind. She was in such emotional turmoil that anything was now possible.

This was a critical moment. She leaned far back in her chair, took a huge, long breath and this time stared upwards as if she were reading an answer from the ceiling.

She couldn't look at me and whispered, "There is a little bit of money. I…" She stopped. I never found out where the money came from, but it was enough to help me buy the air ticket from Cairo to Beirut and have a small reserve for train fares. Over the next few days the final plans were made and I could barely sleep for excitement. My mother was still in a state of partial shock but was resigned to see me off, and after tearful goodbyes I headed for Khartoum railway station with Saleem for the journey to Cairo.

I could write a separate story about my first trip to Europe and the many adventures I had on the way. I kept my visa and passport close to me all the time, zipping them under my shirt, and I was thrilled by the plane journey to Beirut. As the train pulled out of the station I saw the Nile snaking its way north to Egypt and made a mental snapshot of it. It was my spiritual anchor and I craned my neck to have a last look and say goodbye to it.

Saleem and I soon learned that sharing was the best way to travel. Our money was lasting and we shared taxis with others – usually a lot older than ourselves, to keep the cost down. These other people also shared their bread and olives as we moved north from Beirut to Damascus and Turkey. From there we hitched lifts in huge wagons.

Sometimes we helped the driver load them before setting off from the depots, and at other times we were allowed to sit in the back, open to the sun, becoming dusty and tanned as we reached Turkey. I remember one driver passing loads of oranges and bread to us, one hand on the wheel and the other stretched out backwards out of the window, only just managing to keep the wagon from careering off the road. I did keep my promise and sent postcards to my mother, although I didn't tell her about this bit of the journey.

At night we slept in cheap hostels. The food was basic and the mattresses hard and lumpy, but we were full of energy, burning the magic fuels of youth, and we couldn't have cared less. Soon we had reached Skopje in the then-Yugoslavia and we had a mighty stroke of luck. We met up in a youth hostel with an 18 year old Sudanese student called Jaffar. He was smartly dressed, and to our young eyes, very sophisticated. He was on his way to Paris and though he had an international driving licence he hadn't quite enough money to buy a car. He suggested that if we were to pool our resources we might be able to get an old second-hand one and then sell it when we got to Paris.

This was quite a gamble for us, as it would use up most of our cash. My mother's voice kept ringing in my ears.

"What if the car breaks down? What if you have a crash? What if Jaffar is a crook?" There was also Zainab. "Go on! You'll be OK. Trust your own judgement!"

Zainab won and we went ahead. The car was a small, light blue, noisy Opel. It was battered and had a messy interior but it started first time. The garage owner looked a bit shifty, but he was happy with the equivalent of £58 sterling we paid for it, and so away we went. It turned out that Jaffar was a capable driver. He was a bit bossy, acting like an older brother, and would become annoyed when we couldn't read the old maps very well. To save money we slept hunched up in the car for a couple of nights, parked at the back of gas stations, but we eventually reached Paris and sold the car for a small profit!

We said goodbye to Jaffar and were now within reach of England, with just enough money to pay for the Channel ferry. I still remember with a smile my encounter with the immigration officials in Dover. My visa and passport were fine, but questions were asked about why I was coming and what was the purpose of my visit. I knew I wanted to find some work and make some money, so I was honest and answered, "Probably to wash dishes." The man burst out laughing and called out to one of his colleagues to come and have a look at this young boy who had come all the way from Sudan to work in a kitchen.

They were still chuckling when they let me through. I think my answer had made their day.

Saleem had told the officials he was going to Manchester to stay with his relatives and we took the train to Victoria Station in London. On the way I stared out of the window for a long time. Europe had become greener as we drove north from Turkey, but I had never seen anything as verdant and rich as the woods and forests of southern England. I had seen pictures of them before but the reality was stunning. The towns and villages were just as enchanting – often the train would pass by the backs of rows of small houses and I marvelled at all the carefully tended flower gardens, the neatly cut lawns and the lines of clothes held out to dry in the wind. To me they somehow spoke of a kindly, well-ordered, good-natured people, and when I met some of them I was not disappointed.

Victoria Station was noisy, bustling and intimidating for two young boys. Cairo Station had been just as busy but here people seemed to walk more quickly and looked more anxious and preoccupied. They all seemed to be carrying umbrellas and hurrying to some desperately important rendezvous or meeting, checking their watches and scanning the timetable boards. The worldly-wise Jaffar had warned us that the big stations in London were sometimes visited by thieves and pickpockets and we stood closely together, holding on tightly to our rucksacks and looking about nervously. We didn't have to worry – when Abdul accidentally bumped into an old lady she immediately apologised as if it had been her fault! He knew that he had to take a tube to Euston Station to travel to Manchester in the north, so we shook hands and said goodbye, hoping to meet up in exactly the same place in a couple of months' time I was now on my own. I was apprehensive and probably still experiencing culture shock, but I reminded myself that I had survived in Cairo and could do the same here. I was used to the commotion, tension and anonymity of big cities, and I took heart from having made the long journey without any major problems. I was also used to hard work. I shouldered my backpack and walked straight towards the central station café.

This was part of my plan. I had found work in Cairo by doing precisely the same thing and I felt confident that the same would happen. Looking back as an adult over 40 years later I am astonished at the innocence, even naivety, of my young self. I was a total stranger in a foreign country, had no friends or relatives, had nowhere to stay and had no job. I had just enough money to see me through two or three days without starving, but that was it.

"Could I speak to the manager please?" I asked.

"I'm the manager. How can I help?" the man replied.

He was a harassed, overweight, red-faced man, but he had a gentle tone of voice.

"I'm looking for a job, sir. I can wash dishes."

"Can you now! Look, son, I'm very busy and we haven't any jobs going. I'll tell you what. There's a café over the road. Ask to speak to James and tell him that Dave sent you. He might be able to help. Good luck, son."

"Thank you!" I replied.

I was puzzled. I was grateful to the man for his help, but why had he called me his 'son'? Also his accent was odd. Not 'BBC' World Service at all! This was a strange country.

I recognised James straight away. He was a balding, middle-aged man jerking levers on a great steaming coffee machine and barking orders to a young waitress. The café was about half full with ten or so people dotted about.

Encouraged by my help from Dave I approached the counter.

"Yes?" He looked at me with narrowed blue eyes.

Young people of my age didn't normally come in for a coffee.

"David sent me," I said.

"David. David who?" he asked.

"David. From the station. The café."

"Oh Dave! Well. What do you want?"

"A job," I replied.

He started chuckling to himself and looked me up and down.

"A job! Just like that! Well, we'll have to see. Don't hold out much hope. We're fully staffed as it is. Where're you from?"

"Sudan," I answered.

"Sudan! You're a long way from home, son. Where're you living?"

"Nowhere," I admitted, "I've just arrived."

He put the coffee cup on the counter with elaborate care and leaned over to have a closer look at me. "Well, well, well. All the way from Sudan. Elena! We've got a visitor." A tall, blonde woman wearing a clean, white apron emerged from a back kitchen. She was taller than her husband and had a cheery, open expression. I liked her immediately and sensed that she would be sympathetic.

"This is? What's your name, son?"

"Kamil," I told her.

"Kamil's come all the way from Sudan to find a job. Isn't that something. Problem is, we've got no vacancies at the moment."

Elena was inspecting me and took a while before she spoke. To me her English was clearer than her husband's and it was obvious she was intrigued by my sudden arrival.

"You got no job, dear?" she asked.

"No."

"Got anywhere to stay?"

"Not yet."

"You worked in a cafe before?"

"No. But I have washed dishes at home and know how to put books together. I've worked in bottling and oil factories and I can make the best mint tea in the world. I am used to hard work."

She was smiling now but James was frowning. I think she must have held my gaze for nearly half-a-minute. The café looked reasonably prosperous, but I could see that she thought hiring me would be a gamble. "You got some sort of visa, dear? How long you staying?"

"Two months." I thought one month wouldn't be of much use to them.

She looked across at James and made a quick decision.

"He can start today. Gillian's away on holiday for two weeks and then Frank goes when she comes back. He can fill in." James was about to protest, but Elena just pursed her lips and dared him to disagree. It was obvious who was the real boss of the café.

Once more it was a woman who had helped me on my way. In retrospect I think it was the innate maternal instinct that played its part. I was trying to be a young man but Elena had seen through my pose and recognised a young boy, thousands of miles from his home.

It got better. Elena found a small room for me at the back of the café. It wasn't much, but there was a bed and a chair and there was a washroom just next to it.

"You can sleep here, dear. We won't charge you and there's enough food in the café for a growing lad like you. We live just round the corner and James opens up at seven o'clock every day. We go to church at ten o'clock on Sundays, so you and Geoff will have to look after the place for an hour or so. He'll show you what to do."

I hadn't met Geoff yet, but it turned out he was their 20-year-old son. He was as friendly as his parents and we got on well together, spending any free time playing cards and ping pong in a back store room. He was fascinated by my unexpected

arrival and couldn't believe how far I had come in search of a
job. The working hours were long, but I knew a good deal when
I saw one. The café was open until well after nine o'clock and
we worked right through the day with an hour off for lunch and
two other small breaks of 20 minutes or so.

Compared to what I had been used to in Khartoum and
Cairo, it was easy for me. The pay was far better and because
I had free food and lodging I was saving just about all of it. I
wanted to show James and Elena that I could work hard without
complaint and be trusted. All the time I was hearing voices in
my head from my mother and Zainab urging me to work hard
and be as honest as possible. I think James and Elena were a
bit surprised at how I spent my free time. I liked playing ping
pong with Geoff, but I was also keeping a diary and would
spend hours in my room writing things up. At other times I
made my way to the British Museum and headed straight for the
antiquities section dealing with the Nile, Sudan and Egypt.

I would wander the corridors in a semi-trance, goggle eyed
at the statues and the fabulous displays of treasure found in the
great pyramids. I wasn't at all lonely, but Elena and James were
convinced I was homesick and I would be invited round for late
evening meals at their home where they treated me like a young
son. It was there that I learned to appreciate the traditional
English Sunday meal of roast beef, crispy potatoes and Yorkshire
pudding.

All the time I was getting a crash course in British culture
and learning a great deal about how to deal with people. I
remember once when a young couple sitting at an outside table
had ordered a coffee, then the man had asked for a muffin.
When I came with the order he said that he hadn't ordered the
muffin and his partner insisted he had. I had been told by James
that in England the golden rule was, 'the customer is always
right,' and I told the couple that there would be no problem in
taking the muffin back. The girl became very red in the face and
started shouting at her partner and when an arm was waved, the
tray of drinks I was carrying would have spilled all over her if I

hadn't whisked it away in time. I was very lucky in being able not to spill anything, and I think this distracted them from their quarrel and they apologised and calmed down. After that they became regulars at the café and gave me generous tips which I put into the 'pool' to be shared with the others. They kept asking me questions about how old I was and where I was from, but James had told me not to give out too much information to customers because of security matters. This little incident was a valuable lesson for me, as I realised that being polite and reasonable with people and remaining calm can help to defuse many potentially disastrous situations.

In the end I enjoyed my stay with the family so much I extended it to two-and-a-half months. This meant that I would be late for school in Khartoum and that I would have to travel back alone without Abdul, but I wasn't too concerned because I had by now saved up enough money to travel all the way by train and air. When it was time to leave, the café was closed for the morning and James, Elena, Geoff and four other friends came to Victoria Station with me to say goodbye. James pressed a leather jacket and a bag of food into my hands. I still have a cameo picture of them all in my mind as the train slowly drew away from the platform. They were smiling and waving. I have never forgotten the warmth and kindness they showed to a young traveller from a foreign land who had unexpectedly arrived on their doorstep.

Now back home and at 16, though still the 'baby' of the family, I considered myself to be a worldly-wise and resourceful individual. I was studying hard at school, helping to support my family through my trials as a child labourer, and I had travelled and made a successful working trip to Europe. Perhaps a bit smugly I considered myself to be mature and confident beyond my years, but the lessons I had learned from these experiences really did colour my outlook on life and my personality. Having to ride on the top of swaying trains, making tea and meals for ferry workers to pay my way, being captured by 'pirates' and living for a week in a Bedouin camp, as well as having to cope with numerous family tragedies, had hurled me into the mayhem of life and I had survived.

And then I was arrested by President Nimieri's security services! I was in my final year at school when one morning two smartly dressed men knocked on the classroom door and addressed the teacher. "We are looking for Kamil Idris. Where is he?" I stood up immediately, my knees shaking. The men hadn't introduced themselves but everyone knew who they were.

They had that unmistakable air of confidence and menace.

"Come with us please." This wasn't a request. It was an order and I have never heard a class of boys so silent as I walked out with the two men. They drove me to their compound a few kilometres away where they kept me for two days. As President of the Student Union I had always thought that something like this might happen, and in a way I was mentally prepared for it. After all, I had done nothing wrong or subversive, apart from overseeing political debates and meetings at the school. During my two days' interrogation I refused to eat or drink and was eventually allowed to go home. I was severely shaken by the incident, but I wasn't physically threatened and I think they were just giving me a warning. What was really upsetting was that when under arrest they had entered my home and confiscated many of my books and documents, which I never got back.

After this I was ready for the next stage – university. I had an instinctive understanding that having a clear goal, a sense of purpose, would be helpful in achieving academic success. I was only too well aware of the fate of students who drifted into University life with a 'let's see what happens' philosophy, without any obvious ambition or career expectation. To me they seemed to accept whatever came their way. I wanted to master my own fate, a hubristic and maybe risky approach, but I thought it worth the gamble. I had two very definite ambitions or aims. One was to become a prominent university professor with an international portfolio, and the other was to join the United Nations in a leading legal or diplomatic capacity.

As ever it was the family that had helped to sharpen and

clarify my approach. I had always confided in my mother and my grandmother Zainab. I felt easy in their presence and valued their shrewdness and advice. To me Zainab was a wise complement to my mother, but she also had a masculine awareness of the outside world and its competitive and complex nature. She had listened quietly to my dreams for the future and had advised me to study philosophy, sciences and law. "You can make sand your bed, and sky your cover, but you can never cover the sun with a blanket" was the essence of her own experience. I was unsure of what this meant, but I think she was trying to tell me that to be a success in life I would have to have cast iron qualifications and work as hard as I possibly could.

Later on, as I matured, I realised there was another, more profound interpretation in her words. She had been urging me to search always for the truth and not to try to compete with God. From the moment that she uttered these words I tried to apply them to all aspects of my life.

I like to think that they helped to add a degree of humility to my character, to look beyond the obvious and accept that all human beings have weaknesses and limitations, and we should show charity and understanding to all, no matter what their race, religion or gender.

My mother and Zainab are still towering presences in my mind and even now, as a grown man, I find I often summon their spirits up in my imagination and ask for their advice. I don't find any embarrassment in admitting to this – atheists may scoff, but if you are a believer in the afterlife, as I am, it makes perfect sense.

I think they would have been proud of what I was undertaking because I would be studying at two different universities at the same time. I knew that this was an enormous risk, as taking just one degree was demanding in itself. At the University of Khartoum I was studying Law, and at the University of Cairo in Khartoum Pure Philosophy and Psychology with some units of Political Science. I also started to learn ancient Greek (so that I could read Aristotle and Plato in the original) and French.

I knew some people thought this was unwise and that I would inevitably fall between two stools, but I had the self-confidence and motivation to ensure that if I micromanaged each day, I could succeed. To balance the two areas of study I would have to reduce my social activities to a minimum and apply rigid self-discipline for the next five years. I devised a daily routine similar to the one I had used at school built around long periods of study and short breaks. I knew I could keep this up because many hours of monotonous misery in the various factories had inured me to hardship. In addition I would now be working for myself and my future, and not for meagre wages. Working on the basis that genius is 1% inspiration and 99% perspiration I vowed to stick to my schedule.

My studies at the Law School were helped by a secret ally. Ami Abdelwahab was the head attendant at Khartoum University's Faculty of Law. He was a tall, imposing character, always immaculate in his clean, white jalabiya and turban, and we knew we had to show him respect as he was in many ways a powerful and influential figure. I think he saw himself as a sort of headmaster, continually on the lookout for troublesome pupils, and my friends and I were careful to keep in his good books. I certainly held him in high regard. My father had once told me that a clue to a person's character can sometimes be seen in the way he or she walks. Ami Abdel walked quickly with his head up and his back ramrod straight, and he had made it clear in the past that he had absolutely no time for lazy or disrespectful students.

Quite out of the blue one morning he beckoned me over. I thought he was going tell me off. His speech was as rapid as his walk and I had to listen carefully. What had I done? It turned out that he had been watching the way my colleagues and I had been staying in the library until it closed late in the evening and he said he wanted to help us. There was a large kitchen next to the staffroom and he had his own premises nearby. He had a room that was empty, and, if we liked, we could use it to study and if need be sleep over without being disturbed. The room turned out to be a huge space right next to the staffroom.

It was from here that Ami Abdel made tea and biscuits for the teaching staff and washed dishes. Whenever we were allowed in he would grin at us and hold up a massive ring of keys in one hand and a finger to his lips as if to say, "Remember, I am doing you a big favour." We worked into the small hours and would let ourselves out quietly when we were done. Some years later, when I had graduated, I thanked him by sending his children some presents, and a pair of sunglasses and reading glasses from New York which I knew he had always wanted.

I did not restrict my reading just to law and my reading was omnivorous. I wanted to find out and explore, rather than stick to rigid orthodoxy. One of my guides was Montaigne, a French philosopher with a refreshingly straight-forward approach to life who said:

"If I study, the only learning I look for is that which tells me how to know myself and teaches me how to die well and live well."

I thought this was sound advice and I stuck to my schedule. The chance to study when everyone else had gone home was a huge bonus, but I also realised that I could not become a recluse or hermit, and so I continued to take a keen interest in daily politics. I was not a member of any particular party, and I liked to think I had independent views, relishing the free exchange of ideas and opinions within the universities. Looking back on it this was a hectic and agreeable time for me. I was beginning to form my own religious and political outlook on life and the ancient philosophers, particularly Plato and Aristotle, and the wisdom of Sufism, were dancing on my mental horizons.

In the background was politics. The country had won its independence from British and Egyptian rule in 1956, close to the year I was born, and as I grew up I had become aware of the succession of revolutions and unstable governments that had come and gone in the following years. As a teenager I was able to understand that tensions between the north and south of the country were the main problem. I was now old enough to appreciate the significance of what was happening, and when Jafaar Nimeiri seized power in 1969, promising to end the civil war, I breathed deeply.

He did face serious opposition and in 1971 was briefly captured in a communist coup, but he escaped over a palace wall and had the leaders of the coup executed. I think he was a popular figure at the time because he promised to address the tensions between the North and the South of the country and introduce radical reforms.

The fact that he was also the son of a postman, a football lover and no admirer of ostentatious display (he stuck to driving his own car when he took over) added to his appeal. He introduced a socialist agenda very much along the lines of the one Nasser had started in Egypt, transforming the economy by nationalising the banks and industries, and encouraging Soviet investment and aid.

During the next ten years there was relative peace but he clashed badly with the late General Gaddafi who attempted to depose him. He once memorably observed that the Libyan leader had, "a split personality, both sides evil". Disillusioned with socialism he began to side with the USA, receiving aid and arms from Washington following his support for Egypt's peace-making efforts with Israel. Nimeiri did make several mistakes, and some of his later initiatives did backfire – perhaps he didn't study the cases carefully enough. There was no doubt he was a dictator, but he had a light touch compared to others, and I and most of my contemporaries tried to debate and argue openly. We were living in a diverse society where different views were mostly accepted and the focus was on the middle way, moderation in all things.

I was managing to stick to my schedule of hard work and intellectual enquiry, while allowing myself periods of free time to socialise and rest my mind. I had now left home and was living in university accommodation, sharing a comfortable study bedroom room with two close friends. I enjoyed their company, but most of my working day was spent at lectures or in the library, or in Ami Abdel's room where I could work in silence, with occasional visits home at weekends. My mother fussed and clucked about the state of my health and eating habits. I usually came away a little heavier from all the food she produced, as she insisted I was starving myself at the university during the week. The fact that I was now self-supporting was a continual source of pride. I was no longer a child labourer, but I was paid reasonably well as a part time journalist, sending off articles on current affairs and topical issues to national newspapers and magazines. I made sure that these were not too controversial or subversive, and I think they helped to clarify my own outlook and philosophy of life.

I had been born a Muslim and during my intensive study of pure philosophy it was inevitable that the great thinkers of antiquity would have an impact on my outlook. Aristotle's belief that thought or reason is the greatest endeavour was intriguing, as was his opposition to moral relativism and its belief that truth is whatever an individual thinks it is. However, it was Plato who interested me the most. His theory of the absolutes, that everything on earth is an imperfect reflection of its own essence and that life is nothing more than the imprisonment of the soul in the body, chimed in with my religious faith. If this idea was followed to its logical conclusion, then the soul pre-existed the body and therefore all knowledge was simply a case of remembering. For example, when Pythagoras's theorem is explained, the natural reaction is to say "of course". I also liked the way Plato explained his most profound ideas by using pictures and metaphors, particularly the story of the cave, the fire, the shadows and the unseen world behind the watchers' backs.

A wonderful by-product of this intense study of philosophy was my discovery of Sufism, the mystical element of Islam which had been introduced to Sudan in the sixteenth century. I admired the gentle and tolerant manners of Sufi academics such as Sheikh Alaraki Elrayeh Eluleish (who became a close friend and who later became a senior Justice of Gezira Province in Sudan), and I particularly admired the highly influential Sheikh Dafallah Elsaim Deema. These men, as well as others, seemed to have a poise, serenity of manner and psychological balance that made them stand apart from others, yet there wasn't the faintest hint of smugness or superiority in their makeup. They were humble, charitable, good humoured and had a well intentioned acceptance of others.

Sheikh Dafallah was a tall, dignified, kindly man with the most exquisite manners. He had thousands of followers and kept open houses where everyone was welcome, and I was impressed by his openness and tolerance. I think there was nothing exclusive in this approach to religion and Christians and Jews were accepted as brothers who shared in the great Abrahamic root of the three monotheistic faiths. Once when I was in Sheikh Dafallah's 'home' (Al Maseed) there was a drunk man who kept falling over. When others would have seen this as a disgrace and thrown him out, the Sheikh asked for calm and the man was shown quietly to a bed in the next room. I was impressed by all of this God-like compassion and wanted to find out more.

I found out that Sufism has its roots deep in Islam. Small groups of men known as 'Lovers of God' began to appear in the Muslim world about 100 years after the death of Mohammed (PBUH). They were known as 'Journeymen', 'Travellers' or 'Wayfarers of the mystical path'. They respected the outer religious laws but their emphasis was on closer union with the divine, the secret yearnings of the heart for a return to the creator. Later these men became known as 'Sufis', possibly because of their purity of heart (safa) and their white woollen clothes (suf). The essence of their approach was love and devotion and an opening of the heart to the grace of Allah. It concerned itself with building bridges between cultures and religions, and regarded all men and women as brothers and sisters. Its lack of dogma and moderate thinking were to me a perfect antidote to the wild extremists of other religions. I found the emphasis on proselytising and aggressive intolerance of some religious followers unacceptable and anathema to a thinking person.

Some of the Sufi's teaching was based on humour and common sense, and they had hundreds of stories to complement the deep truths of their faith. The emphasis all the time was on balance, taking the middle way and not swinging to wild extremes. Here is an example of a Sufi story.

> A woman and man came into Judge Nasrudin's room one day.
>
> The woman complained, "I was just walking on the street the other day, when this man, whom I never met before, came up to me and kissed me! I demand justice!"
>
> "I agree that you deserve justice," Nasrudin said. "Therefore, I order that you kiss him and take your revenge."

These compilations of tales and jokes were used by the Sufis to spread their message of thinking clearly and passing on the wisdom of the ages, helping to harmonise the tensions between differing cultures. This is what made me respect their beliefs. It is a cliché to say that the twenty first century is crying out for such an outlook, where humility and tolerance are the pillars of faith.

To me Sufism holds out a beacon of hope for the future. As an ancient way of belief it has a proud record of embracing free thinkers from all walks of life.

Foremost Sufis in the Arabic world have included the great poet Rumi, Al Ghazali, Al Arabi, Omar Khayyam and Fariduddin Attar (whose stories were later adapted by Chaucer in The Canterbury Tales). In the West Sufi thought has had admirers and followers such as Cervantes, Winston Churchill, St Francis of Assisi and the late Secretary General of the UN, Dag Hammarskjold. I am convinced that if there is to be reconciliation and healing between those who wish to force their beliefs on people and those who advocate more peaceful methods, then Sufism is one of the keys to progress.

The intellectual gates were open and I relished the opportunity to base my ideas on experience and not just dry doctrine. The Sufi belief that God is not remote or unapproachable, and that experience of him can be achieved in this life, was very important. In addition, St Augustine's teaching on the primacy of faith before reason and his explanation of how the soul is longing for its return to its home in the divine were perfectly compatible with this approach. All the time my mind was moving to an inevitable conclusion, and I even had an 'Isaac Newton' moment in our small garden at home. I was eating dates and carelessly threw away a few stones or kernels. A few months later I discovered a small palm tree shoot growing.

I didn't need books of philosophy to explain that there is a force in nature that is independent of human intervention. What was behind this miracle of growth?

What or who set it in motion? How could the universe possibly be understood as a random collection of whirling atoms? There had to be a creator, a mover, a carer, an unseen power beyond human comprehension. I was moving to some answers, while at the same time remembering that the basis of Sophocles' philosophy had been the asking of questions.

I think it was the five years at university that helped to finally shape my outlook on how I should relate to people from all walks of life. I could see the dangers of narrow sectarianism and the hollowness of depending merely on the outward adherence to the rules and rituals of religious duty. These were of course important, but faith without charity and good manners was to me incomplete. The essential message that was coalescing in my mind was that the supreme virtues were kindness, tolerance, freedom of speech, dialogue, basic human rights and acceptance of my fellow men and women while we were temporarily on earth.

Meanwhile I graduated with honours and distinction from Khartoum and Cairo Universities respectively, having relished the challenge of undertaking so much work. To relax I would take evening walks, well away from the city, along the banks of my beloved Nile where the magical smells of wood smoke and spices, and the gentle flow of the shimmering waters, calmed and refreshed my spirits. This was my secret haven, my temporary escape into an unchanging, timeless world where I could find peace and a restoration of energy.

Chapter 7

The Nomad Becomes a Diplomat

Achievement is the result of determination and self knowledge.

(Kamil Idris)

Should I have had a tie? Was it a mistake to have worn a jacket by itself? Was my afro haircut inappropriate? The four interviewers from the Sudan Ministry of Foreign Affairs and other departments opposite me seemed to radiate disapproval. Outside in the brilliant sunshine of the courtyard other candidates walked self-consciously about, waiting their turn. I knew that one of the men across the table from me was a psychiatrist. Was he already analysing me? They were high ranking civil servants and they were interviewing hundreds of applicants for a fresh intake of diplomats. Approximately 15 places were up for grabs and I was determined to be chosen as one of them. Yet had I got off to a disastrous start? It was strange. I had gained one of the top grades in the examination, and up to this point I had been full of confidence, but the jackets and ties opposite me seemed to be saying, "You have no chance... Don't you know the elementary rules of correct dress?" A quick glance outside was reassuring – all the other applicants were tieless.

I was still studying and teaching part time at the universities, but now it was the dreaded interview when one wrong word could affect my life forever. The questions showed that the

133

panel had done its homework thoroughly by researching my background and challenging me on the obvious issues. What had attracted me to Sufism? Why had I taken on two degree courses simultaneously? What were my political views? Why had I studied both law and philosophy, and so on.

Did they know that I had briefly flirted with communism? How could I possibly reconcile these radical views with a career as a civil servant? I decided that the only thing I could do was to reply as honestly as I could. The interview became more of a discussion and exchange of views, especially political ones, and I even questioned the psychiatrist about his own outlook.

This could have been a mistake. I sensed that he had made up his mind that I was not worth considering.

Doubts came crashing in. Maybe I had applied too early, and why was the psychiatrist making so many notes when the others weren't?

Afterwards I was in a state of nervous agitation. I found it difficult to sleep and tried to throw myself into work, but my mind kept wandering. I stayed at home to wait for the letter. If it was a brief note then it was all over.

If it was heavier, with more forms, I had been successful.

Clunk! Exactly two weeks after the interview the heavy letter fell to the floor of my house in Omdurman and I knew I had passed as soon as I heard it. I had made it and was accepted into the then highly prestigious Foreign Service of Sudan and I was so proud.

Funnily enough, one of the first people I met on a later social occasion was the psychiatrist, Professor Hasabu, who had been writing all the notes during the interview.

He smiled, shook my hand, congratulated me and said he had liked the way I had respectfully stood my ground and not given in to authority when the difficult questions had been fired at me.

And so I began my professional life… and if I thought things were going to be easy after all the studying I soon found out differently. The Foreign Service was run on highly disciplined lines. You had to start each day at 7.30 a.m. on the dot, and if you were late, tough luck, as the doors were closed and locked and you then had to explain yourself to a superior. You were expected to wear a smart suit and tie, or a formal long sleeved safari suit, and there were strictly no visitors without clearance from the top. I was quite happy with all these rules and became absorbed in the work, firstly looking at topics to do with public administration, and then spending time in the Arab Research and Legal departments.

Looking back on it now I think this was one of the happiest periods of my life. I was not only a fully occupied diplomat in the Foreign Service, but had also been accepted into the Institute of Public Administration. In addition I had been allowed time out to continue to work as a part time lecturer. This was an exceptionally heavy schedule but my oasis, my sanctuary, was the fact that I was once again living at home. Every evening my mother and sister would welcome me with a large glass of hot milk and on Friday mornings the whole family would gather for a communal breakfast and we would chat about the week's events. Occasionally the idyll could be broken, and my thoughts went back to my childhood hell in the various bleak factories I had worked in. I tried to wrest my imagination away from these memories, but they are still rooted in my mind even today, and I have to force myself to think of happier times and dismiss the flashbacks.

I passed an interesting year there but began to realise that an additional qualification would help to further my ambitions of promotion in the diplomatic and academic fields. I was selected for a scholarship to attend Ohio University in Athens, Ohio, the oldest University in the USA's mid-West. The one year course would lead to a Master's Degree in International Affairs with an emphasis on International Law. In September 1977 I flew from Khartoum to Washington via London and took an internal flight to Ohio. This was my first visit to the USA and I was taken aback by the friendly, extrovert and welcoming nature of the students and staff. Nothing seemed to be too much trouble, and

I was whisked away in a minivan to the campus by a welcoming committee of students. This was early autumn and already the trees' leaves were beginning to change into thousands of shades of gold, yellow and orange. My room, though small by American standards, had everything I needed including a bed, a small closet, desk, bookshelves and a comfortable chair. The 200-year-old university was on a vast campus, and I marvelled at the ease of manner and confidence of the students, the elegance of the tree-lined avenues and the gracious red brick buildings.

I felt I had in a way 'arrived' on the international scene, and that my experiences working and travelling in Europe as a student had prepared me well for a year in the United States. Labouring away as a child and teenager in the back streets of Cairo, the café near Victoria Station in London and in Witney near Oxford, and the small murky factories in Khartoum, had ensured that anything else was a form of paradise. It had been the book-keeping factory experience that had unsettled me most. I remembered my grandmother Zainab's warning about copyright, and an idea began to form in my mind about how it might be safeguarded internationally. Maybe I could do something about this when I became more qualified. In the meantime I had to study hard for my Master's degree.

The start was unfortunate. I had missed some of the early classes because of administrative complications in Sudan and was given a frosty reception by the highly respected professor. He was a scholarly, solemn, elderly-looking man and was taken aback at my unexpected arrival in his class. "You do realise that you have missed the crucial first few lectures?" he stated.

"I am so sorry, I…" The other three students in the room fell silent and I was lost for words.

"You will not be joining this group. There is another one starting in a few months. Kindly leave the room and shut the door after you." In a daze I wandered out of the class and slumped against a wall in the corridor. I had never anticipated such an unexpected setback.

I was devastated and so confused, that I even thought

about applying to another university. However, what would happen to my scholarship? How could I ever recover from this embarrassment? I decided that the only thing I could do was to seek out the professor and explain that my lateness was not my fault. To my astonishment he allowed me back in on a trial basis. I was first to arrive for the next lecture on a Monday morning and was met with some knowing grins and hushed welcomes from the other three students. The professor strolled in and began his lecture on a topic that I had written extensive research on as a student.

It had been a complex matter and the professor asked if any of the others knew anything about the issue. Silence.

None of them had a clue. He was about to continue when I put my hand up. I sensed his impatience, even irritation, but he had asked a question and knew he had to allow me to answer.

I stood up and got completely carried away, rambling excitedly about the details of the issue for about seven minutes. Flushed and triumphant I sat down to an icy quiet. I looked around expecting to see smiles of admiration, but one of the students had put his head on his desk and the professor was staring at me. What had I done wrong? I had only answered his question in full. The professor then rocked me to my core, telling me that I was mistaken.

The first person I spoke to on the phone was my mother back in Sudan. She was sympathetic and reminded me with a telling metaphor that if one faulty rung on the ladder caused a fall, I should immediately step up to the next one. She told me to have courage, that when Allah closes one door he opens another, and that she would pray for me.

Shortly after this incident I was called into the office of my supervisor, the Emeritus Professor of History and distinguished academic who had published definitive books on slavery. She was a tall, soft-spoken, blond-haired lady in her 60s, exuding composure and compassion. I warmed to her immediately as her kindness was reassuring.

The matter was quickly resolved. The professor admitted that

I had been correct in my assessment and analysis of the issue. I was able to continue with the course and was even asked to make some independent contributions to the actual teaching of it. I was grateful for the intervention into the matter and for the integrity of the professor for admitting he had been mistaken. I established a working rapport and friendship with both of them. Some time later the lady even visited my family and me in Omdurman, and I was able to show her some of my favourite havens by the Nile. She had never been to the country before, and as a historian was staggered at the amount of ancient ruins and cultural artefacts to be seen.

I enjoyed my course immensely and by sticking to my well-tested work routine was able to finish my Master's degree well ahead of schedule with distinction.

My stay in America made a deep impression. With my scholarship funds I was able to enjoy a lively social life and I still smile when I remember the evenings out at a wonderful place which I think was called 'Restaurant Oasis'. It lived up to its name, as it was a meeting venue for students and staff where a first-class cuisine was complemented by open, lively discussions. When the meal was over we would return to the university common room and continue until the small hours. There were differences of opinion when the chat moved to politics and religion, but even the most extreme views were listened to with tolerance and good humour. What we were doing was honing and forging our own ideas and philosophies for the future, while at the same time accepting the rich diversity of viewpoints that can find expression in a free society. There seemed to be a mutual understanding between the students and the lecturers that open questioning, interruptions and direct challenges were an accepted part of seeking for the truth. The students weren't in the least bit rude, but it also became clear that this generation was ready for much soul-seeking and I was quite shocked at times at the way they later began to chip away at the country's foundational ethics and beliefs. This wasn't the outright rebelliousness of the late 60s, but change was definitely in the air.

The 70s are sometimes seen in retrospect as the hangover period after the wild, turbulent 60s. This had been a time when the student riots, the challenging of authority and rebellious youth had raised its angry head.

The old order had been challenged by the baby boomers, the rock music, the new technology, the spirit of flower power, radical protest and the excesses of the drug culture.

Now there was a sobering up, a reassessing of the political structures and a calming of the revolutionary temper.

Some of my American friends felt the 60s were an invigorating and refreshing time, when a new generation would usher in a great beneficial society, freed from a conservative past – but I had my reservations. I thought it was foolhardy to tear down existing structures and to rubbish traditional morality when there was a doubt and vagueness with what would be the replacements. I admired the idealism of the youth movements but I was worried about their dismissal of any counter-arguments and in some cases their aggressive intolerance of opposing opinions.

However, in the political arena, the 70s were as turbulent and disturbing as the blockbuster 60s. The international scene was as volatile as ever with the US still involved in Vietnam, despite the growing anti-war protests to bring the troops home. It wasn't until 1973 that the last soldiers left with that iconic picture of the last helicopter leaving Saigon, with stranded civilians clinging to its undercarriage in despair. President Nixon then faced a home grown scandal called 'Watergate' and resigned in 1974 under threat of impeachment. I was only too aware that National Guardsmen had, in the same year, shot dead four anti-war students in nearby Kent State University.

These were nervous times and further abroad instability was rocking the world. In 1973 OPEC, led by the urbane Saudi Sheikh Yamani, caused economic upheaval by raising oil prices. In one year the cost of a barrel of oil rose from $3 to $12, pricing many countries out of the market completely. Unbelievably Japan rode the crisis and witnessed a huge boom, overtaking the economy of West Germany to become the second largest in the world. Later it experienced an economic recession when inflation turned to stagflation with prices dropping alarmingly and investment plummeting. This was one of the first instances of the replacement of Keynesian economic theory with neoliberal economic theory, and other countries took note.

In the same year there was the Israeli/Arab War and Black September activists seized the Saudi Arabian embassy in Khartoum. In Cambodia Pol Pot and his communist Khmer Rouge army overpowered the government and began a drastic reform process. In an attempt to enforce a Marxist agrarian society, they marched hundreds of thousands of civilians into the countryside, denuded the cities and arrested, tortured and killed Buddhists, priests, monks and anyone they considered 'intellectual'. The estimated number of those killed was three million.

The decade was still polarised by the tension between the USA and the USSR, and in an attempt to defuse the situation and put a brake on the alarming nuclear arms race and stockpiling of weapons, an international meeting in Helsinki was called. This led to a signing by 35 countries agreeing to, among other things, the inviolability of all post World War Two frontiers and a respect for human rights. However, 'The Helsinki Accord' was non-binding, as it didn't have the status of a treaty and the eminence grise of US diplomacy, Henry Kissinger, dismissed the whole thing as, "a grandstand play to the left wingers". Another peace-keeping move was the Camp David Accords, a treaty signed in 1978 by both Egypt and Israel. US President Jimmy Carter invited Anwar Sadat and Menachim Begin for secret talks at his Presidential retreat.

Furious with him for making peace with Israel, extremists later assassinated Sadat during a military parade.

Terrorism spread like a plague in Europe. The Baader-Meinhof group and The Red Brigades in Germany and Italy kidnapped and murdered prominent politicians. In the UK the IRA continued its bombing campaign, trying to force the

acceptance of a united Ireland. There was a military coup in
Ethiopia leading to the overthrow of Haile Selassie, one of
the longest-lasting monarchs in world history. In the Lebanon
a vicious civil war broke out with Israel, Syria, the Palestine
Liberation Organisation and Christian Druze forces using the
country as a battleground for their own interests.

The list of conflicts could go on and on. Before the decade
ended there had been the appalling Soweto massacres in South
Africa and the Iranian revolution in 1979, when Shah Pahlavi
was overthrown by Ayatollah Khomeini. This ushered in the
establishment of The Islamic Republic of Iran and a theocratic
government.

All of this painted a grim picture, but it was not all gloom
and doom, as serious international development issues were
started. In many developing countries the green movement had
taken root, investment had increased and poverty levels were
declining. The 60s had been a roller coaster ride but some of its
legacies were bearing fruit – civil and human rights movements,
women's liberation and a growing awareness of the dangers of
pollution and planetary control were increasingly on the agenda.

Like everyone else I was profoundly affected by these world
events, and I was aware that with my recent qualifications I
might be able to play a part in them. My immediate future was
still uncertain, but I had absorbed many lessons from studying
the lives of leading influential statesmen. I was particularly
amazed by the position of Anwar Sadat. He had known that
he was taking a controversial stance when he agreed to the
peace treaty with Israel. Here I am neither commending
nor condemning him – I am simply stating that it is critical
that this conflict be resolved as, in my opinion, and I am
not exaggerating, the Israeli-Arab struggle, along with other
conflicts, could trigger World War Three.

His assassination sent shock waves throughout the world
and added weight to my core belief that violence only begets
more violence, and that somehow the cycle has to be broken. I
think history will eventually prove that dialogue is the essential

ingredient in moves towards peace. At the time I had no idea that in the future I would be able to play some part, mainly through diplomatic channels, in diverting key political figures along this route.

Meanwhile my academic sojourn in the US had come to an end. I had graduated with close to full marks, and with growing self-confidence was ready to fly back to my beloved Nile and The Sudan.

Chapter 8

Return to the Two Rivers. Meditations by The Nile

The worth of a man is judged by the threshold of his anger.
(Kamil Idris)

My time in America had been an eye-opener to the benefits of living in a dynamic democracy and to the charms and energy of its extraordinary people. The country had its problems and its fair share of malcontents and divisive issues, like any other, but I admired its entrepreneurial spirit and 'can do' philosophy.

At the end of the 70s it was still recovering from the seismic shocks of the Vietnam War which had seared its soul and shattered its self-confidence, but its instinct for renewal and progress meant it was once more eager to engage on the world stage. The nuclear standoff with the Soviet Union and Cold War tensions still rumbled away, but the old inbuilt optimism and beliefs in its core values were emerging from its fog of doubt and introspection.

I had appreciated the way I had been warmly accepted into the academic circles and been welcomed as a fellow traveller in intellectual enquiry. A career as an academic had its attractions and was now a possibility, and I wanted to follow up my Master's degree in International Affairs and International Law with a Doctorate, but at the same time an inner voice was urging me to strengthen my deep-rooted affection for Sudan and my family.

It was now 1978. I had been overwhelmed by the heady freedoms and energies of America and its people, but as soon as my plane landed in Khartoum airport, I was once more in my spiritual home. I was anxious to resume my duties at The Ministry of Foreign Affairs and do some more lecturing, and I had also completed a great deal of research for my Doctorate. A busy schedule lay in wait, but first came the warm family welcome and the inevitable gargantuan meals to celebrate the return of the weary nomad. A few days later I took a walk.

Perhaps I had been living in cities for too long. Perhaps there comes a time in everyone's life when the extrovert, noisy, bustling world becomes too much and solace has to be sought elsewhere. I was still energetic and ambitious, but part of me recoiled from the getting and spending, the endless hurry and divided aims of modern life, and the ceaseless quest for status. I was sick of universal savagery, the wars, the killings, the rise of new dictators, the drug cultures and what I perceived as a moral vacuum in the world. I had enjoyed genuine success in a short time, but there was part of me that felt empty and unfulfilled.

Meetings, commerce, deadlines, business and politics had clouded my soul, and I wanted the world to slow down, even stop. I needed some time to myself and one evening, obeying a strange, atavistic instinct, I walked for miles, away from the throbbing hum of Khartoum, to a quiet bank of the Nile. I sat down alone on a sandy shore and let the sunlit waters and whispering currents weave their spell.

As a child I had splashed and played in the Nile's waters and had let my imagination be swept away by its magic. It was more than a legend; it was a living link to an enchanting past. I was looking at a scene that hadn't changed for thousands of years. How many billions of tons of water had flowed past where I was standing? What had happened to the silent, vanished races of antiquity?

The first humans, the fathers and mothers of mankind, the Nubians, the Egyptians, the Romans, the Arabs, the British? I was sure their ghosts were somewhere around.

This landscape was shimmering with their ancient presences and I felt a genius in the air. Through the mists of the years I could almost feel their nearness. What a strange world we lived in. Heirs of the past and custodians of the present, we are all poised between two eternities.

Puzzled and unbidden, we arrive in the world for a short while and are then on our way. If the Nile had a spirit or character, I felt it would confide its secrets to me. It might speak to me. It would maybe tell me that all the mighty empires of the past, all the colourful pageantry of history and the arrogant, posturing lords of the earth, were as nothing when compared to its own eternal stillness and everlasting spirit.

I glanced northwards. In my imagination I swooped away to the bleak, windswept desert and hovered over the remains of the broken and lonely pyramids of Meroe, testimonies to the futility of mankind's search for permanence and immortality. I had been too young to appreciate their significance in the story of Sudan, but in a strange way the memory reconnected me to my earlier self.

I think we all, however old, still carry the small boy or girl in our personas and cherish the innocence and bliss of those early days. Now sitting quietly and becalmed by the Nile I was once more a little boy rocked to sleep by the rickety old train and nestled against my mother's shoulder.

I was as safe and secure as if I was in heaven. And then came the dreams and the nightmares. Where they sprung from I have no idea, but wise old men often talk about 'djinns', 'noonday devils', 'evil spirits', and I sensed from my studies in philosophy and metaphysics that perhaps there are more things in heaven and earth than we can imagine. The modern, enlightened world will scoff at these ideas, but for me they had an element of truth. I had fought these destructive, invasive voices throughout my life and now, when I had achieved so much and was poised for more success, I had a flashback to my childhood fears.

The voices were persuading me to give in. They weren't aggressive or harsh, just oily and gentle, speaking to me as if I were a silly little boy who had been led astray.

Weren't my life and my achievements pitifully small and insignificant in the great scheme of things? Wouldn't I be just as irrelevant and as soon forgotten as the wrecked, broken statues in the deserts and the great achievers?

What was the point of my existence? Why not slide back into nothingness and stop trying to prove myself? My hard work and successes didn't count for much and were not going to make the world any better, so why continue?

These were dangerous, insidious, siren presences, mocking my ambitions, and they wouldn't go away. They kept urging me to escape from all the violence and mayhem of the world, the wars, the killings, the rise of tyrants and zealots. What difference could I make when faced with the type of people who would kill others, convinced they were doing God's good work? These fanatics had been slaughtering innocents throughout history, so why bother confronting them?

Thoughts such as these could drive any man to despair and I prayed for answers. Meanwhile the great river flowed softly on, indifferent to my inner turmoil. Absorbed in its own progress, it seemed to have little comfort for my soul.

Then a strange thing happened. While meditating I had removed my sandals and let my feet nudge into the water.

Tiny wavelets had begun to caress them. Unceasing, insistent and exploratory, they appeared to be trying to wash the dust away and cleanse them. I became so preoccupied by watching them that all my anxieties faded away. The insidious voices of doom vanished and I felt profoundly calmed and refreshed. I felt as if nature was reminding me of a consoling truth – that despite the turmoil, tragedies and trials of life, there was a deep-down, relentless freshness built into the DNA of the earth and that eventually all would be well and all manner of things would be well. Maybe Allah had answered my prayers in a veiled, inexplicable way. This wondrous river kept rolling and rolling along, just like in the famous song, and in its own mysterious way it was insisting that I should stand up, face the future and not be afraid to play my part, however obscure it might be.

I was staring out over the rippling waters, deep in thought when a shadow appeared on the sand next to me.

I looked up and around to see an old man with his hands behind his back. He was dressed in shabby, mud-stained farmer's clothes. He said nothing, as if he was thinking like me, then he smiled, revealing a set of decaying yellow teeth.

"God be with you."

"And also with you," I replied.

"Here. Have these." He handed me some fresh dates.

"Thank you so much. But why are you giving them to me?"

"Because you look a bit sad," he replied. "Your head was in your hands. I thought they might cheer you up. By the way, there are seven of them, food for the soul…"

I looked down at the dates in my hand. There were indeed seven of them. Seven, the sacred number. When I looked up to thank him again the old man had disappeared over the sand hills.

It was spiritual encounters like these brief, semimonastic retreats from the world, that helped me keep my sense of harmony. In other words, there was a fusion in my life. I was able to balance the hectic demands of the professional with the complex questions of existence, the big questions, the ultimate mysteries of life with equanimity. It was as if I could switch from one to the other without losing perspective. I needed this sort of psychological stability, because new responsibilities were arriving thick and fast.

Re-joining the world, I was now engaged with the Ministry of Foreign Affairs and assigned to its Legal Department. After a while I was elected to the Legal Experts Committee of the Organisation of African Unity, now known as The African Union or 'AU'. As a young man, this was quite a step up for me as it put me in touch with some of the leading players on the continental scene.

At the same time, through careful management of schedules, I passed my bar examination and was admitted as an Advocate and Commissioner for Oaths. I was even able to keep up my part-time lecturing in Law and Philosophy.

Then in 1979 I was offered a posting to the country's United Nations mission in New York. This came totally out of the blue, and I leaped at the chance of revisiting old friends in America. I waited and waited for confirmation, but the wheels of the civil service sometimes move slowly, even backwards, and the administration changed its mind, requesting that the position be given to a married person.

Instead I was given a posting to Geneva where I would become a diplomat in the permanent mission of Sudan to the UN. I was lucky enough to be part of an outstanding delegation led by Ambassador Omer Birido, a well-read, highly competent intellectual whose manners and charm I will never forget. I was a relative newcomer to the diplomatic scene and the warmth of his welcome and encouraging remarks helped me to feel at ease. His deputy, Ambassador Ibrahim Hamra, was equally impressive and matched his superior in courtesy, generosity and dedication.

There was also Director Amir Mirghani, Head of the cotton section, another man of innate courtesy, charm and integrity. The team also included diplomats of high calibre and professional performance, such as Abdalla Abbas, Yousif, Mohamed Salah, Mirghani and Hashim.

I was a newcomer to Switzerland but was aware that it was a small land-locked country in Europe that had kept itself out of the wars for hundreds of years, and which had the most discreet banking system in the world. I found it to be a breath-takingly charming and beautiful place, totally untouched by the bombed-out cities of its neighbours. While Berlin, London, Vienna and Budapest had suffered heavy bombing during the Second World War, Zurich, Geneva and Basle had escaped, with their historic buildings and streets perfectly intact. In the evenings I would sometimes wander away from my small bachelor flat and marvel at the quaint old streets and buildings and their air of peaceful permanence. At other times, when I was free from work, I liked to stroll along the shores of Lake Leman for fresh air and exercise. It is one of the largest lakes in Europe, and though it

didn't have the turbulent drama of the Nile, its glassy stillness
had a soothing effect on my mind.

I was now heavily involved in my work and one of the first
meetings I attended in Geneva was called by The United Nations
Conference on Trade and Development, otherwise known as
UNCTAD. I was asked to present a paper to the delegates on
the code of conduct on the transfer of technology, and it must
have gone down well because I was later appointed coordinator
and spokesman for Africa and all developing nations. I
remember this time very clearly because I met and led many
important personalities and senior diplomats.

It also came to my attention that Dr Arpad Bogsch, the then
Director General of WIPO (The World Intellectual Property
Organisation), was interested in the topics we were discussing. At
the time our Mission, along with the Saudi Arabian and Nigerian
Missions and the office of the World Bank, was renting space
in WIPO's premises. During a different meeting at WIPO, I
listened carefully to the items on the agenda and to Dr Bogsch in
particular. What he was talking about struck an immediate chord.
Later that evening my mind drifted back to my early childhood,
working in the primitive publishing factories. I felt that if I could
play some sort of role in protecting the work of authors and
inventors from being hi-jacked, it might go some way to help
developing countries strengthen their own economies.

This was perhaps early reflection, but it galvanised my future
plans.

It became clear during that meeting that Dr Bogsch was
proposing to replace his Deputy, Mme Laubway of Cote
d'Ivoire, with Mr Marino Porzio of Chile. Again I watched
Dr Bogsch closely. White-haired, impeccably dressed, ramrod
straight in his chair, with intelligent blue eyes, he exuded control
and authority. He had that instantly recognisable thing called
'presence'. He was decisive, tactful and firm in his handling of
the meeting, and Mr Porzio was emphatically approved as the
new Deputy Director General. I didn't meet or interact with Dr
Bogsch at the time, but I had had an in-depth introduction to

the workings of WIPO and the way it could offer huge benefits to humanity by protection of intellectual property assets.

Later WIPO increased its numbers of staff and we had to find alternative premises. Just after we moved I was pressed into continuing as spokesman for the group of developing countries on all matters such as technology transfer, business practices, economic development and intellectual property rights. This was a significant opportunity for me to work with ambassadors and high ranking officials. I was now moving in influential circles in Geneva and getting to be better known in the international community. At a comparatively young age I now had heavy responsibilities and duties with an unprecedented work load, and I would sometimes wonder to myself at how far the nomad from two rivers and the child labourer had travelled.

I also realised that my activities and portfolio with UNCTAD were complementary in outlook to those on the agenda of WIPO, in that both organisations were intent on demystifying Intellectual Property and bringing its benefits to all countries – from the most highly developed to the poorest and most needy.

Then came a break. In 1980 I was sent to the UN in New York as part of a Sudan delegation at The Law of the Sea Conference, where I was elected as the Rapporteur for the Third Committee of Marine and Scientific Research. I was there for a few months and the meetings ultimately ended successfully, creating at a later stage The Seabed Authority.

Back in Geneva I was unaware that my progress was being closely observed by WIPO, and in 1982 I was invited to meet up with its Deputy Director, Mr Mario Porzio, an urbane, elegant and sophisticated Chilean lawyer who was acting under instructions from his superior Dr Bogsch. We had a very friendly chat at our mission and I was surprised that I was being considered for a position with them. Later Mr Porzio asked me to come and work at WIPO, but I had to decline the offer because I was currently enjoying a high-profile role as a free voice spokesman and coordinator for an important group of countries, and I did not want to let that group down. Six months later he again approached me, but once more I had to refuse. Finally Dr Bogsch himself asked for a meeting, and when he offered me a position with WIPO I knew I would have to reconsider.

I was unsure of how I should respond and said I would have to think about matters, but eventually I was asked to apply for a post as a Senior Programme Officer in the then Technical Cooperation Division. There was competition for the position with a short list of candidates, but my application was successful and I started working for WIPO on December 31st 1982. The technical division (development cooperation) was divided into three departments: Africa, Asia and Pacific, and Latin America and The Caribbean. I was placed in the former, which meant that I would travel extensively in home territories, and worked under the late Mr Ibrahima Thiam. I remember him warmly as a softspoken, religious man of the highest integrity. Slightly more than two years later a new department was created, the Arab Bureau, and a competition was held for its first Directorship. I was delighted to win the competition and advanced up the international civil servant scale from a P-4 (Programme Officer) to a D-1 (Directorship), an unprecedented promotion.

Now I was dealing very much on familiar ground, and my advisory work involved my visiting all Arab countries. Here I would also have meetings with the leaders of the League of Arab States, influential ministers and ambassadors. Once I had understood the requirements of my work I looked closely at my schedule, as I had done earlier in my life, and I realised that if I was careful and planned the day in detail I could continue with academic studies. I enrolled at the University of Geneva to read for a Doctorate in International Law, and graduated with distinction from the prestigious Graduate Institute of International Studies in 1984. I was proud of this qualification and even more so when Dr Bogsch congratulated me during a daily staff meeting. He started off by waving my thesis in the air in triumph as an example of the rewards of hard work!

Chapter 9

Marriage and the
Top of the Ladder

*Quiet minds cannot be worried or frightened,
but go on in fortune or misfortune at their
own private pace, like a clock ticking in a
thunderstorm.*

(RL Stevenson. Scottish novelist and poet.
1850-1894)

Envy of others is poison to the soul.
(Kamil Idris)

She was tall with long dark hair reaching over her shoulders, dark brown eyes and golden, glowing skin. We had known each other since we were children and every year she seemed to grow more lovely. Azza was 21 years old and still at university studying commerce and business. Her mother had died when she was a small child, and as the eldest sibling, she had taken care of her younger sisters and brothers. She had developed into a mature, kindly and very beautiful young woman and I think she sensed that I was attracted to her.

I was now almost 30 years old and the hints from my family that, "so and so is a nice girl," and, "hasn't so and so become such a beauty," were aimed at my bachelor status. I knew that marriage customs were very deeply rooted in Sudanese culture and that I would have to follow strict protocol if I was to be lucky enough to win Azza as my bride. I also knew that she shared my feelings as we had already met frequently, usually under the gaze of a watchful aunt or two. Azza's father, Mohyeldeen Mabrouk, had remarried after the death of his first wife. He was a highly respected Commander-in-Chief of the Sudan Air Force, the trusted pilot of the presidential airplane, and a qualified lawyer. He was a significant presence in the community and as the families were related we already knew each other quite well, I would have to write a letter of proposal asking him if I could marry Azza.

In general, before a man can marry in Sudan, he is expected to be economically self-sufficient and able to provide for a family. In addition the bride will also expect him to provide her with jewellery and clothes. The two families have to agree to certain traditions in the arrangement, and once these are settled, the preparations for the wedding can begin. This was 1986 and Sudan, like many other countries, still clung to its attitude to old established customs. There are so many diverse cultures and each one has its own particular customs.

The main ceremony took place in a nearby mosque at 5.00 p.m. on Monday 5th May, 1986. Azza and I were not present. We were at our respective homes while our family representatives concluded the formal arrangements on our behalf. This was the more serious and formal time of the day, with the witnesses and guardians observing the legal aspects and then listening to a sermon. Afterwards food and drink were served in the courtyard of the mosque and just to let all the neighbours know that things were now signed and sealed, someone fired a rifle shot in the air.

This was the signal for more fun to begin and we knew what was coming next. Our party was held in the large courtyard in Azza's house with a huge tent and thousands of guests, some inside and some out, some sitting, some standing, with lots of comings and goings.

I had been granted leave of absence from my work and after a short honeymoon in Cairo I returned with Azza to Geneva. The pressures of my position were accelerating and as Director of The Arab Department I was soon back dealing with all the

Arab countries and regional organisations including ALESCO, INESCO, The League of Arab States and the Federation of Arab Scientific Research Councils, as well as others. This involved regular periods of travel and at first I was unsure whether Azza would cope with being by herself in a busy city when I was away. I needn't have worried. She had so many interests of her own that she kept herself very occupied and she also made friends easily. Her main interests were in interior design and visiting all the art galleries and museums in the area, and she loved being able to drive herself around in a four wheeled Jeep that kept her safe on the snow covered roads in the winter. We had bought a small house in the countryside which was in the middle of a vineyard and Azza delighted in decorating it and making it homely, while also improving her French.

I was now working closely with my superior, Dr Bogsch. He was a remarkable man in many ways and it was a pleasure working with him. He was insistent upon accuracy, quality of performance and attention to detail, and you always had to be well prepared for a meeting. A master of his drafts and notes, his style was to ask questions and get as much information as possible before making a decision. The problem was that often I did not know what the topics on the agenda were before the actual meeting, and 'winging' it or hoping for the best didn't always work. I made many overseas journeys with him and he would expect me to know who was whom at the various meetings and conferences we attended. This meant that I had to do some rapid research and memorise names and official positions so that if he was introduced he would know whom he was talking with. He had a formidable reputation and sometimes meetings with his staff became very tense and fractious.

On one occasion the situation became so acute that I questioned him directly. This was a risky thing to do, and it is no exaggeration to say that my whole career could have been affected if he had reacted differently. It was late afternoon in his Geneva office and I and four others had been discussing a problem with the then African Industrial Property Organisation.

It was a hot and sultry day and we were all tired. Dr Bogsch had been firing questions out in his usual manner and wanted a quick fix to the problem.

We could see he was becoming irritated by our concerns and began interrupting everyone, including me. I think he thought we were being unnecessarily pedantic, but we knew that he was ignoring our worries about some political problems and sensitivities in one of the countries within the organisation.

When he interrupted me for the fourth or fifth time I stood up and indicated that I was ready to leave the room in protest. I told him that it was about time that he listened instead of cutting us off, and that there were acute complications that had to be addressed before a decision could be made. There was a stunned silence in the room and Dr Bogsch sat up in his chair, stared me directly in the face and cleared his throat. I thought that was it, I would lose my job. I could see he was thinking carefully about how he was going to react and what he would say.

I don't think anyone had ever talked to him like that before and he was clearly taken aback.

Instead of telling me to leave the room, his voice quietened and he admitted that it would be better if we took more time over the decision. There was no direct apology but I think he appreciated that he had been a bit too hasty. The air was cleared, there were discreet sighs of relief from my colleagues and we moved on.

That was the professional side of the man, but over time I began to see a different side to his character. He was a very private person but sometimes the official mask slipped and the human side would appear. I remember once when my eldest son, still a small child at the time and visiting Sudan with his mother, became sick and Dr Bogsch got to hear about it. We were both then on an official visit to Syria and I was worried that my son wouldn't receive the essential care to help him through.

Dr Bogsch insisted on helping, and before I could do anything he had arranged for the relevant medicine to be flown first-class to Sudan. There were very few people who were aware of this side of his nature, which I think was a pity, because it would have added balance to his legacy. He was highly respected but the kindly side was kept well hidden. I have no hesitation in saying that he was one of the most impressive men I have ever met or worked with, and at times there was a touch of genius about him.

My career was going well. We had settled down to life in Geneva and Azza began to bless me with children. I could enlarge more about how a stable family life can be a foundation for happiness and today, at the time of writing, I have six children. Mohamed (27), Dinas (24), Dahlia (22), Dahd (20), Mumin (15) and Munib (5). Apart from Munib, who is currently at Junior school in the UK, they were educated mostly in the International Schools in Geneva where they were able to form friendships with pupils from across the racial and religious spectrum. I think this helped to broaden their outlook and understanding, and we complemented this by making sure they combined a compassionate religious faith and a belief in kindness, hard work and honesty in all their dealings. I was particularly pleased one day when Dinas brought home a Jewish girl to meet the family. They became and still are close friends. If only others could put their prejudices and preconceptions behind them like young people so easily do…

In 1991 I was elected by the UN General Assembly to the United Nations International Law Commission, a position in which I served until 2000. At first Dr Bogsch and the UN Secretariat in New York had been against my nomination because of potential conflicts of interest. I was reluctantly allowed to stand on the condition that, should I be successful, I would hand in my notice with WIPO. This was the first time that the UN had encountered such a move and they were uncertain as to how to proceed. I accepted this condition and the election took place in the General Assembly of the UN in New York. I am happy to say that, despite there being a long list of strong candidates, I was successful, and when I returned to

Geneva I wrote the expected letter of resignation. I was prepared to leave WIPO and Azza, as ever, gave me unconditional support. We would now be in uncertain territory but her 'let us move on' approach gave me the confidence to continue.

What happened next left me speechless. Dr Bogsch refused to let me leave but gave me an escape clause. I could continue with WIPO and conduct my dealings with the Commission in any annual leave of absence. The UN position was very demanding, but would involve only part-time work. I thought this was a very generous compromise, showing flexibility and common sense on Dr Bogsch's part, and my respect for him soared. I was now wearing 'two hats' and energised by the challenge. As part of my work, I was elected Vice Chairman in 1993 and also served on the Commission's Working Group on drafting the Statute of the International Criminal Court.

I was then re-appointed to an additional term on the ILC from 1996 to 2000 which is an interesting story in itself. I contested elections at the General Assembly of the United Nations for a second term of membership of the UN International Law Commission (ILC). I received confirmations from a large number of delegations to vote for me as they had done for the first term. I left New York one week before the elections.

It was late evening, on the eve of the elections, that a note (true or untrue) was widely circulated by the permanent mission of Sudan in New York withdrawing my candidature from the long list of candidates. Nobody had thought that the note was fraudulent. The result was simple: I was no longer a member this time because my name had been withdrawn. Many people were unhappy but I left the matter there and moved on.

Before the new membership had met, however, one of the members of the Commission had passed away. In which case the members of the Commission themselves vote to fill in the vacancy. My candidature was widely encouraged and submitted. Subsequently, I was elected from a long list of candidates and became a member again after just few weeks of that unblessed attempt. God is great!

Meanwhile I was making progress with WIPO and in 1993 Dr Bogsch sounded me out on a promotion from a D-1 position to a D-2, moving from Junior to Senior Director status. I was flattered to be asked but I thought that if I accepted it would be my last move upwards, and to be honest I had hopes of becoming a Deputy Director General (DDG) instead. Later in that same year Dr Bogsch proposed to the Coordination Committee two candidates for the DDG position but neither was accepted.

After these two unsuccessful nominations, Dr Bogsch approached me about standing for the DDG position.

This was good news but I knew I needed time before accepting the nomination in order to check with member states representatives to see if I could firm up some support. I needn't have worried, as two weeks later I was unanimously approved and served my new day as DDG on July 29th, 1994. My main responsibility was to developing countries throughout the world, and this meant that during the following years I was constantly travelling and meeting with a huge range of heads of state, ministers and senior diplomats.

In 1997 Dr Bogsch announced that the position of Director General (DG) would become vacant and invited member states to make nominations. As his deputy I was in the running. However, I also knew that I was not his first preference because he favoured Mr Francois Curchod, a man with whom he had already established a friendly and long-standing working relationship. Mr Curchod was a dedicated and highly competent professional who held dual nationality in both France and Switzerland. Another internal candidate was Mr Carlos Fernandez Ballesteros, a warm, charming, cigar-smoking Uruguayan extrovert who was also close to Dr Bogsch.

The elections, chaired by the former German ambassador to the UN, Mr Wilhelm Hoenyck, were very fair and transparent. I was impressed by the man's presence and inherent authority and sensed that whatever happened he and the Coordination

Committee would do their utmost to make sure that the best candidate was chosen. There were twelve of us applying, including four internal ones, and after an informal straw poll to gauge preferences the official business began. I was in front during the preliminary rounds, followed by a French candidate, Mr Jack Michell. Thankfully I was able to stay ahead in the final round and won with a clear and comfortable majority. These were tough rounds.

I was now Director General and so proud of the fact that I was the first candidate from a developing country to hold such a prestigious position. Now I had to pick my cabinet or team of strategic advisors. I decided that all internal candidates who contested the election should be maintained in their original positions, and on the day following the election I made the announcement in the presence of Dr Bogsch. It is of course a cliché that strong men will sometimes pick weak people to surround them. They don't want to be challenged and an inner circle of 'yes men' is flattering and safe. In the long term, however, the obvious happens and they lose touch with reality and become detached from the truth.

Some of the politicians and world leaders I had had dealings with were shrewd enough to surround themselves with perceptive and intelligent experts. I wanted to do the same and certainly didn't want those 'yes men'. As a gesture to the outgoing Director General, I named the main WIPO building after Dr Arpad Bogsch.

I also wanted to get to know my staff at every level, from the leaders at the top to the ordinary people below.

My experiences as a child labourer were always with me, and although I was now at the top I understood the trials of long hours working with little reward or recognition, when the fear of the sack or a bullying boss could make life hell. A new internal justice system was put in place so that staff could have a fair hearing if there were any complaints of high-handedness or unfair treatment, and I began to implement improved working conditions and benefits.

Once these internal matters had been addressed it was time to look outwards. I felt I was now in a position where I could articulate and raise the interests of Africa and developing countries without openly challenging the established way of doing things. I was passionate about the need for protecting copyright and patents so that investors and researchers could be confident that their discoveries and ideas would ensure genuine growth and development. For example, in the area of health new and better drugs needed to combat disease would not be introduced without the patents system as there would be an understandable need for secrecy. Other areas needing protection included technology, brands, inventions, education, international law, trademarks and literary and artistic works. These were complex matters, but vital for a developing country in its attempts to modernise and grow. In short, I wanted to transform WIPO by extending and enhancing its position and reputation worldwide and extending a universal helping hand.

The task was enormous, but I believe that small things can make a difference. Not many people receive two salaries, but as Director General I was also the salaried and elected Secretary-General of UPOV (The Union for Protection of New Varieties of Plants).

I earmarked this secondary salary to be given to deserving countries, and instead of flying first class I sat in business or economy class with my colleagues. I genuinely believed that by being open and approachable as a boss and setting an example, the organisation could run more smoothly.

The human touch is so important and when meeting delegates from other countries I would try to put them at their ease by holding consultations in advance of large meetings, reassuring them that their voices would be heard. I think this gave them a sense of being really involved, that their participation counted, and it also helped to minimise unnecessary disagreements during the actual meetings. In addition, although my instincts were to help the growing nations, I tried not to show any obvious partiality to any particular country or region.

At that time it was only in the economically and technologically developed countries that IP was really effective. Others simply didn't have the resources or expertise to equip themselves, or indeed the awareness of how it could benefit them. As a start I decided upon a three-pronged approach to the problem: firstly, the developing countries needed to be informed about the advantages IP could bring. To drive home the point I authored a book on the value of IP as a 'power tool' for economic growth. Secondly, we needed to provide all the necessary technical assistance so that they could record digitally and patent and protect all the knowledge or 'prior art' they already possessed so that it wouldn't be compromised. Thirdly, national laws varied in their approach to IP, and we needed to harmonise them to create an international standard.

In this context I would like to commemorate the memory of two dear colleagues, both dedicated and talented men working under me in Geneva, namely Ludwig Baeumer and Joachim Bilger. The former was a leading expert in the field of Intellectual Property Law and the latter a top Financial Controller. Both of them needed my clearance to travel to the USA on official business, and on one occasion they would both be flying back on separate flights. However, Joachim called me from New York and asked if he could change his flight and return with Ludwig, one day later than his original one, as he still had some outstanding consultations to complete at the UN in New York. I thought this was uncharacteristic of him and I really needed him to come back on the earlier flight, but I had to make a quick decision while in an important meeting and reluctantly agreed to his request.

As a result both men travelled together on Swissair flight number 111 from John F Kennedy Airport in New York on September 2nd, 1998. This was the flight that crashed at 10.31 p.m. into the cold waters of the Atlantic Ocean, just off the coast of Nova Scotia, killing all of the 229 people on board.

We were all devastated by this tragedy and for a long

time there was a strange atmosphere in the offices as stunned colleagues tried to go about their normal business. They just couldn't believe what had happened.

It was a truly sad event, and from time-to-time I wonder to myself what the outcome might have been if I had insisted that Joachim had taken his original flight. As a gesture to their dedication I named two conference rooms after them in their memory. It was the least I could do.

Without losing focus on the industrialised countries, I also tried to steer the agendas of WIPO meetings to reflect some of the concerns of growing countries, and in 2000 an intergovernmental committee on IP, genetic resources, traditional knowledge and folklore was established, which had far-reaching and concrete results.

After the collapse of the former Soviet Union I then had the opportunity in my senior UN capacity of visiting all of the newly-born countries in support of their legitimate demands. The changes that had been made in the brief periods of independence were astonishing as they began to recover their self-confidence and national identities. Interestingly some of the first things they did was to restore their own currencies and the potent symbols of their flags and anthems.

During my time in Geneva one of my proudest achievements was in bringing to Switzerland groups of young Palestinians and Israelis under the context of training opportunities. The two groups had no idea that they would be working together and initially the atmosphere was understandably tense. Over time their mutual suspicions began to vanish and they openly discussed their mutual problems. By the time they had finished they had promised to become pioneers in global healing.

Closer to home, in 1999 tensions between rival factions in Sudan were running high. Hassan El Turabi, the influential leader of the Muslim brotherhood, and Sadig El Mahdi, the former Prime Minister, could not agree on a way forward for the country and the risks of a violent conflict were growing. I decided to try to bring them together and organised a secret meeting in Geneva on May 1st of that year. They were initially suspicious of each other's ideas but in the end the meeting was successful and both men ended the occasion with a firm handshake and a promise of mutual cooperation for the good of the country. They then returned to Sudan to brief their advisory bodies and partners as to the outcome of the meeting. In my view a serious crisis was narrowly avoided; a potential fire, to use a metaphor, was partially extinguished.

Before finishing this chapter I should mention a clerical error that caused some minor confusion. When I joined WIPO in 1982 there were the necessary forms to fill in and my date of birth (26.08.54) was typed as 26.08.45.

This was a simple typing error and I knew that as any UN staff member was allowed to modify any date of birth, I would be allowed to correct the mistake before quitting the system. When I became aware of the error I informed the then Director General and the personnel department but the matter wasn't apparently given much importance.

I was told not to worry as the changes would be made in good time and I would not be awarded any undue benefits.

In short the error was corrected and the record straightened. Sadly some attempts were made to take advantage of the error, suggesting that I had deliberately falsified the information. I have to say categorically that this was certainly not the case. The bottom line was that the whole thing was a simple case of human error. My whole raison d'être was for complete transparency in my professional life and I think some people tried to raise a storm in a teacup. End of story! (See Appendix 4 for documents relating to this issue.)

Nile Crocodile

Sudan elections 2010, riding a camel before addressing a public rally

INTERNATIONAL STUDENT IDENTITY CARD

8/26/54

Idris

Kamil

Sudan

№ C6 05761b

STUDENT

Ohio University

CIEE Student Travel Services
777 UN PLAZA, NEW YORK, NY 10017

Athens, Oh 2, 16, 78

My identity card as a student at Ohio University, United States of America, dated February 26, 1978. Note the correct d.o.b. and my fashionable 'Afro' haircut!

OHIO DRIVER LICENSE
JAMES A. RHODES, GOVERNOR
Robert M. Chiaramonte, Director of Highway Safety

KAMIL E IDRIS
73 N CONGRESS
ATHENS O 45701

SIGNATURE KAMIL E. IDRIS.

LICENSE NUMBER NJ916964

CLASS 1

BIRTH DATE 08 26 54

DATE ISSUED 06 01 78

Registrar, Bureau of Motor Vehicles
Dean L. Dollison

EXPIRES ON BIRTH DATE 81

SEX M HT. 5 10 WT. 136 HAIR BLK EYES BRN

My Ohio Driver's Licence

Old wheezy train, similar to the one on which I sat on top of the carriages and which left me stranded in the desert

The overcrowded ferry from Wadi Halfa to Aswan. Maybe the men are wondering where that boy Kamil is with the mint tea…?

A warm and generous welcome from His Majesty Filipe VI, the King of Spain, during an official visit to that country

One example of a formal ceremony bestowing upon me an Honorary Doctorate

كسلا

أخي الحبيب الى نفسي والقريب الى فؤادي فريد

مع غمرة شوق عارمة بعيداً ونسيم هادئ عليل أرسل اليك سلاماً
حاراً وأشواقاً ساخنة وأمنيات طيبة لك وللأهل جميعاً وأتمنى
أن تكونوا بخير .

... وصلني خطابك التالت وذي اللونين الأحمر والأخضر في مساء
السبت 7/19 على ما أعتقد فقد نسيت التاريخ وكان ذلك بعد رحلة
شاقة وتعبه فقد خذل الطريقة وكاد أن ينتوه لولا عناية الله وحسن الخط ؟
والحكاية إنك كاتب العنوان خطأ وصدرتها - مكتب الأراضي والتعمير
كذا - المديرية - قلتها الأراضي وبذلك ذهب الخطاب الى الأراضي وهي
مصلحة الاستثمار ومن حسن الخط فقد صادف وجود الأخ على معرفته لقد
أصبح موظف في الاستثمار وها أنا في نفس الوقت وقد تألم متسائلاً
يصله الي ؟ وعندما تسلمته كانت الكلمة منتصف الليل وحين أذوب
شيء لينا على معقله وبعد أن صدا وعندما بدأت في قراءته كانت
الساعة صباحاً وبعد ذلك حمدت على أن آتيه لك الرد قبل أن أنام .

أخي كنت كنت الحال بعد هذه الغيبة الطويلة (9) !! أتمنى أن
تعلمها كما أشتغلت العمل في أتم صحة وأتم عافية وخصوصاً الوالدة
العزيزة ومرضعتى التانية فتكذان عنها حار وتحياتي لها أحر
وكذلك الأخت العزيزة ... باره والعمة الحبيبة (هيم) والأخ صديقي
والأخوان كامل وعز الدين مع ت ... لت على لام على خطأ أتم الرقيقة والتي
تعب سماحة عند فتكفه خدتم الصادقه وجبم العيون .

... البلد ها دئة الى حد بعيد وقال لذلك انك تشم جير هباه
القاسي وأنت على بعد شوي أوليت هنا هدوءاً بعث على
الشأم وكاد يجعل الواحد يزعق أعلى صسته ونحن المعدودون على
صصنى العاصمة وضجيجها الفظيع ....

● في خطابك ذكرت أن المظاهرات والمؤتمرات وحالة الطوارئ
والعبارات الثقيلة أصبحت الطابع المميز للمدينه وهذه هو أنها أنباء
حمراء وتلمتويه بالأحمر لذلك للتأكيد إلا أنها من تحري بالرغم من ذلك
أحسن من كثير بكثير والتى أصبحت جماعات الرعندوة (ناشدديابوا)
ذوى الشعر المتين المشبك والمزبل بكميات كبيرة من العرك مما يذكرك
بجماعات الإنسان الأول شآلن الكرومف وكذلك ظاهرات بنات البلو
وهن يحملن العجين فوق مؤخرتهن ونسوان الحلقنقه الجردة وهن
ملمحات والواحدة منهم تشبه شيئا مع استذكارى التجديد لها ...
وكذلك لا تنسى حرية السبحة والمطابخ والقطاوى والضعوط
والجمال والجميد ؟ كل هذه الأشياء هى الطابع المميز لكلها وأترك
لك الحكم بعد ذلك وإن كانت الجنة فهل هذه الأيام هى مهتتل
الجميل وضعاؤها المنحت ..

... ذكرت فى خطابك لى أنك لاحظت فى خطابى ملاحظات إلا ؟ (؟)
وهى إن كانت ما تنجيبك فمعذرة وهذا الخطاب كذ يخلو منها تماماً .
أما من البعث الأخضر فلا أظن أن صديقك حامد إلى الآن وعلمله
أفشى الشر _ وأرجو أن لا يكون كذلك (وفى خطاب كامل يلح
على أن أحلى له القصه وأنا أقول ليه كلها أيام وبعدين
أجى أقول ليه .

... وفى خطاب صديقك ذكر لى أن لعاً قد شطا على المنزل وشرق
في بكلم وشاملتك الجوقيال وصلوا من المال وكذلك فى خطابك لم
تذكر شيئا من هذا القبيل ولعلها كانت مداعبة من صديقك
أما إنها كانت قد حدثت بالفعل _ وأتمنى أن لا يكون _ فمزرابي لم
وجبراً على الضبيعة والخانات آلت من الرايات ...
أرجلك أن نبلوغ شاهم الحار بالى العم العزيز لسيده وقد حاولنا
مرارا أن تتصل بهم فى المنزل وفى كل مره تكون الرد بأن الخط بطال

A school report in mid seventies and a positive observation by the Headmaster

Two 'zeers' or traditional water pots. These usually hung outside houses and were available for other villagers and travellers passing through to help themselves. They were my main source of supply of water when I had been stranded in the desert and was walking to Aswan

حديث المدينة

عثمان ميرغني

إلى كامل إدريس...!!

في مصر.. أعلن الدكتور محمد البرادعي، المدير العام لوكالة الطاقة الذرية السابق ترشيح نفسه في انتخابات الرئاسة في مصر.. وبغض النظر عن قدرته على منافسة الرئيس مبارك أو مرشح الحزب الوطني الديمقراطي فإن المثال عندنا في السودان يجب أن يدخل إلى حيّز النظر السياسي..

في السودان لدينا مفخرة الدبلوماسية السودانية الأستاذ الدكتور كامل إدريس المدير العام السابق للمنظمة الدولية للملكية الفكرية.. إحدى أكبر منظمات الأمم المتحدة.. وهو بما نظير البرادعي عندنا مع الفارق.. فالبرادعي عاب عليه بعض المراقبين أنّه بعيد شيئاً ما عن السياسة، وأنّ شُحّ خبرته فيها ربما لا تجعله مناسباً للرئاسة.. لكن كامل إدريس لعب دوراً مؤثراً في السياسة السودانية ربما أبرزها عندما تولى الوساطة بين الحكومة ممثلة في د. حسن الترابي والمعارضة الخارجية ممثلة في السيّد الصادق المهدي في جنيف.. والتي أفضت في النهاية إلى المصالحة السياسية التي أخرجت العمل المسلح من قاموس المعارضة، وأفضت إلى الأوضاع التي لا زلنا نتابع حلقات تحولاتها..

في تقديري أنّ الدكتور كامل إدريس مرشح مناسب لخوض انتخابات الرئاسة بجانب مرشح حزب المؤتمر الوطني المشير الركن حسن أحمد البشير رئيس الجمهورية.. والمرشح الآخر البروفيسور عبد الله علي إبراهيم .. وهي الأسماء التي على الأقل أعلنت رسمياً حتى الآن..

دخول كامل إدريس إلى حلبة المنافسة الرئاسية سيرفع من درجة التنافس.. وسيُكسب الانتخابات حيوية مهمة للغاية حتى تنال الشرعية المطلوبة.. لأنّ إدريس مسنود بخبرة سياسية وتنفيذية علاوة على البُعد الدولي الذي يحف بهذه الخبرة.. وعلى أقل تقدير فإن دخول كامل للمنافسة يمنح الانتخابات مصداقية دولية مهمة للغاية لحفز التعاون الدولي مع السودان خلال فترة الانتخابات وللاعتراف الدولي بنتائج الانتخابات مهما كانت هذه النتائج محبطة أو سعيدة للمجتمع الدولي.

ولا أقصد من هذه الكلمات ابتدار حملة انتخابية لصالح كامل إدريس.. بل لأحفزه هو للانطلاق في مضمار هذه المسابقة المصيرية في السودان.. وحتى تأخذ الانتخابات جدية ومنافسة أكثر جاذبية للشعب لتشجعه على الاهتمام والمثابرة على تثبيت حقه في قول كلمته في اختيار من يفوضهم لإدارة الحكم والشأن العام خلال الفترة القادمة..

أول من ستفاجئه هذه الكلمات هو الدكتور كامل إدريس نفسه.. لكن للضرورة أحكام ليس مطلوباً ممن يتصدى للعمل العام أن يخطط حياته لنفسه بنفسه.. فكثير من مجريات القدر ترسم أحياناً طريقاً للبعض حتمياً لابد من سلوكه في مرحلة ما.

أتمنى أن يوافق الدكتور كامل إدريس على النزول إلى حلبة الانتخابات.. وأتمنى بعد ذلك أن يأخذ الجميع الانتخابات بجدية؛ لأنها عملية مصيرية إذا لم تتم في موعدها. فالكثيرون يذكرون كيف تحولت الانتخابات الرئاسية في أواخر التسعينات إلى مزحة.. بسبب الفارق النوعي الكبير بين المرشح الرئيسي وعشرات المرشحين الآخرين الذين نزلوا في الحلبة.. للدرجة التي أطلق فيها الشارع السوداني نكتة تقول (انتخبوا بطل السباحة.. لينقذ البلاد من الغرق..) ولا يزال سباحنا الدولي كيجاب يؤكد في مجالسه الخاصة أنّه كان الفائز الحقيقي بتلك الانتخابات.

ليتني أسمع من الدكتور كامل إدريس رأيه.. بالموافقة..!!

osman.mirghani.@yahoo.com

*A column by a well-known journalist (Osman Mirghani) inviting
me to contest Sudan Presidential elections in 2010*

تكريم الدكتور كامل ادريس

من عوتيه و من رقراق سلسله	و مــن دلال تبدى فى ثنئيه
من رافديه و قد جــاء على قدر	الـى لقاء حميم الوصل دانـيه
من عربدات نجـوم فوق صفحته	و مـن تدلـه بدر فى لياليه
ومن اريج ريـاض عند شاطنـه	تهدهد الليل اذ يسجو و تغويه
من شجو طير غريب فوق رابية	يبث لحنا حـزين الوقع باكيه
و مـن حصاراتـه الشماء بـازخة	تختال فى صلف جم و فى تيه
مضى الليالى عليها و هى مـائلـة	تحدث الناس عن امجاد ماضيه
تـدير عقل رهيب فـى تصوره	و صنع كف تعالى الله باريه
و من مشـاعـر جيـل انت نابعه	جيـل العطاء بلا من و تمويه
من كل هذا جمعت السحـر قافيـة	حيـه تتـوارى حين تأتـيه
يا من حمى الفكر فى الامصار مقتدرا	و صان حرمته من كل تشويه
و من رعى قيم الابداع فازدهـرت	منها الحضارة فى شتى مجاليه
قد بايعتك شعوب الارض قاطبـة	و ايدتـك باعجاب و تنويـه
و مـن ينل ثقه الدنيـا باجمعهـا	تسنم المجد فى اعلى مراقيه
عشقت موطنـك الغالى و همت به	و انبل الحب ما يرجى لاهليه
انـا عشقنـاه حتى قد اضر بنـا	ما يـعتريه و ما بتنا نقاسيـه
توافـد الصحب للتكريـم يدفعهم	ود وصدق وفاء انت راعيـه
فاهنا بتكريــمهم اياك انهمـو	احوال صدق نبيل القصد ساميه

دفع الله الحاج يوسف منى

A poem written about me by a well-known Statesman and a senior Lawyer, Dafalla Elhaj Yousif in December 2003

An antique piece of sculpture which belonged to my father

أم درمان

الملازمين

منزل ٢٧ / ٣ / ١

يسيد / الطيب ادريس

*An envelope that contained an important letter addressed to our
old Elmulazmein, Omdurman house no. 27/3/1*

A school report in mid seventies and a positive comment by the Headmaster

My card as a Doctoral student at the Graduate Institute of International Studies, Geneva, Switzerland

كامل إدريس

أصلك هو الفهم والحكمة ليها جليس
قبل الانتخاب ما أنت فينا رئيس...
كل أيامنا ليك من جمعة حتى خميس...
ما بتحتاج دعاية لا دعوة لا تحنيس...
والناس تصطفيك يا الكامل الإدريس...

= =

كل طاقتنا ليك ننهض معاك سويا...
جمعيات رجال وشبابها والنسويه....
أفضالك كتير الخافية والمرئية....
يا الكامل تمام مليان وقار وروية...
دورك عثلمي ومكين الفكري...

== = = =

اتقدم عديل وأملأ المكانة رئاسة....
عاين للوجوه الفيها علم وفراسة...
الدرر النفيسة ما أنت من غطاسها....
شوف كل القبائل تفخر تدقو نحاسها...
رشحتك رئيس الحضرة بي جلاسها...

Another poem written about me by an anonymous author

0047122774057

فريق تصف كامل إدريس بتعلم الفكر وثقا تمحك، وتعيس الجو

Nov 24. 2007. 08:36

أفريقيا تصف كامل إدريس

بعدا فكر وثقا عنك. وسياسي اخبر

شهد يوم أمس نفر رئاسة لاتحد لأوريقي حبث

حضرة أربعا وهم سفرة نحور أفريقية

حصه لدكتور كمل إدريس سير بعه سنصة

لعية لسكية لحكرية وأمبر بعه وأخد

... لاصف ولسية جبية. وإنه رخي

إدريس حطابا فوضع بالتصفيق الحار أكثر من مرة.

شدد فيه على أهمية دور الصناعات الثقافية وأثرها

في لاقتصاد العالمي، الذي استفادت منه الدول

عربية وأمربكا اللاتينية كمصدر أساسي من

مصدر ... القومي بفرق إجمالي دخل دول

... مجمعة. كما أوضح أن لصناعات الثقافية

... في ... لاقتصاد القومي وزيادة الناتج الإجمالي المحلي، وفرص العمل، بل تعد أداة ربط

... لشعوب وتجمعات. وأوضح أن أفريقيا غنية وما زالت بكر في هذا المجال. وبعتبر إدريس

... لسحر هو لمفذ الرئيس لاقتصاد القارة الأفريقية. كما بين في رسالته بأن الرايو هي

... لمستقبل، وعلى أفريقيا أن تنظر للمستقبل من خلال ترقية مصادرها وتراثها وموردها

... حدبا المالية.

... المجموعة الأفريقية الدكتور إدريس بابن أفريقيا وابن النيل، والقائد اعذ

Press release conveying the fullest support of the African Group in Geneva in 2007

INSTITUT UNIVERSITAIRE DE
HAUTES ÉTUDES INTERNATIONALES

GRADUATE INSTITUTE OF
INTERNATIONAL STUDIES

Carte d'étudiant

132, rue de Lausanne   1211 Genève 21

My student card of the Graduate Institute of International Studies, Geneva

Old Swiss driving licence, no. 1733761, dated 1/6/1978

One of my first Sudan diplomatic passports no. 00790 in the late seventies

RÉPUBLIQUE FRANÇAISE

DIRECTION GÉNÉRALE

DE L'AVIATION CIVILE

CARTE

DE

PILOTE STAGIAIRE

N° ST | 0 2 | 0 6 | 0 7 7 4 | 8 9

Cigna - Aviation

My private pilot card no. 0206077489 in the early eighties

UNITED STATES OF AMERICA

INTERNATIONAL MOTOR TRAFFIC

INTERNATIONAL DRIVING PERMIT

Convention on International Road Traffic of 19 September 1949
(United Nations)

FALLS CHURCH, VIRGINIA 22042, U.S.A.

Issued at _____

Valid For One Year From:

Date _____*June 02, 1978*_____

IMPORTANT — This permit is not valid for driving in the United States

J. B. Creal

Authorized signature of the empowered authority

№ 943463

International driving licence, dated 2/6/1978, used when I toured Europe

My Sudan certificate of nationality no. 474173, dated 19/7/1970

My card as an advocate and commissioner for Oaths in Sudan (renewal),
no. 84/490, dated 31/1/1989

My card of membership of Sudan Advocates Association, no.1855, dated 7/1/1991

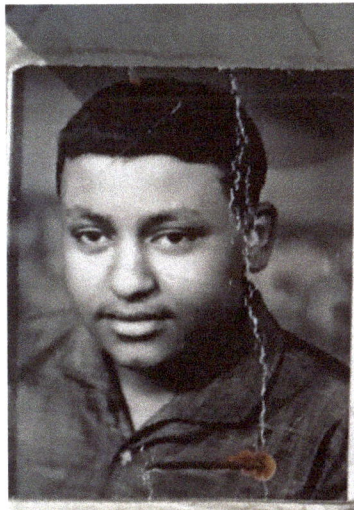

My identification card as actor in the National Theatre, dated 13/10/1972

وَزَارَةُ الخَارِجِيَّةِ

	الاسم	كامل الطيب إدريس
	الوظيفة	سكرتير ثالث
	الإدارة	العربية
	الرقم المسلسل	(١ ١ ١)
	تاريخ الإصدار	١٩٧٧ / ٧ / ١
	التوقيع	

My identification card as third secretary, Arab Department, Ministry of Foreign Affairs, no.000098, dated 1/7/1977

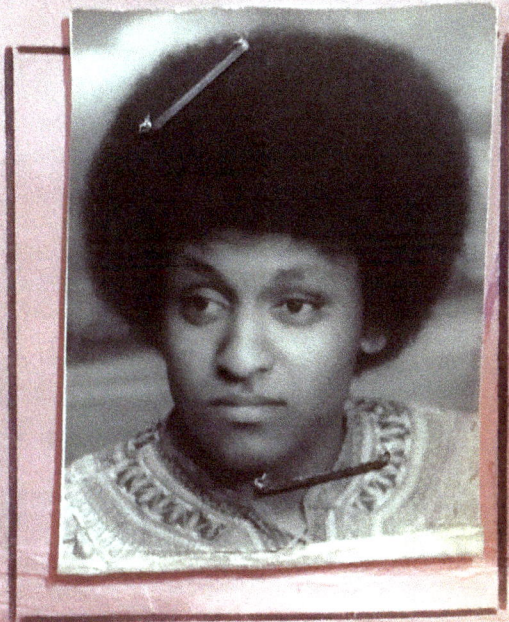

اسم الطالب كامل عبد الحميد أبوزيد
الفرقـه الرابعة / فلسفة
رقم الجلوس ١٠٠
رقم ايصال السداد ٢٠٠٦ / ١
مراقب شئون الطلاب

My identification card as Philosophy student at Cairo university, no.103, in 1974
(I was studying at two universities concurrently: Khartoum (Law) and Cairo (Philosophy)

My United Nations VIP identification card, as Director General, no.304, dated 10/11/1997

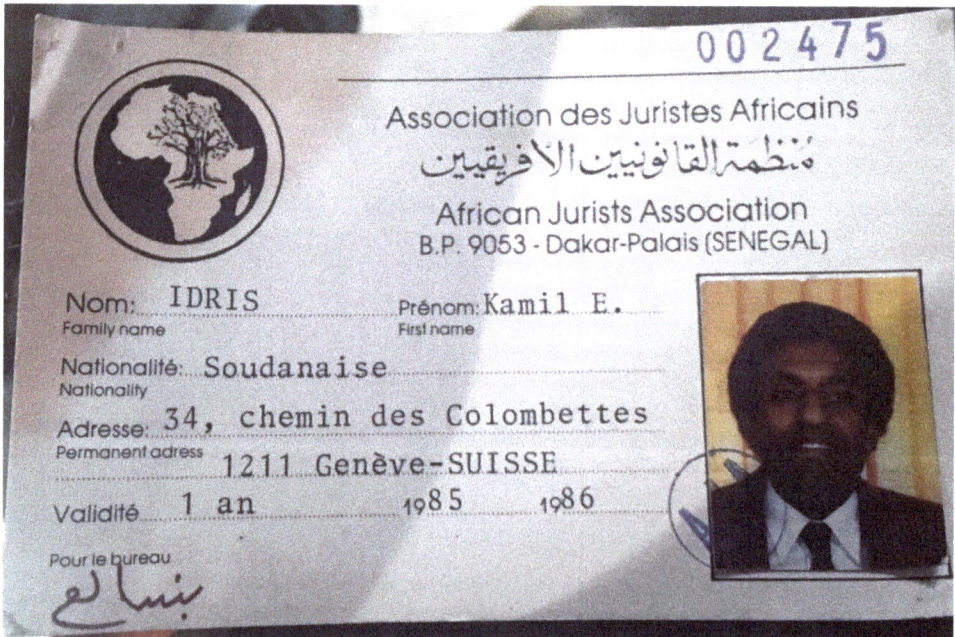

My identification card as a member of the African Jurists Association, no.002475, dated 1985

United Nations, New York
WIPO
SPEC AGENCY
31-Dec-1996
Mr. Kamil IDRIS
Signature:

My identification card of the United Nations, New York, as a representative of a specialized Agency, dated 31/12/1996

My identification card at the Assembly of Headss of State and Government of the then Organization of African Unity OAU (now African Union), dated 2-11/7/2001

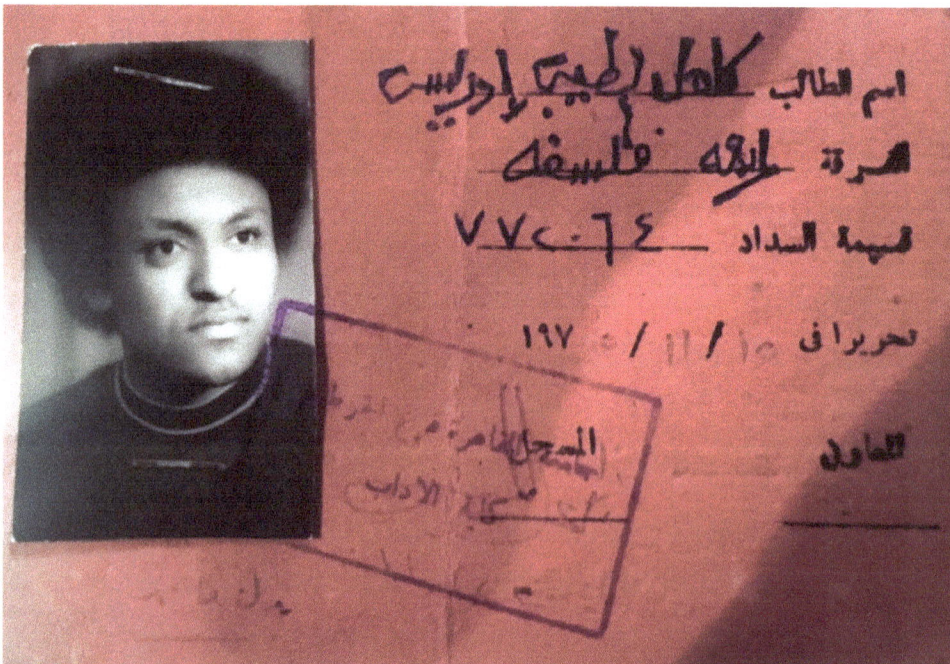

Mu identification card as Philosophy student no.772064, dated 15/11/1975

WIPO SINO-AFRICAN INTELLECTUAL PROPERTY FORUM
FORUM SINO-AFRICAIN DE L'OMPI SUR LA PROPRIÉTÉ INTELLECTUELLE

中非知识产权论坛

BEIJING, CHINA MAY 21-22, 2002

Dr. Kamil Idris

WIPO

0021

DELEGATE

My identification card as Keynote speaker at the Afro-Chinese International Conference, no.0021, dated 21-22/5/2002

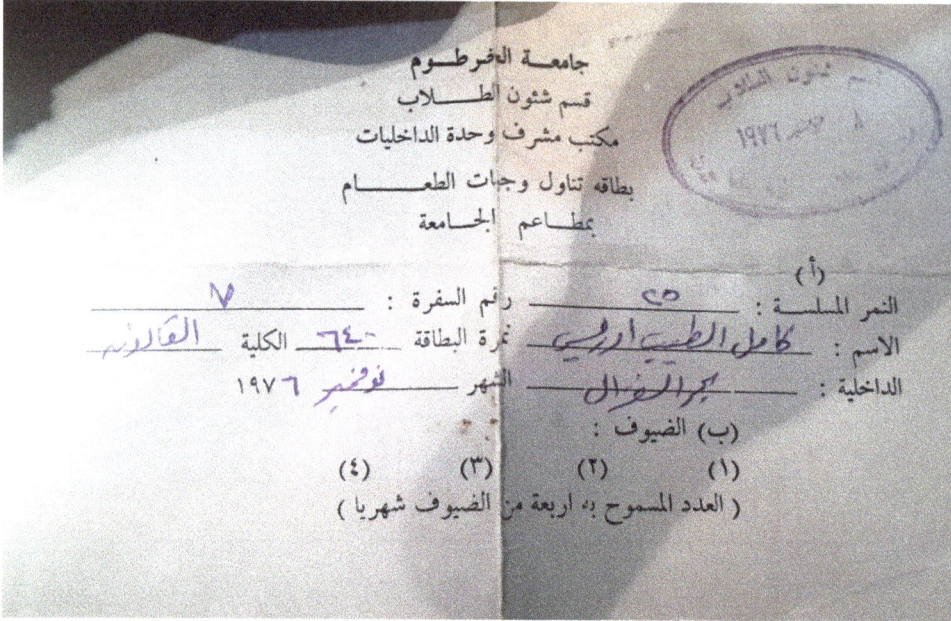

My identification card no.64, dated November 1976 of accommodation "Bahr Elghazal" of the Faculty of Law, university of Khartoum, seating table no.7 (with four guests)

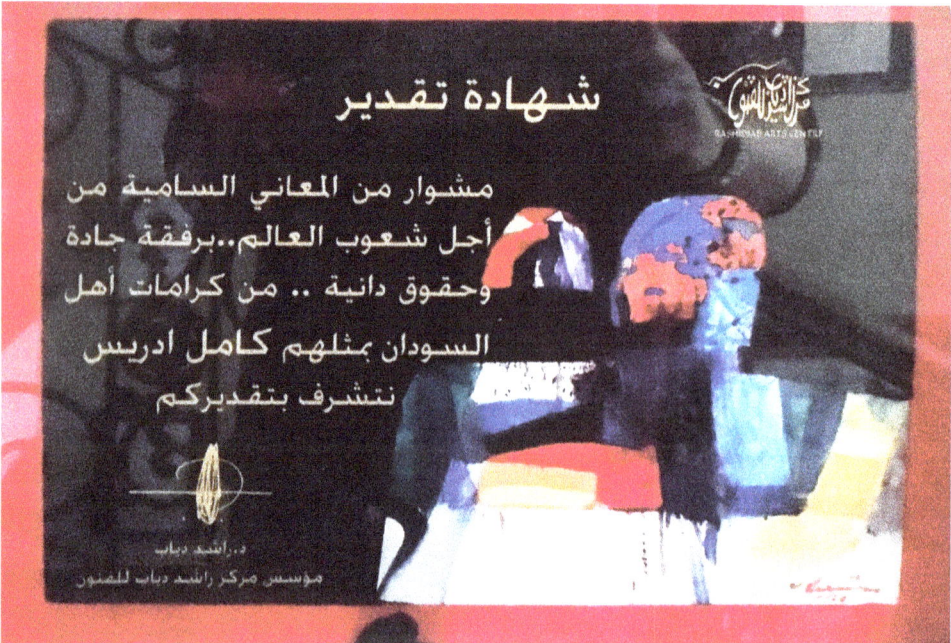

A certificate of appreciation from Rashid Diab Cultural Centre in Khartoum

Федеральной службой по интеллектуальной
собственности, патентам и товарным знакам

НАГРАЖДАЕТСЯ

Доктор Камил ИДРИС
Генеральный директор ВОИС

Памятным знаком в честь 50-летия образования
Комитета по делам изобретений и открытий
при Совете Министров СССР (Госкомизобретений),
правопреемником которого является
Федеральная служба по интеллектуальной
собственности, патентам и товарным знакам
(Роспатент)

Руководитель Федеральной службы
по интеллектуальной собственности,
патентам и товарным знакам

г. Москва
29 сентября 2005 г.

Б.П. Симонов

A decoration in 2005 from a former Soviet Republic

OHIO UNIVERSITY
DEPARTMENT OF SOCIOLOGY AND ANTHROPOLOGY
CARNEGIE HALL
ATHENS, OHIO 45701

June 12, 1978

To Whom it May Concern:

This is in regard to Kamil Eltayeb Idris who has asked me to write a letter of recommendation in his behalf. I have known Mr. Idris during the Spring Quarter 1978 as a student in my Sociology of Organization course and in independent readings. I also served as a member of his qualifying committee for the Masters Degree. In the course of my contacts with Mr. Idris, I have found him to be a very knowledgeable student with a truly remarkable verbal facility. The oral report in my organization class was well presented and displayed his knowledge of detail about an organization in the Sudan. In his oral presentation to the qualifying committee, he demonstrated a great ability to recall and relate the assigned readings to the questions asked.

In short, Mr. Idris is an intelligent and informed student whose ability to pursue advanced graduate training is beyond question. I can recommend him for a course of study leading to the Ph.D. degree without reservation.

Yours truly,

Orville R. Gursslin
Professor of Sociology

OG/dl

A letter of recommendation from Ohio University (USA), dated 17/6/1978

DEPARTMENT OF POLITICAL SCIENCE
BENTLEY HALL

June 8, 1978

To Whom It May Concern:

It is my pleasure to recommend Mr. Kamil Idris to you. Mr. Idris recently completed the Masters of International Affairs degree from Ohio University. An interdisciplinary degree, Mr. Idris pursued course work in the disciplines of Philosophy, Sociology, and Political Science. Mr. Idris completed two courses under my supervision and I was, as well, the chairman of his oral comprehensive exam for the M.I.A. degree.

My opinion of Mr. Idris is very favorable. The coursework which he did with me included "Technology and Politics" (Political Science 613), a regularly scheduled graduate seminar, and "Law and Society" (Political Science 598), an independent study. I greatly appreciated Mr. Idris' participation in the graduate seminar. His attendance was regular, and his oral comments were always pertinent and thoughtful. His written work was equally good. His paper demonstrated an ability to do high quality academic research and it was well written. He has an effective command of the English language. These impressions of Mr. Idris were only confirmed during my conversations with him concerning his independent study. He was thoroughly prepared for our weekly discussions, his oral remarks were cogent, and he showed independence of judgment in the execution of the project.

Mr. Idris passed his oral comprehensive exams on May 26, 1978. The examination committee was composed of myself, Dr. Corrado (Philosophy), and Dr. Gurslin (Sociology). In preparation for his oral exam, Mr. Idris studied "Philosophy of Law" with Dr. Corrado and "Organizational Theory" with Dr. Gurslin, in addition to the coursework which he did with me. Based on Mr. Idris' performance in his coursework and his oral exam, the committee was unanimous in recommending that he be awarded the Masters of International Affairs degree.

It is my opinion that Mr. Idris possesses the scholarly attributes for further graduate work leading toward the Ph. D. I have a very high

regard for him both as an individual and as a promising student. I feel that he would be a most effective teacher.

Sincerely,

Ronald J. Hunt
Assistant Professor

RJH/su

A letter of recommendation from Ohio University (USA), dated 8/6/1978

June 12, 1978

TO WHOM IT MAY CONCERN:

During the past year, Mr. Kamil Idris has been enrolled in a program of study leading to the Master of Arts in International Affairs. He completed satisfactorily all of the requirements for the degree which was awarded on June 10, 1978. Mr. Idris focussed his work on law and society.

Reports from his instructors indicate that Mr. Idris is an intelligent, hard-working student with a deep commitment to educational advancement. His overall grade point average attests to his ability.

On the basis of his record at Ohio University, I recommend him to you without reservation or hesitation.

Sincerely yours,

Edward Baum
Assistant Provost for
International Studies

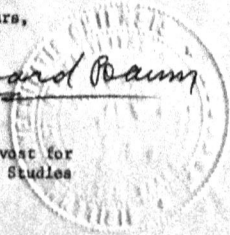

EB/mf

A letter of recommendation from Ohio University (USA), dated 12/6/1978

OHIO UNIVERSITY
CENTER FOR INTERNATIONAL STUDIES
ATHENS, OHIO 45701

African Studies Program
Office of the Director
614-594-5542

June 12, 1978

TO WHOM IT MAY CONCERN:

Mr. Kamil Eltayeb Idris has just completed his M.A. in International
Affairs at Ohio University. As his grades will show, he did extremely
well in our program and I feel that he is the type of person who should
be encouraged to go on to take further degrees, either in law, philosophy,
or political science. He is exceptionally able, intelligent and motivated
and has all the personal qualities necessary for a successful academic
career. I sincerely hope that he will be given the opportunity to continue
his education; particularly as young scholars of his calibre are hard to
find.

Sincerely,

Suzanne Miers

Suzanne Miers
Director of the African Studies
Program
Professor of History

SM:ps

A letter of recommendation from Ohio University (USA), dated 12/6/1978

DEPARTMENT OF POLITICAL SCIENCE
BENTLEY HALL

May 18, 1978

To Whom It May Concern:

I am writing to recommend Mr. Kamil Idris for further graduate work, particularly at the Ph.D. level. This recommendation is based upon his work in an independent study course on "Problems in Legal Theory." The course was divided into two parts. The first focused on the relationship between law and the Islamic religion in non-western political systems. The second was a comparative analysis of selected works by St. Thomas Aquinas and John Rawls. He demonstrated a superior ability to analyze both western and non-western legal theorists and it appears that he enjoys learning.

Sincerely yours,

J. F. Henderson, Jr.

James Franklin Henderson
Assistant Professor

JFH/su

OHIO UNIVERSITY
GRADUATE COLLEGE   OHIO UNIVERSITY
OFFICE OF THE DEAN GRADUATE COLLEGE
WILSON HALL   OFFICE OF THE DEAN
ATHENS, OHIO 45701   WILSON HALL
ATHENS, OHIO 45701

A letter of recommendation from Ohio University (USA), dated 18/5/1978

DEPARTMENT OF POLITICAL SCIENCE
BENTLEY HALL

May 16, 1978

To Whom It May Concern:

I am responding most enthusiastically to a request for a letter of recommendation by Mr. Kamil Eltayeb Idris. This is unusual in view of the fact that I have known Mr. Idris only for a year, not long enough for anyone to hazard a judgment of any other person. That I am willing to do this in the case of Mr. Idris bespeaks of his very outstanding quality as a student and human person.

Mr. Idris is a very intelligent, industrious, and self-reliant person. As a student in independent study (Research in Political Science) with me, he wrote two superior papers dealing with State Responsibility and the Doctrine of Jurisdiction in International Law. The papers were a model of clear thought, sophisticated analysis, and balanced judgment. It was quite remarkable that Mr. Idris required minimum supervision in that intellectual venture, revealing clearly his highly developed research and writing capability.

It is my conviction that Mr. Idris is a person of high moral standards and refined personality. He is always courteous and tolerant of others' faults, including the sins of absentminded professors. And yet, Mr. Idris is assertive and would not compromise his integrity as a person. It has been a rare pleasure for me to have had an opportunity to meet with such a fine young man from Sudan.

Sincerely yours,

Sung Ho Kim,
Assist. Prof. of Political Science

SHK/su

A letter of recommendation from Ohio University (USA), dated 16/5/1978

OHIO UNIVERSITY
DEPARTMENT OF PHILOSOPHY
GORDY HALL
ATHENS, OHIO 45701

June 7, 1978

To Whom It May Concern:

KAMIL ELTAYEB IDRIS worked with me during the Winter Quarter 1978. He
presented to me in weekly recitations the philosophy of Islam. I learned a
great deal. Mr. Idris literally prepared ten lectures of at least one
hour's length. His understanding of the material is very mature and in-
sightful. In particular his ability to draw appropriate parallels between
Islamic positions and Western philosophy displayed a deep grasp of
philosophical issues of both traditions. In addition his application,
especially of jurisprudential and legal philosophy, to contemporary social
issues and positions showed an ability to apply abstract concepts to
concrete instances.

Mr. Idris knows the history of Islam and of philosophy in the West. He
is an original and outstanding scholar.

Sincerely,

Dr. Warren Ruchti, Chairman
Department of Philosophy

WR/lb

A letter of recommendation from Ohio University (USA), dated 7/6/1978

Chapter 10

Swimming against the Current

Paralysis of the heart leads to paralysis of the mind.

(Kamil Idris)

I n the summer of 2003 I attended a closed, head-to-head meeting with President El-Bashir at his official residence in Khartoum. We were discussing the recent unrest in the region of Darfur, where rebel groups had clashed with government troops, and casualties on both sides had run into the hundreds. This was a worrying escalation and I suggested to him that the situation had to be handled delicately, despite the provocation, otherwise there could be a monumental disaster. I could see that he was listening attentively, leaning forward and weighing every word, but as I continued with my thoughts he sat back in his chair and began to fold his arms. To me this body language signalled that he thought I was being too cautious and over-estimating the problem. I tried to press my points home but to be fair I realised that he needed more time to consider his way forward.

He remained at a polite distance for the rest of our discussion and then suggested a meeting later that evening with his then Vice President, Ali Osman Taha, and the then Head of Intelligence, Salah Gosh. I told him I had already been invited to a dinner that night, specially arranged by a highly respected Nationalist businessman called Hassan Kambal. I was the guest of honour and it would very embarrassing for all concerned if I failed to turn up. El-Bashir made a hurried telephone call and we agreed instead to meet after the dinner at 11.30 p.m. The meeting was to take place at Ali Taha's residence in the north of the city and there would just be the three of us as El-Bashir would not be present.

Ali Taha had had an eventful political life, having been once arrested and imprisoned by President Nimieri in 1985, and he was now a very trusted and capable deputy to El-Bashir. Suave, slim, polite, and in an elegant blue suit, he received me warmly when I arrived at his impressive residence close to the Nile at 11.27 p.m. Next to appear was Salah Gosh. As Head of Intelligence he was a very powerful man indeed, and his thick-set build and bustling presence suggested that he was a personality to be reckoned with. He came armed with boxes of files and as it was already very late I hoped we weren't going to be dragged into a tour of their contents.

Once the introductions were over I thought it best to repeat what I had outlined earlier to El-Bashir and I was listened to respectfully. I stressed that in the past centuries Darfur had been an independent kingdom which had later profited from colonial rule; that its diverse population was tolerant and peaceful, and that it had its own historic method of settling disputes called 'Agaweed'. Any disagreements, for example, particularly between farmers and shepherds, would be settled by this informal, traditional method, with the local administration passing decisions which everyone accepted. However, food shortages in the 1980s had led to famine, and many years of tension over land and grazing rights between the mostly nomadic herders in the drier north and settled farmers in the south created a struggle for survival.

Also it was simplistic to caricature the problem as a quarrel between Arabs and Africans, as there had been generations of inter-marriage resulting in a mosaic of tribes, and occupational boundaries were fluid and often crossed. If we were to insist on central government interventions and imposed jurisdiction, it would only cause confusion and disruption. It was fair to say that post-independence, Sudanese rulers had viewed these local administrations as archaic relics of colonial rule and had begun to side-line them. I thought this was perhaps one of the possible factors in the origin of the conflict. I also argued that there were deeply rooted resentments against perceived economic and political inequalities, with Darfur and other outer regions of the country believing themselves ignored and marginalised by the central administration. I hinted that if there were to be any Government interventions they should be low-key, peaceful, swift, certainly not brutal, and that any action out of proportion would be dangerous and unacceptable.

I was relieved to see that the others had gone quiet and were watching me closely and nodding their heads, so I took a breath and made a dramatic proposal.

I suggested that we should attempt to bring the leading players in the conflict to a meeting in a neutral setting.

This would be in Geneva, with two witnesses – myself and the former Prime Minister of Sudan, Sadig Al-Mahdi, who was then living in Cairo; the government would be represented by Salah Gosh. Happily everyone present agreed to the meeting, but first I had to contact Al-Mahdi to persuade him to come. I also made it my business to contact the late Al Turabi, an influential leader of Muslim opinion (and in my view the most eminent contemporary scholar of its history and teaching), to seek his advice and hopefully his goodwill. Unsurprisingly he was in full accord with my mission to initiate a peaceful solution to the conflict and I was given his blessing.

Shortly afterwards I flew to Cairo to be met at the airport by the then Sudan Ambassador, Ahmed Abdelhalim, a warm, scholarly gentleman of the first-rank, dressed in his traditional white jalabiyah and elaborately folded turban, who then took me to meet Sadig. On the way he explained that he was happy to be of any assistance, but because of the sensitive and confidential nature of the meeting he would prefer not to be involved.

This was fine by me as I was sure I could rely on Sadig to

travel to Geneva once he understood the importance of the meeting. Sadig was a highly experienced negotiator and had a profound understanding of Sudan's history and place in the modern world. He was unique in that his western education at Oxford University was underpinned by his deep Islamic faith, resulting in a politically fused philosophy of tolerance, clarity of vision, flexibility, humility and high principle.

I went to Geneva ahead of the others but Gosh, maybe through no fault of his own, failed to appear. I rang his home number and mobile but there was no reply and repeated calls came to nothing. There was only one answer – the initiative had failed and I contacted El-Mahdi and the representative of the rebel faction to break the bad news. In my opinion this was a crucial lost opportunity that could have prevented the savagery and bloodshed that would inevitably follow. The horrors of the war in Darfur are well documented and even to this day, and I am not exaggerating, I have nightmares about the hundreds of thousands of innocent people killed, maimed, and made homeless and starving by the brutality of the war. It could have been avoided. If that meeting had gone ahead it could have had a direct influence on the stability of the country: Sudan might have reached out for some sunlit uplands instead of having to live through one of the darkest periods in its history.

Darfur is a huge region about the size of France and is home to an estimated 7.5 million people and according to authentic sources hundreds of thousands were killed and an estimated 2.5 million displaced. There was a global outcry; international peace-keeping agencies were controversially allowed into the country.

Between 2003 and 2008 I had been heavily involved in initiatives to resolve the conflict and reassure the global community that peace and resolution were top priorities, but when the ICC (International Criminal Court) issued its arrest warrants the situation changed. President El-Bashir asked me to see if I could help to intervene, but before I accepted I had to explain to him that I was an international leader and senior diplomat and would have to act in an independent capacity.

The then Prosecutor of the ICC was a tall, bearded Argentinian called Luis Moreno Ocampo, a fearless and impartially minded man who had come to public attention in 1985 when he was the Assistant Prosecutor in the trial of the Argentinian Military Junta. This trial had been the first since the Nuremberg Trials, when senior military commanders were prosecuted for mass killings, and he was instrumental in obtaining the convictions of five of the nine defendants.

My motive for accepting El-Bashir's request was to try to somehow effect an end to the war. Sudan's reputation was already dire enough and I didn't want it to get worse. I also had a nagging doubt that perception and rumour are sometimes stronger than reality, and that El-Bashir might not have been as fully in control of his military subordinates as people thought.

Ocampo was welcoming and sympathetic, and a series of meetings in The Hague and Geneva took place with the full presence and participation of a Senior Delegation from Sudan. He obviously understood the complexities of the situation and the atmosphere was friendly and open. I continually stressed, both to him and the critical opposition back home, that we needed to prove that the judicial system in Sudan was both willing and competent and could deal with this particular situation internally. If anything was in doubt then the ICC should be able to complement and adjust its jurisdiction accordingly. An objective middle-way would be the best possible solution, and I was asked to make a recommendation, summarised in two points. Firstly, the ICC should be allowed to investigate all aspects of the matter in Sudan, and secondly, on the basis of that recommendation and conclusion, both of the accused should be tried independently from the ICC in Sudan with full representation and defence.

The ICC had been established through a proposal by the UN ILC (International Law Commission) and I had been one of its principal draftsmen. During the debate of the ILC, when we were drafting I had objected to one important point, namely "referral by the Security Council of specific cases to the ICC".

Why? Because such referrals could be selective and subject to veto by any permanent member of the Security Council. The ILC sent the draft statute to the Rome Diplomatic Conference with that point unresolved. Finally the Rome Conference resolved it in favour of the Security Council being allowed to refer cases to the ILC. I thought this was a significant mistake, as justice would be seen to be selective and a trust deficit would inevitably follow. In my view this is now one of the reasons that The African Union and other world governments are doubtful about the ICC's role. My recommendations to resolve the Sudan issue have never seen the light of day. I was not involved in any of the internal domestic discussions relating to this matter, and soon afterwards Sudan rejected any form of cooperation with the ICC.

I thought it was now time for me to stand as a presidential candidate. I knew I couldn't win, but I thought it would help to increase my chances of helping to solve some of the country's problems. I left WIPO in 2008 with one year of my contract still to run, giving me a breathing space to prepare an election campaign. Throughout my years in Geneva I had kept up close ties with Sudan, informally advising on and intervening in a variety of matters of national importance. I had found that speaking from the vantage point of the UN, I was able to demystify many of the preconceptions that people held about the country's nature. This was not just blanket propaganda or outright denial, and I was open and willing to accept criticism about the conflict in the south and the situation in Darfur and other problematic areas. I tried to explain that one of the difficulties the authorities faced was the sheer size of the country. Before South Sudan declared its independence in 2011, it was more of a continent than a country, with close to 40 million people scattered across its 2 million square kilometres. It was a vast area to govern, and added problems included poor roads and limited rail communications. It was emerging from decades of colonial rule and it was no wonder that places farthest from Khartoum had felt a need for increased autonomy and control.

The procedures for the eleven Presidential candidates were highly complex and I needed numerical recognition from all the regional states in my campaign. I also took the risk of demanding a public apology from the authorities for all the atrocities that had resulted from the conflicts in Darfur. This was a dangerous thing to do, but I was deeply moved to receive significant amounts of support from young people, women, the elderly, the more marginal areas of the country, and even from members of historic political parties. Taking into account my extended absence from Sudan I felt humbled by the size of this unexpected mandate.

Then came the death threats. About eight weeks before the election a local journalist who had often interviewed me asked for an evening meeting at a coffee shop in central Khartoum. He was nervous, speaking slowly and quietly, glancing over his shoulder checking on the other customers. He told me that he had heard rumours that if I continued with my campaign my life would be in danger, adding that my popularity was worrying to other circles. He didn't say which circle but it was clear that there were certain groups who wanted business as usual and I was a threat to them. I had to be careful and it would probably be better for me and my family if I withdrew my candidacy. Up to this point I had been canvassing openly with no protection or security, and for a moment I thought about trying to hire some sort of bodyguard but I put it out of my mind. Something deep inside me rejected the idea and I promised myself that I would not be intimidated. The journalist had probably risked his own life in telling me what could happen and I thanked him for his courage. In the end nothing happened but throughout the rest of my campaign I was aware that a shot or a knife might suddenly appear from nowhere.

The election was widely accepted as being unfair, but I was not overly concerned at not winning, as the real object of standing had been to help the nation as a moderate and reforming candidate for change.

I was delighted, however, to be appointed as the Vice

Chairman of The Sudanese Organisation for the Defence of Human Rights and Freedoms. This was an independent body with a remit that assured a distance from government influence. It would have been easy to run this as a sinecure, paying lip service to any recommended policies and issuing non-committal platitudes, but I was determined to stack the commission with the most impressive people from every possible faction, knowing full well that it could be a thorn in the side of the intelligence and security forces. Our overall aim was to try to highlight the need for respect for human rights and freedom of expression, formulate important recommendations for ending the conflicts, and repair the image of Sudan to the international community.

During the hearings the commission listened carefully to my submissions.

The commission was chaired mainly by Professor Faroug Mohamed Ibrahim, a man of complete integrity and one of the most respectable figures I have ever met.

The discussions inevitably touched on sensitive security matters and my active participation in them meant that I would later be placed under surveillance and subsequent arrest.

Chapter 11

Arrest and Interrogation. Stay on the Rock.

Banish your sins and you banish depression.
(Kamil Idris)

The two men, neatly dressed in slacks and well ironed shirts, knocked on my neighbour's door. "Do you know where Kamil Idris is?"

"No. Who are you?" he replied.

"Never mind. Do you know where he is?"

"No I don't. I've already told you." The old man was unafraid. "And even if I did know, I wouldn't tell you!"

He slammed the door in their faces and the men strolled nonchalantly away. They were not going to be put off.

The date is stuck in my mind forever. The next day, 15ᵗʰ June 2012, a relative of mine took a phone call from the same men. They gave him a deadline and demanded that he deliver a message to me. They wanted to talk to me urgently about important government business. Would I please phone them on a given number? My relative was shrewd enough to tell by their tone of voice of the implied threat and contacted me straight away. I was not in the least worried by them. I had nothing to hide and phoned the number. No reply. I knew who they were and why they were looking for me. The country's Intelligence Services were well known for keeping their watchful eyes on any signs of political dissent or criticism of the government.

There were rumours of people disappearing for long periods of time and not being well treated. I was reasonably confident though that whatever happened my international standing and diplomatic profile would be protection enough. Looking back I was perhaps assuming too much.

The next day I was away from my house attending a meeting relating to Darfur and the Nuba mountains. My wife Azza was preparing the midday meal in the kitchen when there was a loud banging from the front of the house. It was the same two men and they threatened to break the door down if she didn't open it. She refused to let them in and they shouted that a very important senior person wanted to talk with me. Azza breathed quietly and said nothing. Silence. She later told me that when they walked away down the path she peeped through a curtain and saw other men looking up at the house, taking notes and photographs.

Twenty-four hours later I was driving my son's blue BMW in central Khartoum when I noticed a white Cressida car following close behind me. Two other cars were to my left and right, and one of them indicated that I should slow down and pull over. I moved to the left side of the road driving north up Elsiteen street, then took another left to Omac street. I wasn't deliberately trying to out-race them, but I just wanted to see how far they were likely to go. I realised they were serious when the Cressida barged through a red traffic light and accelerated after me.

I turned into a car-washing station, got out and was given a seat by one of the workers while the car was being cleaned. The best way to play this, I thought, was to be as calm as possible. A tall safari-suited man in his mid-fifties got out of the Cressida and walked casually towards me.

He smiled and with a polite bow introduced himself as a Colonel in the Intelligence Services. He asked if we could have a talk about an urgent matter.

"Before you ask me any questions, can I see your ID?" I asked.

"Of course." It was genuine.

"Is this an arrest or an official interrogation?"

"We just want to have a chat with you," he told me.

"About what?"

"This and that…"

"Okay, but we are not going to chat here. I will talk with you at my residence."

"Fine. My superior is already waiting outside there."

"Really? My car is nearly ready and…."

"You won't need it," he interrupted. "Better if you leave your car here and come with me." This was a tense moment and there was very little conversation as we drove back to my house. I remember he made one or two calls on his mobile. My name wasn't mentioned, but I realised he was letting his superiors know that he had successfully detained me. He sounded pleased with himself.

"So who is your superior?" I asked.

"You will find out."

"If this is an official arrest I need to know because I will have to cancel an important appointment. I also need to phone my wife to let her know what is happening."

"Okay. Go ahead," he said.

Azza sounded worried but defiant on the phone, mainly because there were three or four Intelligence Service cars parked under the trees near the house, and the neighbours had sensed that something unusual was happening.

I was determined that when we arrived I would try to take control of the situation and keep these men on the back-foot. I got out of the car first and the superior, a heavily-built, red-faced man, introduced himself as Siddig Hamza. I could tell he had probably just made this name up on the spot. He was friendly and charming but I didn't trust him an inch, and I walked briskly to the front door with him as his deputy followed behind. Playing the role of the grand host was the next ploy. Would they like to sit down? How about some coffee and biscuits? These gestures seemed to unsettle them and they sat meekly silent on a sofa while I began to ask the questions.

"Would you mind if we didn't use our mobiles during the 'dialogue' and would you mind if I took notes?" I asked. We all placed our phones on a table and I made sure they could see that I intended to keep a written account of the conversation.

I was determined to take the initiative and launched into the offensive. "Before we begin, I have to let you know that my wife was very upset about the aggressive behaviour of two of your officers yesterday. There was no need to threaten to break the door down! Also, you don't need reminding that the country is undergoing a very difficult time, and without constructive and open discussions the situation will continue to deteriorate. I hope this is important. Before you start let me tell you that I love this nation more than you do. In addition, nothing you can threaten me with can be worse than all the trials and dangers I have already experienced in my life so far.

This includes being a child labourer, balancing on the tops of moving trains, nearly dying in the desert, being eaten alive by wild animals and having a knife held to my throat by pirates. Now what can I do for you?"

The senior man cleared his throat and leaned forward with his hands on his knees.

"Dr Kamil," he said. "First of all I must apologise on behalf of my officers for upsetting your wife, but we have an important message from a senior government official. We know you are respected internationally and appreciate all you have done in the past to help this country. I will come straight to the point. We have to tell you that we have serious concerns about your relationship and recent meetings with El-Turabi, Abu-Eisa, El-Mahdi and Faroug Mohamed Ibrahim…" In other words the opposition.

I paused, frowned, copied his body language by leaning forward and spoke very slowly. "I don't know these people you are talking about. I only know Sheikh Hassan El-Turabi or Dr Turabi, Ustaz Faroug Abu-Eisa, Immam El-Sadiq El Mahdi and Professor Faroug Mohamed Ibrahim. Please, when you refer to these gentlemen, show them some respect by referring to their full names and titles."

There was a short silence as the men weighed the formality of my response. They continued. "Well, we would appreciate it if you broke off contact with these men. Do you realise they could tarnish your reputation as a national and international personality?" He paused and leaned across towards me. "They are good-for-nothing devils." The last words hung in the air like poison and they waited for a reply.

"They are Nationalists, all born in Heaven, and I am honoured to be in their company! Is that the end of your questions?" I asked.

There was no answer so I continued, this time raising my voice, "No one has the right to control my movements or limit my freedom. You in particular are not in any position to advise or warn me, or tell me whom I should meet with. Instead you should focus your energies on solving the real problems of our country. Please tell the people who sent you that if this is the content of their message, it is rejected." As I was speaking I was also writing comprehensive notes. This in itself was a coded message that a proper record of the talk was being kept.

Neither man had anything more to say. They refused the offer of more coffee and I saw them to the door. Before they left the superior turned, looked me in the eye and said, "We will be in touch…"

They were true to their word. About six weeks later at 5.30 in the evening, just when I thought the storm had blown over, I was once again summoned to the door to be met by two different young men. They shook me by the hand and apologetically asked if I would accompany them to the Intelligence headquarters. "Is this an arrest or an interrogation?" I asked.

"I'm afraid it's both. My superiors will tell you more," one of them replied.

"Well first of all I must inform my family."

"No, sir. No time. You must come with us right now," he insisted.

My youngest son, Mumin, was standing next to me and I whispered to him, "Intelligence men!" His terrified glance told me he understood that he was to let Azza know where I was being taken.

On the way the men changed cars from a small Atos to a larger Cressida and we sat in silence throughout the journey with myself in the front seat and the two security men in the back. One of the offices of the Sudan Intelligence headquarters is a non-descript five-storey building in north Khartoum called 'Mawgif Shendi', which means 'the station for all buses travelling to Shendi in the north of Sudan'. This sounds comical enough, but for those unfortunate to be held there it is anything but.

It is a very serious place indeed, with a dubious reputation.

I was led into a featureless grey room and opposite me across a long table were five prison officers. For the next 24 hours, all through the night, they questioned me in teams of one or two. There was no violence but they had confiscated my mobile and the sessions were relentless, broken only by the few times they left me alone, presumably so that I could worry about my fate. Why had I stood for election? Who were my supporters? What had been my role in the ICC? Why was I associating with dissident groups?

There were other questions too but they kept coming back to these central ones. I was surprised because I knew they had the answers already. So was this just a game to unnerve me? To send a warning message? Whatever it was I was determined not to let them win. I kept reminding them of the message I had given earlier to their colleagues about my passion for the country, and noticed that as the night went on they became sleepy and tired. I tried to summon up reserves of energy and take brief catnaps when they left me alone. I also had another weapon. I knew that whatever they did to me I had a secret haven, a place I could go to in my imagination where they couldn't touch me. During the catnaps I went on a journey to the banks of the Nile. If the world was too much I could shut it out by letting my eyes rest on the flowing waters and listen to the gentle swish of the currents. Here was peace and here was history. What was my own life in comparison to the millions of soldiers, farmers, fishermen, explorers and historic legends who had gone before me? Hundreds of years before whole generations had gazed on exactly the same view and had been calmed and inspired by the tranquillity and majesty of the Nile, and now they were in eternity. I tried to remember some lines of Shakespeare which I had memorised as a student:

> We are such stuff as dreams are made on,
> and our little life is rounded with a sleep.

We are only on the earth for a short time, so be brave and stick to the truth or, more simply, the earth is a farm and the harvest will come later. With these thoughts arming my mind my predicament shrank to nothing and I was able to sometimes smile at my interrogators as the sessions continued through the night. I think this confused them and I was able to hold the initiative.

After a few hours I became aware of noises outside the building. It didn't sound like a violent demonstration, but I realised that word had got out about my arrest and the media and some of my supporters were making their presence felt. I was heartened by this and kept on trying to tire the officers out. I also decided to talk to them as if I was addressing a press conference or talking to the social media. This was a reminder to them that a serious mistake was being made. Both parties were now very tired indeed, and without any paper signing or formality I was eventually released at 8.30 a.m. the next morning.

The harassment continued. I had arranged an evening working dinner and meeting at my house for 25 prominent opposition figures, including El-Turabi, El-Mahdi and Abu-Eisa, who were all seeking a durable solution to the country's problems. During the day the ever-present Intelligence men were watching from parked cars under the shade of trees and at

5.30 p.m. the doorbell rang. Two men were once again insistent that I should come with them for another interrogation and possible arrest. While they produced their IDs I asked if I could go upstairs to change my shirt. They were impatient to get away and told me to hurry.

This time the questioning was more aggressive. There was no physical violence, but the officers, again in teams of two or three, were hostile and dismissive of my answers, moving me from room to room, perhaps to disturb me. "Why do you associate with the opposition leaders?" they asked. "Why are you trying to undermine the Government? What went wrong between the ICC and Sudan? Who did you influence in those discussions? What are your future plans?"

My responses were honest but they thought I was being deliberately evasive. "Don't ask me. Ask your superiors or senior government officials. They know the real answers. They can advise you better than I." The monotony continued through the night, but at 9.00 a.m. one of the senior officers drove me back home. There were only the two of us in his car and after a lengthy silence he coughed nervously. "Dr Kamil, I wonder if you could do something for me," he said.

I had no idea what was coming next. "Possibly," I replied.

"You see, I am suffering from high blood pressure and cholesterol levels, and I was wondering if you could bring me back some special medicine when you next travel to Europe." I had to cover up my smile. This was a man who only a few hours previously had been asking threatening questions. It was a revealing insight. Away from his colleagues his bluster and arrogance completely disappeared and he was like all of us, human and vulnerable. In the end I wanted to honour my promise. I did get the medicine for him and called the number he had given me, but there was no answer and it never reached him.

Meanwhile the surveillance continued, sometimes on a comical level. At least two cars were parked permanently outside of the house and I was followed wherever I went.

It became so farcical that I gave the Intelligence men my daily schedule so that if they got lost they could find me.

When they followed me I advised them to drive carefully and that I would look out for them in traffic by using my mirror. Once, when I had a meeting at a restaurant, I even introduced them to my guests and arranged some food and drink for them.

However, things were becoming intolerable. I decided to fly to the UK to deal with an arbitration case and to see my three grown-up children, Mohamed, Dinas and Dalia, who were junior doctors there. Maybe if I took a long break from Sudan the tension would ease. Yet how could I evade the Intelligence men? I ordered a taxi to come to the back entrance of the house at 1.00 a.m., drove to the airport and took a Turkish Airlines flight to Istanbul, intending to fly on to Manchester. At 7.00 a.m. Turkish time I phoned Azza from Istanbul. She was in shock. She told me that the 'watchers' had noted my absence and interrogated and humiliated our house guard Abdelgadir, demanding to know where I had gone. To his eternal credit he had refused to say anything to them and they beat him badly, particularly around the face. When they threatened to kill him he still refused to talk.

However, it got worse. He overheard them discussing kidnapping one of my young children. This was a devastating development and things were becoming serious. The only thing I could do was fly immediately back from Turkey and protect my family. I arrived in Khartoum un-noticed and began making hurried plans to leave the country permanently, taking the rest of my family with me.

We had to move discreetly because the 'watchers' were now on high alert and I thought I could be arrested again at any moment. We had only a few hours before our flights to Istanbul and Manchester to pack a few clothes, collect passports and birth certificates, and cancel several professional and household arrangements. I had to leave some treasured possessions behind, including all my notes and diaries that had been meticulously kept since my student days. There were dramatic goodbyes to

be made, especially to Abdelgadir. The man was crying when
I thanked him for his courage and loyalty, and when I said I
hoped to see him again he just shook his head as if he knew that
it would never happen.

Once again the taxi came to the back door and on the
way to the airport I checked to see if we were being followed.
Unbelievably we were in the clear, although we still had to
get through airport security. Last minute airport arrests were
commonplace and I couldn't relax until the plane had actually
left the ground. Next to me my young children were already
asleep and Azza was quietly mouthing the word 'exile' over and
over. We had had no time to think about the consequences of
our escape, but this is what it was. At that moment I could see
no way that it would ever be safe for me to return to my beloved
Sudan. Seconds before the plane reached the clouds I looked
out of a window and could just make out the dark blue ribbon
of the Nile as it flowed past Khartoum. My mind and soul were
in turmoil. Was I taking a last look at my home, my birthplace
and my anchor in life? And what of the future? My three eldest
children were well established as doctors in the UK and this was
a consolation. Whatever happened at least we would be secure
and together as a family.

The same could not be said for Abdelgadir. Later I learned
from one of his relatives that he had been frightened to death
by the humiliation of his beating and had undertaken a highly
dangerous journey to escape. He had mostly walked all the way
through Sudan, into Ethiopia and had reached the shores of
the Red Sea. He had spent weeks by himself, avoiding the large
towns where he might have been stopped and questioned. Then
he had persuaded some local fishermen to ship him across the
sea to Saudi Arabia and had swum to the shore. I uttered a silent
prayer to Allah for his safety but I never heard from him again.

The plane flew on into the dawn. I slept fitfully and once
again I heard echoing voices from my childhood, "Stay on the
rock! Stay on the rock!"

Chapter 12

My Philosophy of Life. Great Minds and Unseen Powers

A little philosophy inclines man's minds to atheism, but depth in philosophy inclines man's mind towards religion.

(F Bacon. English philosopher, statesman and scientist. 1561-1626)

Continue with your acts of kindness and charity, even if they go unnoticed.

(Kamil Idris)

Where do nightmares come from? Why, secure in a close and affectionate family, do infants run to their parents' bed in the night, rigid with fear? I have a treasured memory of a joyful childhood, but the wolves began circling early. I have no idea where they came from or why, but waves of anxiety and terror would overwhelm me, sometimes during the bright, sunlit day, but mostly during stormy nights when Sahara storms howled around the house. Even when I was safe, nestling close to my mother on a sofa, I imagined that the winds were trying to smash down the walls and blast us into the black pits of hell. Were these winds devils in disguise, demons, or djinns? Where had these monstrous fiends come from? Islam had answers: they were the servants of Shaytan, the exile from paradise who was plotting to ruin Allah's creation. At the time, during my early childhood, this reassuring explanation kept the monsters at bay, but as I grew older I wanted to find out more. Divine interpretations were fine, but I hoped that reason and the intellect would underpin with more sophisticated insights my search for the truth and the land of lost content.

Other mysteries, less threatening, were all around me.

The trips to the pyramids of Meroe and my father's fabulous tales of the beginnings of mankind, our ancestors' first journeys out of Africa and the emergence of Homo Sapiens sent my imagination spinning. Then there was the enduring magic of the Nile, the dramatic backdrop to the pageant of kings, queens, empires, battles, and monumental architecture that still stuns the modern eye. I was curious, astonished and bewildered by these spectacles. Man-made architecture explained itself, though the pyramids were miraculous in themselves, but who or what was the overall architect? What immortal hand or eye had framed the symmetry of the stars and universes?

Where had all this mystery, majesty, genius, colour and creativity come from, and why? What had happened to the billions of human beings that had lived before us?

Also, if djinns and demons were real, as I suspected they were, there would have to be a divine balance. If evil existed, there had to be a presupposition of its opposite, good. If the tiger had a creator, did that creator also make the lamb?

These kinds of thoughts, even when I was absorbed by the innocent delights of childhood play, were never far away, and continued into my teens. They were intensified by the shattering loss of my father, my grandmother Zainab, my aunt Fahima, my sister Awatif, Abdulahi Al Aweer and the diagnosis of my mother's serious illness. I understand now that we all have to deal somehow with the deaths of our loved ones, but these came in such quick succession that I began to despair. Why had they been taken away in the prime of their lives? Why did Fahima have to endure the death of her husband and the misery of a lonely, childless life? Why did the indomitable Zainab, who had cast such a spell of laughter and strength, have to be snatched away from us in the night? The only answer I could find was in religious faith.

I carry precious memories of these people and others in my heart to this very day. It had been Zainab who had encouraged us to listen to the evening news on the BBC.

In the late 1960s I remember that at 7.00 p.m. we would gather round the *Grundig* radio to hear the chimes of Big Ben in London. I had a wonderful picture in my mind of a far-away country of red double-decker buses, foggy streets, busy crowds crossing the River Thames, a charming young queen, small brick houses, neat gardens, red telephone boxes, gentlemen in bowler hats, the changing of the guard at Buckingham Palace, and placid, smiling policemen in tall black helmets. Perhaps this was an idealistic image, but when I later travelled to London I wasn't disappointed. If the Nile was an ally in life, so were the chimes of Big Ben.

As we heard accounts of disasters, accidents, the Israeli-Arab war, the first moon landing and the threat of nuclear war, Abdulahi would call for complete silence, holding his finger to his mouth and he would sometimes snatch his glasses off in annoyance even if we were just whispering. When the news was over Zainab would add her own commentary:

> Always remember we are all the creations of Allah. Muslims, Jews, Christians, Hindus, everyone is somebody's son, daughter, brother, sister, mother or father. There is no difference and we should tolerate each other.

These sad things should remind us that we need to help one another, not fight or kill each other.

Both she and my mother were brave and unflinching in their beliefs, and I loved the way their empathy and sympathy trumped the dictates of the demands of religion. We were a traditional Muslim family, but my mother in particular would insist that we meet and make friends with children of other faiths. We had no problem with this and played, laughed, ate and sang with Christians and Jews, never questioning if we were compromising our beliefs. The thought was simply too ridiculous for words.

Another inspiring person who helped to soothe my childhood sorrows was my friend El-Hadi Adam. He and his family scratched out a living on the banks of the Nile, growing plants and vegetables and catching fish to sell in the markets. They were profoundly poor and knew that at any moment the river could flood and wash away their flimsy wooden homes, but he had no complaints. He never seemed to worry and he joked and smiled his way through each day with a 'que sera, sera' attitude. When I met seriously rich people later in life, I was struck by how many of them were miserable and gloomy. Their wealth had not brought happiness, and I would think of him and wonder at the way status and money were mirages.

Still looking for answers and now a teenager, I had found myself attracted to socialism. I didn't think this was unusual as I was probably in tune with millions of other young people throughout the world. The 'baby boomers', the post-war generations of the USA and Europe, were beginning to drift towards its siren voices in droves. Their politics were a heady cocktail of Marxism, Maoism, existentialism, rock music and a serious questioning of the status quo. I had a mentor in Abdelkahlig Mahgoub, a distinguished scholar and leader of the Sudan Communist Party. He lived close by and during my visits to his house he began to explain his political beliefs in straightforward terms. He was persuasive but also honest and never pressurised me into joining the party. He urged me to read Das Kapital, which I found boring because it was so lengthy and dull. He also wanted me to jump some years in school, assuring me that I had the makings of a political leader. His praise was flattering, but I already had doubts about communism as an answer to the ills of the world. I could see that it had insights into history and economics, but I found its dismissal of spiritual matters disappointing.

Somehow I couldn't accept that religion was the 'opium of the people' and Marxism's unwillingness to explore the ultimate questions of life left me cold. It did have reason on its side but, "the heart has its reasons that reason knows not of," and I wanted more.

'More' certainly came my way in an experience which I still can't believe happened. I visited an extraordinary man in north Khartoum called Kamal Hassanain. He claimed to have the power to contact dead souls. I was highly sceptical about this and went along ready to dismiss this as dubious, and Kamal as some sort of a magician, but I couldn't. There were about seven men seated at a round table with Kamal at the head. He was a friendly, cheerful looking man in his early 50s. He chanted a few recitations which I didn't recognize – they could have been prayers or poetry, and he placed a large bag or pannier on the table. The room was already full of incense which added an exotic flavour to the atmosphere.

He then took a pen and inserted it into one of the small holes in the basket and asked if anyone wished to contact a dead friend or relative. When one was chosen he sat back and slightly distanced himself from the pen, while at the same time keeping one hand on the basket.

He then took a piece of A4 paper and placed it underneath the pen. When a question was asked the pen started to write scrawny words very quickly as answers.

I know what a reader is now thinking – this was a sophisticated trick and everyone was being taken in. I have to say that I inspected every possible thing. I picked up the bag, looked under the table checking for magnets or other devices, but I could not find any rational explanation. Kamal hadn't touched anything once the pen had been put down, and neither had any of the people round the table.

Then it became even stranger. The bag levitated two or three metres above the table close to the roof. Once again I couldn't see any sign of human interferences. At this stage Kamal was sitting well back from the table and asked all the audience to stretch up and pull the basket back down. We all stood and tried to drag the basket back to the table, but it resisted heavily as if it had a mind of its own. Eventually, after several attempts, we got it back into position and some of us were now breathing heavily.

The basket now made three distinct knocking sounds on the table, demanding attention. Kamal was watching us closely and smiling, while the pen once again started to write that the session had now resumed and questions could continue!

I was absolutely staggered by this and when I got home told my wife Azza and her father what had happened. She was astonished. "How can a man who is so deeply immersed in philosophy and mathematical logic possibly be taken in by such things?" she asked.

I replied, "Okay. I can see what you mean. Why don't we invite him here for a demonstration? He said he would be willing to come."

A few days later Kamal arrived at our house and repeated the performance. My family couldn't believe its eyes and we were all left speechless as the incense began to settle. My father-in-law, an intelligent senior army officer and a die-hard realist, insisted that he and I should go to Kamal's for a final session. Two days later we were at his place and witnessed the same thing. We were with a different audience, and this time the basket, instead or remaining stationary near the ceiling, started flying around!

"Can you believe this?" I said to my father-in-law.

"No! I have never seen such a thing in my life," he replied. "Do you think we should pay him?"

"No. He has already told us he never accepts payment."

"Okay. Let us go back home. I need some fresh air…" We drove home in his car in complete silence.

I was left with two questions, which I still haven't been able to answer. Either there was some trick or magic which was beyond my comprehension, or what I had witnessed was a manifestation of an unseen power. Perhaps for a few seconds the veil of reality had been lifted into another dimension… I felt I was once more in a small boat on the Nile listening to the fishermen's tales. There was a full moon, a panoply of stars, and life was full of mysterious wonders.

I still had the Nile. I would often wander away to quiet places on its banks, as far away as possible from the clamour of the crowd. Here my doubts and attendant ghosts kept their distance and I was quietened by its sublime indifference to my spiritual struggles. "Don't worry," it seemed to say.

"Whatever happens, life will continue. I will still be here, even for thousands of years when you are all gone. I am from the world without end and I will never die." I didn't find these thoughts in the least depressing. Strange as it may seem, my spirits were calmed and refreshed. The river's permanence and unchanging beauty were in a way a symbol of the truth I was seeking, and its never-ending journey through time was like a whisper of eternity.

Talking of eternity reminds me that I was fortunate to be alive, having experienced by this stage in my life two serious car crashes and a very nasty incident involving food…

In 1996 I was travelling in a car from Amman in Jordan to lunch with Government officials before flying that evening to Syria. There were four of us in the car, myself, Samir the chauffeur, one of my colleagues and a security man. Of course during the trip I began to chat about this and that with my colleague and when politics entered the discussion Samir decided to join in. He should really have kept quiet as we were travelling along a mountain road and he needed all his concentration to avoid an accident. He was also chain smoking. Out of the blue he entered the discussion on unemployment in various countries. "They should work harder!" At that precise moment we were driving on the edge of a very deep ravine and I decided to politely shut him up. "Samir, I appreciate your comments but please keep your eye on the road."

"Yes, Doctor, Sir. I will do that but I want you to know that I have been driving for thirty years and have never once had an accident. I am the best driver in the whole of Jordan!"

He was driving in the middle of the road and then found himself staring at a huge wagon coming straight for us. He swerved, avoided the wagon and then things seemed to happen in slow motion. I remember that the horizon suddenly changed and we were looking UP at the ground. The car was now poised upside down on the edge of the ravine. Unbelievably none of us was injured. I also remember that even though I was hanging from my seatbelt I could see a front wheel spinning above my head.

I had a brief thought that this sort of thing happened only in films but this was real and we were inches from death.

The security men and I were strangely calm, unable to believe what was happening. There were a few seconds of silence as we all assessed the situation and then Samir panicked. He leant across to the front passenger seat, flung open the door, crawled out and ran screaming round a bend in the road.

A couple of passing cars had by now stopped and somehow we were helped out of the car, kneeling and scrabbling on the road and muttering prayers of relief. We saw a few flames flickering from the bonnet and quickly distanced ourselves, running around the bend in the road.

There was a whoosh and a massive bang and the car was in flames.

To this day I cannot believe that I survived without any serious injury and the incident sharpened my appreciation of just how narrow the gap between life and immortality is.

The second one was in the Slovak Republic in 2003 when I was on the way to a Government Head of State meeting. There were four cars in the motorcade and the first one hit an obstruction on a roundabout. I was in the second car and it smacked into the first one and then was hit from behind by the third one. I was shocked and unhurt but one of my colleagues seriously injured her back and we had to take her straight to a hospital. Sadly she was unable to return to work and had to be formally incapacitated by the UN.

Finally, I nearly died in a Japanese restaurant. It was shortly after winning an election to the International Law Commission in New York and I was enjoying a solitary meal when I choked on a piece of food. I stood up holding my throat gasping for breath. A couple on the next table came to my rescue. The young girl shouted for an ambulance, put one arm on my chest and with the other banged on my back. My breath came back in short bursts, the trapped food in my throat was loosened and I survived. I was so grateful to her and even wanted to pay her but she wouldn`t think of it. I never found out her name but she is always present in my thoughts and I never forgot her quick reactions.

A few years later in Geneva I was dining in a Pizzahut with my family when the same thing happened to someone else. The father of a family on the next table began to choke and his wife panicked. I raced across and started to bang his back. I had to hit him hard three times before he eventually recovered. The lessons of life…

By this time I was studying law at The University of Khartoum and knew that if I was disciplined with my time I could also study philosophy and psychology at the nearby University of Cairo. I started with the giants of the ancient world: Sophocles, Plato, Aristotle and the Sophists, and, to understand them more deeply, I studied ancient Greek. Plato was a revelation. I could see that some of his thought would be mirrored by the great monotheistic religions waiting to be born later. His theory of absolutes, that justice, for example, is universal and transcends the ages and any human context, and his idea that all knowledge is a remembering rather than a discovery, sent ripples of recognition through my mind. His analogy of the cave where mankind sits in front of a fire and sees only shadows of reality flickering on the wall, ignorant of the perfected forms outside, hinted at the existence of a sphere beyond the grasp of human understanding.

The theory of absolutes was a rebuttal of moral relativism, the idea that morality is a fluid concept and that no one culture or historical period is uniquely privileged over all others. In his book, The Closing of the American Mind, published in 1987, Professor Alan Bloom told a story and then asked a question to an undergraduate class.

In 1842 Sir Charles Napier was appointed commander of the British colonial forces in India. He had received reports that a wife of a prominent village chief was to be burnt alive on her dead husband's funeral pyre. Napier had enough soldiers at his disposal to prevent the burning, and when he did so his answer to the chief's objections was this: "My nation also has a custom. When men burn women alive against their will we hang them and confiscate all their property." Apparently the students' reactions to the story were mixed. Some of them, steeped in the fashionable moral relativism of the day, argued that Napier had no right to be there in the first place and that he was imposing his values on a foreign culture and so on.

Others took the view that Napier was absolutely right to intervene.

I read with an open mind. It didn't matter whether it was Muslim, Christian, Jewish, Buddhist or ancient philosophy, I simply wanted to get to the truth. Abu Hamid Al Ghazali, Ibn Rushd, Ibn Al Arabi, Ibn Sinai, El-Halaj, Thomas Aquinas, St. Augustine, Descartes, Thomas Paine, Kant, Hegel and Nietzsche were just some of the minds within my grasp, and I tried to distil the essence of their thoughts into a consensus. I wanted to see if there was any common thread, any clues as to how the universe and the mysteries of life could be explained. I found obvious links between the three monotheistic religions; that charity, kindness, a rejection of violence, goodwill and tolerance were the keys to peace and what Sophocles called 'the good life'.

Metaphorically they were all 'singing from the same song sheet', even if they didn't know it. Perhaps this is a simplification, but maybe that fact by itself was a key to the puzzle. The truth, after all, may be so obvious it can't be seen.

I revered the wisdom and depth inherent in the Holy Qur'an, as interpreted by the great Al Ghazali, the eleventh century philosopher, theologian and Sufi mystic.

He was seeking the key to happiness and he felt his mission was to place more emphasis on a close spiritual encounter with Allah, rather than paying obedience to a set of rules. It was the internal and not the external dimension he was advocating. He would have had a ready answer to extremists and fanatics: "A human being is not a human being while his tendencies include self indulgence, covetousness, bad temper and attacking people." He was no puritan either, reminding joyless clerics that, "he who would ban music as harmful to the soul, let him also claim that the songs of birds are prohibited".

Although I read these great works with delight, at this point in my life I was still verging on deeper thinking. I wanted more than dictates as self evident truths, despite their appeal. I wrestled for a long time with the problems of reason, creation and evolution. Could reason alone sustain a belief in a creator? If it could, where did the power that created reason originate? I found some enlightenment in the inherent logic in Thomas Aquinas's Summa Theologica and his five proofs for the existence of God. They are highly complex and have since been challenged, but I thought they were convincing and compelling.

One of them was the argument from 'contingency'.

This claims that in the world there are varying degrees of perfection. The existence of these variations suggests that there is an ultimate standard of perfection, the absolute.

Another was the 'argument from design' which claims that there are certain observable laws that permeate the universe and that these laws could not have come into existence by themselves. They must have had an originator or creator. I believed therefore that the logical belief in God leads inevitably to reason, and not the reverse, and the only way to perfect reason will be through the utmost metaphysical submission to the will of the creator.

These were deep theological and philosophical waters, and I appreciate that what I have said is a synthesis of highly sophisticated thought. Aquinas and many Islamic philosophers and others were now proving the existence of a creator, and if there was a creator then our reason stemmed from there. In other words reason has to have been brought into being and cannot have just emerged from a vacuum. As far as I know this precept has not previously been openly dealt with. It is incomprehensible that the human faculty of reason could have preceded the existence of matter, and therefore reason cannot be the 'first starter'. This to me then presupposes the existence of a creator supplying the energy for growth, renewal, rebirth and the underpinning of the inherent laws of physics and mathematics. Once the creation is in flow, then the power of reason applies, specifically through mankind alone.

As a complement to these ideas there were other pointers to belief in commonplace observations of life.

For example, so many people complain about the cruelty and injustice in the world and its brokenness and corruption, but where do they get these ideas of justice and fairness from? As CS Lewis pointed out, "A man does not call a straight line crooked unless he has an idea of a straight line." So too GK Chesterton, "It is perhaps the strongest mark of the divinity of man that he talks of this world as 'a strange world' though he has seen no other."

I found myself gradually moving towards a position that had found expression many years previously from Francis Bacon: "A little philosophy inclines man's mind towards atheism but depth in philosophy inclines man's mind towards religion."

Having got this far, I also understood that an acceptance of a religious viewpoint should not allow me to become dogmatic and dismissive of other people's values or beliefs. Voltaire's maxim, "I disapprove of what you say but I defend to the death your right to say it," still held true. In addition, a belief in a superpower that controls creation presupposes the existence of another realm of which we are barely conscious, that there are more things in heaven and earth than we are aware of.

It should also be remembered that human judgements are made in the context of time, but in the context of the absolute or eternity they become irrelevant. That is why I believe human reason has its limits and that trying to equate our lives with the divine is meaningless. The word 'time' is a human construct and just as there are no limits to space there are no clocks in eternity. There is an eloquent reference in The Holy Qur'an: "We have removed from you your veil, so that today your sight is perfect" (Sura Qaf-Ayah [verse] 22), a thought which finds an echo in The King James Bible: "For now we see through a glass darkly" (Corinthians 13.12). In other words, as humans we have intimations of the divine, the numinous, the undiscovered country, but our vision is cloudy and indistinct. Clues to its existence can be found in great poetry, music, the lives of holy people and also in the mysteries of the world around us. In my opinion the real purpose of education therefore is to open the eyes of children to these wonders. They should marvel at the fact that every cloud since the beginning of time has had its own shape, that every human being, including identical twins, has a unique face and set of finger prints, and that every single snowflake that has ever settled on the face of the earth has had its own structure.

I believe these facts are miracles in themselves, as are the strangeness of sleep and dreams. I admire the story of the ancient Chinese philosopher Chuang Chou of his dream that he was a butterfly:

> Once upon a time I was a butterfly, fluttering here and there happily without a care in the world and unaware that I was Chou. Soon I awakened and there I was, veritably myself again. Now I do not know whether I was a man dreaming I was a butterfly, or whether I was a butterfly dreaming I was a man.

In broad daylight this seems preposterous and common sense asserts itself. Of course we are real. Our physical body confirms it. But when we consider that one third of our lives is spent asleep, the idea doesn't seem so ridiculous after all. Jung and Freud spent much of their time puzzling about this odd counter-world. So did Shakespeare.

In his play, A Midsummer Night's Dream, after the wedding feast, the newly wedded humans blow out the candles and go upstairs to sleep. Onto the stage trips the good fairy Puck with a final farewell to the audience. Who is real? The humans or the fairies?

Throughout my life I have been trying to synthesise these complementary and contending voices of religion and philosophy. Like most people I can be swayed here and there by the arguments for and against, and by the noble examples of those who try to live up to their respective demands. As I grow older though I sense that a conclusion may be within my grasp. We come from we know not where, and we go to we know not where, is a bleak, atheistic view which I cannot accept. I cannot believe that we are a random collection of atoms whirling around in a dark meaningless universe. I would rather side with the collective wisdom of the ages which acknowledges, mainly through religion, music, art and poetry, that there is another dimension to life – that though we are living a mystery there is a divinity that shapes our ends.

Albert Einstein reflected on these kinds of thoughts:

> I'm not an atheist and I don't call myself a pantheist. We are in a position of a little child entering a huge library with books in many languages. The child knows someone must have written these books; it does not know how. It does not understand the languages in which they are written. The child dimly suspects a mysterious order in the arrangement of the books but doesn't know what it is. That, it seems to me, is the attitude of even the most intelligent being towards God.

It is how that belief in Allah is interpreted and practised that is the key to peace and brotherhood. The three great monotheistic religions of Islam, Christianity and Judaism all share a common father in Ibrahim (Abraham) and the belief that we are each blessed as creations of Allah and precious in his sight. They share the precept that suicide and murder are sacrilege and that no religion has the right to force its faith on others.

Throughout the centuries Ibrahim's descendants have fought and warred, but now is the time for reconciliation and mutual forgiveness for the sins of the past. Perhaps we don't go far enough: As Jonathan Swift, the author of "Gulliver's Travels", wrote, "We have just enough religion to hate one another and not enough to love one another."

I would add a corollary to that by saying that even if love is not there, there is a moral obligation to tolerate and respect each other's differences. Metaphorically speaking we are all playing separate instruments, and therein lies the power of the orchestra – but we have to follow and listen to the single conductor for the music to reveal its beauty.

Untune that string and hark what discord follows... We need at best to celebrate our differences and at worst to accept them with kindness. As The Holy Qur'an puts it:

Lakum deenukum waliya deen.

or

Unto you your religion and unto me mine.

(Surah Alkafirun Verse 109:1-6)

And as ever it was the Nile which seemed to radiate its own form of agreement. It had no words, no philosophy, no rules of life, but it had its own majesty, its own music and its own enduring magic. I think that there is in everyone, deep down in his or her nature, something rooted in a memory of an earlier, fresher life. Some religions will call it 'The Garden of Eden', other cultures 'The Golden Age'. Whatever it is, I could hear its siren voices and feel its pull when I rested by its banks.

I have a complete list of sincere thanks in the appendix to all those who helped me in some way during my professional life, but I would like here to make special mention of members of my advisory committee. Their worldly wisdom, thoughtful participation and generous giving of their time in our many meetings across the globe were invaluable.

They are:

Prince Hassan of Jordan; the late Julius Nyerere of Tanzania; the late Boutros Boutros Ghali, Secretary General of the UN; the late former President of Malta, Guido de Marco; the former President of The Philippines, Fidel Ramos; the late Foreign Minister of Sri Lanka, Lakshman Bruce Lehman; the distinguished Chilean lawyer Marino Porzio; the equally distinguished USA lawyer Bruce Lehman; the former President of the OAU, Amara Essy; the Minister of Trade for Egypt, Mrs Faiza Abu El-Naga, and many other dignitaries.

For making a unique contribution to this noble endeavor through this book, I wish to thank the authors for their penetrating foresight and deep concern for the underprivileged sections of our society. May God bless them in all their future efforts in this direction.

Mandela

Nelson Mandela,
Johannesburg, South Africa
Former President of South Africa

Nelson Mandela's introduction to and commendation of my co-authored book "A better United Nations for the new millennium in 1999/2000."

With Imam Sadig Elmahdi, former Prime Minister of Sudan, taken in March 2016

With Robert Mugabe in Harare, in March 2000. Frank exchange on reform.
A Regional African Training Centre in Zimbabwe was named after me

With Yasser Arafat, in June 1996. I gave him honest advice which he highly appreciated

*With Ilham lliev, President of Azerbaijan, after the award of Doctor
Honoris Causa by the University of Azerbaijan in 2006*

*With Georgia Parvanov, President of Bulgaria and his Government, after an Honorary
Doctor Causa by the University of National and World Economy in 2002*

The Venice Award of Intellectual Property, presented by the Mayor of the city of Venice, Paolo Costa and the Minister of Industry, Antonio Marzano, in 2004

With Alexander Lukashenko, President of Bellarussia on the occasion of an award of Doctor of International Law and title of Professor from the Bellarussia State University, in 2007

With A.P.J. Abdul Kalam, President of India, accompanied by distinguished dignitaries, awarded the Doctor Honoris Causa from Indira Gandhi National University, on Saturday 5th March 2005

With the Japanese Imperial family in Tokyo, in 2003

With the Prime Minister of Portugal, Jorge de Sampayo, who conferred upon me the award of the Grand Cross of the Infante D. Enrique, in 2004

With Sultan Qaboos bin Said al Said of Oman on the occasion of bestowing upon me the Award of Oman (the highest), in 2004

With Jiang Zemin, President of China. China awarded me the
honorary professor of Law, Peking University in 1999

With President Jiang Zemin of China on a formal state visit during which I was
awarded the Doctor Honoris Causa by Fudan University (Shanghai), in 1999

With the Prime Minister of China, Zhu Rongji, during a state visit in 2000

With king Hassan II of Morocco in 1998. He invited me to give him advice on a critical matter. I met him alone and gave him my honest opinions which he appreciated and adopted

An Award by the International lawyers' Muslim Association, in Ankara, in 2014

Chapter 13

The Awakening of an Ancient Civilization and the Future of Historic Sudan

All the great things are simple, and many can be expressed in a single word: freedom, justice, honour, duty, mercy, hope.
(Winston Churchill. 1874-1965)

A man's word is the foundation of the world.
(Kamil Idris)

I hope that those who have read so far have understood that my heart and soul belong to the intimate connections of birth and family. Sudan is my home and my anchor in life. It made me what I am and I passionately want it to stand up proudly amongst the other nations of the world. If I were brutally honest I would have to admit that at the moment its image internationally is unfortunate. Civil war, Darfur and social unrest have been the dominant headlines for too long. I could go on at length about other problems, particularly economic ones, but I feel the time is now ripe for reconciliation, acceptance of past failings, and a shared vision of the future.

Some cynics might dismiss this as political grandstanding or clichéd opportunism, but believe me I mean what I say. Throughout the book I have tried to convey the essential warmth and goodwill of the ordinary Sudanese people, their astonishing history, their deep cultural roots and their innate generosity, aspirations, energies and hospitality. Of course there are tribal and religious differences but my experiences in the wider world

have convinced me that people are remarkably similar in their
wish for a peaceful place where they can nurture their children,
get through life and create loving and tolerant communities.
The desires, hopes, struggles, worries, fears, joys and sorrows are
common to all, regardless of race or creed. As I conclude this in
late 2016, the thousands of refugees from Syria and other war
damaged countries journeying on foot into the heartlands of
Europe looking for a haven for their families is testament to that
ideal.

I base my outlook not just on my experiences as an
international diplomat, leader and scholar, but also on the
simple truths and lessons I learned as a child growing up in
Omdurman. If it's true that children learn by example then
there are some towering figures that are still spiritually with me.
They are members of my moral arsenal and whenever in doubt
I still consult them. I was very young when my father died and
so he didn't play as large a part in my upbringing as my mother
Amouna, but I remember his great 'presence', his profound faith
and his sympathy for the poor and needy. My mother's bravery
in the face of his death, her unending generosity to strangers,
and her fierce unconditional love for her children is another rock
in my daily life. My Grandmother Zainab was insistent that we
should know the details of our history but that we should also
accept that the world was becoming a smaller place, that we were
in a global village and that we had to live in harmony with our
fellow men and women, even those of different faiths. She had
a profound conviction that we were living a preparation for the
next life, that what we did and how we behaved on earth would
have to be answered for in eternity when all our lives would be
one. Added to that list would be my aunt Fahima who tried so
hard to give me a precious present before she died of grief.

I'm sure that most fortunate people will have similar
reverence for the giants of their childhood and they will
understand if I say that these three women and my wife were
and are like goddesses for me. My childhood mentor Abdulahi,
the enigmatic philosopher king and one of the kindest men I

have ever met, had a similar philosophy. He was always urging us to forgive the sins of history and look to the future. It would have been so easy for him to have become embittered by the bloody slaughter of Omdurman and the colonial assumptions of the British and Egyptians, but he pleaded for tolerance. In his opinion the present generations shouldn't be blamed for the mistakes of their fathers and he turned our eyes to the lessons to be learned. He was adamant that human reason was limitless, that saving lives, resilience in the face of hardship and avoidance of violence were the keys to the future. In his opinion the battle of Omdurman could easily have been avoided if the leaders of the two sides had sat down to talk as rational human beings. He also pointed out that the legacy of the British included railways, hospitals, a legal system and a university, and that Sudan had been able to build on and develop these after independence.

It was these seminal characters, and of course others, who helped shape my outlook on life and gave me the realisation that although history is often written by the victors, the underlying impulses of human nature that yearn for brotherhood and good fellowship will eventually trump the darker forces.

That is why I am convinced that although Sudan is currently travelling on a hard road, there is a way through and a brighter future awaiting. I am fully aware of the peril of half-baked, grandiose political initiatives, talking shops and slick slogans. There have been too many false dawns later eclipsed by selfishness and corruption, and I know my ideas could be judged as yet more recipes for doomed strategies. In 2011 Sudan became two countries and the tension between the north and south continues to rumble on. Droughts, shortages of food, tribal aspirations and the national debt are just some of the nightmares that have to be faced, so why my optimism?

So far my memoir has been a glimpse of the past, an affectionate description of a misunderstood and loveable country that has been allowed to drift into chaos and horrific civil war. I want to finish with a vision, not a hopeless fantasy but a realistic plan, that could unite and harmonise the vast potential of its people, and harness its huge land and mineral resources. It should be remembered that Sudan stands at the very crossroads of Africa, a unique strategic position, and when it was united, it was the largest country in the continent. I passionately want it to shake off its past, take a lead and re-join the family of nations.

Every country on earth has had its struggles and dark ages, but I am deadly serious when I predict that Sudan, and indeed the whole continent of Africa, can grow and develop into prosperity. My vision is based on experience and close academic analysis of national and world economic structures. I am not boasting at all when I say I have the confidence to know what I am talking about. I would even go so far as to say that what I am suggesting is a promissory note to future generations who will hopefully reap the rewards.

My recommendations are the result of years of consultations, studies and successfully realised economic publications that have had international recognition. They receive more attention in my recently published book, Sudan 2025: A Realistic Path to the Future, but the plans can be summarised in ten major points.

The bed-rock for future progress must be a necessity to learn from the mistakes and failings of the past.

1. Sudan has enormous fertile areas and huge land, oil and mineral resources, including recent discoveries of gold and diamonds, and it has a strategic continental position, linking north and south and east and west. It also has an ancient, fabulous history that arguably predates that of Egypt. Its potential as an international tourist venue has hardly been tapped. It was one of the first African countries to gain independence, but its development is stalling because of mis-management, an absence of vision and weakness of the current plans. Its political and economic performance is not reflecting the legitimate aspirations of its people.
2. There is an obvious and urgent need to end the wars and disputes that are diverting the energies of the people. Ethnic and tribal questions have to be countered by an emphasis

on national reconstruction. There is therefore an additional need for a new constitution that ensures general freedom and human rights for all, regardless of religion or gender. Given the latent talents of the mainly youthful population and the dormant wealth of the country, it should be possible to effect these plans in a relatively reasonable short space of time.

3. It is critical to have an agreed governmental system which will take into account the potential problems that could arise from a new constitution. The differing political frameworks, ethnic folkloric lifestyles and tribal traditions must be respected and allowed for in this process.

4. The most valuable asset of the country is its people. The human factor, allied with education for all, becomes its axis of development.

5. Social justice, an accountable, respected and independent legal system is the safety valve of society and should form a protective shield against religious or political intolerance.

6. The aim of these reforms will be to stabilise the country. To encourage stability and investment the government will have to issue public apologies, where necessary, as a cure to heal past wounds. Transparency, openness, accountability and an avoidance of any form of corruption or favouritism are crucial in this process.

7. It is of critical importance to follow UN guidelines on development. Some of these have been itemised above but the following are mandatory:

   A. The struggle against poverty and hunger is the first priority.
   B. Elementary and secondary education for all.
   C. Gender equality.
   D. Reduction of the national death rate.
   E. Improvement of mothers' health.
   F. The fight against malaria and other diseases.
   G. International investment in a partnership for development.

8. It is critical that the branding of Sudan should concentrate on improving its negative image in the international community. To attract foreign investment it needs to restore the confidence that it can provide goods and services to the outside world.

9. Sudan should learn from the example of successful countries, whether small or large, such as Singapore or the United States, where national priorities override the more local ones. A federal system will only work when the cultural identity is national and not regional. Human experience proves the truth that diversity is an important principle and a precondition for the building of a country. This should be recognised and accepted, but national priorities are a necessary unifying factor.

10. The healing of a country such as Sudan is not an unrealistic dream. By taking into account all of the above it can be achieved. Clear, competent planning, coordination of efforts and efficient follow-up are the ingredients of success. In this context it is worth emphasising the importance of youth. The young are the potential catalysts of the future and we need to nourish and inspire them. The role of women in the transformation process and the protection of children is also of major importance.

Conclusion: This is a monumental task but it is within our capabilities. There has to be a national consensus that unites all factions in an honest and consistent effort to achieve not only reform but transformation. We cannot rely on windy rhetoric and the work has to be a dynamic daily tool overseen by a government that is trusted to show fairness and integrity in all its dealings.

Chapter 14

Nelson Mandela and a Promise for Africa

No one is born hating another person because of the colour of his skin or his background, or his religion.

People must learn to hate and if they can learn to hate they can be taught to love, for love comes more naturally to the human heart than its opposite.

(Nelson Mandela. 1918-2013)

Perhaps the sky is blue and fair, because we humans are not there.

(Kamil Idris)

All men dream, but not equally. Those who dream by night in the dusty recesses of their minds, wake in the day to find it was vanity; but the dreamers of the day are dangerous men, for they may act on their dreams with open eyes, to make them possible.

(TE Lawrence, The Seven Pillars of Wisdom)

Before he wrote an introduction to one of my publications I had a one-to-one meeting with Nelson Mandela at his home in South Africa. He called me 'a true son of

Africa'. It was an unexpected and spontaneous tribute and I was humbled by it. At the same time he urged me to write this memoir and I have tried to justify his faith in me. I sensed that he thought my story would be of interest but that he had a more pressing agenda in mind. He wanted his own dream of a peaceful and prosperous continent to be realised and perhaps to reach expression through the book. So in a way this is a dual message, and many of my hopes for the future mirror those of Mandela himself. Our shared vision is not fanciful dreaming and has been made with open eyes. The fact that Mandela achieved a personal triumph in overcoming hatred and bitterness, uniting his country by personal example, gives me enormous confidence that great things can be done. Through sheer determination he championed freedom and justice and shone a blinding light into the future. He can be followed.

It was a moment of genius when Mandela presented the rugby world cup wearing a Springbok rugby shirt, a potent symbol for the white Afrikaners. The sensational gesture instantly reached out a hand of friendship and reconciliation to the whole nation. How easy would it have been for him to avenge his persecutors in a series of public show-trials in savage recrimination for his years of imprisonment? Instead he walked another path, the path of forgiveness, and it made all the difference. The 'Rainbow Nation', the country of many colours, became a reality.

It reminded me of another heroic figure who had also been imprisoned and ridiculed after exposing the sufferings of people living in the Soviet Union. In his novels and essays Alexander Solzhenitsyn was an outspoken critic of his government and, just as Mandela refused to be released from jail unless all other political prisoners were freed, so Solzhenitsyn defied the state by continuing to write in secret. He simply would not allow his voice to be broken and was eventually deported against his will from the country he had fought for during the Second World War.

His exposure of the brutality meted out to starved slave labourers in the hellish Siberian gulag reached the ears of the free world and, as the essayist Christopher Hitchens described it, "something terminal happened to the edifice of Soviet power". It began to creak, and eventually it collapsed under the weight of its own absurdity.

I think that these two pivotal men were living proof that the individual is the most precious asset of humanity.

They were the embodiment of the oft-quoted phrase, "Poets are the unacknowledged legislators of mankind."

They refused to be intimidated and shamed their oppressors into eventual silence and disgrace. We should honour their memory.

There were other brave individuals who passed under the radar of public recognition when defying the thugs, bullies and dictators, but Mandela and Solzhenitsyn were the most prominent in the great vanguard of humanity.

They were towering figures and I hope to endorse their example in any way that I can. I feel I have a moral obligation to communicate my shared vision to as wide an audience as possible. Hence the memoir.

One of the quotations at the beginning of the chapter is a warning though. It is very easy to dream and then wake in the morning and do nothing. If the vision is to be acted on it needs daylight practicalities, energy and dedication to bring it to life.

Here was the ultimate grandiose question: one which had buzzed in my mind for years. How could Africa face its challenges and realise its enormous potential? It is something that I would like to address in more depth in another book as the question is so huge in its scope.

It was Mandela who offered a blisteringly honest diagnosis. When he came to power in 1994 he addressed a summit meeting of the then Organisation of African Unity, the OAU, reminding the audience that for 2,000 years Africa had been exploited, subjugated and economically drained by foreign colonialists. However, he also reminded them that a succession of African leaders had made no major improvements, paraphrasing Cassius from Shakespeare's 'Julius Caesar'.

> We must face the matter squarely that
> where there is something wrong in how we
> govern ourselves, it must be said that "the
> fault is not in our stars but in ourselves".

He insisted that if Africa was to join the developed world it needed to look itself in the mirror and face the truth. Fifty years after independence, many of its countries were in poverty, with wealth in the hands of a small minority. There were question marks about the ultimate destinations of foreign aid, there was a perception that 50% of the sub-Saharan population was existing on one dollar a day with low levels of life expectancy, as well as high levels of unemployment and illiteracy.

Addressing this situation will not be easy, but I sincerely believe that progress is still possible. It will take time, forethought and tough decision making.

In 1945 the continent of Europe was in ruins. Millions were homeless and destitute, economies had been smashed and mass starvation threatened. Hitler was gone but his apocalyptic mania had impoverished everyone. A group of very flinty-eyed US senators suggested a rescue scheme. It was called 'The Marshall Plan' and its idea was to grant funds and low interest loans to the entire continent so that it could regain its feet. The low interest loans were vital, in that growing economies would be able to absorb the cost of repayment without being crippled.

The aims of the plan were unambiguous and clear – the rebuilding of war devastated regions and cities, the removal of trade barriers, the modernisation of industry, the removal of petty regulations hampering business and the prevention of the spread of communism were paramount.

It began in 1948 and within four years Europe was experiencing its fastest period of growth in its history. The results were sensational, with agricultural and industrial production exceeding pre war levels, particularly in West Germany, which underwent an extraordinary 'economic miracle'.

I believe the example of such an inspiring plan could be a

basis for serious discussion at the highest level, although the implementation would have to have a difference. Africa is bigger than the USA, Europe, China and India put together. It is so huge that the process would have to become sub-regional. In addition every country that accepted funds would have to be subject to rigorous inspection by an approved neutral body, and the emphasis would concentrate on business development with social needs as secondary. This is because I believe that harnessing the vast natural resources on a sound economic basis could lead to growing prosperity and the betterment of social conditions. In simplistic terms, the only way to improve the lives of the African people would be to provide them with the tools to do the job, rather than allowing temporary help through yet more cash grants. Grand aid schemes are emotionally beneficial but they address the symptoms and not the roots of the problem itself. The key to making a breakthrough is to ensure that political and economic conditions can ensure growth. This was precisely the diagnosis that persuaded those US senators to risk sending vast amounts of money to Europe after the Second World War. A dramatic recovery was the result, and I see no reason why a similar one, although not 'one size fits all', could not be effected in Africa. To ensure success there is a need to fight corruption, improve oversight and strengthen accountability. The requirements for transparency, commitment, honesty and integrity are crucial.

I appreciate that at the moment this is a hypothetical issue. The idea of a type of Marshall plan for Africa has been raised before but never acted on, and I am wary of high level talking-shops that end in empty promises and inaction. My faith in its success, however, is based on two factors. The first is the example of Mandela himself. I have no doubt at all that were he alive today he would be channelling his efforts into making that plan realistic. The second factor is the knowledge I have gained from almost thirty years' experience as a senior UN Executive. In all modesty, I feel I am in a position both to help analyse the challenges and bring together the key resources, including political and academic, that could begin to address the task, enormous though it may be.

Underlying this faith, my bedrock optimism, is something else. Wherever I have travelled in the world I have kept, in a secret chamber of my heart, a constant companion. Throughout this book there has been a recurring theme – my ultimate source of inspiration and hope for Africa has been the River Nile itself. All my life I have cherished its image and its beauty whispers to me of another world just beyond our human vision.

Down the kaleidoscope of centuries it has seen the coming and going of kings and queens, dynasties and tyrants, the why and wherefore of many things, and in my mind I seem to see it smiling quietly at the folly and inconsequence of it all. There is a belief that smells can take you instantly back to childhood and whenever the political world has been too much for me I have taken a mental trip to its sandy banks.

There I can conjure up the smell of wood smoke, dust and damp reeds, and I am at one with my ancestors, inhaling the same scents as they did hundreds or even thousands of years ago. The Nile, unchanging, timeless, flows on. I can see the sunshine turning the water into flickering diamonds, the herons standing still as ancient statues, swallows and kingfishers swooping here are there and weather beaten fishermen casting their nets from their small boats. I am home again and somehow I know that all will be well and all manner of things will be well.

Eventually.

Chapter 15

Tune the Strings and Harmony Will Follow. Peace and Universal Healing

Wisdom is the wealth of the wise.
(Kamil Idris)

In 1989 Francis Fukuyama's essay, 'The end of History', argued that with the collapse of Soviet communism and the supremacy of western liberal democracy, the world could enter an era of minimal conflict, and human life might enjoy an unprecedented peaceful future. The defeat of fascism and communism had brought huge benefits and there was a collective sigh of relief that the Cold War, with its threat of nuclear annihilation, was over. Democracy wasn't perfect, but in its commitment to human rights and individual freedom it was held out as the model for progress. The grand old man of US diplomacy, Henry Kissinger, declared that he now hoped for, an inexorably expanding cooperative order of states observing common rules and norms, embracing liberal economic systems, foreswearing territorial conquest, respecting national sovereignty, and adopting participatory and democratic systems of governance.

It is easy to sound wise after the event, but I was dubious about Fukuyama's assessment from the beginning. All welcomed the fall of communism, but the lessons of history inform us that when one hydra head is chopped off another one takes its place. In retrospect I think the celebrations at the fall of the Berlin Wall were an over-reaction, and it was short-sighted to assume that humanity would just proceed in a straight line of progress towards a sunlit future without applying the necessary intelligence to the facts.

Instead of getting better, things got worse. In Afghanistan, for example, there was the assumption that once the Soviets had been defeated the path to liberal democracy would be open. It never happened. The same can be said for the period shortly after the invasion of Iraq. If there is a power vacuum then it is highly likely that it will be filled by opportunists and not by the automatic will of the people or the strongest force. In other words the dynamic maintenance of the solution to a problem is more important than the solution itself. If there are to be realistic approaches to international crises, half-hearted, superficial initiatives will always fail, and things should never be taken for granted.

By the 90s and the start of the new millennium world events were not going according to plan: optimism was fading; there was 9/11; the long drawn out Israeli-Arab conflict rumbled on; civil war broke out in Syria; ISIS began to fight for its caliphate, and in Africa Boko Haram emerged; Iraq continued to live in the shadow of its invasion and subsequent crisis; the Iranians pushed for nuclear power; and Russia started to flex its muscles in Ukraine. In the Middle East, in particular Yemen, Tunisia, Libya and Egypt, there were stirrings of discontent and unrest. The 'Arab Spring' was a case in point.

An ageing population in Europe, cossetted by decades of borrowing and overspending, was looking nervously at its outlying countries where near economic meltdown ushered in drastic austerity measures. Greece was in economic free-fall. Spain, Ireland and Portugal, and even France and Italy, were seeing record levels of unemployment. In the Mediterranean thousands of desperate refugees from North Africa, Syria and other countries were trusting that Italian and Greek rescue boats would tow them to safety and a new life. For thousands the rescue boats never appeared. After the UK's democratic decision in 2016 to leave there was even talk of the eventual disintegration of the EU itself.

International tensions persisted. Negotiations with Iran over its nuclear plans were underway and in the developing and least developing countries poverty, unemployment and the threat of famine would not go away. International organisations, in particular the UN and regional bodies, were and still are struggling to solve the problems and in many instances losing the battle.

In 2005 there had been riots in the Clichy-sous-Bois suburb of Paris, one of the banlieues surrounding the city, and home to restive immigrant families. Unemployment and resentment at being side-lined and ignored were the chief complaints, but cultural tensions were also in play.

Disaffected youths saw economic and moral decay all around them in a post-Christian society that was in nervous retreat from its earlier worship of multiculturalism. In 2008 French politicians were outraged when the national anthem was booed before a friendly match against Tunisia. Denmark issued leaflets dissuading immigrants from entering the country. France banned the wearing of the veil in public and in Oxford there was controversy over a request for minaret loudspeakers to broadcast daily prayers. In Paris in 2015 the Charlie Hebdo attacks and the November killing of 129 civilians sent European security into a tailspin. It shouldn't be forgotten either that suicide bombings in Turkey and Lebanon were having a similar effect on morale, though defiance and a determination to protect themselves and their values remained.

This ominous international scene was a million miles away from Fukuyama's vision of economic growth and a lowering of the Kalashnikovs, but I refused to accept that all was doom and gloom. I did have a flashback to those nervous days in the 1960s when the headlines were full of the horrors of the Vietnam war and Nikita Khrushchev was banging his shoe in anger at the UN. At the time nuclear war seemed imminent and, as the song went, we were, "on the eve of destruction". I could see the worry in Abdulahi's eyes, even though he pretended to be unconcerned. However, the destruction never came.

Determination, resilience and common sense combined to defuse many of the international flashpoints, and the world moved on.

There were more lessons from history:

In the seventeenth century Europe endured the Thirty Years War when Catholics and Protestants literally tore, burnt and tortured each other to pieces. Then came the era of reform, and the Enlightenment when faith and dogmatic belief was tempered by reason. The faith wasn't diluted or compromised, it was re-examined and refined, with the core values of faith, hope and charity still intact.

It also began a process of preaching its tolerance and respect for other faiths and championing the belief in human rights. There was still a long way to go, especially in the church's relationship with Islam and Judaism, but at least the door of reconciliation was beginning to creak open. It culminated in an unprecedented initiative by Pope John Paul II in 2000 when he made a sweeping apology for 2,000 years of violence, persecution and blunders, calling for centuries of hate to be replaced by forgiveness and compassion. He called for an end to divisions between Christians and to hostility and suspicion towards those of other religions. He didn't name the crusades, the inquisition or the holocaust, but the references and implications were clear. Some senior clerics were worried that others might see this as weakness, but later popes continued to echo his apologies in more detail. I didn't see this as a weakness at all – in fact, I saw it as a form of confidence and strength. By reaching out to other faiths, the example of mutual forgiveness and acceptance of differences was being set.

It is perhaps not widely known that a similar initiative of reconciliation began in the Muslim world when The Ottoman Royal Decrees of 1839 and 1858 abolished poll taxes on non-

Muslims and granted citizenship rights to all, regardless of faith. This is still a work in progress but the good news is that it is being widely welcomed. The universal values of human rights, freedom of expression and liberty of conscience have been embedded in The Holy Qur'an for hundreds of years and are reflected in direct accord with the 1948 UN Declaration of Human Rights.

Like any sane man or woman, I have thought deeply about these matters. In the long hours of the night I have sometimes woken up and wondered what sort of world my six children and future generations will inherit. If we allow ourselves to be cowed by chaos the abyss of darkness beckons. Then another voice joins in. This voice tells me that throughout history humanity somehow emerges triumphant from wars and discord. Deep in its DNA there is a recognition that dialogue, reconciliation, forgiveness, compassion and tolerance are the supreme virtues. With these thoughts in mind, I would like to set out a list of proposals that could begin to address the tensions in our midst. They are by no means comprehensive but I feel they could be worthy of consideration. After all, the longest journey always begins with a single step.

1. International and credible research institutions should embark on studying and analysing seriously, objectively and transparently the root causes of terrorism. The said-studies are required to dissect the historical, social, economic and political dimensions of this dangerous phenomenon.
2. Accelerate reform of the United Nations System of International Organizations as outlined in my Book A Better United Nations for the New Millennium.
3. Establish a Global Dialogue Forum (GDF), with a clear vision and open mission to mainly address issues of International Terrorism. As matters progress, it could include representatives from warring factions. The aim is to gradually establish global healing and universal

reconciliation. The structure of the Forum and its finances could be discussed separately.

4. Encourage tolerance across the globe through appointing Tolerance Ambassadors.

5. Give a new intellectual input to resolve the Israeli-Arab dispute and encourage contacts and dialogue amongst and between the youth from both sides. This would ensure consensus amongst future generations. (I tried this at the UN and it worked well.) Israel and Palestine need to co-exist peacefully through a Permanent Peace Treaty (PPT).

6. Build new international mechanisms to fight hunger and provide food security.

7. Build new mechanisms to work on poverty reduction and eventually poverty eradication.

8. Encourage the international, regional and national media to support this vision, and ensure that national policies avoid double standards.

9. Create enlightenment campaigns focussing on the noble mission of Religions and humanity.

10. Emphasize the necessity and importance of reformation of dogmas, ideas, systems and regimes.

11. Create international incentives in support of the above objectives and projects.

Epilogue

*And never say of anything, 'Indeed, I will do
that tomorrow', except when adding, 'If Allah
wills'.*

Surah 18. Al-Kahf, Ayah23

No matter how hard I have tried, this memoir has developed into something beyond itself. What started out as a simple narrative, a story of a child labourer and his progress towards the international stage, has assumed a life of its own. Politics, history, religion and philosophy have wandered in, as have the insistent, haunting voices of long-gone generations.

Perhaps this is just as it should be. We are all the inheritors of the past, the results of dynamic currents flowing through us, our characters and DNA shaped by our ancestors. As the saying goes: "When a baby is born, it is already a thousand years old." So I feel these byways into other worlds are as much a part of my life as the factual account itself.

There is an additional strand, parallel to the narrative and complementary to these diversions. It is my story but it is also a portrait of a colourful, vibrant and strong country: my personal tribute to the people of Sudan and their rich, wondrous heritage. The common perception is of an unfortunate nation torn by factions, a fractured and struggling place where tension and violence are unchecked. But there is another, deeper dimension which transcends this picture – and it can be found in the happy lives, ancient traditions and supporting communities of the people themselves who are deeply rooted in the land.

I go back to a chapter in the memoir when I was stranded in the deadly Nubian baadiya, the desert furnace where I stared in horror at a train leaving me alone to my fate. I was rescued by a small Bedouin community that was still living by the disciplines and ethos of its ancestors. I was the helpless stranger, totally dependent on charity and I was made a temporary member of the family. For a few days I was privileged to share their lives and I have never forgotten their kindness, dignity and humanity. There were precious moments, magical firelit evenings under the stars when the wisdom of centuries found expression in their myths, stories, proverbs and fables. The silence of the desert, the daily milking of the camels, the collecting of firewood, the cooling breezes flowing through the tents during the sunsets, are images that have stayed with me all my life. This was a community at ease with its past and secure in its identity, hence its confidence in its traditions and dress. I know that, away from the bustle and dislocation of the cities, there are thousands of communities just like the one I am describing, and they are the real Sudan.

I hope that young people in particular who have read so far can be encouraged by this engaging picture. They should know that they also are the inheritors of a culture rooted in warmth, generosity and continuity.

I have been so fortunate in my diplomatic life to have had the opportunity to visit a huge range of countries. I have given lectures, talks, and received commendations and decorations from all over the world but I have never lost the feeling that, amid all the ceremonies and glittering occasions, people are very much the same wherever I have gone. Kindness, tolerance and goodwill seem to me to be the root virtues of mankind. This is also so in the settled democracies where security, freedom of speech and human rights have been the norm for centuries. There is little fear of authority in countries such as the UK, the USA or Switzerland, to name just a few, but the levels of honesty, transparency and personal responsibility in these countries is something I would like to commend. The fact that the UK has a highly respected Queen in the twenty first century for example is extraordinary. She has no political power but her influence for the good is tremendous. She is universally loved and I would like to single her out as an example of dedication to duty, stability and personal integrity of the highest order. As a young student in the US I was welcomed with tolerance and kindly consideration and I cannot have wished for a finer place to pursue my career than in Switzerland.

I am now at the stage where there is much to look back on and I often have to smile to myself when I realise how far I have come in what seems to be such a short space of time. Whenever I have been listening to the speeches of powerful world figures, handing out prizes, or addressing vast audiences I have always been aware of a little boy in a dark bottling factory and of the times when the smells of oil, swimming in the Nile and wandering in the spice soaked souks of Omdurman sweep me back to the magical times of childhood.

Aromas that triggered the nostalgia of my childhood memories still follow me to this day. Whether I shake hands with kings or dignitaries, or ordinary people, my sense awakens my memory of my child labouring at the oil factory: my hands smell of oil. The emotional part of my brain reminds me of the signature of my memory. Scents from my childhood make a lasting impression. They are stronger than sounds, pictures or words.

The scent of the grass by the River Nile happily drifting by on an early winter breeze. Not far from this is the smell of fish stocked in farmers' baskets. The burning charcoal early in the morning when my mother was struggling to cook tea in the courtyard of our old house; the smell in hot summer of a round, cold, sweet and juicy watermelon and the smell of camels' skin in the desert. All these smells linger in my mind, bringing back powerful memories.

Perhaps this is one of the great secrets of life: to have a permanent sense of wonder at its colour, variety and ultimate mystery.

I have already expressed my pride in the majestic endurance of the mighty Nile but there is another aspect of my country that complements and enriches it. I have already mentioned the pyramids of Meroe in earlier chapters when I was perhaps too young to fully appreciate their significance.

Many years later satellite photographs are able to reveal the full extent of the great civilisation that supported and surrounded them. Hidden under thousands of years of wind and sand the skeletal remains of cities, roads, palaces and tombs are now being uncovered. I mentioned the outstanding work of Charles Bonnet, the French archaeologist who was one of the first to realise that Sudan had a history and culture to rival that of ancient Egypt. Since 2012 the momentum of discovery has been undertaken by the generosity of Qatar Museums, working closely with its equivalent in Sudan to form The Qatar-Sudan Archaeological Project (QSAP).

The teams have made stunning discoveries and the area is now a UNESCO world heritage site. More than 250 pyramids have been uncovered, dating from 2500 BCE, when the kingdom of Kush, based around Meroe in northern Sudan, was the centre of a fabulous civilisation and the pyramids are thought to be the burial grounds for 30 kings, eight queens and at least three princes. It was no wonder that when Bonnet had said he went to Sudan to find traces of Egyptian civilisation he came to understand that the Kushite or Nubian stood alone with its own powerful identity.

Kush occupied a hugely strategic position; it lay in a fertile basin at the crossroads of desert routes linking Egypt, the Red Sea and the heart of Africa to the south. Controlling these routes meant it could export gold, iron, metal, ebony, incense, copper, precious stones, and even ostrich feathers. It grew very rich and quickly became an epicentre of innovation and culture.

It also played a crucial role in shaping Egypt from the 8th century BCE when its Middle Kingdom was in decline. Around 730 BCE the Nubian king, Piye, sensed a weakness and invaded and conquered Egypt, gaining control over the entire Nile valley. He was known as one of the "Black Pharaohs" and established the 25th Egyptian dynasty (ca 770-656 BCE).

What is extraordinary is that this process of discovery is really just beginning. Who knows what other treasures are lying under the sands of centuries waiting to be uncovered? I am supportive of the ambitions of QASP who are keen to build visitor centres and museums for tourists and to continue digging to find out more. This an enormous chance for the country to reclaim its place among the brotherhood of nations and celebrate its ancient splendours. It is already happening. The British Museum in London recently had a special exhibition of just some of the discoveries and in Germany the jewels of Meroe's first century BCE Queen Amanishakheto are on display for all to wonder at.

I take immense pride in the rediscovery of Sudan's former glories. As a child I grew up in Meroe and was taken by my father to wander around its ruins. I saw with the blank eyes of youth but now realise that something must have entered my soul, some connection with those people, a deep-rooted spiritual link with my ancestors, which lay dormant until adulthood. Now my imagination races when yet more discoveries are made. The past is not a foreign country and I believe it can inform and speak to the present in its own unfathomable way. Whispering down the centuries come messages of greatness, stability, order, trade, fabulous palaces and all the gorgeous splendours of Nubia and Africa. Such is the inheritance of Sudan.

The message behind this historic and ancient civilisation is that Sudan needs to improve its corporate image, restore its credibility and have the courage, determination and skills to rejoin the broader community of Nations.

Finally, I hope my memoir can be a message of reassurance. There is a saying that you can judge the quality of a civilization by the value it places on an individual's life. I would add to that by arguing that a civilization is built on the bedrock, the cornerstone, of loving families – families that accept those of different faiths and cultures with tolerance and good humour. As such, I hope the portrait of my own family and the numerous characters – eccentric and welcoming, kindly, generous communities that are described in the book – can go some way to broadcasting a signal to the wider world.

I have been involved in world affairs for many years and I understand that grand promises and lists of resolutions can sound magnificent on paper but, unless they are acted on, they become hollow and meaningless.

My 'signal' therefore is that global healing and reconciliation, particularly between the three great Ibrahimic faiths of Islam, Christianity and Judaism, tolerance of differences and mutual understanding, is not a fool's paradise or a pipedream. It was Nelson Mandela who understood the importance of forgiveness and, by not seeking revenge for his imprisonment, he captivated the world's attention. My sincere wish is that my memoir might help to add a few more pages of endorsement and hope to his mighty example.

Preview of Forthcoming Book on World Leaders

There has not been space in this book to include reminiscences of meetings with a host of world leaders. (See Appendix 7 on page 352 listing dignitaries, statesmen and stateswomen.)

Mostly these leaders were friendly and hospitable but there were occasions when I had to call on all my patience and self-control. One of them, not listed above, insisted that he should be commemorated with a special medal.

When I gently pointed out to him that it had to be earned first, he shot me a withering look and called me a "son of a b***h"! Arabic linguists will understand that the translation is highly insulting.

There was another time when I arrived for an official visit to The King of Jordan in a taxi because the official driver was late, and another in a different country when the close presence of security guards chilled me to the bone.

It will take another volume to relate my full impressions of these people but here is a snapshot of just one. In 2002 I met with the recently retired President of Cuba, Fidel Castro, in Havana.

It was my habit before these meetings to fully research the history and background of each individual so that I always knew what to expect. I must make it clear here that I was in no way sympathetic to his politics or philosophy but I also have to be fair to the man. Wearing his customary khaki uniform and offering us coffee and biscuits, Fidel Castro was warm, charming and attentive, and as we talked around a simple wooden desk he took notes of everything we discussed, scribbling furiously away as he took in each point. At one stage his simple Bic biro ran out of ink but he wasn't in the least embarrassed.

Straight away he asked me to call him Fidel and for two hours we roamed around the world's problems, discussing possible strategies that might help Cuba's plight, in particular the international embargo and the relationship of Cuba with the UN and USA.

We also talked about other global issues and establishing justice, and I was well aware of Cuba's questionable human rights record, but by the end of the meeting I was convinced he was genuine in wanting to canvass my opinion. One of the initiatives we discussed was his willingness to send Cuban doctors to developing countries, mainly in Africa. One part of me suspected that there might be a political motive behind the move, but when he added that Cuba would be paying their salaries and that the list of countries was random I was reassured.

As I mentioned before, I was aware that in western eyes he was not to be trusted. After all, this was the man who had been at the centre of a potentially cataclysmic period in world history, the 1962 Cuban missile crisis.

Even though I had been a small child at the time, I remembered the atmosphere at home vividly. The whole world had held its breath as Soviet warships carrying nuclear rockets headed down the Atlantic for Cuba.

President Kennedy, already alarmed at the presence of nuclear missiles only 90 or so miles from Florida, had encircled Cuba with his own warships, effectively blockading it. It was 'high noon' on the open seas and a case of who would blink first. If neither Khrushchev nor Kennedy backed down nuclear war was the next option.

At the time it appeared that Khrushchev lost his nerve and ordered his ships to turn round, but years later confidential documents revealed that secret talks had been underway and that a deal had been hammered out.

Khrushchev had pointed out that the US had nuclear missiles in Turkey aimed at the Soviet Union. Kennedy refused to de-commission these but offered a promise not to invade Cuba. Khrushchev agreed and the world breathed again. Both sides had saved face but Castro, having been completely left out of the negotiations, had felt humiliated.

This was the man who was now facing me across the table. When the final details of the offer of medical help had been discussed and a number of other matters resolved, Castro leaned back in his chair and the talk drifted to his early days as a revolutionary leader. I had heard that he loved to reminisce about the heady times of the late 1950s when he and Che Guevara and their small band of guerrillas had led a rebellion against the corrupt regime of Fulgencio Batista, the then President. He told me that people in the west had forgotten how grotesque Batista's rule had been. Cuba had been nothing more than a gambling paradise for the American mafia and assorted criminals. An example of just how corrupt it was, was that Batista's brother-in-law controlled 10,000 slot machines and the revenue from every single parking meter. When he was eventually forced out of office, Batista flew out of the island at night with 300 million dollars stashed away in offshore accounts and subsequently lived a life of luxury in Marbella. He died in 1973, two days before a Cuban assassination team could carry out its plan to kill him.

As a young man Castro had been more interested in baseball and basketball than academic matters, but as he grew into manhood the gap between the wealthy elite and the struggling poor in Cuba outraged him.

Intelligent and well educated by the Jesuits, he had a profound sense of right and wrong and when he entered the University of Havana Law School his political antennae sharpened. Ironically, his own upbringing had been privileged. He was the grandson of a Spanish immigrant whose own son had become a wealthy landowner. This was something of an embarrassment for the fiery Marxist revolutionary:

It doesn't sound too good to say that I am the son of a landowner, so let us say that I am the grandson of exploited

Galician peasants.

He founded the Ortodoxo Party and expected to win the 1952 election, but inevitably the voting was rigged and in 1953 he and 150 supporters began a rebellion. He was arrested and jailed for 15 years, but released in 1956, fleeing to South America where the plight of the poor intensified his sense of mission. He was now convinced that the only way to eradicate poverty was through a Marxist inspired violent revolution. The rest is history.

He returned to Cuba with 81 followers. Batista's forces captured most of them but Castro, his brother Raul and Che Guevara escaped to the mountains where they continued the fight. Batista began to lose popular support and when defections from his army became impossible to replace he vanished, and the 31-year-old Castro assumed power.

This was his finest hour. He was a conquering hero, a saviour of the country, a charismatic, bearded gift from heaven, and if he was a twentieth century Napoleon, Che Guevara was the incarnation of Lord Byron, a handsome, romantic icon whose poster would adorn millions of student bedrooms throughout the world, especially in the turbulent 1960s when to be left and liberal was an essential, even fashionable necessity.

Castro immediately implemented drastic far-reaching reforms on classically socialist lines. He nationalised sugar and tobacco plantations, forbade farmers from owning property and established huge 'collectives' where nobody really owned anything, except of course the state. The farmers became state employees and the press was muffled. There was to be no criticism of Castro's policies and if people did not like it they could leave. There were purges of disaffected military leaders and inevitably the established US companies suffered from loss of revenue.

True to form, Castro opened diplomatic relations and aid links with the Soviet Union, which did not go down well with the Eisenhower administration in the US. When he bought oil from them at knock down prices the US companies in Cuba refused to process it. In retaliation Castro simply took them over.

Alarmed at the presence of a Soviet ally on its doorstep, the US made a serious mistake in backing an invasion by Cuban exiles in 1961. This was the infamous 'Bay of Pigs' fiasco which had the reluctant backing of the new president, John F Kennedy. Trained by the CIA, hundreds of the exiles were killed and over 1,000 captured.

Castro was indignant but triumphant. He announced an immediate end to democratic elections and denounced American imperialism. It was a public relations god-send for both Cuba and the Soviet Union, but it also triggered a full US economic embargo that was not lifted until the rapprochement in 2015.

As a further snub to the Americans he began to export his version of Marxist philosophy to developing countries in Asia, South America and Africa. The Soviet Union continued to prop up his regime but the sanctions affected Cuba's export trade badly and soon trickles of refugees began arriving in Florida. Although a reformer with a genuine sympathy for the poor, Castro could not abide opposition and civil liberties were almost non-existent.

Workers had no right to strike, independent newspapers were shut down, religious institutions were harassed and executions and imprisonments whittled down the numbers of political opponents.

Meanwhile it was rumoured that the CIA was doing its best to assassinate him. When Castro told me that he had been the target of over 600 attempts to kill him I thought he was probably exaggerating, but there were too many documented reports of bizarre methods of getting rid of him to be ignored. These methods included sending him a fungus-infected scuba diving suit, exploding cigars and Mafia-style shootings.

His own behaviour was also becoming increasingly eccentric. It was said that he used to keep live chickens in his hotel bedroom and when he was invited to speak to the UN in 1960 he talked for 4½ hours non-stop. He bettered this during the

1986 Communist Congress when meal breaks were included to give the delegates a breathing space.

It could not go on. With the collapse of the Soviet Union in 1991, Cuba's economy went into free-fall. There were no more markets for sugar and Cuban cigars and no more cheap oil imports. The US refused to lift the embargo and so Castro took a leaf out of the Chinese book of economic growth and started encouraging small businesses. He also courted international investors and began promoting Cuba as a tourist venue. In 1996 he visited the US and invited exiled Cubans to return and start their own businesses.

I think we had had a fruitful meeting and I must say that I enjoyed meeting the man. There was a naturalness and complete lack of pomposity about him that appealed to me, and he did reveal a very generous side to his character. Before we left he took me to one side and assured me that I would receive a special package from Cuba once a year. I had no idea what this might be but sure enough a few weeks later there was a delivery to my office – a box of the finest Cuban cigars. Being a non-smoker myself I made sure they found an appreciative home with some of my grateful colleagues and friends!

I was accompanied during this historic visit by three assistants: Ambassador Khamis Suedi (Tanzania), Ambassador Dolores Jimenez-Hernandez (Mexico) and Mr Roca Campana (Cuba).

Appendix 1

Awards, Certificates and Publications

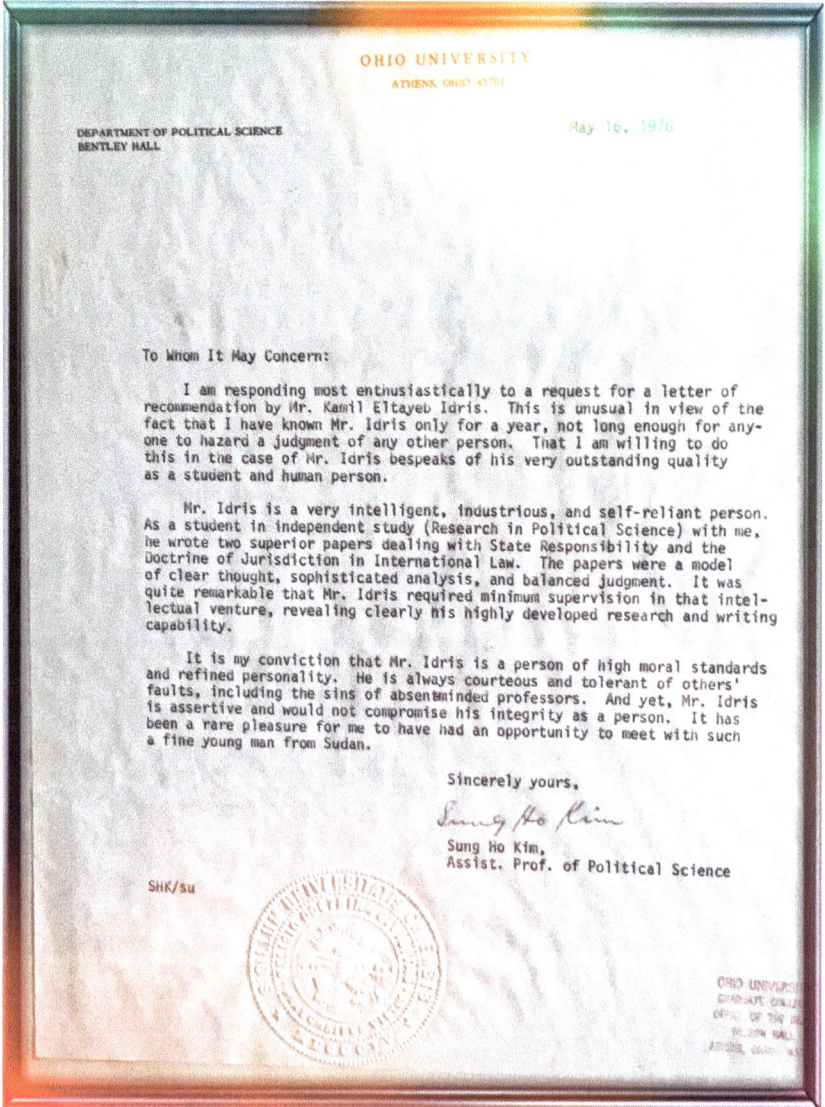

OHIO UNIVERSITY
ATHENS, OHIO 45701

DEPARTMENT OF POLITICAL SCIENCE
BENTLEY HALL

May 16, 1978

To Whom It May Concern:

I am responding most enthusiastically to a request for a letter of recommendation by Mr. Kamil Eltayeb Idris. This is unusual in view of the fact that I have known Mr. Idris only for a year, not long enough for anyone to hazard a judgment of any other person. That I am willing to do this in the case of Mr. Idris bespeaks of his very outstanding quality as a student and human person.

Mr. Idris is a very intelligent, industrious, and self-reliant person. As a student in independent study (Research in Political Science) with me, he wrote two superior papers dealing with State Responsibility and the Doctrine of Jurisdiction in International Law. The papers were a model of clear thought, sophisticated analysis, and balanced judgment. It was quite remarkable that Mr. Idris required minimum supervision in that intellectual venture, revealing clearly his highly developed research and writing capability.

It is my conviction that Mr. Idris is a person of high moral standards and refined personality. He is always courteous and tolerant of others' faults, including the sins of absentminded professors. And yet, Mr. Idris is assertive and would not compromise his integrity as a person. It has been a rare pleasure for me to have had an opportunity to meet with such a fine young man from Sudan.

Sincerely yours,

Sung Ho Kim,
Assist. Prof. of Political Science

SHK/su

A distinguished American Professor making a recommendation about me

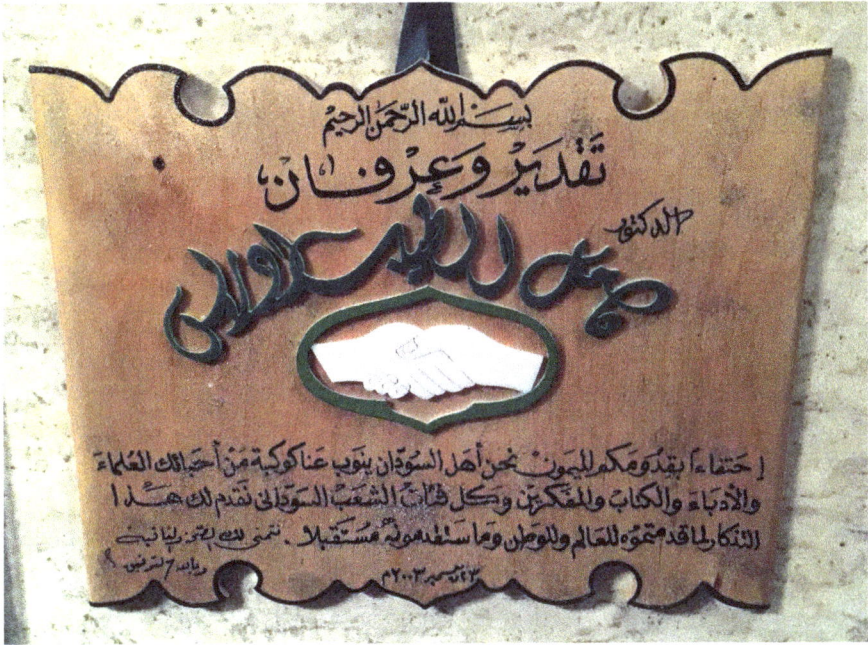

Commemoration by scholars, artists, authors and thinkers on behalf of the peoples of Sudan

Honorary Doctorate of Law conferred upon me by the University of Khartoum

Republic of Bulgaria
Ministry of Foreign Affairs

The Minister of Foreign Affairs

AWARDS

Dr Kamil Idris

Director General of WIPO

with the commemorative medal

"60 Years UN,
50 Years Bulgaria in the UN"

Minister:

Sofia Dec 2005

Ivailo Kalfin

Commemorative Medal Award by the Minister for Foreign Affairs of Bulgaria

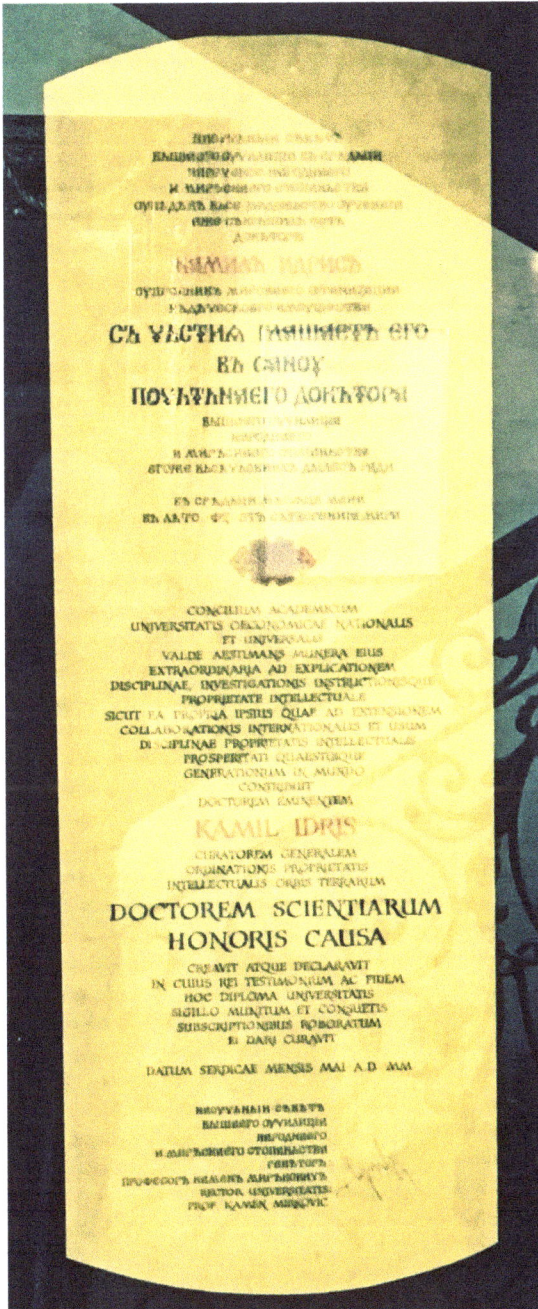

Degree of Doctor Honoris Causa from The Russian Federation

INDIRA GANDHI NATIONAL OPEN UNIVERSITY

AWARD OF THE DEGREE OF DOCTOR OF LETTERS (*HONORIS CAUSA*)
TO
Dr KAMIL IDRIS
Director General
World Intellectual Property Organization

Citation

Vice-Chancellor, Sir, it is my privilege to present to you this citation in honour of Dr Kamil Idris, Director General, World Intellectual Property Organization who has graciously accepted our invitation to receive the award of Doctor of Letters (honoris causa) on the occasion of the Sixteenth Convocation of the Indira Gandhi National Open University.

Dr Kamil Idris, a national of Sudan, is an erudite scholar of repute in the field of International Law. He began his association with WIPO as Senior Programme Officer, Development Cooperation and External Relations Bureau for Africa in 1982, became the Director, Development Cooperation and External Relations Bureau for Arab Countries in 1990 and Deputy Director General in 1994. He assumed charge as Director General of World Intellectual Property Organization in 1997 for a period of 6 years. During his first term as Director General of WIPO, he led the organization with a visionary zeal and aimed to highlight the central role of intellectual property as an important tool for social development, economic growth and wealth creation. His vision for WIPO has had an outward focus based on relevance, empowerment and inclusion and an inward focus based on clarity, efficiency and transparency.

In view of his dynamic leadership, Dr Idris received unanimous support from the Organization's General Assembly and member states and was formally re-appointed to a second term as Director General of the World Intellectual Property Organization in 2003. He is committed to build on his achievements of the past and to ensure that intellectual property gains its rightful place on the agenda of policy-makers at the highest level and is recognised as a powerful tool for social and cultural development in the global economy.

Dr Idris is also Secretary-General of the International Union for the Protection of New Varieties of Plants (UPOV) since 1997. Before joining WIPO, Dr Idris served in various capacities – as Attorney-at-Law, Advocate and Commissioner for Oaths, Sudan; Professor of International Law; Ambassador, Sudanese Foreign Service; Legal Adviser, Permanent Mission of Sudan to the United Nations Office, Geneva; Coordinator and Spokesman of the African Group and the Group of 77, Geneva. He was also a Member of the United Nations International Law Commission (ILC) from 1992 to 1996 and from 2000 to 2001.

Dr Idris has been decorated in recognition of his achievements by Sudan, Egypt, Senegal, Russian Federation, Saudi Arabia, Slovakia, Syrian Arab Republic, Portugal, Romania, Mexico, Republic of Moldova, Cote d'Ivoire and Poland. He has also been conferred Honorary Degrees by The State University of Moldova, Franklin Pierce Law Center, Concord, New Hampshire, Fudan University, Shanghai, University of National and World Economy, Sofia, University of Bucharest, Hannam University, Deajeon, Mongolian University of Science and Technology, Ulan Bator, Matej Bel University, Banska Bystrica, and National Technical University of Ukraine, Kyiv Polytechnic Institute, Kiev. He is Honorary Professor of Law, Peking University, China since 1999.

Dr Idris had his early education at Khartoum University, Sudan and Cairo University, Egypt. He did his Master's in International Law and International Affairs from Ohio University, USA and his Doctorate in International Law from the Graduate Institute of International Studies, Geneva University, Switzerland.

In his current stint as the Director General of the World Intellectual Property Organization, Dr Kamil Idris is championing the rights of indigenous peoples, and respect for their distinct cultures, communities and values and encouraging steps to respond to the needs and aspirations of the world's indigenous people, so as to enhance their effective participation in policy processes on matters that concern them. In the field of intellectual property (IP), this translates into greater respect and recognition for the cultural and intellectual framework and knowledge systems in which traditional cultural expressions, traditional knowledge and associated genetic resources are developed, maintained, and transmitted to future generations within the traditional or customary context. In this perspective, he shares the vision and mission of our university. We are indeed privileged that Dr Idris has agreed to accept our invitation to receive the Degree of Doctor of Letters (honoris causa) at the Sixteenth Convocation.

Sir, may I have the honour of presenting Dr Kamil Idris to the Sixteenth Convocation of the Indira Gandhi National Open University, and to request you to confer on him the Degree of Doctor of Letters (honoris causa).

Indira Gandhi National Open University, the largest on planet earth, awards me Doctor of Letters (Honorius Cause) given by the President of India, Abdul Kalam

Dr. Kamel Idris

Director General
World Intellectual Property Organization

In recognition of his outstanding contribution to
publishing in the Arab region and worldwide

and

His ongoing work to promote development and
progress through the promotion
and protection of copyright

January 2007

INTERNATIONAL PUBLISHERS ASSOCIATION

Ana Maria Cabanellas, President

اتحاد الناشرين العرب
ARAB PUBLISHERS ASSOCIATION

Ibrahim El Moallem, President

Recognition and citation by the International Publishers'
Association and the Arab Publishers' Association

277

THE WORLD INTELLECTUAL PROPERTY ORGANIZATION

HEREBY EXPRESSES ITS GRATITUDE

TO

Kamil IDRIS

FOR SERVICES RENDERED TO WIPO

DURING A PERIOD OF

25

YEARS

Geneva,

MARTIN I. UHOMOIBHI
Chair
WIPO General Assembly

Recognition by the World Intellectual Property Organization

بسم الله الرحمن الرحيم

نحن قابوس بن سعيد بن تيمور سلطان عمان

تقديرا منا لما قدمه من خدمات

ممتازة في أعماله التي قام بها

سعادة الدكتور كامل إدريس ـ مدير عام المنظمة العالمية للملكية الفكرية

قررنا منحه

وسام عمان من الدرجة الثانية

وأمرنا بإصدار هذه البراءة وقد أبلغنا بذلك

صدر عنا بقصرنا في مسقط

في اليوم العاشر من شعبان عام ١٤٢٥ الهجري

الموافق الخامس والعشرون من سبتمبر عام ٢٠٠٤ الميلادي

بأمر جلالة السلطان

*The Decoration of Oman conferred upon me by Sultan
Qaboos bin Said, of Oman (Arabic text)*

279

The highest Medal from Mexico bestowed upon me

بسم الله الرحمن الرحيم

جمهورية السودان

رئاسة الجمهورية

إلى الدكتور / كامل الطيب إدريس

تقديراً لخدماتك الجليلة التي أديتها للدولة فقد منحناك

وسام النيلين

من الطبقة (ــ الأولى ـ)

وأمرنا بإصدار هذه البراءة ليذاع وليعلن

تحرر بالقصر الجمهوري بالخرطوم
الخرطوم في يوم التاسع عشر شهر ربيع الثاني سنة ١٤٢٣ هـ
الموافق يوم التاسع والعشرين شهر يونيو سنة ٢٠٠٣ م

رئيس الجمهورية

*The Nilein Decoration (first class) conferred upon me. It is
the highest decoration in Sudan (Arabic citation)*

281

RÉPUBLIQUE DU SÉNÉGAL

ORDRE NATIONAL

DU LION

Le Président de la République du Sénégal

Grand Maître de l'Ordre National du Lion

Nomme ce jour, par décret N° 98 - 319

Monsieur KAMIL IDRIS

DIRECTEUR GÉNÉRAL DE L'ORGANISATION MONDIALE DE LA PROPRIÉTÉ INTELLECTUELLE (OMPI)

né le _____ à _____

COMMANDEUR

de l'Ordre National du Lion

pour prendre rang du MÊME JOUR

et jouir de tous les droits et prérogatives attachés à cette qualité

Fait à Dakar, le 16 AVRIL 1998

Le Président de la République,

Scellé et enregistré sous le N° 2.127

Le Chef du Service des Décorations

Le Grand Chancelier de l'Ordre National du Lion

The President of the Republic of Senegal bestows upon me the National Order of Lion

282

FRANKLIN PIERCE LAW CENTER

KAMIL IDRIS

You have served your nation, the international community of nations and the international intellectual property community with extraordinary insight, understanding, compassion, and skill.

As a scholar and teacher, you have encouraged, enlightened, and touched the lives of many, shedding light on the often obscure and arcane worlds of international affairs and intellectual property.

As a political leader representing your nation and the world of nations, you have demonstrated a remarkable ability to see issues from all sides and to chart a course forward that strengthens all and diminishes none.

In service to the international intellectual property community, you have applied your considerable intellect and compassion to provide leadership and vision in a world of fast changing economic, technological, social, and political circumstances.

As a leader of men and women, you have exhibited extraordinary inspiration and capacity for work and deep respect for the professional and personal lives of those you lead.

For all of these accomplishments and the many other ways in which you have truly improved the lives of countless people, FRANKLIN PIERCE LAW CENTER is proud to confer upon you the honorary degree of

Doctor of Laws

this fifteenth day of May, nineteen hundred and ninety nine.

The prestigious Franklin Pierce Law Center of the United States of America awards me Doctor of Laws, with the citation above

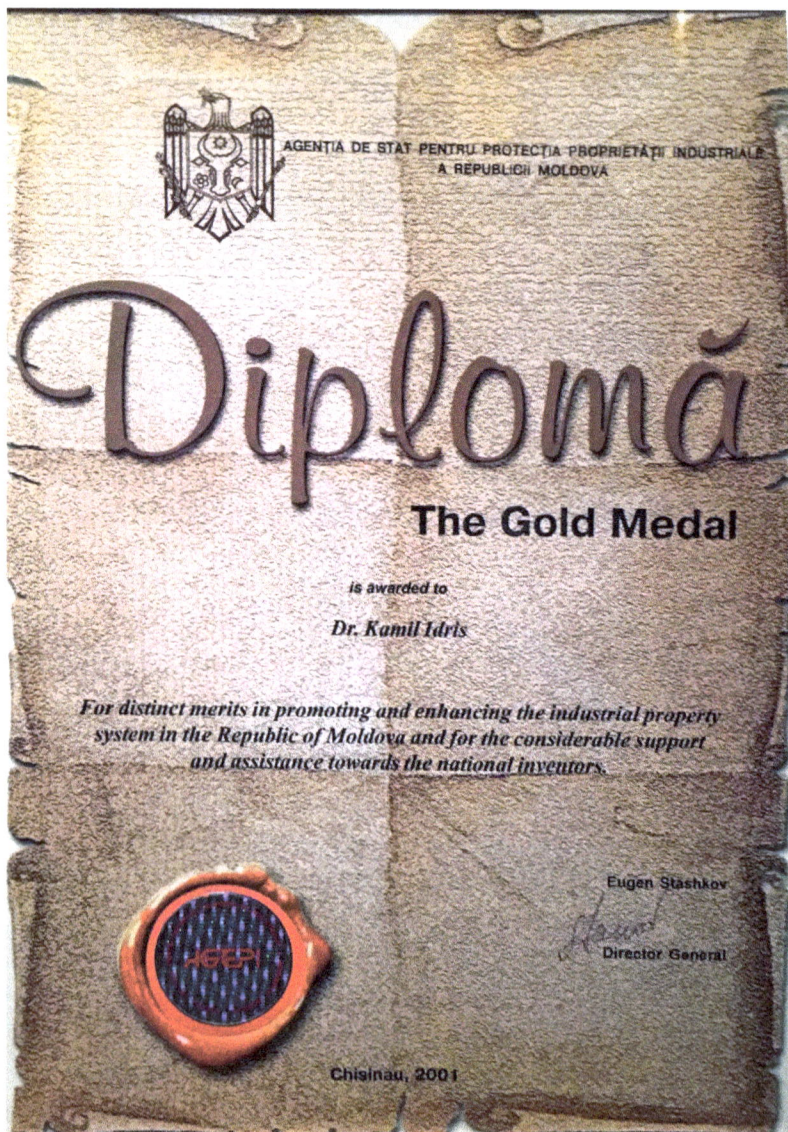

AGENTIA DE STAT PENTRU PROTECTIA PROPRIETĂȚII INDUSTRIALE
A REPUBLICII MOLDOVA

Diplomă

The Gold Medal

is awarded to

Dr. Kamil Idris

For distinct merits in promoting and enhancing the industrial property system in the Republic of Moldova and for the considerable support and assistance towards the national inventors.

Eugen Stashkov

Director General

Chisinau, 2001

The Republic of Moldova bestows upon me The Gold Medal presented by the President of the Republic

بسم الله الرحمن الرحيم

University of Elimam ELmahdi

جامعة الإمام المهدي

In recognition of his outstanding contribution in the field of intellectual property and in appreciation of his valuable efforts in developing the World Intellectual Property Organization (WIPO) one of the organization of the united nation also for the great confidence that expressed by all countries of the world for his appointment as the director general of (WIPO) for a second term the senate of the University of Elimam Elmahdi in its 3ʳᵈ meeting on the 5ᵗʰ of July 2003 has decided to a ward.

اعترافاً بإسهامه المتميز في مجال الملكية الفكرية وتقديراً لمجهوداته القيمة التي بذلها في تطوير المنظمة العالمية للملكية الفكرية التابعة لأمم المتحدة (الوايبو) وللثقة التي منحتها له دول العالم قاطبة بإعادة إنتخابه مديراً عاماً لهذه المنظمة نقدر قرر مجلس أساتذة جامعة الإمام المهدي في جلسته الثالثة في الخامس من يوليو ٢٠٠٣م.

The Degree of Honorary Doctorate

منح درجة الدكتوراه الفخرية

Of LAW

في القانون

TO

إلى

Dr. KAMIL ATAEB IDRIS

الدكتور كامل الطيب إدريس

Vice Chancellor

المدير

The university of Elimam Elmahdi confers upon me the degree of Honorary Doctorate of Law

UNIVERSITY OF GEZIRA

جامعة الجزيرة

SUDAN

السودان

By the authority of Senate we, the Undersigned, hereby certify that:

نحن الموقعين أدناه نشهد أن مجلس الأساتذة

KAMIL IDRIS

قد منح :

Has been awarded the degree of the University Doctorates (Honoris Causa)

كامل إدريس

درجة دكتوراه الجامعة الفخرية

Given at Wad Medani this day Monday 14 Rabi I 1428 Hij - 2 April 2007

وذلك تحريراً بود مدني في يوم الإثنين ١٤ ربيع أول ١٤٢٨هـ الموافق ٢ إبريل ٢٠٠٧م

Dean of Academic Affairs

Vice-Chancellor

مدير الجامعة

عميد الشؤون العلمية

The University of Gezira awards me the degree of Doctor Honoris Causa

AFRICAN REGIONAL INTELLECTUAL PROPERTY
ORGANIZATION (ARIPO)

Certificate of Honour

This is to certify that

Kamil Idris

in his capacity as the Director General of the
World Intellectual Property Organization (WIPO) has
made significant contribution towards the development
of ARIPO and intellectual property worldwide.

In recognition of his contribution, the ARIPO Training
Centre building has been named after him.

Dated this 15th day of February, 2006.

G.H. Sibanda
DIRECTOR GENERAL

*The above certificate represents one of my major contributions to the African
Continent – in recognition of this a major training centre was named after me*

The Franklin Pierce Law Center in the USA confers upon me the Honorary degree of Doctor of Law in 2016

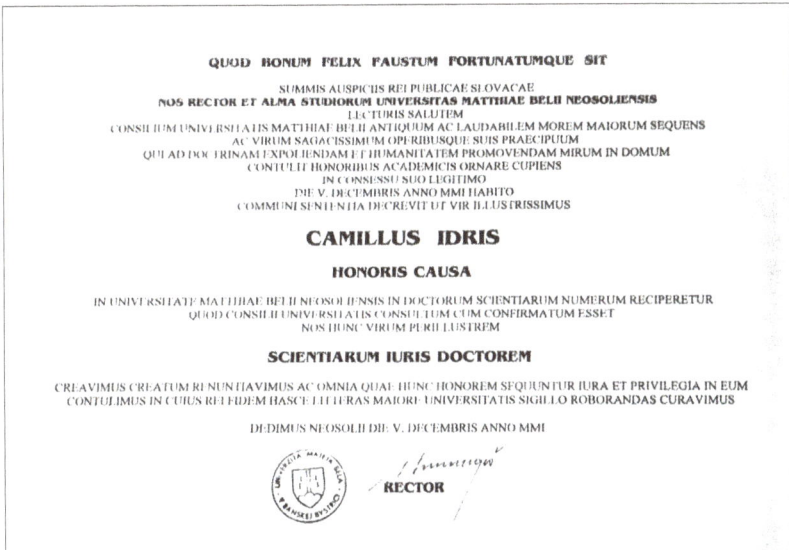

Doctor Honoris Causa in 2001 from Matej Bel University,, Slovakia, and Doctor Honoris Causa in 2002 from the National Technical University of Slovakia

Extract from a poem in Arabic of relevance to me

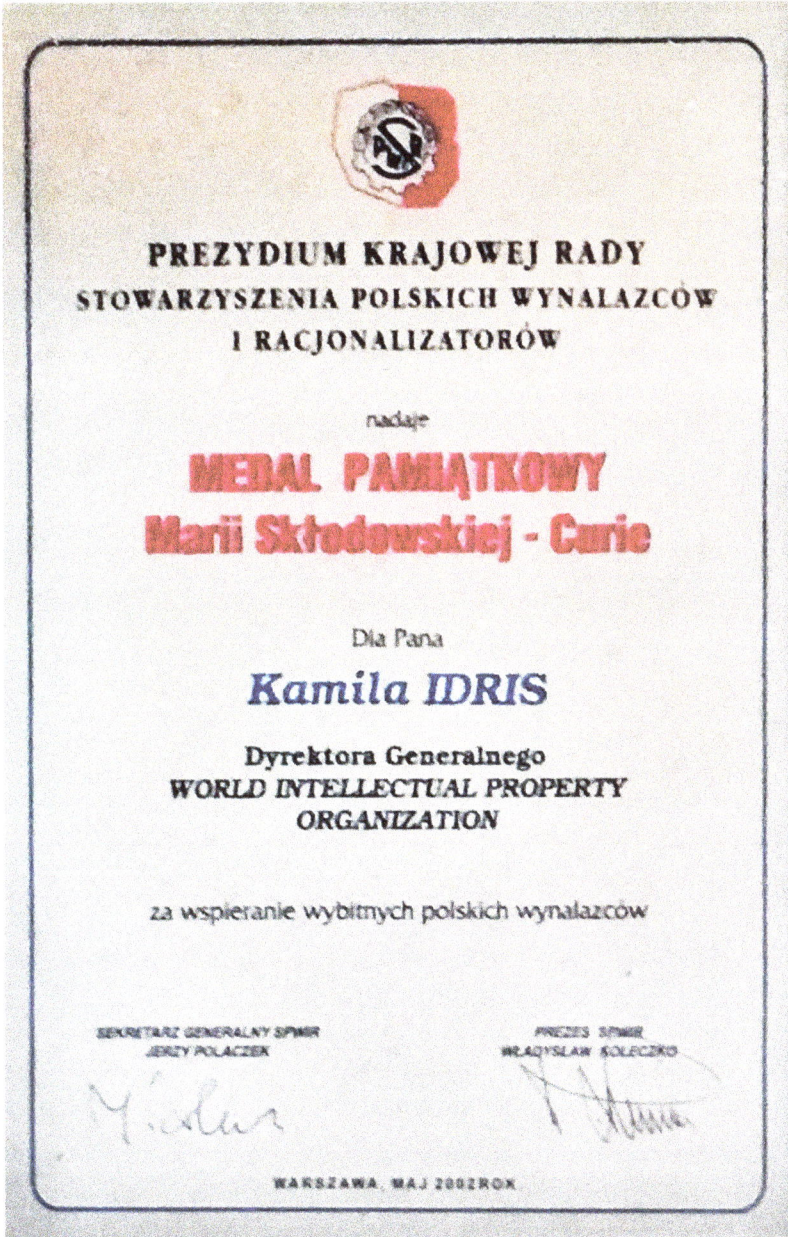

PREZYDIUM KRAJOWEJ RADY
STOWARZYSZENIA POLSKICH WYNALAZCÓW
I RACJONALIZATORÓW

nadaje

MEDAL PAMIĄTKOWY
Marii Skłodowskiej - Curie

Dla Pana

Kamila IDRIS

Dyrektora Generalnego
WORLD INTELLECTUAL PROPERTY
ORGANIZATION

za wspieranie wybitnych polskich wynalazców

SEKRETARZ GENERALNY SPWIR
JERZY POLACZEK

PREZES SPWIR
WŁADYSŁAW KOLECZKO

WARSZAWA, MAJ 2002ROK

Awarded the Maria Sklodowska-Curie Medal from
the Association of Polish Inventors, in 2006

289

Awarded the title of Honorable Professor by the Kyrgyz State National University, by Kurman Bakiev, President of the Republic and Prime Minister Igor Chudinov

Congressional Record

United States of America

PROCEEDINGS AND DEBATES OF THE 105th CONGRESS, SECOND SESSION

Vol. 144   WASHINGTON, TUESDAY, MARCH 3, 1998   No. 20

Senate

WELCOMING DR. KAMIL IDRIS, DIRECTOR GENERAL OF THE WORLD INTELLECTUAL PROPERTY ORGANIZATION

Mr. HATCH. Mr. President, I rise today to welcome to the United States Dr. Kamil Idris, the Director General of the World Intellectual Property Organization (WIPO). As many of my colleagues know, Dr. Idris was elected Director General in November 1997, succeeding Dr. Arpad Bogsch, who served in that capacity for 25 years. As Director General, Dr. Idris is responsible for overseeing WIPO's strong efforts in promoting intellectual property protection across the globe.

Dr. Idris has had a long and distinguished diplomatic career on behalf of his native Sudan. He is particularly well-known in international intellectual property circles through his 16 years of effective service to WIPO, most recently as Deputy Director General. I was pleased to visit with Dr. Idris informally shortly after his election as Director General and once again wish him success in his new position.

I would note that Dr. Idris is taking the helm of WIPO at a critical juncture in the evolution of international intellectual property protection. Nations throughout the world will look to his leadership in promoting a global fabric of intellectual property protection in the ever-explosive digital age. The WIPO Copyright Treaty and the WIPO Performances and Phonograms Treaty, both signed in Geneva in December 1996, are important components of that fabric. The United States has an opportunity to set standards for the world to follow by ratifying and implementing these treaties in a timely fashion. I have joined with my colleagues Senator Leahy, Senator Thompson, and Senator Kohl to introduce legislation to do just that. I look forward to Dr. Idris' support of similar efforts to implement these treaties in an effective manner in the remainder of the WIPO member countries.

Dr. Idris' visit today marks his first official visit to the United States. He will be accompanied by the Commissioner of Patents and Trademarks, Bruce Lehman, who will join Dr. Idris in meetings with the Secretary of Commerce and other agency officials who play important roles in safeguarding and promoting American ingenuity. Dr. Idris will also have the opportunity to meet with many of the leaders of our creative sectors, among them the pharmaceutical, motion picture, software, information technology, broadcasting, publishing, and recording industries. Each of these industries depend on the work of WIPO to assist them in securing effective protection for their intellectual property in the international marketplace.

I am pleased that Dr. Idris has made this important visit. I am sure I am joined by my colleagues in welcoming him today and in wishing him the best in his activities here. I look forward to continuing to work with him in a close and cooperative relationship.

United States Congressional record showing welcome of my visit to the USA in March 1998

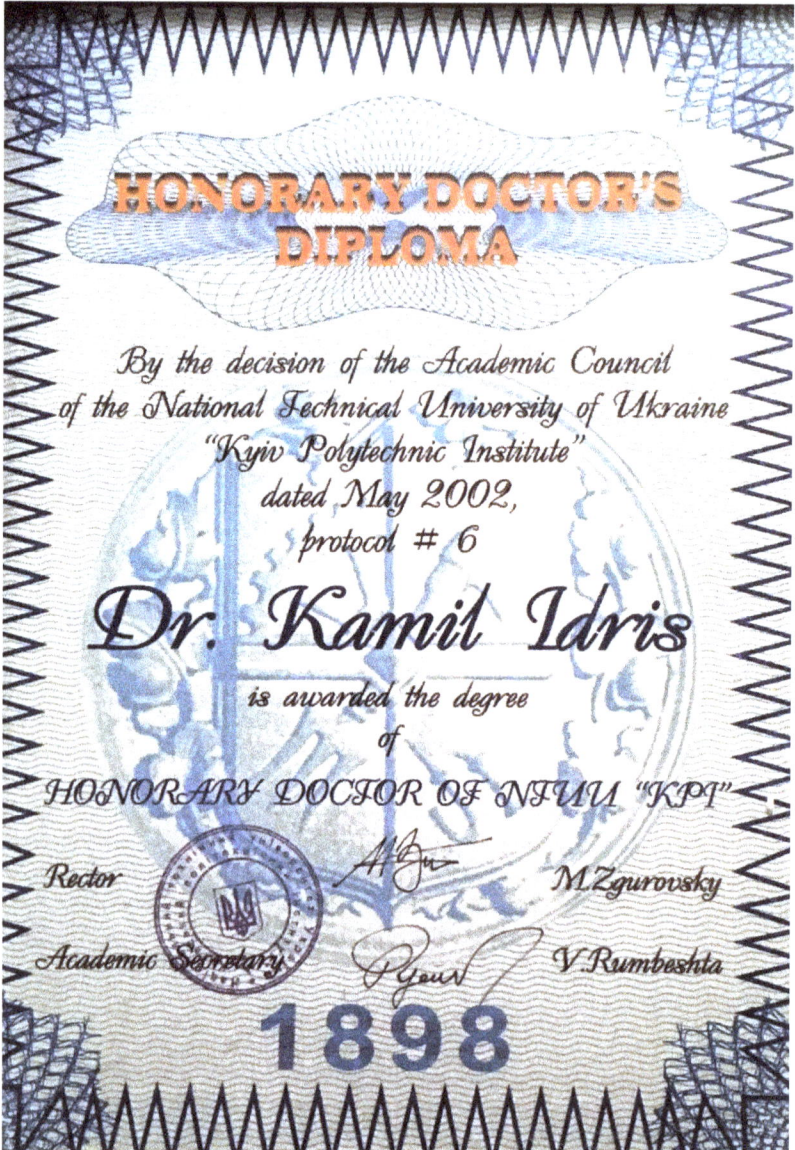

HONORARY DOCTOR'S DIPLOMA

By the decision of the Academic Council
of the National Technical University of Ukraine
"Kyiv Polytechnic Institute"
dated May 2002,
protocol # 6

Dr. Kamil Idris

is awarded the degree
of

HONORARY DOCTOR OF NTUU "KPI"

Rector   M.Zgurovsky

Academic Secretary   V.Rumbeshta

1898

*Honorary Doctor's Diploma from the National Technical
University of Ukraine in May 2002*

*Certificate of appreciation by the People's Support
Association in Sudan in April 2007*

*Invitation from the Minister of Culture of Sudan for a Presidential
evening to decorate me on the 4th of September 2008*

Another poem of relevance to me, dated 4th September 2008

Details of my BSC Philosophy degree (in Arabic), dated November 1976

غنـــــوة فــــرح

يا كامل الأدريس   يا العالم الانسان
أبشر وصلت الميس وشــــــــــــرقت امدرمان

● ● ●

من أهلك الطيبين حزت العـــــــــلم والدين
وأحمى لاخ وأصغير بك العابدين ناس الفضــــــل واللين
ختيت بصماتك للراحوا والجـــــــــايين
يالعالم الانسان
شرقت امدرمان

● ● ●

من كافة البلدان توجت بالتيـــــــــجان
وجمدت للانسان ايه في ـــــــمة الفنان
بقائد الفرسان فى اصعـــــــــب الازمان
نهديك انا امدرمان
ممزوجة بالالحان

● ● ●

اهلك فى بيت المال ختوك فى الاحــــــداق
شالت غناك عزة زحمة فـــــــرح دفاق
وغنوك للاطفال انشـــــــــــــوة فى الاعماق
وضموك فى الوجدان
ياكامل الانسان

● ● ●

وتعظيم فى حى السور المنـــــــو شع النور
وايضاً لنهر النيل البرى خيـــــــر وهدهور
والعرفو سر الليل البيـــــــك زادو حبور
انشوة ليها زمان
من بلدة ضوها بان

● ● ● ●

يا كامل التهذيب فيك الرجــــــــاء ما بخيب
من قمت انت تجـــــــيب وللحاجة انت حبيب
فى الرفقة حزت نصيب علـــــمك غزير ومهيب
ب العام   يالعالم الانسان
شرفت امدرمان

A song that carried my name and was performed in 2006 by a female band

296

*A certificate of appreciation awarded to my wife Azza by
Imam Almahdi University, dated December 2003*

An article (in Arabic) on me, dated 2010

Office of Registration, Student Records,
and University Scheduling
614/594-6911

OHIO UNIVERSITY
Chubb Hall 108, Athens, Ohio 45701

MARCH 20, 1978

TO WHOM IT MAY CONCERN:

THIS IS TO VERIFY KAMIL ELTAYEB IDRIS, 888-88-4262, COMPLETED
THE FOLLOWING GRADUATE COURSES FALL QUARTER 1977-78:

COURSE		HOURS	GRADE
PHIL 692	SPECIAL STUDIES	5	A
POLS 591	RESEARCH IN POLITICAL SCIENCE	5	A
POLS 598	PROBLEMS IN POLITICAL SCIENCE	5	CR
INST 500	INTRO/GRAD STUDIES	2	CR

MR. IDRIS EARNED 17 GRADUATE HOURS AND A GRADE POINT AVERAGE OVERA
OF 4.000 ON A 4.000 SCALE.

KENNETH H. SLATER, DIRECTOR
OFFICE OF STUDENT RECORDS

MBO'

My overall grade at Ohio University (USA), dated March 1978

CAIRO UNIVERSITY
KHARTOUM BRANCH
FACULTY OF ARTS

TO WHOM IT MAY CONCERN

This is to certify that Mr.RAMI EL TAYEB ????? has obtained
the B.A.degree from the department of Philosophy of this Faculty
in March 1976 with the Grade " Very Good" "Honours"

The credits he got in the examinations ?????? the four years
of regular study at this degree are as follows:-

FIRST YEAR 72-1973

1-   NATIONAL SUBJECT . . . . .GOOD
2-   ISLAMIC CIVILIZATION . . . . .GOOD
3-   ARABIC LANGUAGE . . . . .VERY GOOD
4-   FRENCH LANGUAGE . . . . .VERY GOOD
5-   ENGLISH LANGUAGE . . . . .VERY GOOD
6-   History. . . . . .DISTINCTION
7-   PHILOSOPHY. . . . . .DISTINCTION
8-   SOCIOLOGY . . . . .GOOD
9-   GEOGRAPHY. . . . . .GOOD
10- GENERAL ESTIMATE. . . . . .VERY GOOD .

SECOND YEAR 73-1974

1-   GREEK PHILOSOPHY. . . . . .DISTINCTION
2-   MEDIEVAL PHILOSOPHY. . . . . .DISTINCTION
3-   AESTHETICS. . . . . .DISTINCTION
4-   FORMAL LOGIC. . . . . .VERY GOOD..
5-   CHILD PSYCHOLOGY. . . . . .DISTINCTION
6-   GENERAL PSYCHOLOGY. . . . . .DISTINCTION
7-   GREEK LANGUAGE. . . . . .VERY GOOD..
8-   ENGLISH LANGUAGE . . . . .DISTINCTION
9-   NATIONAL SUBJECT. . . . . .VERY GOOD..
10- ISLAMIC PHILOSOPHY. . . . . .VERY GOOD..
      GENERAL ESTIMATE. . . . . .DISTINCTION

THIRD YEAR 74-1975.

1-   ISLAMIC PHILOSOPHY . . . . .VERY GOOD..
2-   MODERN PHILOSOPHY. . . . . .DISTINCTION
3-   MORAL PHILOSOPHY . . . . .VERY GOOD..
4-   MODERN LOGIC. . . . . .DISTINCTION
5-   SOCIAL PSYCHOLOGY. . . . . .VERY GOOD..
6-   ECONOMIC AND POLITICAL THEORIES. . . . . . .GOOD. . . .
7-   ENGLISH LANGUAGE. . . . . .DISTINCTION
8-   GREEK LANGUAGE. . . . . .GOOD..
9-   GENERAL ESTIMATE. . . . . .VERY GOOD..

FOURTH YEAR (B.A. DEGREE) 75-1976.

1-   ISLAMIC PHILOSOPHY AND MYSTICISM. . . . . .GOOD..
2-   CONTEMPORARY PHILOSOPHY. . . . . .VERY GOOD..
3-   METAPHYSICS. . . . . .DISTINCTION
4-   PHILOSOPHY OF SCIENCE. . . . . .DISTINCTION
5-   ETHICS. . . . . .DISTINCTION
6-   PHILOSOPHICAL TEXTS IN ENGLISH. . . . . . .
      LANGUAGE. . . . . .VERY GOOD..
7-   SPECIAL DISSERTATION . . . . .VERY GOOD..
8-   GENERAL ESTIMATE. . . . . .VERY GOOD)
                                                  HONOURS.

M. El Hefni
REGISTRAR
21/11/1976

DEAN
Professor Samuel B Hanna.

Details of my BSC Philosophy degree (in English), dated March 1976

Award of distinction and cultural innovation by the
Minister for Culture of Sudan, dated August 2007

*Medal of appreciation from Khartoum Development
Association, dated September 2008*

Award by the Quran and Islamic Studies Association, dated
December 2003, on the occasion of a decoration bestowed
upon me by Sudan Criminal Investigation Bureau

Appendix 2

Testimonials and Commendations

The following are a selection of testimonials and commendations.

Dr P.S. Rao, Former President of the UN International Law Commission (India)

Dr Kamil E Idris is a many sided person. He is many things for many persons. It is difficult for anyone to fully comprehend his myriad qualities and get a composite picture of him. As a young man he endured difficulties and got himself educated well both at home and abroad.

He earned degrees in law and other fields. He worked hard and saw some hard times. He understands the problems of young people in the making. He is realistic but has courage to dream big and make it happen. He worked with small and humble people and at the same time endeared himself to people in high position around the world. He worked with Heads of State and Government and was much decorated for the services he rendered to different countries and regions.

When Dr Kamil Idris was first introduced to me in Geneva at the Palais des Nations in 1991, when I was attending the meetings of the International Law Commission (ILC) as a member, it was a summer morning and he came across to me as a cool person. The chat we had was brief but he impressed me in no time that he is highly focused and determined to make a mark in public life. Besides he exhibited great energy and enthusiasm for things he was doing and wanted to do. He was full of smiles and his handshake was warm and firm. We struck an instant contact with each other and I readily agreed to give my support which he sought for his candidacy in the ensuing elections to the ILC next November at the UN General Assembly in New York.

The election to the ILC as always was very competitive and full of excitement. Several highly placed persons, regarded professionally and politically as important and respected were in the sway. None of us could take the election as granted. All major players of the UN and big powers from the five continents are competing with each other for the limited number of seats earmarked for each of the five regions: Africa, Asia, East Europe, Latin America and the West Europe and others (the USA, Canada, Australia and New Zealand). Dr Kamil Idris and I both got elected to the ILC for a term of five years commencing from 1992 ending in 1996. Dr Idris in the process earned the unique distinction of being the first person in the history of the ILC to become its member even as he was holding a senior position in the secretariat of the World Intellectual Property Organization (WIPO), which is a specialized Agency within the UN system. He was the first international civil servant to seek the ILC membership. In contrast, it may be noted that members of the UN secretariat cannot seek election as members of the ILC.

Following our election, we came together as members of the ILC during the next five years (1992-1996) and spent a lot of time both within the meetings of the ILC and outside.

Now as fellow members of the ILC we not only got to know each other well but became very attached to each other. We used to walk to his office at the WIPO after the meetings in the evening, which is right across the Palais des Nations.

Most of our time in these get-togethers was spent for a start in reviewing the day's proceedings of the ILC but soon would encompass personal and family matters as well as other subjects of common interest. Kamil always exhibited a great sense of humour no matter how serious the issue we are discussing. His comments often betrayed his strong commitment to enhance and ensure equality and dignity of nations coming out of the colonial yoke in the comity of nations.

He was equally committed to increase the level of representation, both in numbers and stature, of persons coming from these countries within the Secretariat of the WIPO and the UN.

As a member of the ILC, he took keen interest in its proceedings. These involved highly technical matters involving international law and policy. Even when dealing with them the policy orientation and broad brush of Dr Idris always provided fine touch to the discussion at hand.

He was deft in locating common areas even when others appeared to have lost in pursuing arguments against each other's preferences. His presentations were forceful, to the point, never pontificating and most of the time trending in the middle of the road and often persuasive. He spoke in English but was equally proficient in French and later in Spanish also. He used his mother tongue, the Arabic, as appropriate and as the occasion demanded. As a member of the ILC, Dr Kamil Idris was able to articulate the interests of Africa and the third world always playing a moderating role in the debates and negotiations, which usually accompanied the development and drafting of articles on various subjects on its agenda. His skills of negotiation, quick grasp of core issues involved and ability to identify points of common interest were an asset to the ILC. To my surprise, however, Dr Idris did not seek reelection, even though he was initially a candidate when elections for a new and in his case a second term of five years for the ILC were held in November 2001. The reason was, as I gathered later, that about the same time he was nominated and got elected as the Director General of the WIPO in circumstances not entirely preconceived.

Dr Idris thus established another global record when he became in the history of WIPO the first African and indeed the first third world professional/diplomat who secured election as the Director General of the WIPO.

However, we as members of the ILC got another opportunity to induct him as a member of the ILC when in mid-term (1987-2001) a vacancy arose in the African quota of membership when our senior colleague from Senegal Doudou Thiam passed away after serving the Commission for nearly 29 years, the longest anyone ever served it. The re-induction of Dr Idris as a member of the ILC in 2000 was a mark of respect he earned from all of us, members of the ILC, for the active role he played and contribution he made to its work as a member in his first term. As noted above, as matter of fact neither before his election to the ILC in 1991 nor after he left the Commission finally in 2001 no other person serving in the secretariat of WIPO or any other universal international organization sought or got elected as a member of the ILC. Idris's is the unique case and difficult to be repeated as election to the ILC requires some higher standing in the field of international law and some special aptitude to contribute to the process of codification and progressive development of international law, being the mandate of the ILC as prescribed under Article 13 of the UN Charter.

The election as the Director General of WIPO gave a new opportunity to Dr Kamil Idris to reorient his priorities as a person as much as the senior-most functionary of an important international organization invested with the functions and duties to promote and protect intellectual property rights world-wide. Working with WIPO and heading it put Dr Idris in a special and unique role. On the one hand he had to enlarge even as he continued the traditional role of WIPO as a promoter and defender of intellectual property rights which until then mostly respected and protected in the economically and technologically developed countries. This meant spreading the message within the developing countries concerning the value of IPRs. Simultaneously the developing countries also would have to be motivated and equipped with necessary tools to protect and enforce within their jurisdiction the IPRs recognized by other countries. On the other hand, he had to respond to the developmental priorities of the developing and least developed economies of the world which are ill-equipped to profit from the existing regime of IPRs until they were able to secure necessary financial and technological resources to cultivate their own arts, culture and genetic heritage into commercially viable products earning their own IPRs competitive enough in the open market. To reconcile the apparent divergent goals, Dr Idris chose a three pronged approach: First to disseminate necessary information in the developing countries about the important role IPRs could play in developing the economies of the poor and technologically underdeveloped countries. To drive the point, he authored an important book on the value of IPRs as a 'power tool' for economic growth. Second to provide necessary technical assistance to them to enhance their capacity to property and digitally record such knowledge or 'prior art' they already possess, in terms of genetic resources, traditional knowledge, and folklore and to utilize it as a base to improve the same or create new knowledge which was capable of earning IPRs. Third, as national laws varied in their protection and enforcement of IPRs, to focus on harmonization of these laws; and create best practices and establish new international standards. He largely succeeded in his effort to bring the value of IPRs to all major countries in Africa, Asia and Latin America through various technical assistance programs and seminars and workshops organized on the value of their traditional knowledge, genetic resources, folklore and other products.

As the Director General of the WIPO, he further encouraged reorienting the agenda of the WIPO meetings to reflect the priorities of the economically less and least developed countries which were in need of protecting their traditional and genetic knowledge, for example in herbal and ayurvedic medicines, ethnic designs, folklore and music. It was during his time as the Director General that the WIPO started focusing seriously on the development agenda of these countries. As a consequence the WIPO established in 2000 an intergovernmental committee on intellectual property and genetic resources, traditional knowledge, and folklore. There was also a separate item on the development agenda of developing countries, sponsored by Brazil. He established offices at the headquarters of the UN to bring home to the diplomats of countries' members of the UN the programs and priorities of the WIPO often involving them in exchange of views for mutual profit. He also established regional offices in Singapore and an office in Washington, DC.

The WIPO also established an Academy to promote the study and research into legal, technical, scientific and policy matters connected with the promotion and protection of intellectual property rights. These were innovative steps at the time which have now become a part of parcel of the broad architecture of the WIPO.

Through these institutions, Dr Idris strenuously worked to enlarge schemes aimed at building the capacity of developing countries which were in need of establishing national institutions and authorities based on international standards first to create IPRs of their own and then to promote and protect IPRs of those countries in pari pasu with promotion and protection of IPRs granted and recognized by the developed countries in the international market. Partly due to the efforts of the WIPO under the wise and energetic direction of Dr Kamil Idris, as a matter of record, IPRs are gaining ground as a value in the countries referred to as the emerging economies and other developing countries which are on the move in economic and technological terms.

As a person Kamil has been kind, understanding and outgoing, even as he values and protects his privacy. He is a quintessential family man proud of his mother, his wife and children and always cherished his large family of brothers and brothers-in-law. He has been very loyal to his close associates and friends. He used to be very considerate to the members of the service staff and others he met. He would offer instant help and extend generous assistance to persons in need. He has a talent to identify gainful qualities of persons he happened to meet, even if he met some of them only casually. He took great pleasure as the Director General of the WIPO in securing their services for its broad and specialized missions. When it came to take decisions he seeks advice from the right quarters but always takes his own decisions and will stand by them. To his credit, during his time as the DG of WIPO, more persons from the third world and countries in transition were recruited and promoted to important positons in its secretariat than ever before.

Dr Idris showed great fortitude and resilience in the face of some opposition and criticism of his actions and decisions. He never loses his cool even in the face of a crisis and sometimes as the going got tough he got tougher to overcome the same. Some of the problems he faced as the Director General in my view were the result of dreaming big and not having the right assistance at the right time to turn them into reality. Even as he well developed the art of diplomacy, the courage to dream big, practised the art of delegation of powers and functions in the interest of time and efficiency, and put these qualities of his in the service of WIPO as its Director General, Dr Idris was preparing himself for a bigger and perhaps even more a challenging task, that is, to serve his country Sudan following his retirement as the head of the WIPO.

He is thus well equipped and otherwise well-known in diplomatic and political circles of the world to serve his beloved country Sudan. Given his energy, unique qualities and great experience as a highly valued international civil servant, it would appear to be only a matter of time before he is engaged in some important and prestigious positon in the service of his great nation.

Dr Kamil Idris is a man of destiny and would no doubt be a man for all seasons! May Allah shower his choicest blessings on Dr Kamil Idris and his beloved country Sudan which he is destined to serve for a long time to come!

Dr Larry Allman, International Copyright Specialist (USA)

My Friend, my mentor and my protector.

I went to work at WIPO in March of 1995. It was an

incredibly wonderful, prestigious place to work with an outstanding reputation worldwide. Kamil Idris was then Deputy Director General in charge basically of Cooperation for Development. I was in the Copyright Law Dept., so I had little contact with him, in terms of my official duties. I saw him every morning at the Courrier. I could tell he was special. I went to his office during my first year there, and asked him if I could take him to lunch. He surprisingly agreed. We had a great time, shared stories of our coming to WIPO, and he treated me like an equal – I was so wet behind the ears, it showed how accomplished he was, how gracious. From that point onward, until we both left in 2008, he was always kind and supportive, and when he became DG, he really looked out for me. He has a unique skill to make everyone and anyone feel comfortable, even special, when in his presence.

In the summer of 1997, when he had been officially nominated as the next DG, but was not yet in office, there was a Ministerial Conference in Trinidad which he attended. I was there as part of the WIPO team. He just charmed every one of those Ministers; we saw it first hand. At one point during the Conference, Kamil took a few of us to meet the Prime Minister of Trinidad and Tobago. It was the first time I was in the direct presence of a PM. Because Kamil was there, the PM treated all of us with such respect, it was clear Kamil had the touch, the ability to make people feel important, respectful, and part of the moment. He had a great skill with people. He left the Conference early with two other colleagues. Two days later, we all left to fly back to WIPO via London. When we got on the plane, an ADG (Carlos Fernandes Ballesteros) and I had got ourselves into the first class section of the 747. Just before the plane took off, Kamil and the two colleagues got on the same plane, and went to their seats back in business class, much less spacious than our first class seats. Their prior flight had been cancelled, and they were last minuted onto this one. Once we took off, I went back and offered Kamil for him to take my seat in first class – he refused, sat in the back with his colleagues, and handled it just like one of the guys. He never, in my experience, imposed himself on anyone, never used his high standing to get an advantage.

When he was installed as DG, he formed what was considered his cabinet, the Office of Strategic Planning and Policy Development, and he chose me to be in there, to look over the copyright stuff. He also had me representing WIPO at the WTO. It was a great honour.

After about six months, I had a lunch with the assistant to the US Trade Representative. I'm still not sure why, but I thought I could talk to her like a normal person (maybe because she too was American), but a serious misunderstanding took place and affected my relationship with my country. Kamil handled the whole thing with such grace and precision. He sent for me, explained what had happened, told me that I would be given other important assignments, that this was nothing to worry about, and just made me feel that I had a friend. He dealt with it in such a way that I was able to learn from it, and that I knew that he understood me, a not too easy task.

Later on there was a similar incident and once again Kamil was able to resolve it with exceptional tact. I think there were few people in WIPO who received this kind of special treatment and I thank him every morning in my prayers for making my life at WIPO so pleasant.

My last project at WIPO was the development of a book I had proposed, the History of WIPO from 1992 until 1997, a period of time which followed the other huge history of WIPO book prepared under Dr Bogsch. I proposed it mainly because I thought the organization should do something special for Kamil, as he had transformed it a lot, extended and enhanced its representation worldwide. He green lighted the project, but asked that I do it with a working group. I proposed the top people in the organization with, what I thought at the time, the requisite skills to make the project the best possible. One aspect of that book was to be short biographies of Kamil and Dr Bogsch. I got to work with Kamil several afternoons, in his office, unbelievably cool sessions in which he would go over his life, and I would take notes, and turn those into written pages. I learned so much about him, but mainly, I got to share time and space and history with him, just the two of us, and it was just the kind of thing one remembers one's whole life. It was just so, so special. I finished the short bio, five pages, but in the end, Kamil decided not to include either one (I wrote Bogsch's too, taken from his autobiography/ memoir). I would say that no other employee of WIPO ever got to do something that special, with such a great man.

Towards the end of our time together, in 2008, when I learned that he would be leaving WIPO, I knew it was time for me also to leave; there were other circumstances for me, but his leaving was the biggest factor. There were two ways for me to leave, one of which (eliminating my post) paid me a much larger exit package than simply retiring, but which required special authorization from the DG. I asked to see him – he always accommodated me with a quick meeting, which was not the same for everybody else. I explained what I would like to do, terminate my post and leave with a package. He got it immediately, gave the special authorization, and even shepherded it through the course of many different hoops and obstacles. One time, when there was obvious blockage, and I told him about it, he asked to see in his office the top four people from the various departments necessary to push it through, like the Director of HR, Legal Counsel, Chief of Staff, that level, and explained to them, in front of me no less, that he wanted my termination/exit package to go through smoothly and efficiently, and on time. Consequently, and thanks only to him, I left WIPO with a nice exit package, some great, great memories, and thoughts of how lucky I was to have had a friend like Kamil Idris.

Ms Heidi Hawkings, Personal Executive Assistant (USA)

One of the things that stand out most to me about Kamil Idris'
approach to being Director General of WIPO is that he was
truly there to serve, rather than to be served by others. Being
named to such a post was not so much an achievement to
him but rather a responsibility asked of him to fulfil a rather
challenging role. Certainly, he achieved many things during
the 11 years of his mandate – among them transforming the
organisation into one that is outward-looking, and open to
evolving with the changing world (in particular in relation to the
growing importance of intellectual property to many countries
and business). He accomplished these changes in many ways
and through various strategies (political and managerial, for
example), but the fact that he was so successful in this seems
to me to be, above all, thanks to his great gifts in working with
people.

Kamil Idris always had time to talk to people, to listen to
them and to be concerned for their welfare. Working closely
with him, I was witness to the countless times that he put others'
needs before his own – not just because he thought it was the
right thing to do (which he did), but because he genuinely cares
about others and likes people generally. For example, the needs
of the staff of the organisation were dear to his heart, and many
of the changes he implemented involved improving working
conditions and benefits to staff. He worked tirelessly to ensure
that a new internal justice system was put in place in the hopes
that staff at all levels could have a fair hearing and access to
justice. He would also take time to consider individual cases of
staff – meeting with them directly where necessary, in particular
where others had given up hope of finding a solution. He simply
cared enough and believed that everyone – in particular those
with less hierarchical power – should have a fair shake or a
second chance.

He was also keen to work with colleagues and with
representatives of countries and other organisations on the

basis of consensus building. Although he would not shy away from taking difficult decisions where that was required, he was always open to listening to all sides of an issue – and was self-confident enough to be willing sometimes to change decisions in the light of new information. He had a wonderful way with delegates from all countries – making each one feel important and that their views were valued. I can't remember him showing any partiality to particular countries or regions, but rather I discerned a desire on his part to ensure that everyone was welcome at the table to discuss and decide on the way forward. He held countless consultations with groups of delegates in advance of big meetings, to ensure that they would understand, and could have their say on, the issues involved. This investment paid off, as it gave delegates a sense of really being involved and that their participation counted. It also helped to minimise unnecessary disagreements during the committee meetings themselves. To my mind, this was brilliant from both a management and a political standpoint.

This outstanding ability to bring all players on board as it were, brought with it certain challenges – one of which was that people were veritably clamouring to see him. This was understandable, and yet there were only so many hours in a day in which to organise meetings, to bend and stretch the schedule to meet the demand. This sometimes made for humorous situations in managing the logistics of simultaneous or overlapping appointments. It was not uncommon for the front office staff (myself and two others) to bring coffee and tea to one group in the waiting room, run to take a round of coffee/tea to another group in Mr Idris' study, all while he met with yet a third party in his main office. As it was my job to ensure the smooth running of the schedule, this was sometimes a bit frustrating. I sometimes suspected that this amused Mr Idris from time to time – no doubt the best attitude to adopt amidst such a frenzy of activity. However, I would say that the three of us in the front office certainly learnt much about diplomatic courtesy from Mr Idris. Even when visitors had to wait to see Mr

Idris, he always made them feel so welcome that they left in a good mood.

Kamil Idris was never interested in receiving anything extra in relation to his role, no particular perks per se, because he was the head of an organisation. At the very beginning, he even resisted having a driver. When it became clear though that it was a matter of practicality, he accepted the necessity, but I believe that he would sit in the front of the car next to the driver rather than behind him. At that time in WIPO, the organisation's rules allowed Directors General to fly first class, while other members of staff were to fly in business. However, Mr Idris preferred to travel with his colleagues instead in business class – which not only saved money for the organisation but also showed his colleagues that he valued them more than his own comfort. All this is not to say that he did not uphold the dignity of his position, for he certainly did that as well. He simply was not "in it for himself", or for whatever benefits he might have obtained. For example, one of the first things he did upon becoming Director General was to relinquish the second salary that had traditionally been paid for the role of Secretary General of UPOV (a role automatically held by the WIPO Director General as well). He decided that this second salary should instead be earmarked for assistance to developing countries – one more in a long list of admirable qualities.

Over the years, I have learnt much from Kamil Idris – much about being true to one's values and beliefs, and to oneself, in the face of pressures to do otherwise. Both justice and mercy are important to him, and no matter what the behaviour of others, he would always say that we should "rise above" the situation – meaning that we should neither retaliate nor deviate from kind behaviour. These are ideals that I too embrace, but Mr Idris embodied them so thoroughly that I shall always remember his example. Perhaps these reminiscences do not seem very glamourous; however, when all the trappings of the position fall away, these are the things that I remember most.

H.E. Ambassador (Dr) Alfredo Maiolesi, Secretary General of the World Organisation of States, International Parliament for Safety and Peace (Italy)

The magical River Nile is a colourful backdrop to the inspiring story of Kamil Idris's journey from child labouring, being kidnapped and risking his life on the roofs of trains in search of work, to eventual high office on the international stage with the UN.

The memoir is also a vivid cameo of a rarely seen Sudan, of a loving family hit by numerous tragedies, of eccentric characters, old souks, camel markets and of a fabulous historical heritage that is only just being unearthed. At one time under house arrest, Kamil emerges from this wonderful tale as a champion of tolerance, dialogue and human rights.

I found it a richly rewarding, memorable read and would unhesitatingly recommend it.

Dr Miranda Brown, international advocate and human rights defender (UK/Australia)

Kamil Idris is a wise politician who commands respect on the international stage, as well as in his own country, the Sudan. This book is a moving account of his life tracing the journey from his boyhood in Sudan, where he worked as a child labourer to support his family, through his teenage years surrounded by his eccentric relatives in Khartoum, to his adulthood and rise to international recognition, as a global leader at the United Nations and authority on the Sudan. His love of his home country shines through, yet he does not shy away from describing the horrors of the civil war and conflict in Darfur. His commitment to human rights and lasting peace in Sudan are an inspiration.

Dr Marino Porzio (Attorney-at-Law, Funding partner of the law firm of Porzio, Rios, García in Santiago, Chile. Formerly Deputy Director General of WIPO between 1979 and 1987. President of WIPO's General Assembly 1999-2001) (Chile)

I had the privilege of having been involved in the recruitment of Kamil Idris at the World Intellectual Property Organization (WIPO) in Geneva, in 1982, originally for working with one of the units of the Development Cooperation Department which was under my supervision as Deputy Director General of WIPO.

I had been impressed by Kamil Idris, having observed him acting at several international meetings as a young Sudanese diplomat attached to the Sudan Permanent Mission in Geneva. His great diplomatic ability accompanied by an excellent knowledge of the most important topics being discussed at different UN organizations in Geneva, made his participation noticed and important, in particular for developing countries whose interests Kamil Idris used to readily represent. He thus became an important asset for WIPO in particular for African and Arab member countries.

Kamil Idris had a successful career with WIPO being eventually elected, in 1997, as the Director General of the Organization and re-elected for a second term in 2003. Dr Idris thus became the third Director General of WIPO and had the satisfaction of having been the first Director General coming from a developing country, which in view of the nature and complexity of WIPO's specialized topic, was certainly a major political achievement.

I left WIPO in 1987, for returning to Chile, my country, where I resumed my private legal practice, but, in the following years, I still had the chance of visiting Geneva as a Chilean delegate which gave me the possibility of following more closely Kamil's early years as Director General. I was thus able to collaborate with him in some of his activities, mainly as a member of the Policy Advisory Commission, a body he established to receive advice from a number of specialists from different countries and eventually, in my capacity as President of WIPO's General Assembly, for the term 1999-2001.

I am glad Kamil Idris has decided to write this book containing his own views of the important period he spent at the head of WIPO, complemented by so many other biographical facts related to his important professional career, as well others of his more personal life.

Professor Makram Khoury-Machool, Director, The European Centre for the Study of Extremism, Cambridge, England (Palestine/ UK)

Kamil Idris's book is an exemplification of how the once survivalist instincts of a child, which was subliminally enhanced over time, reached the finest plateau of human development, mental ability, and creative professionalism.

Idris's journey is an embodiment of the symbiotic relationship apparent between a simple-social-local context, (acting as an unstable springboard within a murky much-larger regional field), that suddenly transforms and harmonises into the most sophisticated global structures on earth. This odyssey mirrors the stamina, compassion and tolerance that typify Kamil's life.

H.E. Mr Henri-Philippe Sambuc, Swiss International Business Lawyer (Switzerland)

During numerous professional discussions with Dr Kamil Idris, then Director General of the World Intellectual Property Organization, in his large and elegant office overlooking the quiet Geneva Lake, I did not know the story of his young years of hard work, determination and daily courage. For me, he was a brilliant intellectual, with top diplomatic talents and extensive multi-cultural know-how. This early perception is now complemented by the image of a child, son of the giant Nile River, metaphorically digging with a spade in the dry soil in the heat of silent Sudan to unearth as much knowledge of his beloved country as possible.

Dr Idris' book is a lesson in humility for all those who have forgotten how narrow is the path of life and powerful the human imagination and a tribute to those who follow their personal vision.

H.E. Dr Mohamed El Baradie, Former Director General of the International Atomic Energy Agency (IAEA), Nobel Prize Laurette (Egypt)

An inspiring memoir of a life journey enriched by different cultures and values. His experience exposed him to the intricacies of national and international politics. He rubbed shoulders with the simple folk and those in high places. A testament to the powerful bond of humanity that defies the fault lines of colour, religion and ethnicity and a worthy guide for those in pursuit of a world based on peace and human dignity.

H.E. Ambassador Brunson McKinley, former Director General, International Organisation for Migration (IOM) (USA)

From the banks of the Nile to the shores of Lake Geneva, Kamil Idris has accomplished a remarkable odyssey and has recorded his experiences in this fascinating and highly readable memoir, full of insights into human nature and international politics. I recommend it to all readers, especially those interested in how the globalised world really works and how it could work better in the future.

H.E. Dr Amre Mousa, Former Minister for Foreign Affairs and former Secretary General of the League of Arab States (LAS) (Egypt)

It is a success story, and a fascinating one indeed. I have had more than one occasion to hear or read about several stories of success in our community of nations in Africa and the Arab World. But Kamil Idris is unique. From working as a child labourer to sitting at the helm of one of the most important specialized agencies in the international multilateral system... From sitting on top of the train in the Sudanese desert on his way to Cairo to find work and pursue chances of education to running for the presidency of the Sudan... from a boy somewhat lost in the laborious life of the poor in a poor country to a young man determined to "make it"... to a well-educated and an accomplished gentleman.

When Kamil Idris discusses the formation of his outlook on life he underlines the influence of the River Nile. This influence, I myself have grown under the same influence, instills patience, perseverance and determination in addition to entrepreneurial spirit.

Throughout the book we read, not only on Kamil, but on the Sudan, this vast fascinating but underestimated country. He speaks about Africa and its young people who should find in Kamil an example to follow and should learn that achieving in life and full success, while not easy, is doable. I invite schools in Africa and the Arab world to make this book available to the young generation. It would certainly contribute to their positive formation.

I am one of those who recognize the true potential of Kamil Idris as a true son of Africa and as an example of healthy activism, effectiveness and the pursuit of excellence.

Professionalism is apparent in his style of work. When he refers to those world leaders with whom he had "in depth discussions" we find Bill Clinton and Saddam Hussein. We also find the Emperor of Japan and Robert Mugabe, quite a variety of persons, ideologies and ways of governance.

Nelson Mandela was right when he urged Kamil Idris to write his autobiography and it is my pleasure to write a commendation to this moving memoir.

H.E. Ambassador Dr Martin Ihoeghian Uhomoibhi, Joint Special Representative/ Joint Chief Mediator of the United Nations – Secretary General and African Union Chairperson, African Union – United Nations Hybrid Operation in Darfur, Sudan (Nigeria)

Odyssey on the Nile is the moving story of a daring African who clings tenaciously to the hope that world peace is achievable even in the face of daunting international pressures, the contradictions in politics, the controversies in cultures and the differences in religions. This well articulated book breathes new life into accepted history and is a welcome addition to the collected store of world philosophy. Odyssey on the Nile is a must read for those who believe and those who doubt that North, South, East or West, the world is one.

Judge Michele Weil, Former French Judge and Former Diplomat (France)

The moving, extraordinary story of a child of Africa, boosted by his roots, who travels the world, meets global leaders and becomes an open-minded man of peace and brotherhood among nations, his destiny driven throughout by the meaning of his name: "patient and capable of high office..."

Appendix 3

Curriculum Vitae

Prof. Dr (Mult.) Kamil E Idris CV

President
The International Court of Arbitration and Mediation (ICAM)

Former Director General
World Intellectual Property Organization (WIPO)

Former Secretary-General
International Union for the Protection of New Varieties of Plants (UPOV)

Former Member
United Nations International Law Commission (ILC)

Former President
World Arbitration and Mediation Court (WAMC)

Member
Permanent Court of Arbitration (PCA), The Hague

Professor of Law

Academic Distinctions
- Sudan School Certificate (Distinction)
- Bachelor of Arts, University of Cairo (Division I with Honours)
- LLB (Law), University of Khartoum (Honours)
- Diploma, Public Administration (Management Department), Institute of Public Administration, Khartoum (Top Division)

- Master in International Affairs, University of Ohio, USA (First Class Average)
- Doctorate (PhD) in International Law, Graduate Institute of International Studies, University of Geneva (Distinction)
- Doctorate Thesis: "Case study on the Treaty Establishing a Preferential Trade Area for Eastern and Southern African States

Academic Interests

Certificates
- International Economics, Graduate Institute of International Studies (Geneva)
- International History and Political Science, Graduate Institute of International Studies (Geneva)
- International Law of Development, Graduate Institute of International Studies (Geneva)
- The Law of International Waterways, Graduate Institute of International Studies (Geneva)
- International Law of Financing and Banking Systems, Graduate Institute of International Studies (Geneva)

Languages
- Arabic
- English
- French
- Spanish (good knowledge)

Teaching
- Lecturer in Philosophy and Jurisprudence, University of Cairo (1976-1977)
- Lecturer in Jurisprudence, Ohio University, USA (1978)
- External Examiner in International Law, Faculty of Law, University of Khartoum (1984)
- Lecturer in Intellectual Property Law, Faculty of Law, University of Khartoum (1986)
- Lecturer in several international, regional and national

seminars, workshops and symposia
- Member, International Association for the Advancement of Teaching and Research in Intellectual Property Law (ATRIP)

Decorations
- Awarded the Scholars and Researchers State Gold Medal, presented by the President of the Republic of the Sudan (1983)
- Awarded the Scholars and Researchers Gold Medal, presented by the President of the Academy of Scientific Research and Technology of Egypt (1985)
- Awarded the decoration of the Commandeur de l'Ordre national du Lion, Senegal (1998)
- Awarded the Medal of the Bolshoi Theatre, presented by the Director of the Bolshoi Theatre, Russian Federation (1999)
- Awarded the Honorary Medal, presented by the Rector of the Moscow State Institute of International Relations, Russian Federation (1999)
- Awarded the Honorary Medal of The Gulf Cooperation Council (GCC), Saudi Arabia (1999)
- Awarded the Golden Plaque of the Town of Banská Bystrica, presented by the Mayor of Banská Bystrica, Slovakia (1999)
- Awarded the Golden Medal of Matej Bel University, presented by the Dean of the University, Banská Bystrica, Slovakia (1999)
- Awarded the Silver Jubilee Medal of the Eurasian Patent Organization (EAPO), presented by Mr. Viktor Blinnikov, President of the Eurasian Patent Office, Russian Federation (2000)
- Award of Distinguished Merit, presented by the Egyptian Supreme Council for Science and Technology, Egypt (2000)
- Awarded a Plaque from the Syrian Inventors' Association, Syrian Arab Republic (2000)
- Awarded the Grand Cross of the Infante D. Enrique, Portugal (2001)
- Awarded a Medal from the People's Assembly of Egypt, Egypt (2001)

- Awarded a Medal from the Constitutional Court of Romania, Romania (2001)
- Awarded a Medal from the Parliament of Romania, Romania (2001)
- Awarded the Golden Medal Dolores del Río al Mérito internacional en favor de los derechos de los artistas intérpretes from the National Association of Interpreters (ANDI), Mexico (2001)
- Awarded the Golden Medal from The State Agency on Industrial Property Protection, Republic of Moldova (2001)
- Awarded the decoration of the Commandeur de l'Ordre du Mérite national, Côte d'Ivoire (2002)
- Awarded the Maria Sklodowska-Curie Medal from the Association of Polish Inventors and Rationalizers, Poland (2002)
- Awarded the decoration of The Order of the Two Niles, First Class, from the President of the Republic of Sudan, Sudan (2002)
- Kamil Idris Library, University of Juba, Sudan (2002)
- Kamil Idris Conference Hall, Intellectual Property Court, The Judiciary, Sudan (2002)
- Awarded the Dank Medal (medal of glory), from the President of the Kyrgyz Republic, Kyrgyzstan (2003)
- Award from the University of National and World Economy, Bulgaria (2003)
- "Venice Award for Intellectual Property", presented by the Mayor of Venice (2004)
- Awarded the Medal of Oman, presented by His Royal Highness Fahid Bin Mahmud Al-Said, Deputy Prime Minister of the Council of Ministers, Oman (2004)
- Awarded the decoration of the Aztec Eagle, presented by Ambassador Luis Alfonso de Alba (Permanent Representative of Mexico to International Organizations in Geneva) on behalf of Presidente of Mexico Vicente Fox, (2005)
- Kamil Idris Building, Regional Training Center, African Regional Intellectual Property Organization (ARIPO),

Harare, Zimbabwe (2006)

- Awarded a Medal commemorating the 60 years of the United Nations, Bulgaria (2006)
- Awarded a Medal commemorating the 60 years of the Independence of Jordan, Jordan (2006)
- Award of Distinguished Leadership presented by the International Publishers'Association (IPA) and the Arab Publishers Association, Egypt (2007)
- Awarded a Medal on the occasion of the Fujairah International Monodrama Festival, Fujairah,United Arab Emirates (2007)
- Awarded a Medal on the occasion of the Intellectual Property Day presented by The Regional Institute for Intellectual Property of the Faculty of Law, University of Helwan, Egypt (2008)
- Awarded The Distinguished Medal of Cultural Innovation, Sudan (2008)
- Awarded The Family Club Decoration, Sudan (2008)
- Awarded The World Intellectual Property Organization (WIPO) Medal, Geneva, Switzerland(2008)
- Awarded The International Union Of The Protection Of New Varieties Of Plants (UPOV)
- Medal, Geneva, Switzerland (2008)
- Awarded The Distinguished Medal Of The Sudanese Centre Of Intellectual Property, Khartoum, Sudan (2009)
- Awarded The Medal Of Kenana sugar Company, Khartoum , Sudan (2009)
- Awarded The Decoration Of Loyalty And Gratitude Of Omdurman National Broadcasting Station, Sudan (2010)
- Awarded The decoration (WISHAH) of the Syrian revolution (2013)
- Awarded The decoration (WISHAH) of Rashid Diab cultural center, Khartoum , Sudan (2013)
- Awarded The Medal of Distinction by the International Association of Muslim
- Lawyers (2014)

Honorary Degrees

- 1999 Honorary Professor of Law, Peking University, China
- 1999 Doctor Honoris Causa, The Doctor's Council of the State University of Moldova, Republic of Moldova
- 1999 Doctor Honoris Causa, Franklin Pierce Law Center (Concord, New Hampshire), United States of America
- 1999 Doctor Honoris Causa, Fudan University (Shanghai), China
- 2000 Doctor Honoris Causa, University of National and World Economy (Sofia), Bulgaria
- 2001 Doctor Honoris Causa, University of Bucharest, Romania
- 2001 Doctor Honoris Causa, Hannam University (Daejeon), Republic of Korea
- 2001 Doctor Honoris Causa, Mongolian University of Science and Technology (Ulaanbaatar), Mongolia
- 2001 Doctor Honoris Causa, Matej Bel University (Banská Bystrica), Slovakia
- 2002 Doctor Honoris Causa, National Technical University of Ukraine "Kyiv Polytechnic Institute" (Kyiv), Ukraine
- 2003 Doctor Honoris Causa, Al Eman Al Mahdi University (White Nile State), Sudan
- 2005 Degree of Doctor of Letters (Honoris Causa), Indira Gandhi National Open University (IGNOU), India
- 2005 Doctor Honoris Causa, Latvian Academy of Sciences, Latvia
- 2006 Doctor Honoris Causa, University of Azerbaijan, Azerbaijan
- 2007 Doctor Honoris Causa, University of Al-Gezira, Sudan
- 2007 Doctor of International Law and Honorary Professor, Belarussian State University, Belarus
- 2007 Doctor Honoris Causa, University of Khartoum, Sudan
- 2007 Doctor Honoris Causa, Ss. Cyril and Methodius University (Skopje), The Former Yugoslav Republic of Macedonia
- 2008 Doctor Honoris Causa, Kyrgyz State University

of Construction, Transport and Architecture (Bishkek),
Kyrgystan
- 2008 Certificate of Appreciation, Ahlia University,
Khartoum, Sudan

Experience

Professional
- Part-time Journalist, El-Ayam and El-Sahafa (Sudanese)
newspapers (1971-1979)
- Lecturer, University of Cairo (1976)
- Assistant Director, Arab Department, Ministry of Foreign
Affairs, Khartoum (1977)
- Assistant Director, Research Department, Ministry of
Foreign Affairs, Khartoum (January-June 1978)
- Deputy Director, Legal Department, Ministry of Foreign
Affairs, Khartoum (July-December 1978)
- Member of Sudan Permanent Mission to the United Nations
Office, Geneva (1979-1982)
- Vice-Consul of Sudan in Switzerland (1979-1982)
- Legal Adviser of Sudan Permanent Mission to the United
Nations Office, Geneva (1979-1982)
- Senior Program Officer, Development Cooperation and
External Relations Bureau for Africa, World Intellectual
Property Organization (WIPO), (1982-1985)
- Director, Development Cooperation and External Relations
Bureau for Arab and Central and Eastern European
Countries, WIPO (1985-1994)
- Ambassador, Ministry of Foreign Affairs, Sudan (current
status at national level)
- Deputy Director General, WIPO (1994-1997)
- Director General, WIPO, since 1997
- Secretary-General, International Union for the Protection of
Plant Varieties (UPOV), since 1997

Special

- Member of The Academic Council, University of Khartoum (Sudan, April 2007)
- Member, Board of Trustees, Nile Valley University (Egypt, June 2000)
- Member, United Nations International Law Commission (ILC) (2000-2001)
- Member, Advisory Council on Intellectual Property (ACIP), Franklin Pierce Law Center (Concord, New Hampshire, 1999)
- Member, United Nations International Law Commission (ILC) (1992-1996)
- Vice-Chairman of the International Law Commission (ILC) at its 45th session (1993)
- Representative of the ILC in the 35th session of the Asian-African Legal Consultative Committee (AALCC) (Manila, March 1996)
- Member, Working Group of the ILC on the drafting of the Statute of the International Criminal Court
- Member, Drafting Committee of the ILC
- Legal expert in a number of Ministerial Committees between Sudan and other countries
- Member of the Legal Experts Committee of the Organization of African Unity (OAU), which formulated several regional conventions
- Legal adviser in the Ministerial Councils and the Summit Conferences of the OAU (Khartoum, July 1978) (Monrovia, July 1979)
- Participant in several meetings and international conferences of WHO, ILO, ITU, WIPO, Red Cross and the Executive Committee of the High Commissioner for Refugees
- Member of Special Committees established for fundraising for refugees in Africa
- Rapporteur of the Third Committee (Marine Scientific Research) of the summary Ninth session of the Third UN Conference on the Law of the Sea (Geneva, 1980)

- Head of Sudan Delegation to the OAU Preparatory Meeting on the Draft Code of Conduct on Transfer of Technology (Addis Ababa, March 1981)
- Spokesman of the African Group and the Group of 77 on all issues pertaining to Transfer of Technology, Energy, Restrictive Business Practices and Technical Co-operation among Developing Countries at the twenty-second and twenty-third sessions of the Trade and Development Board (Geneva, February and September 1981
- Head of Sudan Delegation and Spokesman of the African Group and Coordinator of the Group of 77 at the fourth session of the UN Conference on the Code of Conduct on Transfer of Technology (Geneva, March-April 1981)
- Spokesman of the Group of 77 on Chapter 9 (Applicable Law and Settlement of Disputes) at the UN Conference on the International Code of Conduct on Transfer of Technology (Geneva, March-April 1981)
- Head of Sudan Delegation and Chairman of the Workshop on Legal Policies on Technology Transfer (Kuwait, September 1981)
- Chairman of the African Group and the Group of 77 at the first session of the Intergovernmental Group of Experts on Restrictive Business Practices (Geneva, November 1981)
- Chairman of the Permanent Group of 15 on Transfer and Development of Technology, within the United Nations Conference on Trade and Development (UNCTAD) (Geneva, 1980-1983)
- Spokesman of the African Group and the Group of 77 at the meeting on the Economic, Commercial and Developmental Aspects of the Industrial Property System (Geneva, February 1982)
- Coordinator of the African Group and the Group of 77 at the first, second and third sessions of the Interim Committee on the International Code of Conduct on Transfer of Technology (Geneva, March, May, September-October 1982)
- Coordinator of the African Group and the Group of 77

at the Meeting of Governmental Experts on the Transfer, Application and Development of Technology in the Capital Goods and Industrial Machinery Sectors (Geneva, July 1982)

- Coordinator and spokesman of the African Group and the Group of 77 at the Intergovernmental Group of Experts on the Feasibility of Measuring Human Resource Flows on Reverse Transfer of Technology (Brain-Drain) (Geneva, August-September 1982)
- Coordinator of developing countries on the drafting of the resolution concerning the mandate of the Office of the United Nations High Commissioner for Refugees, during the thirty-third session of the Executive Committee of the UNHCR (Geneva, October 1982)
- Coordinator and spokesman of the African Group and the Group of 77 at the Meeting of Governmental Experts on the Transfer, Application and Development of Technology in the Energy Sector (Geneva, October-November 1982)
- Coordinator and spokesman of the African Group and the Group of 77 at the fourth session of the Committee on Transfer of Technology (Geneva, November-December 1982)
- Member, Board of Patrons, IP Management Resource (On-line version of Intellectual Property/Innovation Management Handbook), 2007
- Co-President, Foreign Relations Committee, Ministry of Culture (Sudan, 2011)
- President, Sudan Foundation for the defense of Syrian people (2012-2013)
- Vice-President, Sudan Foundation for the defense of Rights and Freedom s (2012-2013)
- Member, Sudan Foundation for Reconciliation and Religious co-existence (2012-2013)
- Judicial Experience and Professional Membership of Associations
- Member of the United Nations International Law Commission (ILC) (1992-1996) and (2000-2001)
- Member and Chairman of several legal experts committees

established within the OAU
- Professor of Public International Law, University of Khartoum, Sudan
- Member of the Sudan Bar Association (Khartoum)
- Member of the African Jurists Association (Dakar and Paris)
- Alternate Chair, Council of Foreign Relations, Ministry of Culture, Sudan
- Registered Advocate and Commissioner for Oaths in the Republic of Sudan
- Vice President, Sudan Organisation for the Protection of Fundamental Rights and Freedoms
- Member, Sudan High Level Committee on Judicial Reform

Projects and Documents
- Formulated and negotiated, on behalf of WIPO, numerous projects relating to development cooperation in the field of intellectual property
- Organized, on behalf of WIPO, various seminars and workshops and presented several lectures
- Drafted various documents on developmental aspects of intellectual property
- Supervised and managed the administrative and substantive aspects of projects executed worldwide

Conferences, Seminars, Courses and Symposia
- Represented Sudan in numerous international and regional conferences; participated in many seminars, symposia, discussion groups, and addressed graduate students on various international academic disciplines
- Represented WIPO, in various international meetings, seminars and symposia
- Represented WIPO on several UNDP Policy and Operations Programmes
- Undertook a study tour at the Max Planck Institute (Munich) in the field of teaching of intellectual property law (1986)

Publications

- Euro-Arab Dialogue, June 1977
- State Responsibility in International Law, September 1977
- The Theory of Human Action, September 1977
- The Philosophy of "Haddith" and "Sunna" in Islamic Law, January 1978
- The Doctrine of Jurisdiction in International Law, December 1978
- American Embassy in Tehran Case, March 1979
- The Legal Regime of the Nile, December 1980
- Issues pertaining to Transfer and Development of Technology in Sudan, May 1981
- China and the Powers in the 19th Century, May 1981
- Legal Dimensions of the Economic Cooperation among Developing Countries, June 1981
- The Common Fund for Commodities, June 1981
- General Aspects of Transfer of Technology at the National and International Levels, November 1981
- Preferential Trading Arrangements among Developing Countries, February 1982
- North-South Insurance Relations: The Unequal Exchange, December 1984
- The Law of Non-Navigational Uses of International Water Courses; the International Law Commission's draft articles: An overview, November 1995
- The Theory of Source and Target in Child Psychology, January 1996
- A Better United Nations for the New Millennium, January 2000
- Intellectual Property – A Power Tool for Economic Growth, 2003
- Sudan, The Year 2020: Lessons and Visions, 2004
- The Intellectual Property-Conscious Nations: Mapping the Path from Developing to Developed, 2006
- Sudan 2020, (2008)
- Sudan: From Least-Developed to Fast Developing, 2008

- Arbitration: A Vision for the Enforcement of Justice, 2009
- Arbitration: Critical Review Of Sudan Legislation On Arbitration, 2009
- Sudan 2025: The Correction of the Path and the Dream of the Future, 2015
- Seven Deaths on the Nile, 2015
- Sudan's Path to the Future: A realistic dream for 2025, 2016
- JASTA, 2017
- My Nile Odyssey, 2017

Articles
- A number of articles on law, economics, jurisprudence and aesthetics published in various newspapers and periodicals
- Russia's Invasion of Crimea: Is it a violation of International Law? Two mistakes will not make a right. Article published by The Hague Center for Law and Arbitration (HCLA) April, 2014
- Law Reform in Sudan: March, 2015

Appendix 4

Record of Achievements

World Intellectual Property Organization

- Strategic Program and Budget for the 1998-99 biennium (and the vision for WIPO) and its unanimous approval by the member-states.
- The Budget and Premises Committees approved the proposals of the International Bureau and authorized the financing from the Special Reserve Fund and purchase of the Steiner lot for additional premises.
- Establishment of the senior management structure, including the Senior Management Team (SMT), Policy Development Group (PDG), Policy Implementation Meetings (PIM) (discontinued) and Policy Oversight Committees (POC). Establishment of the Professional Information Meetings (PRIM) each Tuesday morning.
- Reorganization and transformation of the Secretariat of the International Bureau, including new concepts such as staff development, gender issues, the Office of Strategic Planning and Policy Development, the Office of Global Communications and Public Diplomacy, improved press relations, visitors' center, the WIPO Worldwide Academy and distance education, Least-Developed Countries Unit, etc.
- Improvement of WIPO's corporate image, including demystification of intellectual property and the creation of a new WIPO logo.
- Observance of the World Intellectual Property Day on April 26, the day on which the WIPO Convention came into force (as of April 26, 2001).

- Human Resources Management Division and Staff Development.
- Geographical distribution of posts.
- Progressive development of international law and codification of law.
- Assistance in meeting obligations under the Agreement on Trade-Related Aspects of Intellectual Property Rights (TRIPS).
- Nationally Focused Action Plans (NFAPs).
- Indigenous populations and traditional knowledge, including the creation of a WIPO Intergovernmental Committee, which will deal with the intellectual property aspects of access to genetic resources and benefit-sharing, traditional knowledge and expressions of folklore.
- Decision by the General Assembly to widen the use of the Portuguese language, particularly in cooperation for development activities for Portuguese-speaking developing and least developed countries.
- Reorientation of the main WIPO treaties: PCT and Madrid Agreement.
- The launch of a process of fundamental reforms of the PCT through the setting up of a special body of PCT member-states to consider proposals which will lead, in the first instance, to further simplification of PCT procedures, taking into account the provisions of the Patent Law Treaty.
- Relations with non-governmental organisations.
- WIPO Arbitration and Mediation Center and Internet domain name dispute-resolution services.
- Computerization projects: WIPOnet, PCT Impact project.
- Collection of Laws for Electronic Archive (CLEA).
- Establishment of WIPO's web page in English, Arabic, French and Spanish, and of the WIPO electronic bookshop.
- Offering of personal computers and work stations to Permanent Missions of developing countries in Geneva.
- Establishment of the Policy Advisory Commission (PAC) and Industry Advisory Commission (IAC).

- The adoption by the Policy Advisory Commission of the World Intellectual Property Declaration.
- Establishment of the Advisory Panel on Privatization.
- Constitutional reform initiative.
- Diplomatic Conference for the Adoption of a New Act of The Hague Agreement concerning the International Deposit of Industrial Designs (June 16 to July 6, 1999).
- International Conference on Electronic Commerce and Intellectual Property (September 14 to 16, 1999).
- Diplomatic Conference for the Adoption of the Patent Law Treaty (PLT) (May 11 to June 2, 2000).
- Diplomatic Conference on the Protection of Audiovisual Performances (December 2000).
- Program Implementation Overview and Program Performance (Internal Audit and Oversight Division).
- The establishment of a special program of work aimed at helping small and medium-sized enterprises worldwide to realize the benefits of intellectual property in enhancing their competitive edge and business performance (SMEs' Division).
- Improvements to working conditions, such as part-time work, improvements in the Staff Rules pertaining to annual leave, salary adjustments, medical insurance, sick leave and travel and removal expenses (regularized practices existing within the United Nations common system).
- Decision by the General Assembly to declare as WIPO holidays the two days of Islamic feasts, Id al-Fitr and Id al-Adha.
- Renovation on the former WMO building.

Appendix 5

Official Missions as Director General

1997

- Visit to Japan (with Messrs Gurry, Suedi and Yu), November 3 and 4
- Visit to Sudan, December 26 to 30

1998

- Visit to France (with Messrs Gurry, Bilger, Ntchatcho and Mrs Rog), February 24
- Visit to the United States of America (with Messrs Gurry, Suedi, Owens and Wilder), March 1 to 7
- Visit to Germany (with Messrs Bæumer and Bilger), April 1
- Mission to Lebanon (WIPO Arab Regional Conference on Intellectual Property, Beirut) (with Messrs Saadallah, Starein and Tabbaa), April 21 and 22
- Visit to Senegal (with Messrs Suedi, Thiam, Osman and Fall), April 27 and 28
- Commandeur, Ordre National du Lion INTA Meeting, Boston (with Messrs Bæumer, Machado and Tramposch), May 13
- Mission to Brazil (AIPPI Congress in Rio de Janeiro) and visit to Brasilia (with Messrs Curchod, Castelo, Bæumer, Rubio, Suedi and Tramposch), May 23 to 26
- ARIPO Ministerial Council Meeting, Mombasa, Kenya (with Messrs Suedi, Thiam and Osman), May 28 and 29
- Visit to Tunisia (with Messrs Saadallah, Osman and Mrs Daboussi), June 8 and 9
- Visit to Morocco (with Messrs Saadallah, Osman and Mrs

Daboussi), July 13 and 14, 1998
- Visit to Sudan, July 18 to 21
- Visit to Italy (with Mr Castelo, Mrs Graffigna, Mr Pautasso and Mrs Toso-Dunant), September 24 and 25
- Visit to Finland (with Mrs Jimenez), September 29 and 30
- Visit to Canada and OECD Meeting, Ottawa (with Mr Gurry), October 7 to 9
- Visit to Jordan (with Mr Suedi, Mrs Haidar and Mr Osman), October 11 and 12
- ACC Meeting, New York (with Mr Suedi, Mrs Haidar and Mr Osman), October 29 to 31
- Visit to Tunisia, November 16
- Visit to Argentina (with Mr Rubio and Mr Osman), November 24 and 25
- Visit to the Islamic Republic of Iran (with Messrs Sabharwal, Suedi, Mrs Haider and Mr Moayedoddin), December 12

1999

- Visit to EPO, Munich (with Messrs Curchod and Castelo), January 21
- Visit to China (with Messrs Castelo, Sabharwal, Suedi, Eckstein, Gal Lulin, Ms Wang and Ms Shamoon), January 26 to 28, (honorary doctorate)
- Visit to India (with Messrs Castelo, Sabharwal, Wilder, Jaiya, Miss Wang and Mrs Schrott), February 8 and 9
- Visit to the Russian Federation (with Messrs Eckstein, Osman, Khlestov, Khabirov and Ms Shamoon), February 24 and 25, (Honorary Medal, Moscow Institute of International Relations), (Medal, Bolshoi Theatre)
- Visit to Slovakia (with Mr Uemura, Ms Wang and Ms Schilling)
- March 8 and 9, (Golden Medal, Univ. of Matej Beli), (Golden Plaque, Banská Bystrica)
- Visit to Japan (with Messrs Uemura, Suedi and Mrs Sagiati), March 15

- PhRMA Meeting (Florida) (with Messrs Suedi and Wilder), March 24
- Visit to Austria (Centenary of Office) (with Messrs Curchod, Machado and Suedi), April 22
- Visit to the Republic of Moldova (with Messrs Uemura, Suedi, Ms Wang and Mr Zotine), April 23, (honorary doctorate)
- Franklin Pierce Law Center (with Messrs Suedi, Sinjela, Fasehun, Gra a Aranha, Osman and Sankurathripati), May 15, (honorary doctorate)
- Visit to Norway (with Messrs Curchod, Castelo, Arneberg and Mrs Kippelen), May 19
- Visit to OHIM, Alicante (with Messrs Curchod, Machado and Osman), June 10
- Visit to Zimbabwe (with Messrs Castelo, Suedi, Onyeema and Sery-Kor), June 21 and 22
- Visit to the Center for Strategic Studies, and visit to the Ministries of Culture and Justice, Khartoum, Sudan June 30 to July 2
- Visit to Jordan (PAC) (with Messrs Saadallah, Osman, Mrs Sagiati, Mr Tabbaa and Mr Neale), July 19 and 20
- Visit to Japan (with Messrs Uemura, Takagi, Eckstein, Ms Wang and Ms Tabuchi), July 22 and 23
- Visit to Tunisia, Festival International de Carthage (with Mrs Daboussi), July 31 and August 1
- Visit to Bulgaria (with Messrs Uemura, Ms Wang and Mr Yossifov), October 6
- Visit to China (Shanghai, Kunming and Beijing) (with Mr Suedi and Ms Wang), October 11-13, (honorary doctorate, Fudan University, Shanghai)
- ACC Meeting, New York (with Mr Suedi), October 29
- Visit to Japan (with Messrs Curchod, Uemura and Suedi), November 16
- Visit to Denmark (with Mr Blomqvist and Ms Wang), November 23
- Visit to Israel (with Messrs Suedi, Eckstein, Mrs Sagiati, Mrs

Schwab and Ms Goren), November 30
- WTO Ministerial Meeting, Seattle, United States of America (with Mr Suedi), December 1
- Organisation of the Islamic Conference, Jeddah (with Messrs Suedi and Thiam), December 10
- Visit to China (return of Macao to China) (with Mr Suedi, Ms Wang and Mr Osman), December 19 and 20

2000

- Visit to Sudan (Ana-Alsudan), January 3
- Visit to EPO, Munich (with Messrs Curchod and Castelo), February 7
- Visit to Sweden (with Messrs Takagi, Blomqvist and Eckstein),
- February 9
- UNCTAD Meeting, Bangkok, Thailand (with Messrs Castelo, Suedi, Wilder, Shenkoru and Osman), February 12
- Visit to Oman (with Messrs Suedi, Saadallah and Tabbaa), February 16
- Visit to Washington, D.C. (WIPO Committee, USPTO and PAC, with Mr Suedi, Mrs Jimenez, Messrs Wilder, Osman, Salmon and Neele), February 29 and March 1
- Visit to Mexico (with Mr Rubio, Mrs Jimenez, Mrs Rog Messrs Osman and Toledo), March 2
- Visit to Australia (with Messrs Gurry, Sabharwal and Suedi), March 6 and 7
- Visit to Uzbekistan (with Messrs Suedi, Eckstein, Ms Wang and Mr Khabirov), May 17 and 18
- Visit to Cuba (with Messrs Rubio, Suedi, Mrs Jimenez, Messrs Roca Campana and Osman), June 6
- Visit to Costa Rica (with Messrs Rubio, Suedi, Mrs Jimenez and Messrs Roca Campana and Alvarez), June 7
- Visit to Bulgaria, University of National and World Economy (with Mrs Rog, Messrs Yossifov and Bensid), July 4 and 6, (honorary doctorate)

- Visit to Egypt (with Mrs Heider, Mr Saadallah and Ms Zahran), July 15 and 16
- Visit to Tunisia, Festival International de Carthage (with Mr Osman and Mrs Daboussi), July 23 and 24
- Visit to Sudan, United Nations Association for Sudan, August 20
- Visit to China (with Messrs Suedi, Eckstein and Ms Wang), October 10 and 11
- Visit to the Eurasian Patent Office, Moscow (with Messrs Suedi, Khabirov, Khlestov, Osman and Oushakov), October 12
- ACC Meeting, New York (with Mr Suedi), October 27
- Visit to Nigeria (with Messrs Suedi, Onyeema, Fasehun and Ms Odibo), November 15
- Visit to the European Commission, Brussels (with Mr Takagi and Mrs Rog), November 23

2001

- Lecture at the United Nations Association of the Sudan, Khartoum, and visit to government, January 3 and 4
- Visit to Spain (with Messrs Castelo, Blanch, Carrasco and Osman),
- January 30
- Visit to Portugal (with Messrs Castelo, Carvalho, Osman and Bensid), January 31
- WIPO High-Level Interregional Round Table on Intellectual Property for the Least Developed Countries, Lisbon, Portugal (with Messrs Castelo, Osman, Shenkoru and Bansid), February 1
- Milan (Italy) Forum on SMEs (with Mr Castelo,Mrs Graffigna, Messrs Starein, Osman, Ms Nanayakkara and Ms Shamoon), February 9
- Visit to EPO, Munich (with Messrs Curchod and Castelo), February 13
- Visit to Kyrgyzstan (with Messrs Suedi, Khlestov, Osman,

Ms Shamoon and Mrs Tlevlessova), February 21
- Visit to Kazakhstan (with Messrs Suedi, Khlestov, Osman, Ms Shamoon and Tlevlessova), February 22
- ACC in Nairobi, Kenya (with Messrs Suedi, Fasehun and Neele), April 2 and 3
- PAC Task Force Meeting, New York(with Messrs Suedi, Takagi, Neele and Osman), May 3
- Visit to Bulgaria (Conference with President Stoyanov) (with Messrs Suedi, Eckstein and Yossifov), May 29
- Visit to Romania (with Mr Eckstein, Ms Wang and Mr Khlestov), June 6 and 7, (honorary doctorate)
- Visit to South Africa (with Messrs Suedi and Onyeema), June 20 and 21
- Mission to Sudan, consultations, July 6
- OAU Summit Meeting, Lusaka, Zambia (with Messrs Suedi, Onyeema and Bensid), July 9
- Visit to ARIPO, Harare, Zimbabwe, July 10 to 13
- Visit to the Republic of Korea (with Mr Suedi and Ms Wang), November 19, (honorary doctorate)
- Visit to Mongolia (with Mr Suedi, Ms Wang and Mrs Paguio), November 20, (honorary doctorate)
- Visit to Slovakia (with Mr Bobrovszky, Ms Wang and Mr Khlestov), December 4 and 5, (honorary doctorate)
- Visit to Organisation of Islamic Conference and Islamic Development Bank, Jeddah (with Mr Thiam), December 13 and 14
- Visit to Sudan, December 17 and 18

2002

- Muscat Forum, Oman (with Messrs Suedi, Saadallah and Ms Zahran), January 21 and 22
- Visit to Mauritania (with Messrs Suedi, Sery, Mrs Daboussi, Messrs Osman and Bensid), January 29 and 30
- Visit to Jamaica (with Messrs Rubio, Roca Campana and Osman), March 11 and 12

- Visit to Côte d'Ivoire (with Messrs Suedi, Sery-Kor and Thiam), April 7 and 8
- ACC Meeting, Rome (with Messrs Suedi and Neele), April 10 and 11
- Sino-African Forum, and PAC Task Force Meeting, Beijing (with Mr Castelo, Mrs Hayes, Messrs Suedi, Takagi, Ms Wang, Mr Neele, Ms Goren, Mrs Nessi), May 20 to 24
- Visit to Ukraine (with Mr Petit, Ms Wang, Messrs Khlestov and Osman), May 28 and 29, (honorary doctorate)
- Visit to Germany (with Messrs Takagi and Schmidt-Dwertmann), June 19
- Visit to Sudan, July 31 to August 4
- Visit to Tunisia, Festival International de Carthage (with Mr Suedi and Mrs Daboussi), August 17
- Visit to the Organisation of the Islamic Conference, Jeddah (with Messrs Suedi and Thiam), November 27 to 30
- Visit to Sudan, December 13 to 18

2003

- Visit to Belarus (with Mr Suedi, Ms Wang and Mr Khlestov), June 10 and 11
- Visit to Sudan, July 31 to August 8
- Visit to Bulgaria (with Messrs Suedi and Yossifov), October 12 and 13
- Visit to Egypt and Sudan, October 27 to 31
- Visit to Romania and PAC Meeting, Bucharest (with Mrs Hayes, Messrs Suedi, Takagi, Ms Wang, Messrs Eckstein, Oushakov, Rai, Neele and Mrs Nessi), November 13 and 14
- Ministerial Meeting, Antigua and Barbuda (with Messrs Suedi and Roca Campana), November 27
- Mission to Sudan, December, (honorary doctorate)

2004

- Visit of or to EPO, Munich (with Mr Gurry), March 9
- International Venice Award for Intellectual Property and the International Design Conference (with Mr Rubio, Mrs Graffigna, Mr Gra a Aranha and Ms Shamoon), May 12 and 13
- JIII Centenary Celebration, Tokyo (with Mr Takagi and Mr Uemura), May 25 and 26
- Mission to Sudan August 3 and 4
- Mission to Oman (with Mr Saadallah) September 25

2005

- Casablanca, Morocco: Informal Consultation Meeting concerning Future Sessions of the Standing Committee on the Law of Patents (Messrs Gurry, Yu, Saadallah and Bæchtold), February 16
- Visit to India (with Mr Rai) Indira Gandhi National Open University March 5, 2005, (honorary doctorate)
- Visit to Latvia (with Messrs Petit, Yossifov, and Svantner), April 6 and 7, (honorary doctorate)
- Visit to Colombia (with Messrs Roca Campana, Alem and Mrs Weil-Guthmann), November 7 and 8
- Visit to Sudan: Ministerial Session of the Forum on Intellectual Property: A Power Tool for Economic Growth (with Messrs Shenkoru and Yassin), November 30
- Visit to Sudan: Visit to government and opening session of Symposium for Engineering and Computer Science (Association for the Promotion of Scientific Innovation), December 17 to 20

2006

- Visit to ARIPO and Zimbabwe (with Messrs Takagi, Onyeema, Sinjela, Syed, Mrs Chikowore), February 15

- Celebration marking the 50th anniversary of the Sudan Judiciary, Khartoum, February 21
- Visit to Azerbaijan (with Mrs Weil-Guthmann, Messrs Yossifov and Zotine), March 3, (honorary doctorate)
- Visit to Singapore (plus Diplomatic Conference TLT), (with Messrs Yu, Rubio, Saadallah, Ms Wang), March 13 and 14
- Visit to Republic of Korea (with Messrs Yu, Saadallah Abeysekera), March 15 and 16
- Mission to Sudan, March 24 to 26
- Mission to Portugal (Conference of Ministers of Portuguese-speaking Countries) (with Mr Yu), April 28
- Mission to Madrid (inauguration of new Spanish Patent and Trademark Office) (with Mr Carrasco), September 7
- Mission to Sudan, December 23 and 24

2007

- Visit to Egypt (with Mr Saadallah, Mrs Haider, Mr Abdelaziz and Ms Zahran), January 26 to 28
- Visit to Belarus (with Mr Khlestov), January 31 and February 1
- Visit to Sudan – Gezira University, April 2 and 3, (honorary doctorate)
- Visit to Sudan – University of Khartoum, April 28 (honorary doctorate)

Appendix 6

Marriage Documents

Written letter to my prospective father-in-law dated 21st January 1986, requesting permission to marry his daughter Azza.

The following page shows his reply dated 15th February 1986 (about three weeks later) granting his agreement.

Following this is the official wedding invitation, Monday 5th May 1986.

بسم الله الرحمن الرحيم

جنيف ۸٦/۱/۲۱

أخى العزيز حمى الدين ..

السلام عليكم ورحمة الله تعالى وبركاته - والشكر كل الشكر على
ما وجدناه منكم من ترحاب، وعلى أنباء توافدى بالسودان فى
ديسمبر الماضى .. جزاكم الله عنّا خير الجزاء ..

أود - عبر هذه الرسالة المقتضبة - أن أؤكد ما تمّ
صد بقنا الوفق عبد المنعم - وناقشتم فيه يوم الأثنين عبدالله
حول ذلك الأمر الخير .. والذى استخرت فيه الله كروبلة.
وأنا إذ أقدم على ذلك ، فإنّى أعبّر عن تشوقى لوركم
وتقديرى لإنقانكم .. وأدرك جيدا أصالة العلاقة
وحمظرى المعرفة وصفاء المعشر ..

وكما ذكرت لك عبر الهاتف يوم الأربعاء ۱۹۸٦/۲/۱۲ ، فإنى
أستبجلك عذرا لعدم تمكّن من الحديث حول حول الأمر لأهمّية
وجودى بالبيت ، ولعلك أدرى و أدرك بملابسات وأقام
تلك الأيام .. لكل شىء موعد وللدموع يمشينة.
أقول قولى هذا ، وأنقل لكم الشكر والعرفان لحسن
استجابتكم ونبل مشاعركم ، وأسأل الله لى ولكم العفو
والعافية فى الدين والدنيا والآخرة ·

آمل أن يحضر السودان فى الأشهر القليلة القادمة،
فقطا للحديث معك معهمود والتشاور فى ما بئس من أيام.
مطلق لجياس وميارك أصهيات وسلام لمؤسسة القربينة
وجميع الأهل · ولتبقى كلمة الله هى .. من أخيك حامد

347

بسم الله الرحمن الرحيم

المحترم من ١٠/٥
٨٦

السيد الفاضل والاخ الكريم كامل

لك التحية والشكر أجزله للتقه الكبيره
التي خصصتنا بها أبنتي وثمرة جهادي وزهرة
حياتي عزه . بارك الله لك في أختيار
أولاً . وبارك لك في مستقبل أبايتك
والله أسأل أن تكون لك صيماً لهذك
أبراً . أعرف أنك استمرت الله في أمرك
فالخير دائماً فيما يختاره الله . ويقين أن
هذا الامر سهّل . والا لما كان رفضها
ومجاراة كل من تقدم لها . كانت دائماً أنظر
اليها بنظرة من الاستغراب . وهي ترفض
كل من يتقدم لطلب يدها . وكانت تعرف أكثر
استغراباً هذه المرة . لندما قبلة
وبعض الرجله . شكراً لك فقد
أكرمن لندما أختارك أنة لها . من أكبر
بنات وأبناء خصصناها بكل حبنا وحنانها
من صغات نعيشها فنشأت . والله . وارادة
الله . وهذه آية . ٩ - أن تفقد . والدتها تعرض
ذلك كثيراً . وجزمت من أجلها . ولكنها يقين
أن الله ما أخذ الا ليعطي رضي بك أنت
وأنت ما سنة تحققان كل أمل من حياتها
فيد أهلك إلا من . أبارك ما خلفه الله

في الأزل نأمة بيتك ويبنة سريرك
ينعم من يصاهر وما لمزه ولامل الا
ثمر فيه لتنجب هذه الأسره التي
نتمنى برزقها وتماسكة وسيقيمة من
أصلك أبائنا واجدادنا الطيبه وطاح حيه
وبرزك وه سيم
                    والى لقاء
محي الدين

349

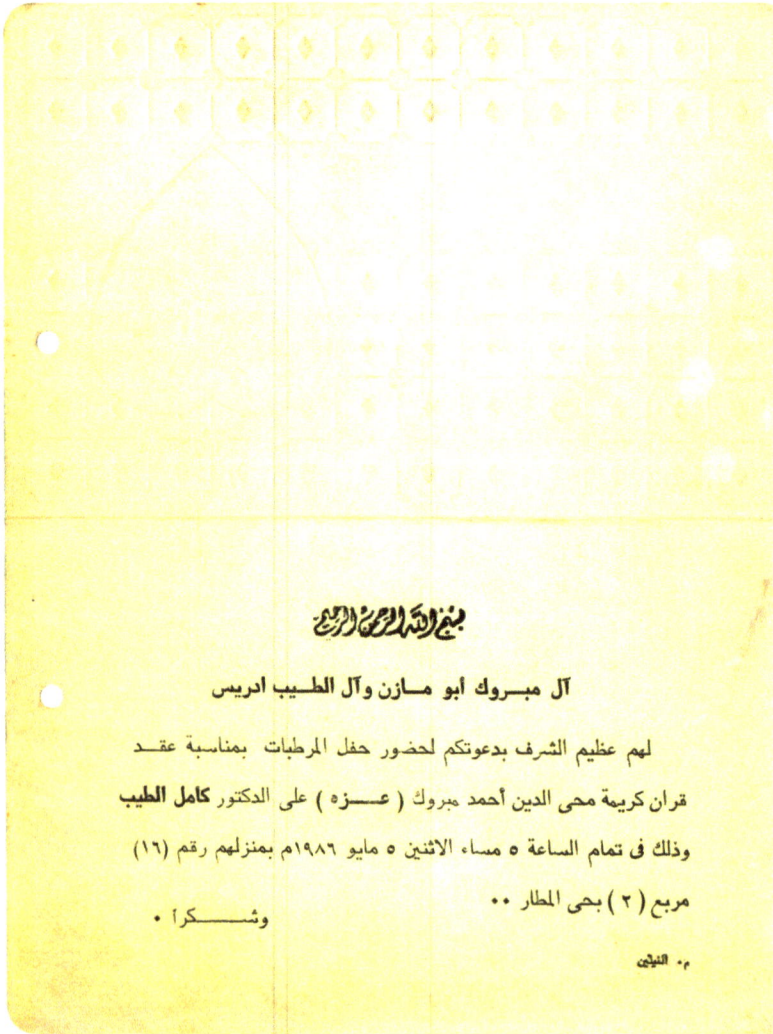

بسم الله الرحمن الرحيم

آل مبـروك أبو مـازن وآل الطـيب ادريس

لهم عظيم الشرف بدعوتكم لحضور حفل المرطبات بمناسبة عقـد

قران كريمة محى الدين أحمد مبروك (عــزه) على الدكتور كامل الطيب

وذلك فى تمام الساعة ٥ مساء الاثنين ٥ مايو ١٩٨٦م بمنزلهم رقم (١٦)

مربع (٢) بحى المطار ٠٠

وشـــكرا ٠

م. النيلين

Our marriage cocktail invitation, on Monday 5th May 1986, at 5pm.
Address: House no. 16, Square no. 2, Airport District

Appendix 7

List of Thanks

My biography would be incomplete if I failed to thank the many colleagues and friends who worked with me in the United Nations, in particular when I was leader of WIPO and UPOV and one of the leaders of the UN International Law Commission. Naturally, it is not possible to mention the thousands of men and women who cooperated closely with me. My apologies for any oversights.

I cherish the memories of meetings with high ranking dignitaries and the subsequent friendships cemented.

I would also like to pay special tribute to the following senior members of my extended family. I am indebted to them for their wisdom, patience, generosity and devotion to us all. They are:

Mohy-Eldeen Ahmed Mabrouk
Hassanain Ahmed Mabrouk
Sharaf-Eldeen Ahmed Idris
Farid Eltayeb Idris
Izzeldeen Osman Ahmed

and:

Suad Ahmed Mabrouk
Amal Khalil Hassanain
Samira Eltayeb Idris
Sumia Mohamed Mabrouk

DIGNITARIES AND STATESPEOPLE:

A.N.R. Robinson
A.P.J. Abdulkalam
Abdelbaki Hermassi
Abdelrahman Elkhalifa
Abdelrahman Shalgam
Abdelrahman Suwar Eldahab
Abdelsalam Eltiraiki
Abderrahmane Youssoufi
Abdou Diouf
Abdul G. Koroma
Abdul Rahman ibn Hamad al-Attiyah
Abel Alier
Abu-Bakr Osman Mohamed Salih
Achi Atsain
Adil Hamid
Ahmed Abdelhalim
Ahmed Elmahdi
Ahmed Elmirghani
Ahmed Mohamed Ali
Alain Pellet
Alberto Szekely
Alexander Korchagin
Alexander Lukashenko
Ali Elmadih
Ali Mahmoud Hassanain
Ali Osman Taha
Amara Essy
Amin Mekhi Medani
Amir Bhatti
Amre Moussa
Andreas J. Jacovides
Ann Veneman
Antonio Guterres
Anwar Alsadat
Ashok Soota
Askar Akayev
Assim Atta
Awn S. Ai-Khasawneh
Babikir Elnoor
Baha-eldeen Mohamed Idris
Bakri Hassan Salih
Benazir Bhutto
Benjamin Mkapa
Beshir Elbakri
Bill Clinton
Bola Adesumbo Ajibola
Bona Malwal
Boutros Ghali
Bruno Simma
Brunson Mckinley
C. John R. Dugard
Carlos Moniem
Carlos Roberto Liboni
Celso Amorim
Celso Lafer
Chieh Liu
Chusei Yamada
Clare Short
Dafalla Elhaj Youssif
Daniel Bernard
Derek William Bowett
Doudou Thiami
Edmundo Vargas Carreno
Edouard Dayan
Ekmeleddin Ihsanoglu
Elgizouli Dafalla
Elnoor Ahmed Elnoor

Elrasheed Eltahir
Elsadig Elmahdi
Eltayeb Suleiman Nail
Emil Constantinescu
Emmanuel Akwei Addo
Emperor Akihito of Japan
Eltigani Elkarib
Faroug Abu-Eisa
Faroug Hamdalla
Fathelrahman Elbashir
Fidel Castro
Fidel Ramos
Fidel Ramos
Francesco Frangialli
Francis Deng
Francois Lagrange
Gaffar Nimeiri
Georgi Parvanov
Gilberto Amado
Gudmundur Eriksson
Guido de Marco
Guido de Marco
Guillaume Pambou-
  Tohivounda
Hashim Haju
Hassan Elturabi
Haydar Kheiralla
Heinz Bardehle
Henry Olsson
Herman Sprujit
Hillary Clinton
Hisamitsu Arai
Hosni Mubarak
Huang Huikang
Husain M.Al-Baharna
Ibrahim Ahmed Omer

Ibrahim Gambari
Idriss Al gazairi
Ilham Aliyev
Ion Iliescu
Ion Iliescu
Ismail Haj Mousa
Issam Hassoun
Issam Salih
Izzeldeen Elfatih
Izzeldeen Hamid
Jacob S. Selebi
Jacque Diouf
Jacques Chirac
James Cochrane
James Lutabanzibwa Kateka
James Richard Crawford
James T. Morris
Jan Eliasson
Jean-Claude Aimé
Jian Song
Jian Zemin
Jiuyong Shi
Jkob Kellenberger
Joel Schoenfeld
John de Saram
John Garang Mayardit
Jorge Amigo Castañeda
Jorge Sampaio
Juan Somavia
Julius Nyerere
Kamal Nasreldeen
Kandeh Yumkella
Katsuo Ogawa
King Abdullah of Jordan
King Fahd bin Abdulaziz Al
  Saud of Saudi Arabia

King Felipe VI of Spain
King Hassan II of Morocco
King Hussein of Jordan
King Hussein of Jordan
Kofi Annan
Koichiro Matsuura
Lakshman Kadirgamar
Laurent Gbagbo
Lee Hsien Loong
Lee Jong Wook
Louise Arbour
Luigi Ferrari Bravo
Ma Lianyuan
Mahathir Mohamad
Mahdi Mustafa Elhadi
Mamoun Awad Abu-Zeid
Mansour Khalid
Mariam Elmahdi
Marilyn S. Cade
Marino Porzio
Martin Uhomoibhi
Mary Robinson
Mayer Gabay
Mazin Abdalla
Michael K. Kirk
Michel Jarraud
Michio Naruto
Mo Ibrahim
Mochtar Musuma-Atmadja
Mohamed Abdelhalim
Mohamed Ahmed Elmadih
Mohamed Ibrahim Nugud
Mohamed Khreissat
Mohamed Mirghani Mubarak
Mohamed Omer Beshir
Mohamed Osman Elmirghani

Mohammed El-Baradie
Mohammed Bennouna
Mustafa Medani
Nabil Elarabi
Nadhmi Auchi
Nand Kishore Singh
Nasser Judeh
Natsagiin Bagabandi
Nelson Mandela
Nicolas George Hayek
Nursultan Nazarbayev
Olusegun Obasanjo
Omer Elbashir
Othman Yeop Abdullah
Paolo Costa
Pascal Lamy
Patrick Lipton Robinson
Paul Biya
Paul Wolfowitz
Pemmaraju Sreenivasa Rao
Petar Stoyanov
Peter C.R. Kabatsi
Petru Lucinschi
Pitiu Lucinschi
Prince Hassan of Jordan
Robert Mugabe
Robert Rosenstock
Roberto Ago
Romano Prodi
Salifou Fomba
Salim Ahmed Salim
Salva Kiir
Samih Shukri
Sergei B. Krylov
Sergio Marchi
Sheikh Zayed bin Sultan Al

Nahyan of the United Arab
Emirates

Siddig Mohamed
Sir Ian Brownlie
Sultan Qaboos bin Said al Said
of Oman
Talal Abu-Ghazaleh
Thomas Philipson
Tony Blair
Wagdi Mirghani Mahgoub
Wail Omer Abdeen
Walter Gyger
Wilhelm Hoynck
William M. Daley
Yassir Arafat
Yoshio Utsumi
Yusuf bin Alawi bin Abdullah
Zein-Elabdeen Abdelgadir
Zhu Rongji

AMBASSADORS

Abbas Almoutasim
Abbas Elmutasim
Abbas Mousa
Abbas Mousa Mustafa
Abbas Osman Alkhalifa
Abdalla Abbas
Abdalla Goubara
Abdelal Synada
Abdelbasit Elsanosi
Abdelgaffar Abdelrahman
Abdelghani Elnaeem
Abdelhadi Alsiddig
Abdelhalim Babu Fatih

Abdelmagid Ali Hassan
Abdelmagid Ali Hassan
Abdelmahmoud Abdelhalim
Abdelmajid Bashir Alahmadi
Abdelmoneim Mustafa Alamin
Abdelmoniem Mabrouk
Abdelrahim Khalil
Abdelrahman Bakheet
Abdelrahman Hamza
Abdelwahab Alsawi
Abdulla Ali Gabir
Abu Algasim Abdelwahid
Abu Bakar Osman Mohamed
Khir
Abubakr Salih Mohamed
Nour
Abuzeid Elhassan
Ahmed Abdel Wahab
Goubartalla
Ahmed Altayib Alkourdufani
Ahmed Diab
Ahmed Elmutsaim
Ahmed Youssef Al Tinay
Al Fatih Abdullah Youssef
Al Fatih Ibrahim Hammad
Alfaki Abdalla Alfaki
Ali Abdelrahman Elnimeiri
Ali Adam
Ali Ahmed Sahloul
Ali Hamad Ibrahim
Ali Hassan Haj Elsiddig
Ali Khalid Elhussein
Ali Yousi Ahmed
Alnour Ali Suliman
Altahir Mustafa
Amer Al Mardi

Asmaa Mohamed Abdalla
Attala Hammad Bashir
Awad Alkarim Fadalalla
Awad Mohamed Hassan
Awad Mohammed Al Hassan
Awad Moursi Taha
Babiker Ali Abdel Karim
Babikir Ali Khalifa
Bakri Elazhari
Bashir Mohamed El Hassan
Charles Manyang
Dafaala Elhaj Ali
Dafaala Mohamed
Eisa Mustafa Salama
El Tayeib Ahmed Hummeida
Elamin Bushra
Elnagrashi Abdelmageeg
    Hamadto
Elrasheed Abushama
Elsadig Elfagih
Eltayeb Suleiman Nail
Farouk Abdelrahman
Fatima Elbili
Gaffar Abu Haj
Gaffar Kibeida
Gaffar Taha Hamza
Galal Attabani
Hafiz Abdelrahman
Haj Elfaki Hashim
Hamad Alnil Ahmed
    Sidahmed El-Hardalou
Hamad-Elnil Ahmed
    Mohamed
Hamid Eltinay
Hashim Abdelrahim
Hashim Abdelrahman

Hashim Abdelrazik
Hashim Eltinay
Hashim Osman
Hassan Abdeen
Hassan Abdel Aziz Farag
Hassan Adam
Hassan Beshir Abdelwahab
Hassan Jadkareem
Ibrahim Abdelmoniem
Ibrahim Ahmed Abdelkarim
Ibrahim Elkhalifa
Ibrahim Hammra
Ibrahim Mirghani
Ibrahim Mohamed Ali
Ibrahim Taha Ayoub
Isaac Shankouk
Isam Abu Gidairi
Isam Hassan
Ismail Abdeldafi
Ismail Ahmed Ismail
Izzat Babiker Aldeep Adellatif
    Abdelhameed
Izzeldin Saeed osman
Jamal Mohamed Ibrahim
Kamal Kineida
Kuwal Manyang
Mahagoub Al Basha
Mahgoub Ridwan
Mahmoud Bannaga
Mahmoud Hassan Al Amin
Mahmoud Hassan Elaminrd
Mahmoud Tamim Eldar
Mamoun Ibrahim Hassan
Mirghani Alnour Gaweesh
Mirghani Khalil Sulaiman
    Achol Deng

Mirghani Mohammed Salih
Mohamed Adam
Mohamed Al Maki Ibrahim
Mohamed Beshir
Mohamed Elabbas Abasaeed
Mohamed Mahmoud Abu Sin
Mohamed Noor Taha
Mohamed Osman Alnougomi
Mohamed Salah-Eldin Abbas
Mohamed Sharif Abdallah
Moubarak Hussein Rahama
Moutasim Al Birair
Mustafa Mohamed Mustafa
Nagib Alkhair Abdelwahab
Nahid Abu Akar
Nasreldeen Ahmed Mohamed
Noureldin Satti
Nouri Khalil Siddig
Omar Abbas Agabna
Omar Abdelmagid
Omar Al Alim
Omar Hydar
Omar Shouna
Omar Youssef Birido
Omer Dahab
Omer Elsheikh
Omer Salih Eisa
Omer Siddig
Osman Alsmahoni
Osman Dirar
Osman Eldirdiri
Osman Elsayed
Osman Naffie
Rahamt Alla Mohamed
    Osman
Saeed Saad

Salah Ahmed Mohamed Salih
Salih Al Nail Al Shafie
Sayed Galal-Eldeen
Sayed Sharif Ahmed
Siddig Abu Agla
Siddig Ahmed Mohamed
Simon Haj Klusika
Sirajeldeen Hamid
Siralkhatim Alsanousi
Sulliman Moustafa
Yahia Abdrlgalil
Yousif Alhadi
Yousif Fadul Ahmed
Yousif Saeed
Youssef Mukhtar
Zeinab Mohamed Mahmoud

LEADING PUBLIC FIGURES

Abbas Abushama
Abbas Haj Hussein
Abdalla Adam Khatir
Abdalla El-Ashal
Abdalla Elashaal
Abdalla Eltayeb
Abdalla Idris
Abdalla Medani
Abdel Aziz Khalid
Abdel Bagi Elzafir
Abdel-Aziz Elhilu
Abdel-Gadir Mustafa Elhaj
Abdel-Moniem
Abdelaziz Farag
Abdelbagi Elawad

Abdelbasit Sabdrat

Abdelgadir Elkitayabi

Abdelgadir Warsama

Abdelhai Kijok

Abdelkarim Ahmed Humeida

Abdelkarim Elkabli

Abdelmohsen Elgahtani

Abdelmoniem Abdelbagi

Abdelrahim Abdelhalim

Abdelrahman Elsadig

Abdelrahman Mousa

Abdelwahab Elafandi

Abdelwahab Himat

Abdou Haj Hussein

Abu Bakar Salih Mohamed
  Nour

Adil Abdelghani

Adil Agib

Adil Elbaz

Adil Mohamed Elhassan

Adil Mufti

Ahmed Abdel Rahman

Ahmed Awad Elkarim

Ahmed bin Yousif Alabd

Ahmed Dagash

Ahmed Elbalal

Ahmed Elbashir Elhadi

Ahmed Elgaali

Ahmed Eltigani

Ahmed Hussein

Ahmed mahmoud Yousif

Ahmed Mohamed Fadl

Ahmed Shibrain

Ainus Abdelmalik

Alaa Naji

Ali Elbashir Gadalla

Ali Gailoub

Ali Karti

Ali M.O. Yassin

Ali Mahdi

Ali Majok

Ali Shumu

Ali Suleiman

Almusalami Elkabashi

Amgad Farid

Ami Bhatti

Amin Hassan Omer

Amir Abdallah Mirghani

Amir Bella

Amir Eltigani

Anne-Marie Petit

Antony Hill

Anwar Dafalla

Arku Manawi

Atta Elbathani

Awad El Karsani

Awad Elhassan Elnour

Ayman Ramadan

Azmi Abdelrazig

Azzam Ibrahim

Babiker Albakhit

Bakri Elmadani

Bakri Osman Saeed

Bernard Kessedjian

Beshir Sahl

Bruce Lehman

Bushara Haj El Fadl

Bushra Eltom

Charles Manyang

Dafalla Elsaim

Dia-Eldeen Bilal

Dina Sheikh-Eldeen

Dominique Boyer
El Fatih Erwa
El-Nour Hawad
El samawal Khalafalla
Elamin Awad
Elaraki Elrayah Eluleish
Elbagir
Elbagir Mohamed Abdallah
Elbukhari Elgaali
Elfadil Saeed
Elfatih Elbadawi
Elfatih Elhaj
Elfatih Hassanain
Elfatih Kashif
Elhadi Adam
Elhadi Nassr-Eldeen
Elhadi Shalouf
Elhaj Warag
Elharith Idrees
Elhindi Izzeldeen
Elmahboub Abdel Salam
Elrayah Elsanhouri
Elsadig Suleiman
Elsawi Bella
Elshafie Khidir
Elsheikh Mousa
Eltahir Fadl
Eltaj Alam
Eltayeb Elabbas
Eltayeb Mustafa
Eltayeb Salih
Eltayeb Yousif Salih
Eltayeb Zein Elabdeen
Eltigani Haj Musa
Eltigani Saeed
Elwathig Kamer

Fadlalla Burma
Fadlalla Mohamed
Faisal Abdelrahman Ali Taha
Faisal Abdelrahman Kibeida
Faisal bin Hamid Malaa
Faisal Mohamed Salih
Farid Eltayeb Idris
Farouq Mohamed Ibrahim
Fathelrahman Elnahas
Fathelrahman Elsheikh
Fathelrahman Shabarga
Fatima Abdel Mahmoud
Fatima Ahmed Ibrahim
Fayza Abu Elnaga
Filosous Farag
Gaffar Abbas
Gaffar Mirghani
Galaa Elazhari
Galal Mohamed Osman
Ghazi Salah Eldeen
Gibril Ibrahim
Hani Nouri
Hashim Abu Elhassan
Hashim Siddig
Hassan Abashar Eltayeb
Hassan Bayoomi
Hassan Elbishari
Hassan Kamal
Hassan Kambal
Hassan Maki
Hassan Tag Elsir
Hassan Taha
Hatim Elsir
Haydar Dafalla
Haydar Ibrahim
Haydar Kheiralla

Henri-Philippe Sambuc
Hugh Dias
Hussein Elnaeem
Hussein Khogali
Hussein Sidahmed
Ibrahim Dagash
Ibrahim Draig
Ibrahim Elamin
Ibrahim Elsalahi
Ibrahim Elsanosi
Ibrahim Elsheikh
Ibrahim Gandour
Ibrahim Hamid
Ibrahim Mohamed Elhassan
Ibrahim Mohamed Osman
Imam Mohamed Imam
Ismat Elalim
Issam Elturabi
Izzeldeen Osman
Jamal Hilal
Kamal Abusin
Kamal Elgizouli
Kamal Hamza
Kamal Hassan Bakheit
Kamal Nasr-Eldeen
Kamal Omer
Kamal Shadad
Khalafalla Elrashid
Khalid Aleisir
Khalid Altowayan
Khalid Bushara
Khalid Satti
Khalid Uweis
Khalil Ibrahim
Mahasin Haj Elsafi
Mahgoub Abbas

Mahgoub Erwa
Mahgoub Hussein
Mahgoub Mohamed Salih
Mahgoub Sherif
Mahmoud Fadl
Mahmoud Giha
Mahmoud Shahat
Maisra Elhaj Elsiddig
Makawi Awad El-Makawi
Makram Khouri
Malik Agar
Malik Hussein
Mihaira Hassan Babikir
Miranda Brown
Mirghani Mohamed Elhassan
Mohamed Abdelaziz
Mohamed Abu-Zeid
Mohamed Ali Kakoom
Mohamed Alim
Mohamed Ammar
Mohamed Elameen
Mohamed Elfatih Hamid
Mohamed Elkhateeb
Mohamed Elmahdi
Mohamed Elshoosh
Mohamed Haj Hussein
Mohamed Hussein
Mohamed Faroug
Mohamed Ibrahim Eltahir
Mohamed Ma-Elinain
Mohamed Mahjoub Haroun
Mohamed Mirghani
Mohamed Nour
Mohamed Wardi
Mohamed Yousif Haydoub
Mohamed Yousif Mohamed

Mohi-Eldeen Mabrouk
Muaz Elsaraj
Mubarak Beshir
Mudawi El-Turabi
Mujahid Awad
Munir Sheikh-Eldeen
Munir Zahran
Mustafa Elfagih
Mustafa Elkheir
Mustafa Idris
Mustafa Osman
Mutasim Elharith
Mutaz Elbireir
Mutaz Kashif
Muwafi Awad
Nabil Adeeb
Nasr-Eldeen Elhadi Elmahdi
Nassr-Eldeen Shulgami
Omer Abdelaziz
Omer Elfaroug Shumeina
Omer Elguzali
Omer Eltayeb Eldosh
Omer Mustafa Sherkian
Omer Zain
Osama Mohamed Ali
Osman Abdalla
Osman Haba
Osman Khalid
Osman Mirghani
Osman Ridwan
Osman Shabona
Osman Taha
Peter Dovy
Qasim Badhri
Rashid Diab
Rihab Taha

Roda Elhaj
Saad Beshir
Saad Gunaim
Saeed Elamin
Salah Bandar
Salah Gurashi
Salah Hamadto
Salah Karar
Salah Mandil
Salah mohamed Ibrahim
Salah Omer
Salih Elameen
Salih Mohamoud
Sara Abo
Sattie El Haj
Sayed Abuseifain
Sayed Issa
Sayed Suleiman
Seifeldeen Mohamed Ahmed
Siddig Eltursbi
Siddig Yousif
Suad Ibrahim Eisa
Suleiman Fidail
Tag elsir Elshoosh
Taha Ali Elbashir
Taha Yousif
Tahir El Mutasim
Tajeldeen Banaga
Vivek Shanker
Yahia Haba
Yassin Ahmed
Yassir Arman
Yousif Fadl Hassan
Zuhair Elsarag
Zuhair Hassan Babikir

UNITED NATIONS

Albert Tramposch
Alejandro Roca Campaña
Ali Yassin
Allan Roach
Anne Craven
Anne-Marie Nallet
Arpad Bogsch
Binying Wang
Bojan Pretnar
Brett Fitzgerald
Carlos Fernandez-Ballesteros
Carlotta Graffigna
Caroline Schwab
Carolyn Davies-Alonso
Christian Ignasse
Cornelio (Lio) Ruzol
Dolores Jimenez-Hernandez
Dominique Delmas
Edward Kwakwa
Elisabeth Cassiau
Elspeth Leicht
Ernesto Rubio
François Curchod
Geoffrey Onyeama
Giovanni Tagnani
Guy Eckstein
Heidi Schrott-Hawking
Henri-Philippe Sambuc
Herman Ntchatcho
Ihab Osman
Inayet Syed
Izzeldin Osman
Jacques Schweitzer
Jaime Sevilla

Jaiya Guriqbal Singh
James Neale
Jean Sagiati
Jenö Bobrovszky
Jiahao Li
Joachim Bilger
Jørgen Blomqvist
José Graça-Aranha
Judith Zahra
Khamis Suedi
Lakshman Kadirgamar
Lalao Rakotomalala
Larry Allman
Lesley Sherwood
Ludwig Baeumer
Marcelo Landicho
Marie-Christine Porcel-
  Sanchez
Marino Porzio
Mawunu Chapman Nyaho
Mayer Gabay
Mercedes Martinez-Dozal
Michele Petey
Michèle Weil-Guttman
Mihály Ficsor
Moncef Kateb
Mpazi Sinjela
Mubarak Rahamtalla
Nahla Haidar
Narendra Sabharwal
Nelson Landicho
Ola Zahran
Orobola Fasehun
P.S. Rao
Patience Häfliger
Paulette Kippelen

Philip Thomas
Philippe Favatier
Philippe Petit
Pietro Rossi
Rama Rao Sankurathripati
Ranjana Abeysekera
Raquel Cousin
Richard Owens
Richard Wilder
Rita Hayes
Rowena Paguio
Sally Legge
Sheila Cornish
Sheila Ginger
Sherif Saadallah
Simon Ouedraogo
Tamara Nanayakkara
Todd Larson
Tony Keefer
Victoria Menezes-Miller
Yoshiyuki Takagi

Appendix 8

Journalism Example

An example of my journalism written when I was a student in Khartoum. The article is discussing a philosophical matter.

Appendix 9

Selected WIPO Documents

WIPO
WORLD
INTELLECTUAL PROPERTY
ORGANIZATION

30 May, 2010

TO WHOM IT MAY CONCERN

This is to confirm that Dr. Kamil Idris, Director General of the World Intellectual Property Organization (WIPO) from 1997 to 2008, did not engage in any activity contrary to the staff regulations and staff rules of WIPO. In this regard, the story concerning his age that appeared on the Internet, was only in connection with an administrative error in the files of WIPO, which have since been rectified. That error has also since been rectified by the United Nations Joint Staff Pension Fund (UNJSPF) in its records. The error had no financial implications for the Organization.

Please do not hesitate to contact me, should you have a need for further information or clarification.

Sincerely,

Edward Kwakwa
Legal Counsel

WIPO
WORLD
INTELLECTUAL PROPERTY
ORGANIZATION

May 30, 2010

According to the official records of the World intellectual Property Organization (WIPO), I hereby state the following facts regarding the former Director General of WIPO, Dr. Kamil Eltayeb Idris ("Dr Idris"):

1. Dr Idris was born on August 26, 1954. He was elected Director General of WIPO in 1997 for a six-year term, and was re-elected by consensus in 2003 for a second six-year term.

2. Dr. Idris's second term of office as Director General would otherwise have expired on November 30, 2009. But in 2007, he informed the Chair of the WIPO Coordination Committee of his decision to advance the process for nominating and appointing a new Director General of WIPO to replace him. The newly-elected Director General of WIPO took over on October 1, 2008.

3. Throughout the period of his tenure as Director General of WIPO, Dr Idris donated his corresponding salary (as Secretary-General of the Union for the Protection of Plant Varieties, UPOV) to developing countries.

4. An External Investigation Report by Ernst & Young categorically stated that it "could not conclude that certain employees of WIPO and third parties concerned committed fraud or dishonest acts"

5. Upon leaving office in 2008, Dr Idris did not accept any extra package or remuneration apart from his routine entitlements as Director General.

Edward Kwakwa
Legal Counsel

WIPO
WORLD
INTELLECTUAL PROPERTY
ORGANIZATION

Appendix 10

Selected List of Supporting Statements

The following documents are available online:

WO/GA/XXI/13
dated October 1, 1997

A/38/3
dated May 27, 2003

The Delegation of Cameroon made the following statement:

"My Delegation and I are quite delighted and extremely satisfied at the election by acclamation of Dr Kamil Idris to the post of Director General of WIPO. For us on the Cameroonian Delegation, as for many others, the election of Dr Kamil Idris is an exceptional event, a real turning point – indeed, a new start for our Organization. For, in the recollection of the Members of this Organization, it is the first event of its kind experienced by us in the present setting in almost a quarter of a century. This in itself is proof that the world is moving, that the United Nations and the other specialized agencies are moving, and that WIPO was also bound to move, without just reacting to a fashion trend but rather by working on the topmost rungs of the ladder. While delighting in the elegance with which this change is taking place, we must not forget that the search for success at this session of the General Assembly and our concern to facilitate the confirmation of the election of the new Director General of WIPO were at the centre of the work of the last session of the

Coordination Committee, which took place here on March 18 and 19, 1997, under the so worthy and exemplary chairmanship of the Ambassador of Germany, His Excellency Mr Wilhelm Hoynck. On behalf of my Delegation, I wish to congratulate him on the clear-sightedness, efficiency and impartiality that he showed throughout the difficult eliminatory stages involving the ten gallant candidates, qualities that do credit to his country and to himself.

"As for Dr Kamil Idris, this worthy son of Africa, I wish to convey to him all the happiness and pride that my Delegation and I feel as a result of his brilliant election. Once again we address to him our sincere and fraternal congratulations as well as our heartfelt wishes for every success in his new position. We are certain that his personal charisma, his innate sense of human relations, his perfect knowledge of the Organization, and his intellectual and moral values will be his best assets when he faces all the challenges arising from the internationalization that he has just spoken of and from the dispensable convergence that it dictates. We should like to think that, in electing him by acclamation a moment ago, the Member States wished to signal not only that they had decided to place their lasting trust in him, but also that they were willing, should the occasion arise, to give him their backing and support. We have just listened attentively and with great pleasure to the first official speech of the new Director General. We have been pleased to note the creative spirit that characterizes his program, and the priority that he is according to certain categories of both multilateral and national projects, such as the creation of the Worldwide Intellectual Property Academy, the reaffirmation of the necessity and importance of development cooperation for the benefit of developing countries, the placing of appropriate means of taking action at the disposal of staff, the guarantee of staff independence, the introduction of transparency, the creation of two high-level Advisory Commissions, the giving of priority to national projects and the reinvigoration of cooperation between States and the private sector, to mention only those. All this reflects a clear vision of the future of our Organization, and testifies to a pressing need for change at WIPO with respect to many areas of concern. We cannot but support the new Director General in this direction.

"I am now coming to the last point of my statement. The area of intellectual property, like other areas, has during the last years passed a phase of dramatic development of information technologies, and it has become evident that there is a need to find uniform solutions to the specific application of those technologies in intellectual property. The purpose of such uniform solution would first and foremost be to safeguard functioning communications between the various offices and organizations that operate in this area. In July, a Working Group on Information Technologies for Intellectual Property was convened here in Geneva. The Working Group adopted a number of conclusions and recommendations, which are contained in document WO/GA/XXl/5. Let me already at this point state that my Delegation fully agrees with those conclusions and recommendations."

The Delegation of Germany made the following statement:

"The first congratulations of my Delegation to you, Ms Chairperson. I am glad, Madam, to see you as Chair of our Assembly during this biennium.

"Dr Idris, on behalf of the German Government, I want to congratulate you on your new responsibility. We are glad we could find such an able and worthy successor "My country has always attached special importance to the cooperation efforts undertaken by WIPO to help and assist the developing countries, and once more takes this opportunity to reaffirm its will to see that cooperation develops further to enable such countries not only to make the necessary adjustments to their legislation but also to ensure the implementation of intellectual property protection.

"That is why, to reply to these driving priorities, the new Director General should be dispensed of the need to wait for a time in order to effectively exercise his mandate. My country would wish that this august Assembly should give him an explicit mandate in that sense to create a flexibility of operation that is indispensable and that would facilitate the passage of the relay.

"In such a case, the Director General could already now initiate appropriate consultations on the most urgent structural reforms, decide his program, set his budget for the next biennium and give greater impetus to north-south cooperation which should constitute one of the true dimensions of WIPO's activities.

"It may be noted that his policy speech opened up interesting prospects in that respect. My Delegation particularly welcomes the new approach that is emerging within WIPO both as concerns the introduction of new internal consultation procedures and the strengthening of the role played by the Organization in the regulation of norms, the introduction of new communication technologies within the new information society."

The Delegation of China made the following statement:

"First of all, I would like to extend, on behalf of the Chinese Delegation and in my own name, warmest congratulations to Dr Kamil Idris on his appointment as the new Director General of WIPO.

"Dr Kamil Idris has great attainments in international law and intellectual property laws as well as rich experience from his long involvement in the diplomatic field and international organizations. After working for nearly 15 years in WIPO, he knows WIPO and its Member States very well and has a good command of several languages. We have every reason to believe that, under his guidance, WIPO will continue its efforts to promote intellectual property causes in the world, to enhance the status and the role of intellectual property in all countries, and to expand coordination and cooperation in the intellectual property field and in the area of development for developing countries. China will, as always, support WIPO in its work and enhance cooperation with WIPO. We hope that, in the future development of intellectual property rights in China, we will continue to get assistance and support from Dr Kamil Idris and WIPO.

"The Chinese Delegation maintains that, without the high attainment and long-term unremitting efforts of the current Director General Dr Arpad Bogsch in the intellectual property field, WIPO could not have had such a high prestige and influence in the world and developed into an international Organization with 165 Member States and nearly 20 unions under it. As a result, Dr Bogsch is held in very high regard by the intellectual property community and the science community worldwide. Cherishing friendly feelings towards the Chinese people and a keen interest in China's intellectual property undertaking, Dr Bogsch has all along supported and assisted China in the establishment and development of an intellectual property regime, the training of intellectual property professionals, intellectual property legislation and its cooperation and exchanges with the rest of the world in this field. He has thus won wide acclaim from the Government and the intellectual property community in China. The Chinese Delegation wishes to express again its profound gratitude to Dr Bogsch.

"I wish to emphasize once again on this occasion that China is a member of the Asian countries and also the largest developing country in the world. Within the regional grouping of WIPO, China is an independent party. China's remarkable achievements in the intellectual property area have won her an extensive appreciation throughout the world. However, up to the present day, there has not been a single Chinese ever positioned in the leading echelons of WIPO. The Chinese Government has recommended Dr Gao Lulin, the present Commissioner of the China Patent Office, to WIPO. Dr Gao meets WIPO's requirements for its senior posts in terms of qualifications, knowledge, experience and capabilities. It is embodied in the recommendation that China attaches great importance to WIPO. I believe that Dr Gao Lulin, an outstanding founding member of China's intellectual property system, will go all out to assist Dr Kamil Idris to open an even brighter future for WIPO. Accordingly, the Chinese Delegation would like to request Dr Kamil Idris, the newly appointed Director General, and Member States of both WIPO Coordination Committee and the General Assembly, to take China's view into full consideration."

The Delegation of India made the following statement:

"The Delegation of India would like to join the other delegations in extending to you, Madam, and to the other elected office-bearers our warmest felicitations. We are confident that the spirit of harmony and cooperation which has always characterized WIPO would be further strengthened under the very able stewardship of you and your colleagues.

"We are delighted that the next Director General is going to be an eminent son of Africa who represents the hopes and aspirations of the entire developing world. The problems in the area of intellectual property rights are, by and large, common to all developing countries. These relate to lack of proper infrastructure for intellectual property rights administration, lack of awareness among the general public about intellectual property rights matters, the absence of a well-developed collective administrative system in copyright and neighbouring rights, the neglect of intellectual property rights studies by academics and the absence of a group of articulate and well-informed intellectual property rights professionals. These deficiencies would need to be addressed promptly. We therefore look towards the new Director General with great hopes and expectations to help us in this endeavour. Dr Kamil Idris is known to all of us – apart from his disarming smile, refreshing candour and suave manners – for his readiness to face and sort out contentious issues and his uncanny ability to grasp. We have had an opportunity to know from him first-hand about his vision, his keen desire to ensure transparency and accountability, his determination to reorganize and broaden the management pattern and his resolve to emphasize nationally-focused action programs. We are particularly happy to note from Dr Idris' statement that he intends to endeavour, through the program of cooperation for development, to mitigate the disadvantageous effects of rapid change on developing and least developed countries.

"These are undoubtedly priorities which we would all share and support in full measure. He will no doubt have a heavy burden to bear, but I would like to assure him that in this task he would have a fund of goodwill and unstinted cooperation from all of us.

"We also take this opportunity to offer our special regards and thanks to Dr Arpad Bogsch who would be demitting his office soon after an eventful career. During his long and distinguished tenure, WIPO grew from strength to strength and became one of the most vibrant UN Organizations. The identification of Dr Bogsch with WIPO was total. We wish him continued happiness and good health in the days ahead."

The Delegation of the United Kingdom made the following statement:

"I am delighted to join other delegations in giving the warmest of welcomes to Dr Kamil Idris as he assumes responsibility for guiding the World Intellectual Property Organization.

"May I pay an equally warm tribute to his predecessor, Dr Arpad Bogsch, whose achievements as a distinguished international civil servant have been chronicled by the representative of the United States and other speakers?

"It is through the leadership and commitment of Dr Bogsch that WIPO has become what it is today. He has helped to harmonize the world's intellectual property systems and has also promoted international registration systems – under the Patent Cooperation Treaty and the Madrid Protocol – which directly benefit users of intellectual property.

"The United Nations family as a whole owes a considerable debt to Dr Bogsch for the success of this Organization. It is a testament to him that one of his own Deputy Directors General has been chosen to build on the foundations he laid. So I join others in wishing him all possible happiness and contentment in his future life.

"Dr Kamil Idris could not be better qualified for this post. His broad experience in the field of intellectual property, his personality and intellect, and his skills as a leader and a diplomat will ensure that WIPO goes from strength to strength. In his statement today, Dr Idris has hit the ground running. He has set a road map for the Organization's future development. No time should be lost, and we agree with the representative of Cameroon and others who have argued that the new Director General should begin his consultations with the staff and the Member States straightaway.

"We welcome the emphasis Dr Idris has placed on accountability, transparency and effective communication with Member States, and much look forward to working with him.

"Madam Chairman, as the Chair has noted, there are important issues to be discussed this week, including those raised by my own and other delegations which are under consultation with the regional groups. These will be taken up at appropriate points in the agenda, but today is the time to express our sincere gratitude to Dr Bogsch and our strong support for his successor, Dr Idris."

The Delegation of Egypt made the following statement:

"Allow me, Madam, to express our congratulations upon your election to preside over the WIPO General Assembly. I should also like to congratulate your two Vice -Chairmen. We are confident that due to your expertise and skill, you will be able to crown our work with success.

"On behalf of the Egyptian Delegation, I should like to express our sincere congratulations to Dr Kamil Idris upon his election to be the new Director General of WIPO. Dr Idris is a model of one of the sons of the African continent who have honoured the African continent in many international forums. He is also one of the sons of Sudan, another Arab country with which Egypt has had very strong ties for many generations and centuries. The history of Dr Idris is full of achievements which make him worthy of becoming the Director General. He is an expert in international law, he is an eminent diplomat, and since working with WIPO in 1982, he has occupied many important posts in which he has demonstrated extreme skill and efficiency. His appointment as a Deputy Director General in 1994 was a natural result of the success that he has achieved so far in the Organization. Appointing Dr Kamil Idris as the Director General comes at a very important juncture of the history of this Organization. Not only for the Organization but also for the international community as a whole"

"What we heard yesterday from Dr Kamil Idris in his forward-looking and very substantive statement further convinced us that we have made an especially happy choice in reposing our trust in him. His stress on development cooperation, on human resources development, on country-focused programs, and his determination to remain at the cutting edge of technological change are truly welcome. We have also heard with great care the several important questions he has posed to us, the Member States, and we assure him that we shall be actively considering these questions.

"Madam President, we look forward to the new Director

General expeditiously commencing to address the many challenging tasks before him, especially on matters relating to the program and budget. And we are hopeful that the full resources of the International Bureau will be placed at his disposal during the transition period.

"In conclusion, Madam President, we would like to assure the new Director General, Dr Kamil Idris, whom our Delegation is proud to call a brother, of the unstinting support and cooperation of our Delegation in his endeavors to make WIPO an Organization fully responsive to the demands of the present fast-changing times."

The Delegation of Mexico made the following statement:

"Madam Chairman, the Delegation that I represent would like first to congratulate you on your election to preside over our work in the coming biennium. This quite simply is recognition of your long professional career in intellectual property.

"Secondly, the Delegation of Mexico endorses the expressions of respect and gratitude conveyed to Dr Arpad Bogsch, and wishes to pay tribute to the man who has, for the sake of this Organization and many of its members, dedicated a large part of his life and of his thoughts, sufferings, ideals, goals and challenges during a period of many, many years.

"Thirdly, the Delegation of Mexico most sincerely congratulates Dr Kamil Idris, unanimously elected Director General of WIPO, and wishes him the utmost success in the discharge of such an important responsibility.

"Dr Idris, we know that the times to come are going to be times of change and challenge for WIPO and its Member States, and we are sure that under your leadership we shall face them successfully. You may be assured henceforth of the full cooperation of the Government of Mexico.

"Madam Chairman, in the coming weeks we shall be going through an intensive period of preparation for the short-term action associated with the transition to a new administration.

"We all know that the experience accumulated by the outgoing Director General, Dr Arpad Bogsch, in the promotion of the objectives of the Organization and its administration over two decades accumulated by the outgoing Director General, Dr Arpad Bogsch, are a reference whose value in the new era will be better appreciated inasmuch as that experience will be shared with the new administration."

"I have thus had the opportunity to entertain direct relations with both persons, and to my way of thinking, it is not so much an era coming an end because the Director General is leaving, but rather an era that is continuing, and, as Mr Idris is himself one of the leading lights of WIPO, his rise to the head of the Organization seems to me the crowning event of an eminently brilliant career. The content of his address is for us an indicator of the new vitality that he is going to instil in WIPO in his capacity as Director General, and he has all the qualities for the purpose. We therefore feel justifiably proud to see him at the head of this World Organization. Nevertheless, it is not sufficient for him to be elected to this supreme responsibility: he himself must also be aware that our continent of Africa has a part to play within the Organization, and that our Africa should not be just a mere spectator but an effective actor, an actor at the design stage, at the stage of the development of projects and at the stage of the implementation of those projects. And so I wish to express the most fervent wish that Dr Kamil Idris, that diplomatic and intellectual paragon of our continent, whose qualities are known to all, may not only make dramatic achievements, but may also succeed in adapting WIPO to the workings of the next millennium, not only thanks to his own talents but also thanks to the contributions of other intellectual leaders who are willing and able to work in the supremely commendable cause of this World Organization."

The Delegation of Trinidad and Tobago made the following statement:

"We join with the others, Trinidad and Tobago, to offer our sincere congratulations on your appointment as President and on the appointment of the others who will assist you in this Assembly. Madam Chair, when you made your request that the distinguished delegate of Burundi speak before Trinidad and Tobago, I knew that you were demonstrating the utmost good sense, because as long as he continues to speak of the century of women, I know that we will allow him to speak again and again. Thus far, Madam Chair, you have demonstrated all the qualities so essential in an efficient and yet humorous and heart-warming Chairperson. We have no doubt that for the rest of your term of office you will continue to chair this Assembly and others in great stead.

"The Delegation of the Republic of Trinidad and Tobago extends our warmest congratulations to Dr Kamil Idris on his election to the post of Director General of WIPO. Madam Chair, in the age in which we live today, the things that we are doing here and now as we speak can be seen and heard anywhere in this global village. And so, over the 24 years that Dr Bogsch has led this Organization, we have seen tremendous developments, and it has been because of the remarkable qualities of Dr Bogsch that WIPO has reached where it is today. He has brought us to the brink of the new millennium and, as I said to him only recently, his life has only just begun. And so Trinidad and Tobago pays tribute to Dr Bogsch. We wish him Godspeed and God's blessing as he embarks on this new phase of his life.

"As we approach this new millennium, we will no doubt witness further tremendous changes in this information age that will have so many other implications for the protection of intellectual property in the world. Dr Idris will bring, in our respectful view, the continuity and a new dynamism that are so essential to take WIPO forward. We recognize, and with him we sympathize, because we know that his task will be no easy one for he must now meet the demands of the developing world."

"Again, I would like to wish the new Director General the best of health, the best of luck, and again I would like to emphasize the great assistance and support that Dr Bogsch has given to us. I would wish him happiness and health in the future and I hope he never stops his active life. I am sure he will continue to become wiser and more experienced. I do not think he is simply retiring and going to get his pension. He is doing that, of course, but I think he is also going to continue to work in the interests of WIPO and its activities."

The Delegation of Saudi Arabia made the following statement:

"Madam Chairperson, allow me first of all to express Saudi Arabia's congratulations to you for your election to the presidency of our General Assembly I would like to wish you full success. We are fully convinced that your experience and abilities will guide us towards a successful Assembly.

"Madam Chairperson, allow me to express my admiration for the outstanding services rendered by Dr Arpad Bogsch during his directorship of this Organization. His wisdom, his knowledge, his abilities, have made WIPO an Organization that has achieved many an outstanding feat. His abilities, his sound guidance, have undoubtedly guided this Organization towards a better knowledge of the needs of developing countries in the field of intellectual property. This Organization has provided such countries with technical assistance that has undoubtedly enabled them to achieve their ambitious technical programs. We would like to wish Dr Arpad Bogsch success, further health, happiness, in the forthcoming phase of his life.

"Madam Chairperson, on behalf of the Government of the Kingdom of Saudi Arabia, I would like to express our happiness and welcome the election of Dr Kamil Idris as a Director General of the World Intellectual Property Organization. I would like, on behalf of my Government, to express our sincere congratulations on his election. Dr Idris, I am fully convinced of your abilities to guide this Organization due to the faith and outstanding abilities and personal qualities and the undoubted experience in the field of diplomatic endeavour. Dr Kamil, you have shown a technical ability, you have proved that you have a very outstanding position in the field of intellectual property, you have shown your dedication to your work throughout your career within this Organization. Dr Idris, we have listened very carefully and in great hope to your opening statement and acceptance speech which indicated your sincere intentions to achieve ambitious goals for this Organization. They are transparent and are very soundly organized from the administrative point-of-view. You have expressed and shown your courage vis-á-vis the challenges of the future. One of the first challenges currently facing developing countries, Sir, is the implementation of the TRIPS Agreement within the World Trade Organization. We are fully convinced that this matter will be the object of Dr Idris' concern and attentions and will be the centre of all consultations he is planning to undertake. We express our full support for his work in this field.

"We sincerely hope that this commitment to ASEAN in the technical cooperation activities of WIPO, as demonstrated by Dr Bogsch would continue under the leadership of Mr Kamil Idris. The ASEAN Delegations would like to extend to Dr Bogsch our very best wishes in his future endeavours.

"On a personal note, allow me to express a wish for a dear friend of many years, Dr Bogsch, that he may have a long and happy life, and perhaps above all. knowing his nature and concern for the Organization, may you, Dr Bogsch, discover that there is life after WIPO.

"Finally, Madam Chairperson, the ASEAN Delegations would like to once again warmly congratulate Mr Idris on his appointment, and offer him our fullest support and cooperation in carrying out his duties as the new Director General."

The Delegation of Nigeria made the following statement:

"Madam Chairman, my Delegation is taking the floor at this time for three main reasons.

"The first is to congratulate you and the two Vice-Chairpersons on your deserved elections to the highest offices of this Assembly.

"The second is to express the happiness of our Delegation, and indeed our country, over the appointment of one of the great sons of Africa, Dr Kamil Idris, as the next Director General of WIPO. We wish therefore to take this opportunity to congratulate him and thank all the distinguished delegates, for the unanimous decision.

"Several Delegations who spoke before us have extolled the great qualities of Dr Idris which have contributed to his suitability to succeed Dr Arpad Bogsch.

We agree entirely with those delegations. The appointment of Dr Idris is a source of great joy and pride to my country, and indeed all Africa, as it must be seen as recognition of his competence, professionalism, excellence, integrity and sagacity.

"It is a tribute to the new crop of African professionals and leaders who Dr Idris amply represents. Nigeria has no doubt that he will bring his wealth of experience as a scholar, an accomplished diplomat and administrator to WIPO to ensure that this Organization continues to be the number one specialized agency of the United Nations system of organizations.

"The acceptance speech of Dr Idris yesterday gives new hope to us in the developing countries, of which his country is one, that WIPO under his leadership will be responsive to the needs of developing countries in their quest to use their vast cultural assets and resources, to develop their economies and contribute to world knowledge and progress.

"Indeed, Dr Idris' background places him in a vantage position to appreciate the need for developing countries to be empowered in all fields of endeavours so that they can march together with the rest of the world into the next millennium.

"Mr Chairman, the African Group is cognizant of the other positive efforts of the Director General in upholding WIPO's vision to put intellectual property at the centre of economic, social and cultural development. We agree that, on its own, intellectual property is not an end in itself. We encourage the Director General to continue to translate this vision and improve the welfare of all people. The African people will continue to support WIPO's policy that translates the vision into practical integration of the development dimension into WIPO's work program.

"Mr Chairman, the work of WIPO brings me to another visionary point which is that if developing countries are to be regarded as partners in the development of the IP system, then predictability and certainty of funding of WIPO's activities that concern their interests must be a core principle of WIPO. In particular, since 1997, when Dr Idris took office, the surplus of WIPO has been strategically used in the investment in the modernization of WIPO's infrastructure benefiting Member States, including developing countries. It coincided with the beginning of developing countries redoubling efforts to establish review and modernize the intellectual property institutions and we do appreciate WIPO's technical assistance for modernizing the IP infrastructure and capacity-building. These efforts and momentum should be maintained and enhanced in the era of knowledge based-economy as IP has become an important component in the development strategy. The need in the developing world for more international cooperation and WIPO assistance is definitely greater. It is widely recognized today that IP has cross-sectoral implications for important public policy goals so that the protection of public health and biodiversity is effected, and we hope with this regard that WIPO will further take into consideration this cross-sectoral impact in its work program.

"Mr Chairman, one important mechanism through which developing countries are pushing IP is the work of the WIPO

Worldwide Academy. The Academy is doing an excellent job in assisting African countries and other developing countries to build capacity in issues of IP in order for them to reap the necessary benefits. IP protection must go hand-in-hand with an educational component. In addition, we need education and training to be able to fully use the various services of WIPO, such as the PCT and Madrid systems. This is why Members should support an increased funding for the activities of the Academy in order for it to meet the demand and training of nationals from developing countries. Mr Chairman, an adequate intellectual property system and a business-friendly environment are key to the smooth operation of IP systems. The African Group is proud of the Director General, Dr Idris, and his commitment to the creating of an intellectual property system where developing countries would reap benefits. We look forward to Members providing all the resources to the Director General to accomplish the important tasks ahead of him.

"In conclusion, Mr President, allow me to express our sincere thanks to all the regional groups of this Organization for the support which they have expressed for the nomination of Dr Kamil Idris for a second term as the Director General of WIPO."

The Delegation of Portugal made the following statement on behalf of Group B:

"Speaking on behalf of Group B, I would like to express my warm congratulations to Dr Kamil Idris for his appointment as Director General of WIPO, for the period 2003 to 2009.

"We recognize, with appreciation, the efficiency with which he has been organizing WIPO's work and the importance of the reform strategy he has established for the Organization, so that intellectual property will better serve the causes of economic growth and sustainable development.

"Group B particularly wishes to pay tribute to his active

outreach to all Member States and to thank him for his constant efforts to promote intellectual property throughout the world.

"I wish to convey to Dr Kamil Idris that Group B is willing to cooperate fully with him during his second term of office, and contribute to the successful pursuit of a vital global agenda for intellectual property, an ultimate goal for WIPO. Group B is confident that WIPO's achievements will grow in the future under the leadership of Dr Kamil Idris, thanks to his management capacity, vision and skills."

The Delegation of Brazil, speaking on behalf of the Group of Latin American and Caribbean States (GRULAC), made the following statement:

"On behalf of the Group of countries of Latin America and the Caribbean (GRULAC), I am honoured and pleased to congratulate Dr Kamil Idris on his reelection to the position of Director General of the World Intellectual Property Organization (WIPO).

"Dr Kamil Idris carried out his first term as Director General with great commitment and energy, and contributed greatly to the modernization of WIPO and of its working methods. We consider it fair and fitting that he should be re-elected with the unanimous support of the Member States of this Organization.

"We reiterate our appreciation and gratitude for various initiatives undertaken in the course of his first term. Our Group considers it particularly important to proceed with the strengthening and promotion of the program of cooperation for development. Also of great importance to the Group is the establishment of the Intergovernmental Committee on Intellectual Property and Genetic Resources, Traditional Knowledge and Folklore.

"Intellectual property is a subject that is acquiring ever-greater prominence on the international agenda. Recent developments in various forums have highlighted the relation between intellectual property, development and important areas of public interest. The activities of this Organization will take on growing significance to the extent that they help lend greater depth to the discussions. Intellectual property has to function as an efficient instrument for the promotion of economic, social and cultural development in all nations.

"We are therefore in favour of the integration of development as a dimension of all WIPO activities.

"Once again we congratulate Dr Kamil Idris on his reelection, and express the wish that his second term of office will be as successful as the first."

The Delegation of Pakistan, speaking on behalf of the Asian Group, made the following statement:

"Mr Chairman, on behalf of the Asian Group, it gives me pleasure to congratulate Dr Kamil Idris on his reelection as Director General of WIPO for another term. This re-election by acclamation is indeed a reflection of the continued confidence that the Member States repose in him.

"Dr Idris' re-election is also an expression of support for the policies he has pursued, and speaks of his success in turning the Organization into an extremely dynamic entity within the UN system. Equally, it is a manifestation of the respect that the Member States have always had for his professionalism, diplomatic skills, innovative approach, and ability to balance the diverse interests of all stakeholders.

"Mr Chairman, it would be remiss of me not to recall before this august gathering some of the important achievements of WIPO under Dr Kamil Idris that testify to his qualities as a leader of this important Organization. Dr Kamil Idris' initiatives to establish the WIPO Worldwide Academy, introduction of the subjects of Genetic Resources, Traditional Knowledge and Folklore to the Organization's agenda, and a program for Small and Medium-sized Enterprises have received wide appreciation and support. Through these initiatives of the Director General, most Member States were offered the opportunity to develop their human resources, identify, protect and benefit from their assets such as traditional knowledge, and be encouraged to use intellectual property as a stimulus for economic development. As a secondary benefit, the demystification of intellectual property was achieved to a considerable extent and its respect, particularly amongst the developing countries, was increased visibly.

"The success of WIPO's Digital Agenda, launched several years ago, is another important achievement of Dr Kamil Idris. In the new millennium, projects such as WIPONET, IMPACT, Intellectual Property Libraries and Office Automation Assistance Programs are expected to bring far-reaching benefits to all Member States.

"Mr Chairman, the Asian Group has always welcomed development-friendly initiatives of the Director General and extended all possible support for their success. It was indeed remarkable that, while charting WIPO's way forward, Dr Idris never lost sight of the interests and constraints of Member States that were unable to fully benefit from the potential of intellectual property in their economic, social and cultural development. In this context, the Nationally Focused Action Plan has been of tremendous help to a large number of WIPO Member States. The flexibility of the program to adjust to peculiar conditions prevailing in each country guaranteed its acceptance, cooperation of the host country's intellectual property officials, and its successful implementation.

"Mr Chairman, the Asian Group is fully aware of Dr Idris' commitment to the promotion of intellectual property worldwide. The initiatives taken by WIPO under his leadership have provided opportunities to its Member States to articulate their expectations of the global intellectual property system. The invaluable experience gained during the recent in-depth and candid discussions held amongst the Member States on key issues of interest and concern would no doubt be useful to all Member States in their deliberations on important intellectual property issues under consideration in WIPO as well as other organizations.

"The Asian Group also appreciates Dr Idris' untiring efforts in highlighting the role of intellectual property in a knowledge economy and admires his insights in this area. In this context, I would like to commend him for his very well-written book entitled Intellectual Property: A Power Tool for Economic Growth. The book contains a wealth of information on how best to use intellectual property for economic advancement. I am confident that this book would be a valuable source of input to the intellectual property policy-making community worldwide.

"Before I conclude, on behalf of the Asian Group, I would like to assure Dr Kamil Idris of our continued support and wish him great success during his second term in office."

The Delegation of Romania, speaking on behalf of the Central European and Baltic States, made the following statement:

"On behalf of the Central European and Baltic States, it is an honour and a pleasure to congratulate Dr Kamil Idris on his re-election as Director General of the World Intellectual Property Organization.

"Mr Chairman, as on other past occasions, our group has joined the unanimous view and expressed its appreciation for the outstanding way in which the Organization under the able leadership of Dr Idris has implemented its policy agenda and carried out its planned activities. During this period, WIPO has established itself as one of the leading Organizations in the new knowledge-based economy. Its impressive and predictable development as well as sound finances have been an important feature in the sometimes turbulent international environment. Today, the Organization is well prepared to meet the challenges of the future. At this fourteenth extraordinary session of the General Assembly, our regional group wishes to pay tribute and

highlight the personal contribution by Dr Idris for securing
the impressive and dynamic performance of the Organization.
Indeed, the vision of the Director General has allowed WIPO
to pursue a rich and diverse agenda. The Organization has
implemented projects and initiatives which, on the one hand,
have met and even surpass the expectations of the Member States
and, on the other hand, have enhanced WIPO's transition from
a predominantly regulatory body into a dynamic Organization
with an integrated vision where intellectual property serves as
a tool for economic and social development. We believe, Mr
Chairman, that the presentation just made by Dr Idris was
most impressive in results and ambitious goals for the future.
Indeed, there have been many significant achievements by the
Organization over the past years. I would just mention a few
examples, such as the adoption and entry into force of new
international treaties in the field of patent law, industrial designs,
and copyright and related rights, the launching of digital
agenda and WIPO's successful initiatives in the Internet domain
names dispute resolution, the successful start of the activities
of the WIPO Academy, the WIPONET project improving
connectivity with national IP Offices, the attention paid to issues
relating to small and medium-sized enterprises, the new focus on
traditional knowledge, genetic resources and folklore. Time does
not allow for me to go into greater detail and to expand upon
this list.

"Taking into consideration the role of intellectual property
in the knowledge-based economy, WIPO is constantly called
upon to extend its contribution in a world facing increased
complexity and ever-greater challenges. With its dynamic,
transparent and modern pattern of activities and current
leadership, WIPO can provide a substantive and meaningful
contribution to this process. The range of issues on WIPO's
agenda reflects its commitment and ability to assist countries in
their social and economic development. Indeed, in recent years,
WIPO has gained much visibility in the multilateral system
and has enhanced its role. We encourage Dr Idris to continue

these endeavours and to further build upon WIPO's record during his second term of office. Moreover, Mr Chairman, we consider that, over the past six years, significant attention has been given to issues that are of particular interest and concern to the countries of our region. The modernization of our intellectual property systems as well as their use for economic and social development in the region have been well addressed in the work of WIPO, taking into account existing dualities and sensitivities. We have embarked upon new fields and forms of cooperation. Under the current policy framework and working modalities in the Organization, our countries can now pursue even more ambitious goals in the future, further develop their intellectual property systems, actively participate in international cooperation in enhancing both international IPR system and benefit-sharing from the existing regimes, raise the level of awareness in our societies on the importance of the intellectual property rights and assets, and last but not least, contribute to the development of the IPR system within the Organization itself. We hope that the countries from our region will continue to receive appropriate attention and assistance in the future as well, and we in turn are determined to bring our own specific contribution to the important work conducted here at WIPO.

"In conclusion, Mr Chairman, and against this background, the group of the Central European and Baltic States wishes to reiterate its full appreciation of the performance of Dr Kamil Idris as Director General of WIPO, its satisfaction with his re-appointment and to wish him every success during his second mandate as Director General of the World Intellectual Property Organization."

The Delegation of Belarus, speaking on behalf of the Central Asian, Caucasus and Eastern European countries, made the following statement:

"On behalf of the Regional Group for Central Asia, the Caucasus and Eastern Europe, I wish once again to express support for Dr Idris' candidacy for re-election to the post of WIPO Director General for a second term of office.

"I would like to say that we highly value and respect Dr Idris, and support all his initiatives aimed at expanding the range of the Organization's activities.

"We welcome Dr Idris' efforts, as WIPO Director General, to transform intellectual property into a potential instrument for the economic, social and cultural development of the Member States of WIPO.

"The efficiency, transparency and dynamism shown by Dr Idris are inalienable features of his leadership of the Organization. Under his leadership, WIPO has become one of the leading United Nations specialized agencies in the knowledge-based economy.

"It is essential to emphasize the inclination of Dr Idris toward the successful modernization and rationalization of WIPO's working methods – for example, through the introduction of greater openness, transparency in establishing the Organization's Program and Budget, and also the implementation of decisions based on modern technologies – in particular, the project to computerize the PCT system.

"In 1998, the WIPO Worldwide Academy was set up with Dr Idris' direct participation and has been called upon to assist the Member States of WIPO to develop human resources for the training of specialists in matters relating to IP policy.

"Under Dr Idris' leadership, many new trends have emerged in WIPO's activities. In particular, WIPO has begun to implement a special program aimed at creating, in developing countries and countries in transition, collective copyright management in the interests of creators such as authors, composers and performers.

"Since 1999, WIPO has adopted the digital agenda – a program of work for the Organization in the coming years based on conditions of interaction between the Internet, digital technologies and the intellectual property system.

"We believe that one of the important aspects of WIPO's works has been the initiative of Dr Idris to attract small and medium-sized enterprises (SMEs) to participate in its activities so that such enterprises have broader possibilities of using the potential of the intellectual property system to develop its commercial activities and enhance competitiveness.

"In conclusion, I would personally like to wish Dr Idris great creative undertakings and physical strength in realizing the tasks facing WIPO, including the application of trends such as:

– a sense of what is most important; – correct leadership; – influence on the way things stand; – a corporate image; – mutual dependency.

"We hope that, by resolving these tasks and enhancing the role of intellectual property in new areas of activity such as the Internet, environmental protection and the protection of traditional knowledge and folklore, WIPO will help to create the essential conditions for creative activity, inventiveness, and the guarantee of the prosperity of future generations."

The Delegation of China made the following statement:

"I would like to express, on behalf of the Chinese Government, our most sincere and heartfelt congratulations to Dr Idris on his re-election as Director General of WIPO for a second term.

"As we have all witnessed during his first term, the Director General has brought to full play his wisdom and talents as well as his organizing ability to ensure an important role for WIPO in addressing international affairs and providing assistance to developing countries. Under his leadership, WIPO has established various forums and mechanisms of vital importance to economic development, such as the Intergovernmental Committee on Intellectual Property and Genetic Resources, Traditional Knowledge and Folklore, and the creation of a unit in the Organization responsible for protection of intellectual property for SMEs to pursue its efforts in this regard, the protection of intellectual property on the Internet, the introduction of modern management systems, the launching of the WIPONET, and the completion of projects concerning information technology management. In brief, we appreciate very much the unremitting efforts of the Director General in realizing these objectives and successes so far achieved during his first mandate.

"We are deeply convinced that, during his second term, Dr Idris will build on his past experiences and use his talented organizing and managing ability as well as his sharp insight on newly emerging things to actively open up new horizons, to attach further importance to cooperation for development, and to enhance its efforts in providing assistance to developing countries, thus creating a new prospect of intellectual property for economic development in all countries.

"As always, China will continue to support the Director General in his work. It is our hope that we could strengthen our cooperation with WIPO under his leadership and make our own contribution to the protection of intellectual property."

The Delegation of the United Arab Emirates, speaking on behalf of the Arab Group, made the following statement:

"We are pleased to extend our congratulations and thanks to Dr Kamil Idris on behalf of the Arab Group. On behalf of this group I spoke in the March meeting and I spoke about the objective conditions that have led us to support the second mandate of Dr Kamil Idris to lead WIPO. This is an attitude for which the Arab Group and other Groups have supported

Dr Idris. We have all expressed our support for his nomination, given his accomplishments during his first term. For this reason, today we support the successes achieved by WIPO that is now embodying economic development in the world, including the promotion of traditional knowledge, genetic resources, folklore, art and research on how to enhance this knowledge. We take this into account for the future to enable all cultures and peoples to come together to appreciate a rich patrimony in heritage for the development of all countries. Mr Chairman, on the reelection of Dr Idris, we support the constitutional reforms and various implementations to conserve folklore and heritage. We seek collective ways to enlarge culture and protect humanity's heritage. All this is possible through the current means, given WIPONET and other opportunities. All this requires developing current means also, given that WIPO works together with the WTO, and that – thanks to the agreement between the two organizations – these have made it possible to agree on the commercial aspects of intellectual property. All this requires continuous work to enable our work in this international scope to resolve in a balanced way everyone's challenges. In our Arab region, we hope to consolidate our relations with WIPO through the Arab Bureau. In the past few years, we have seen a great number of round table discussions take place, work has been achieved within the framework of the Arab Group bringing together experts from WIPO and other Arab experts; this has given rise to intellectual and cultural achievements and has also brought about the modernizing of intellectual property in Arab States. Intellectual property is also a way to develop for the future all the activities of fraternity and enrich the heritage of all peoples. Once again, on behalf of the Arab Group, I would like to extend our congratulations to Dr Idris. We wish him great success in his work as he said in his presentation."

The Delegation of Greece made the following statement on behalf of the European Union, the ten acceding States and the associated States:

"On behalf of the EU, the ten acceding countries and the associate countries Bulgaria, Romania and Turkey, please let me express my sincere congratulations to you, Dr Kamil Idris – or Dr DG, which is the honorary title Ambassador Sha has given you for your appointment as Director General of WIPO for a second term. During your first term, you succeeded in putting and keeping intellectual property firmly on the international agenda; you have done so in a balanced way, addressing the interests of all concerned. We are fully confident that WIPO's vital role in contributing to economic growth and development will be further enhanced under your able guidance during the coming years. Be assured of the continuing full support of the European Union, the acceding countries and the associated countries in assuming your leadership. I wish you success in running this intellectual property Organization with your intellectual excellence to which we have all become accustomed. I would like to thank you very much, and the EU can only be happy at this event."

The Delegation of Myanmar made the following statement on behalf of the Association of South-East Asian Nations (ASEAN):

"Mr President, I am taking the floor on behalf of the ASEAN countries that are Members of WIPO. We, the ASEAN countries, would like to associate ourselves with the statement delivered by Pakistan on behalf of the Asian Group. Like the Delegations that have spoken before us, we too would like to congratulate Dr Idris for his re-election for his second term as the Director General of WIPO. The overwhelming support that Dr Idris has received towards his re-election is the reflection of his achievements in WIPO and the confidence that the Members have placed in his qualities to continue providing effective leadership in WIPO. On behalf of the ASEAN countries, we would also like to assure Dr Idris of ASEAN's continuous full support and cooperation in thrashing out the international intellectual property regime (IPR) agenda during his second term."

The Delegation of Uruguay made the following statement:

"Uruguay would like to express its pleasure and full support concerning the re election of Dr Kamil Idris as Director General of WIPO. We would also like to endorse and share the comments expressed by Brazil on behalf of GRULAC. We believe that the Director General has transformed WIPO into a more modern, efficient and open Organization with greater capacity to respond to the needs and aspirations of its Member States and of developing countries in particular. It is because of these achievements that my Government expresses to the Director General its gratitude and support. The path to be covered however is not exempt from difficulties. The Director General has to face the tremendous challenge of freeing the Organization within a very difficult international environment. The technological financial breach between developing and developed countries is growing, hence the possibilities of research and development are being reduced, and hence the capacity for creating intellectual property in the developing countries themselves. We are everyday witnesses to the reverse transfer of technologies through which scientists and researchers and highly qualified professionals are educated in developing countries at very high cost, migrate to industrialized countries, and there exercise their profession, their innovative capabilities…

"…the vision of the Director General, Dr Idris, 'Intellectual Property Instrument for Wealth Creation', was adopted unanimously at the Brussels United Nations Conference on Least Developed Countries (LDCs). This moral commitment continues to define the work of WIPO in the eyes of those who most look to and depend upon the Organization for support. This moral authority cannot be built upon abstractions, but only upon real service to people. Today, this is what WIPO is doing for LDCs throughout the world by its international program of 'WIPO Deliverables for LDCs'. Through its mission, objectives and the different activities in different countries, theories are tested by concrete action.

"Since development efforts must respond to particular national needs, priorities and circumstances, no single theory or set of priorities can be applied to the development efforts of all countries at any one time. It is here that the importance and uniqueness of the innovative approach of WIPO's Nationally Focused Action Plans for LDCs, which aimed at providing assistance tailored to the specific needs of individual countries, lies. Because of the fact that development requires a perpetual balancing of priorities, emphasis and continual reassessment of needs and policies, the role of leadership is crucial. In this regard, we highly appreciate the contribution of Dr Kamil Idris since he assumed leadership of WIPO.

"While we applaud the Director General for his past achievements, we are confident that he will continue to advance the interest of developing countries, particularly the least developed ones. Intellectual property must be accessible to all so as to make its role in social, cultural, technological and economic development better understood by governments, the private sector and the public at large. WIPO should further strengthen its effort in helping developing countries to harness their creativity, to receive the full benefit of their citizens' creativity as well as those of the outside world.

"Finally, I would like to conclude by expressing my best wishes for the success of the Director General, Dr Kamil Idris, during his second term in office."

The Delegation of the United States of America made the following statement:

"The Ambassador of the United States of America, the Honourable Kevin Moley, has asked me to present to you his congratulations and those of the United States Government. Ambassador Moley is unable to be here due to a conflict with the solemn observances of the United States holiday of Memorial Day.

"The United States of America has instructed me to convey its appreciation of the Director General's vision and accomplishments, and our pleasure at the prospect of working with Dr Kamil Idris over the coming years. I believe I can say the same of a plurality of WIPO's stakeholders, those who are United States nationals.

"And briefly, on a personal note, I have learned a great deal about leadership from the Director General.

"A leader is the person who sees the terrain and the dangers someone whose long experience and keen intuition tell him how to deal with them. That person gathers his support team and his companions to venture into new territory. Dangers and unexpected difficulties may await them; the inhabitants may be uncomprehending or even hostile.

"Some of the company may have ideas and needs different from his and different – markedly different – from those of the rest. Every expedition worth undertaking faces those obstacles, as well as doubt and inertia.

"What is required is someone who can see the goal – not only where the group has been and where it is going presently – but where it should go, what it should do to achieve success. And someone who has the eloquence and charisma to bind us together. Kamil Idris is that person."

The Delegation of Australia made the following statement:

"Like the others before me, I would like to offer strong support and congratulations to Dr Kamil Idris for his reelection as Director General. I do so on behalf of the Government of Australia and on behalf of the Australian Ambassador, Mr David Spencer, who regrets very much being unable to be here this afternoon.

"Australia believes that, as Director General, Dr Idris will be able to continue his important role of promoting intellectual property through all sectors of society and throughout all regions of the world. Australia offers its full support to this work.

"Australia has also strongly supported reforms introduced by Dr Idris over the past six years. The emphasis on increased transparency, modernization, accountability and results-oriented projects has been welcomed.

"We also appreciate the Director General's determination to grapple with immediate challenges to the effective operation of the international intellectual property system, as well as to apply strategic thinking to the longer-term view. Australia reaffirms its commitment to participate in WIPO's forums to harmonize intellectual property laws, engage in debates on emerging issues, and to provide technical assistance when appropriate.

"The Asia-Pacific region is, of course, a key interest to us, and we have been pleased to undertake a number of projects through our Regionally Focused Action Plan.

"In conclusion, Mr Chair, I would like to reaffirm Australia's strong support for Dr Kamil Idris. We look forward to continuing to support WIPO's work program during his next term of office."

The Delegation of Canada made the following declaration:

"It is a particular pleasure for me, on behalf of Canada, to add her voice to our regional coordinator statement, namely Portugal, on behalf of regional Group B, as well as the other delegations that we have heard, and no doubt the delegations to come, in supporting and saluting for a second term the leadership of Dr Idris.

"In Canada's view, his first term has been an unquestionable success. A success for a number of reasons that members have alluded to. Firstly, I think his leadership has been wise and astute, and I think the United States delegate just moments ago put it so well. I think, when you look at his leadership, it embodies a great deal of experience. Experience and leadership are indispensable and intertwined.

"It is a great honour for me to speak in the name of the Least Developed Countries (LDCs) to the fourteenth extraordinary session of the WIPO General Assembly, a session essentially devoted to the renewal of the term of office of the Director General of the World Intellectual Property Organization (WIPO), Dr Kamil Idris, who has spent several years working hard at the head of WIPO.

"Allow me to mention here that the Director General of WIPO, in his recent work entitled Intellectual Property: A Power Tool for Economic Growth, reaffirmed his conviction that intellectual property is a powerful instrument of development, but one which has unfortunately not been used to the best advantage by all countries.

"With that in mind, he has ensured that WIPO has rapidly formulated and implemented its commitment towards LDCs which, through me, convey to him their sincere gratitude.

"For it is thanks to his devotion and, above all, to his very hard work that our Organization has achieved great progress. We cannot but be proud of this. It is normal, therefore, that a person who has given body and soul to our Organization should be allowed to continue to lead it towards still more brilliant successes.

"Having always militated for the upward development of WIPO, he is well placed to understand the subtleties of this process and to ensure that WIPO contributes to the introduction of intellectual property machinery that will generate economic prosperity and peace.

"If WIPO is today an Organization that is held up as an example, that is undoubtedly due to the energy of its Director General and his team.

"WIPO has indeed contributed to the creation of institutions in the fields of intellectual property and cooperation for development.

"I should therefore like to pay special tribute to the Director General of WIPO, not only for his exceptional qualities, but also for the efforts that he has made to reform the Organization, to bring new blood into it, to give a new impetus to the work of the Secretariat, and to devise new programs, including the program for LDCs, which has been reviewed in the light of the challenges of our time.

"Throughout the world, WIPO symbolizes not only the will to protect and promote innovation, but also progress and peace. All the Organization's efforts are leveraged by his intention to protect the product of human intelligence and that of development.

"This moral commitment cannot rely solely on abstractions, but rather on a genuine service offered to peoples. We can safely state that it is to this that WIPO is devoting itself in the interest of LDCs.

"WIPO is committed to the development and promotion of the peoples of the Least Developed Countries.

"In conclusion, I wish to join the other members in expressing recognition, once again, for the significant work done by Dr Kamil Idris, and to assure him of my country's firm support and will to cooperate throughout his second term of office, which we trust will be successful."

The Delegation of the Russian Federation made the following statement:

"First of all, on behalf of the Delegation of the Russian Federation, I would like to congratulate all the Members of WIPO, all the participants in the Assembly, and all the staff of the International Bureau on a historic event – the appointment of Dr Kamil Idris as the Director General of WIPO for a second term in office.

"The unanimity and consensus of virtually all the Members of WIPO in assessing Dr Idris' activities as Director General are connected with his boundless energy, high level of professionalism in assessing problems in the intellectual property sphere, clarity in the establishment of tasks and programs, and openness and transparency in interaction with Member States.

"Almost six years ago, Dr Idris himself spoke of the way in which he envisaged the development of WIPO's activities, which, thanks to his experience, authority and activities, are performed, year in, year out, with the full support of WIPO Members.

"The Delegation of the Russian Federation has always valued highly and supported all the Director General's initiatives, based on comprehensive knowledge of the problems existing in the intellectual property sphere.

"I would like to express great respect to Dr Kamil Idris for his effective and talented work as Director General, which in particular has influenced the emergence in the Russian Federation of new IP laws, taking into account all the worldwide trends developing in this sphere, and also Russia's accession to a number of WIPO agreements.

"I would also like to thank Dr Idris for the efficient work done by the WIPO Worldwide Academy. The creation of a Russian-language version of the distance learning course on the foundations of intellectual property has already provided training for around 1,000 specialists this year from various regions of Russia that have expressed the wish to undergo such training.

"Dr Kamil Idris has a unique ability to formulate, in a clear-sighted and convincing manner, the strategic and tactical tasks facing WIPO in the field of intellectual property. The proposals heard today for the further development of WIPO's activities enjoy our full support.

"I would like to join all the congratulations expressed today to Dr Idris, and I am certain that, under his wise leadership in the coming years, we will achieve together new tangible successes in increasing the role of IP in the provision of stable economic growth in all countries on all continents."

The Delegation of Japan made the following statement:

"I am very pleased today to express my heartfelt congratulations for the re appointment of Dr Kamil Idris to his second term in office as Director General."

The Delegation of Cuba made the following statement:

"Beyond any doubt, intellectual property has become an important subject of heated international debate in all political, economic and social forums, which only stresses its importance as a tool for development and as a wealth generator.

"During the first term in office of Dr Kamil Idris, with the energy and effectiveness that are his distinctive qualities, WIPO has undergone a radical modernization that has transformed it into a forum ready to face, in a very transparent way, all the challenges brought by the new millennium.

"One of the great values of Dr Idris is his ability to promote, through important development cooperation and technical assistance, activities geared for developing countries, and the development of human resources as a key factor in the establishment and development of national intellectual property systems. We are certain that, in the future, the growth and increased resources assigned to continue, increase and diversify development cooperation activities, will continue to provide concrete and positive results for WIPO and its Director General.

"Aware of the extraordinary complexity of developing new international intellectual property standards and programs, we are sure that Dr Idris has the full capabilities to carry them out, taking into consideration, as usual, the needs and opinions of developing and Least Developed Countries, and facilitating negotiations, making a reality of his vision of intellectual property as a tool for development.

"We are very pleased to witness the Director General's effort in promoting vitally important projects, such as the use of intellectual property and SMEs; the intensive use of new information technologies, such as WIPONET and PCT-SAFE, among others; the establishment of the Intergovernmental Committee on Intellectual Property and Genetic Resources, Traditional Knowledge and Folklore. We look forward to the successful conclusion of all those projects."

The Delegation of Malawi made the following statement:

"The Delegation of Malawi also feels highly honored to have this opportunity to congratulate Dr Idris and to reaffirm our full support for his re-appointment to the post of Director General of WIPO, as already expressed by the Representative of the African Group as well as the Representative of the LDCs. During the last Assembly meetings, my Delegation expressed support for the nomination of Dr Idris because we have confidence in his leadership qualities, as exemplified by the excellent and outstanding results achieved by the Organization during his first term of office. As Dr Idris' remarkable achievements have been well stated by many delegations, it will suffice for me to say that my Delegation wishes to fully associate with those sentiments and to put on record our satisfaction with the clear vision of Dr Idris which has transformed WIPO into an Organization that is responsive to constantly evolving trends and demands of intellectual property systems such as in the areas of traditional knowledge, genetic resources and folklore. The development of the intellectual property system as a tool for economic and social development has witnessed a welcome integration of developing and least developed countries like Malawi into the intellectual property system."

"We are certain, Mr Chairman. that the re-election of Dr Kamil Idris will benefit all members of WIPO, who will not fail to take advantage still more, in the course of this new term of office, of the Director General's forward-looking policies, his wide and rich experience and his various innovative proposals.

"Dr Idris referred this morning to the merits of intellectual property as a vector for creating a federation of all nations on the planet, irrespective of their cultural diversities.

"May the work done in this regard under Dr Idris' leadership light the way in order to meet the many challenges faced in the world today."

The Delegation of Argentina made the following statement:

"In the past few years, WIPO has achieved extraordinary results which are the fruit of management imbued with the spirit of initiative shown by Dr Idris. His dedication has transformed WIPO into an Organization better prepared to meet the challenges which it currently faces.

"Dr Idris has promoted the active participation of all the Members of the Organization. His management style, based on openness and dialogue, is undoubtedly worthy of praise, and has strengthened the principle of consensus and participation in the decision-making process.

"Dr Idris has significantly expanded WIPO's programs

and has provided it with an integrated vision and modernizing initiatives. He has been able to organize the work of this Organization effectively by using it to enhance the economic, cultural and technological development, by means of modern working methods, undertaking transparent and global discussions, and ensuring that it deals with matters of vital importance for all its Members and, in particular, for developing countries.

"Dr Idris' strategic vision to integrate developing countries into the intellectual property system in positive terms is the result of the new momentum that he has managed to instil in WIPO's work. The strengthening of cooperation for development and the establishment of the WIPO Worldwide Academy have been decisive for these purposes.

"During his first term of office, he has stimulated the development of the technologies by means of projects of great importance such as IMPACT and WIPONET. His initiatives in relation to small and medium-sized enterprises, electronic commerce and domain names – with the establishment of the Arbitration and Mediation Center – are vitally important contributions. Similarly, constitutional reform, with a view to modernizing the Organization's institutional structure, the entry into force of the WCT and the WPPT, have been some of the results of important innovative and dynamic activities.

"Our country attaches great importance to cooperation with WIPO. In this regard, a powerful stimulus was generated for our cooperation by the official visit of a WIPO delegation, headed by Dr Kamil Idris, to our country in 2001.

"During this visit, a meeting was held between the President of our country, Dr Kamil Idris and the WIPO delegation, which defined the future prospects for cooperation between Kyrgyzstan and WIPO. A program of cooperation between our national Government and WIPO was signed.

"WIPO has always provided support to us in the establishment and development of the patent system and the IP system in our country as a whole, which will shortly mark the tenth anniversary, in June, of its founding. This assistance is multifaceted, and is in the form of technical and consultative services, as well as support in the training of managers through relevant courses, the organization of seminars and so on.

"The support of WIPO and cooperation with the Organization have been especially active in the past few years, as a result of the attention devoted by Dr Kamil Idris who, as Director General, has shown sensitivity toward countries such as ours, a significant step for which we are deeply grateful to him.

"Our Delegation is convinced that WIPO, under the leadership of Dr Kamil Idris, will continue its future dynamic development for the benefit of the intellectual property community to generate economic progress and cultural advancement for all countries; in this connection, we will take all possible steps to offer our support to Dr Kamil Idris. In conclusion, we once again congratulate you, Dr Idris, on your re-election for a second term in office."

The Delegation of Israel made the following statement:

"The Delegation of Israel would like to congratulate Dr Idris on his unanimous re-appointment for the post of Director General of WIPO. Dr Idris' achievements are well documented and so are his unusual leadership and diplomatic skills. One only need listen to the statements made by the Delegation in this hall today to fully appreciate Dr Idris' contribution to WIPO and to the field of IP. With your permission, I would like to say just one word about Dr Idris' contribution to the relationship between WIPO and Israel. Since Dr Idris has taken office, the relations between WIPO and Israel have improved dramatically. Dr Idris makes us feel at home in WIPO. He has made a real effort to cooperate with Israel and to promote IP in our country. He honoured us with a visit to Israel in December 2000, this visit and his follow-up actions exemplify the way Dr Idris puts words into practice. Dr Idris also believes that IP can serve as a bridge for peace in our region and works hard to promote this vision. For all these reasons, let me once again congratulate Dr Idris and wish him great success and pledge our fullest cooperation and support."

The Delegation of Portugal made the following statement:

"First of all, Portugal wishes to congratulate Dr Kamil Idris for his re-election as Director General of WIPO.

"On this important occasion, we would like to express our satisfaction for the work accomplished by the Director General during the last six years.

"Our wish at OAPI is that our efforts are unified still further, that our solidarity is strengthened to support in an ever more vigorous manner the policy which is defined for each of our organizations.

"In the past few years, cooperation between OAPI and WIPO has taken on a new dimension and scope.

Particularly sensitive to the problems of developing countries, Dr Kamil Idris has spared no effort in this direction. We thank him and his staff for those efforts.

"We remain confident that the new era which is beginning will see this cooperation strengthened in the mutual interest of both our organizations.

"Long live cooperation between WIPO and OAPI."

The Delegation of the African Union made the following statement:

"Once more, it is a privilege and an honour for the African Union to have been afforded the opportunity to address this august Assembly on the re-election of Dr Kamil Idris as Director General of WIPO. We have had occasions, like several Member States of this Organization, to comment on the eminent credentials and impeccable performance of Dr Idris. The testimony that has been given during the 37th WIPO Assemblies and the sixteenth extraordinary session of the Coordination Committee of WIPO speak volumes for the abilities and capabilities of Dr Kamil Idris. As we sat through all these sessions and heard the expressions of unanimous support for Africa's candidature, a feeling of pride, joy and gratitude overwhelmed us. All Africans, and indeed the Heads of State and Government who sponsored his candidature, would have felt the same. Now that the Representatives of Member States have spoken and given concrete manifestation of their support, by overwhelmingly electing Dr Kamil Idris for a second term as the Director General of WIPO, allow me, Sir, to add my voice to what the Representative of the African Group has said in the expression of our heartfelt gratitude and sincere thanks to all those who made this unique event possible. To Brother Kamil Idris, let me just say that Africa is proud of you and wishes you even more success in the second term of your office. God Bless."

The Delegation of Sudan made the following statement:

"I have waited for a long time but with great happiness anyway. In Arabic, we say, 'The best comes last'. Mr Chairman, the two rivers, the Blue Nile and the White, sing together in happiness. The great land of this river shimmers in joy, the children of Africa, its sons and daughters, beat the drums of their forests, and their flutes sing of joy. They celebrate the success of one of their sons, a great thinker, a fine diplomat, a confident leader and manager. He comes from and belongs to all this. He is the pride of his land, his people, his continent and his nation. He has high ambitions and he shall reach them.

"Congratulations from your nation, Dr Kamil Idris, on the words praised to you. Your nation is happy for you have a great personality, though modest and always ready to help others. Congratulations to your dear family and your wife and to the Sudanese community in Switzerland, to your friends and colleagues. It is a great moment for your civilization in the Nile Valley that pioneered in discovering science and technology which first used the water where the shadoof, the plow, the pallets and the scale."

Appendix 11

List of publications

My quotations and my Philosophy of life

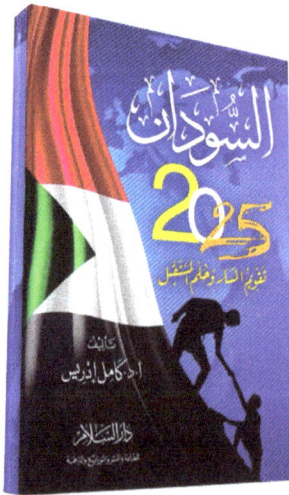

Sudan 2025
Sudan's path to the future: A realistic dream for 2025

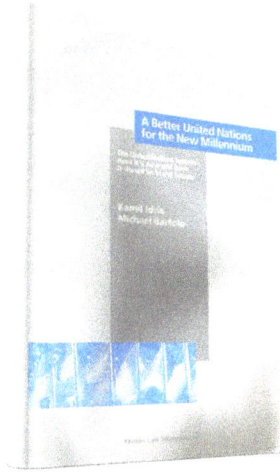

A Better United Nations for the New Millennium

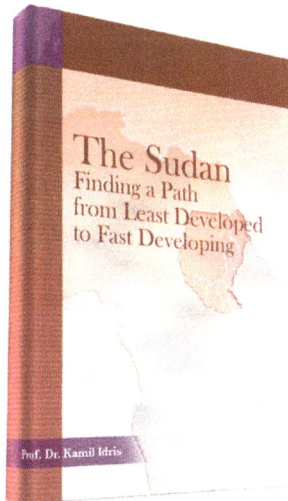

The Sudan - Finding a path from Least Developed to Fast Developing

Sudan 2020

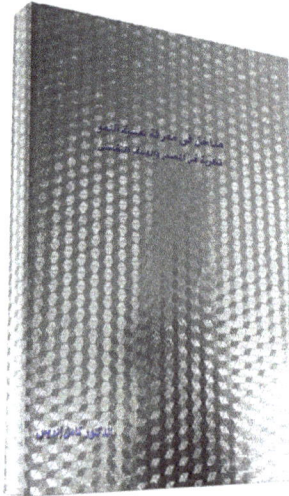

Approach to the Knowledge of Infant Psychology

مداخل في معرفة نفسية النمو
نظرية في المصدر والهدف النفسي

الدكتور كامل إدريس

Theory on the Source and Target of Infant Psychology

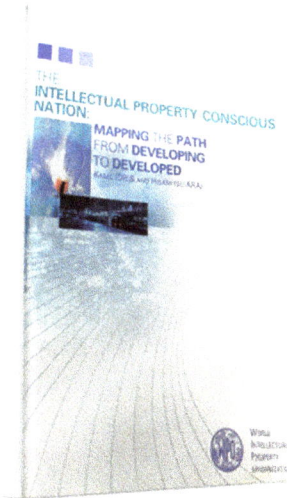

The Intellectual Property - Conscious Nation:
Mapping the path from developing to developed.

413

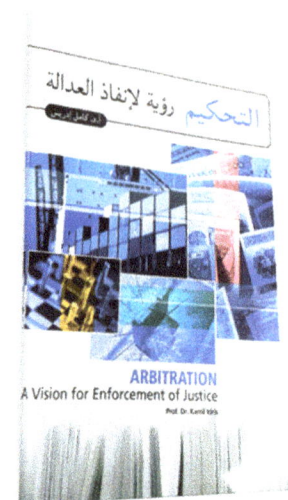

التحكيم رؤية لإنفاذ العدالة
ARBITRATION
A Vision for Enforcement of Justice
Prof. Dr. Kamil Idris

Arbitration – A Vision For Enforcement of Justice

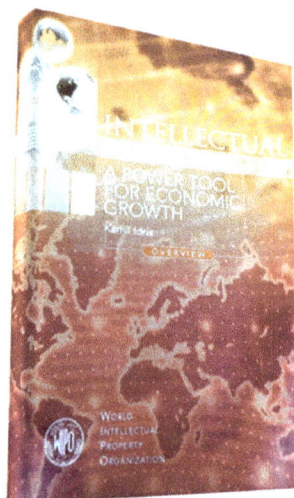

Intellectual Property – A Power Tool For Economic Growth
(Books with the above title were published in different languages – see following pages)

Intellectual Property – A Power Tool For Economic Growth

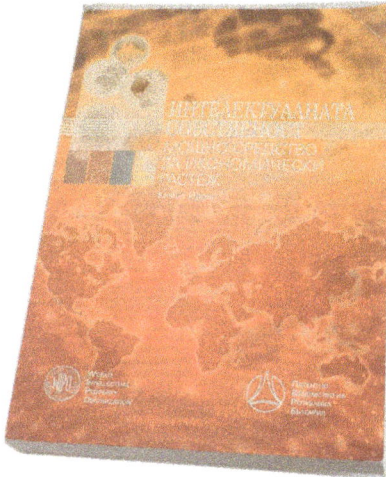

Intellectual Property – A Power Tool For Economic Growth

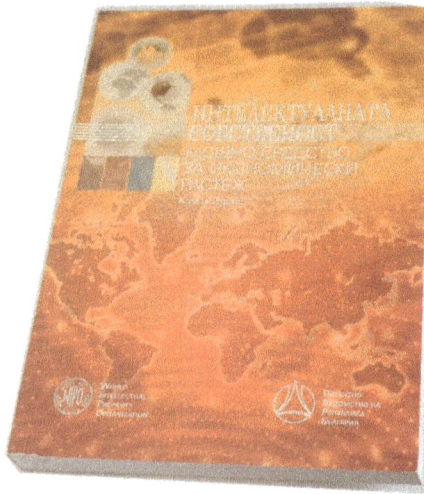

**Intellectual Property – A Power
Tool For Economic Growth**

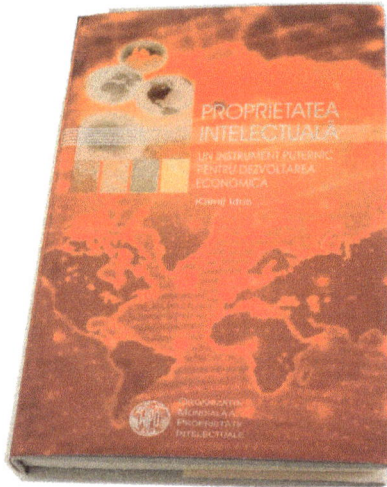

**Intellectual Property – A Power
Tool For Economic Growth**

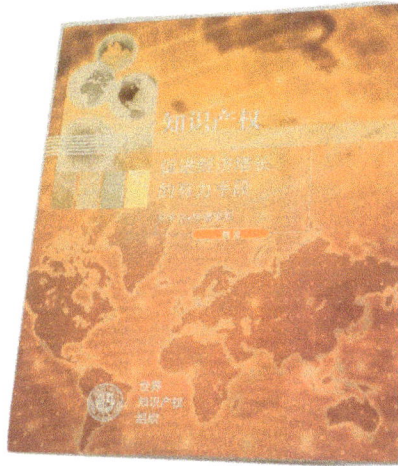

**Intellectual Property – A Power
Tool For Economic Growth**

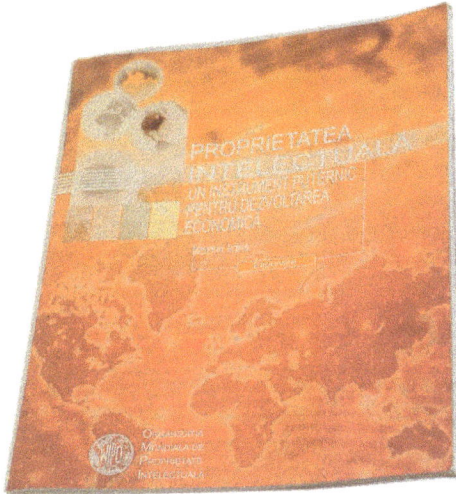

**Intellectual Property – A Power
Tool For Economic Growth**

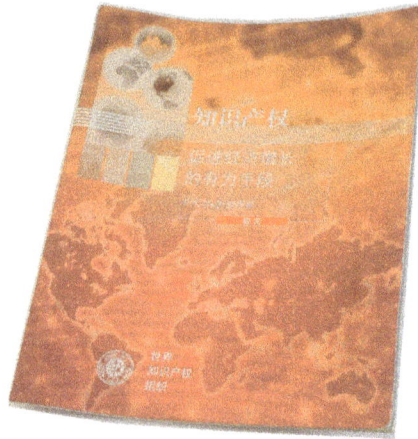

**Intellectual Property – A Power
Tool For Economic Growth**

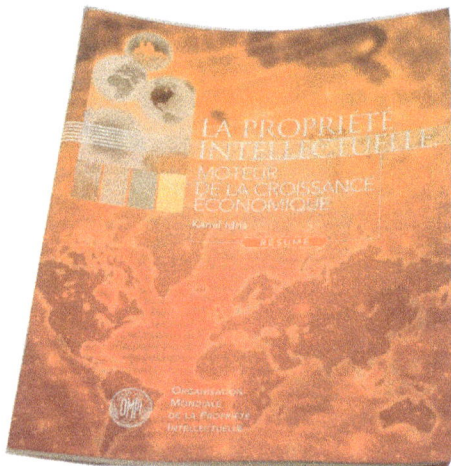

**Intellectual Property – A Power
Tool For Economic Growth**

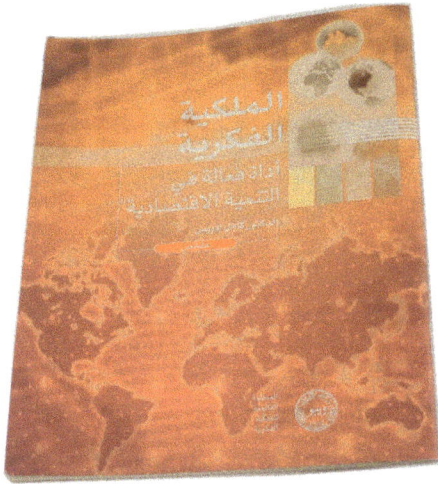

**Intellectual Property – A Power
Tool For Economic Growth**

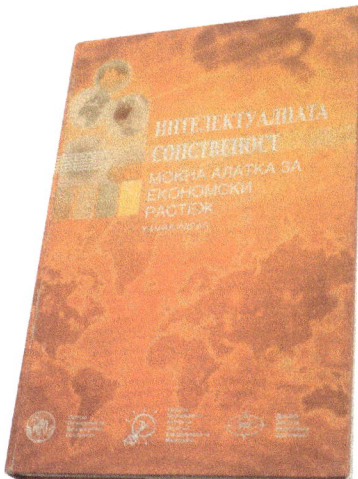

**Intellectual Property – A Power
Tool For Economic Growth**

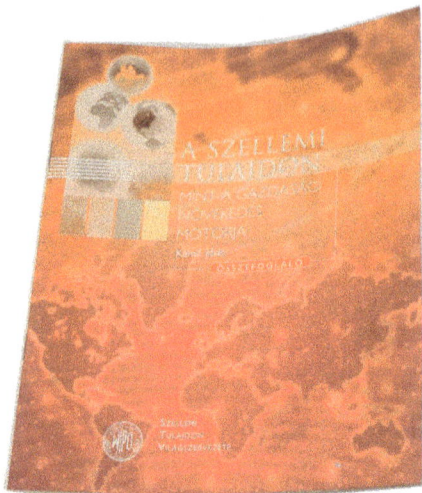

**Intellectual Property – A Power
Tool For Economic Growth**

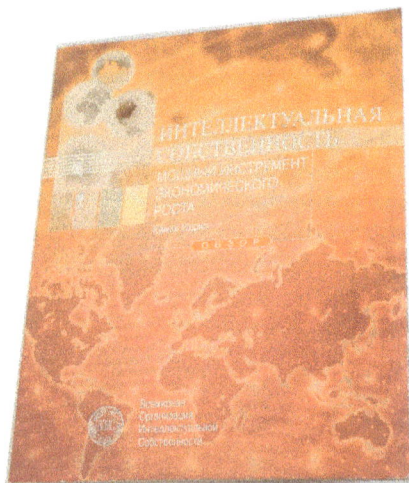

**Intellectual Property – A Power
Tool For Economic Growth**

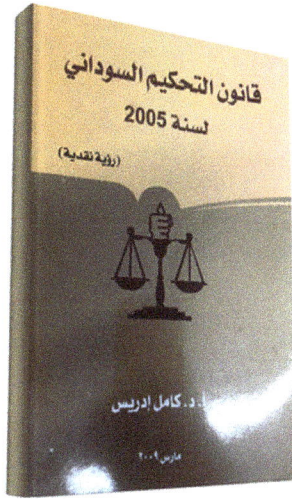

Critical Outlook of Sudan's Arbitration Law of 2005

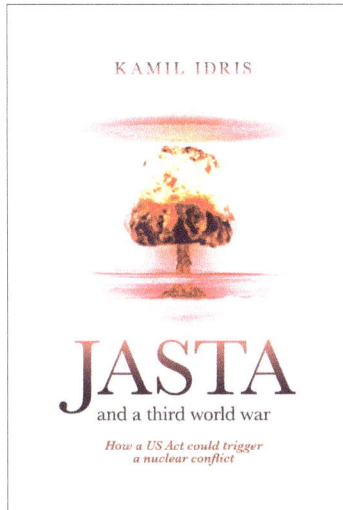

JASTA and a third world war

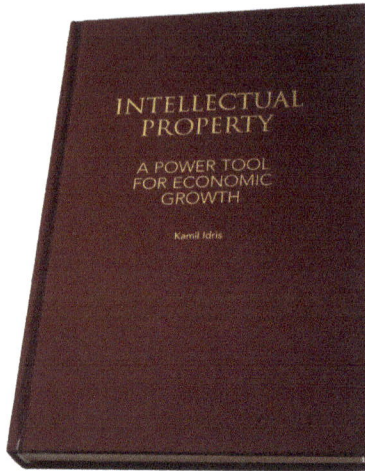

**Intellectual Property – A Power
Tool For Economic Growth**

**The Intellectual Property Conscious Nations: Mapping
the path from developing to developed 2006**

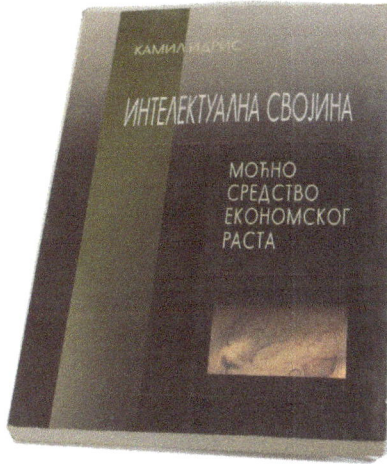

Intellectual Property

Kamil Idris Days (1983-1984)

Kamil Idris Days (1985)

Kamil Idris Days (1986)

Kamil Idris Days (1988)

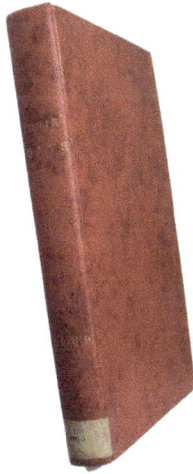

Kamil Idris Days (1989)

Kamil Idris Days (1990)

Kamil Idris Days (1991)

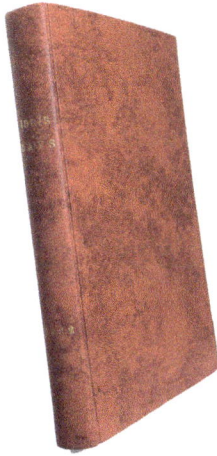

Kamil Idris Days (1992)

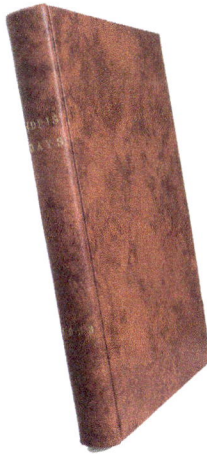

Kamil Idris Days (1993)

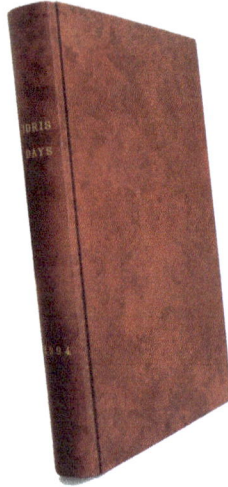

Kamil Idris Days (1994)

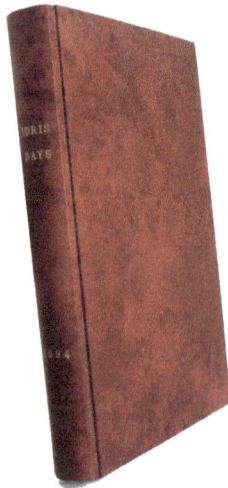

Kamil Idris Days (1995)

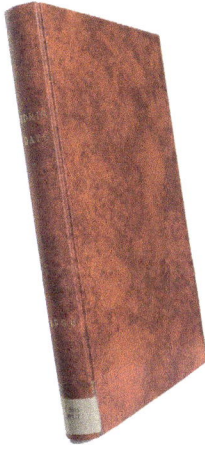

Kamil Idris Days (1996)

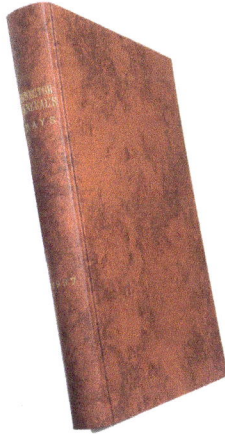

Kamil Idris Days (1997)

Kamil Idris Days (1998)

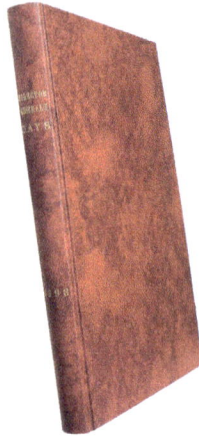

Kamil Idris Days (1999)

Kamil Idris Days (2000)

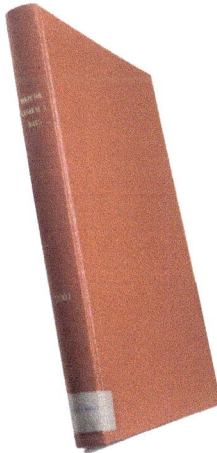

Kamil Idris Days (2001)

Kamil Idris Days (2002)

Kamil Idris Days (2003)

Kamil Idris Days (2004)

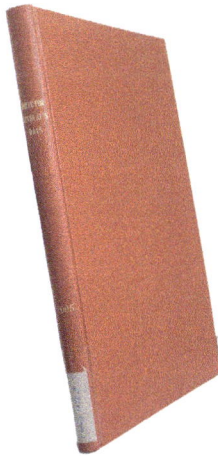

Kamil Idris Days (2005)

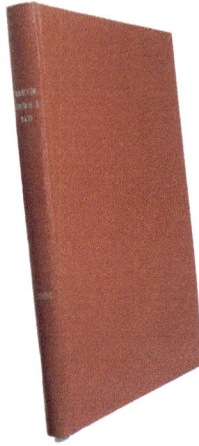

Kamil Idris Days (2006)

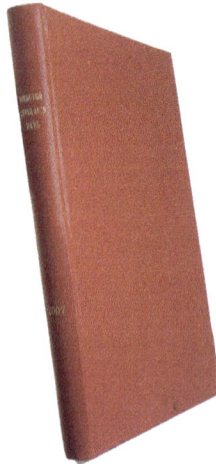

Kamil Idris Days (2007)

More details of these publications can be found on my website:
www.profkamilidris.co.uk

Appendix 12

Historic Omdurman and Khartoum

Historic Omdurman and its sisters Khartoum and Khartoum North are charming cities. Their districts and ancient areas continue to fascinate me:

"Beit Almal" was the ministry of finance of the Mahdia era.

"Elmulazmein" were the guards of the Khalif who accompanied him at all times.

"Beit Alamana" was for storage of weapons and ammunition.

"Hai Alhigra" where the Khalif used to stay seeing off his army before going to the north of the country. He accompanied the army up to the Karari mountains.

"Wad nubawi", named after prince Mohamed Wad nubawi, from "bani jarar" tribe.

"Hai Al-umda", named after Umda Al-maqbool.

"Abu roaf", the name is related to gradual fertility of land.

"Bawabat Abdel-qayoom", named after the leader of the Tabya.

"Umbada", named after prince Mubdi. He was a leader and one of the Mahdia princes.

"Al-arda", where the Mahdi army used to meet every Friday.

"Almorada", a dhow marina for loading and uploading of goods.

"Hai Alumara" was the residence of the princes and leaders of Almahdia.

"Hai Aldubat", an area occupied by army officers.

"Alabasia", most of its inhabitants came from Alabasia Taqali.

"Hai Al-maki", named after Elsayed Al-maki, son of Sheikh Ismail Al-wali, brother of Al-Bakri and grand father of Sayed Ismail Al-Azhari, first Prime Minister of Sudan after its independence.

"Hai wad Al-bana" was named after the famous poet Wad Al-bana.

"Algamair" from gamir. It was a historic site famous for the manufacture of white lime and pottery, along the beach of the river Nile.

"Hai Elshuhada", named after martyrs killed during the war with Kitchener.

"Midan Elrabie", named after Knight Elrabie, one of the Knights of El Mahdia, executed by Kitchener on the same site.

"Hai Elrikabia", named after the Rikabia tribe.

"Wad Albasir" belongs to the Halaween tribe.

"Hai Elmagarba", the site of inhabitants who originally came from Morocco.

"Aldraisa", named after those who were in charge of servicing the railways.

"Alsahafa", named after a well-established newspaper.

"Hai Aldaim or Aldyoom", the colonial power had assembled homeless and poor people around the camp of wad yom.

"Hilat Hamad", named after Elsheikh Hamad wad um Maryom. He is: Hamad bin Mohamed Ali bin Yagoob bin Magli who was a disciple of Arbab Alagaid.

"Hilat Khogali", named after Alsheikh Khogali Abdelrahman, cousin of Alsheikh Hamad.

"Kober", named after an English man called Cooper.

"Aldrooshab", named after a tribe in Rufaa.

"Elhaj Yousif", named after Elsheikh Elhaj Yousif Dhasha.

"Elkabashi" belongs to Elsheikh Ibrahim bin Elamin bin Ali known as Elsheikh Elkabashi. The area of Elkabashi was originally offered by the Kings of Al-Abdallab. Its original name was "Alf'r".

"Elfaki Hashim", named after Elsheikh Elfaki Hashim.

"Al-askila", facing the Friendship Hall, was originally an Italian word, meaning 'port' and the Turks got it from the Italians.

Index

Photo credits and licenses

Cover: